I0084046

Joseph Black

Proceedings of the Zoological and Acclimatisation Society of

Victoria

Joseph Black

Proceedings of the Zoological and Acclimatisation Society of Victoria

ISBN/EAN: 9783741136313

Manufactured in Europe, USA, Canada, Australia, Japa

Cover: Foto ©Thomas Meinert / pixelio.de

Manufactured and distributed by brebook publishing software
(www.brebook.com)

Joseph Black

Proceedings of the Zoological and Acclimatisation Society of Victoria

REPORT OF THE COUNCIL.

THE Annual Meeting of the Zoological and Acclimatisation Society of Victoria, was held on Friday, the 1st day of March, at the office of the Society, 30 Swanston-street.

The Members present being—

DR. THOMAS BLACK, *President, in the Chair*
MR. LE SOUEF, *Honorary Secretary*
MESSRS. C. ALLPORT
   „   G. COPPIN
   „   F. R. GODFREY
   „   R. K. HAMMOND
DR. MOLLOY
MR. A. PURCHAS
DR. PUGH
MESSRS. C. RYAN
   „   G. SPRIGG
   „   H. T. VENABLES
   „   S. WILSON

A letter was read from His Excellency the Governor, expressing his regret that he was not able to be present. A letter was also read from Mr. J. B. Were, regretting his unavoidable absence ; and another from Mr. T. J. Sumner, in which that gentleman conveyed his resignation of the office of Hon. Treasurer. The Hon. Secretary informed the Meeting that Baron Von Mueller had desired him to express to the Members present his great regret at not being able, from press of business, to be present.

Mr Albert Le Souef, the Hon. Secretary, read the Annual Report of the Council, which was as follows :—

THE Council of the Acclimatisation Society of Victoria have now the honor to lay the 'Eighth Annual Report of their proceedings before the subscribers, and they also beg to submit a revision of the Rules of the Society for approval and confirmation. The principal alterations in the rules are that the President, Vice-Presidents, and Honorary Treasurer, will henceforth be elected by ballot at the annual general meeting, and that the yearly subscription of members will be reduced from two guineas to one.

The Council are of opinion that the progress of the Society will be promoted by a change in the tenure of these offices, and that the yearly election of a President, Vice-Presidents, and Honorary Treasurer, from amongst the Members of the Council, will not only be the means of bringing fresh energy and new ideas to assist in the Society's work, but also an additional incentive to Members of Council to exertion in the cause of acclimatisation. At the same time the Council would express their warm appreciation of the manner in which the gentlemen who have filled these offices hitherto have performed their functions.

The latter alteration it is hoped will tend to popularise the Society, by largely increasing the number of its subscribers. The Council think that Melbourne, from its size and importance, ought to number amongst its attractions a good zoological collection; and, if supported in this view by the public, they propose, in the first instance, to form as complete a collection as possible of the Fauna of Australasia, and, hereafter, when in a position to do so, to add those of other countries; but the Council are aware that it is only by the aid of a comparatively large body of subscribers that their wishes and intentions can be carried into effect, as zoological collections are expensive to maintain. The animals and birds already in the Society's gardens are the source of considerable attraction and interest to large numbers of persons who visit the Royal Park.

The Government very liberally placed the sum of £1000 on the estimates for the present financial year for the use of the Society—which sum was voted by the Legislature ; and the Council take this opportunity of thanking the Government and the Parliament for thus enabling them to carry on their useful labours, and trust that the result will prove commensurate with the money expended.

The Council are gratified at being able to state that a considerable amount of success has attended the operations of the Society during the past year. A number of pheasants of the silver (*phasianus, nycthemerus*) and common (*phasianus colchicus*) variety, have been reared, and will shortly be liberated in suitable places. Ducks and other birds have also increased at the Royal Park. Upwards of one hundred and fifty Guinea-fowl have been placed in various secluded spots, in forests far removed from settlement, where it is confidently hoped they will increase, and in a few years afford both food and sport. The Council regret that they are in a measure obliged to carry on their operations in secrecy, on account of the unscrupulous and unsportsmanlike conduct of certain persons, who do not hesitate to shoot pheasants, and other valuable game, just liberated, without any regard to the great injury they are thus inflicting on the cause of acclimatisation.

It is only lately that information was received, that a hen pheasant had been shot up the country at the time she had a brood of chicks too young and helpless to live without their mother : and this is by no means an isolated case. It is the same with hares, which are shot, hunted, and coursed, at all times and seasons, in defiance of the Game Act, to such an extent, that had the hare not have been more prolific in this climate than in England, it would long since have been exterminated. The Council have lately been considering a plan proposed by their Honorary Secretary, Mr. Albert Lesouef, to whose careful supervision and activity they ascribe much of the present prosperity of the Society,—to have a depôt for pheasant breeding somewhere in the ranges, where the birds could go free as soon as they were fledged; but the scheme has not yet been sufficiently matured as to justify their taking any action. If carried out, the risk which these birds run of being illegally destroyed would be considerably lessened.

The vexed question of the sparrow and minah has been dealt with by the exclusion of both birds from the protection of the Game Act.

The Council regret that they were unable, from circumstances beyond their control, to have an amended Game Act introduced last session in Parliament; but a measure has been prepared, and it is hoped that it may become law during the ensuing session.

In September last 2250 brown trout ova were obtained from the Salmon Commissioners of Tasmania, and were hatched at the Society's Establishment at the Royal Park ; some 600 trout fry were also procured by Dr. Thomas Black, the President of the Society, while on a visit to Tasmania ; so that on the whole about 2500 live trout have been placed in different streams during the past season, a large proportion of which were put into the Watts, a splendid tributary of the Yarra, admirably adapted for trout.

Not many deer have been turned out during the past year but those hitherto liberated in many parts of the colony are spreading and increasing rapidly. The Society possess a fine collection of six varieties in their grounds at the Park.

The valuable flock of Angora goats, and the ostriches belonging to the Society, are located at Mr. Samuel Wilson's station, Longerenong on the Wimmera, where they are thriving and increasing.

Although most anxious to encourage and promote sericulture, the Council find it difficult to advance this industry in a really practical manner, so as to be of benefit to the colony. Baron Von Mueller has however, as well as the Society, supplied many parts of the Colony with white mulberry plants, and when these come into bearing, silk growing will, they hope, afford profitable employment to the industry of the Colony. The Society will be happy at all times to furnish every information in their power connected with sericulture.

The Council were of opinion that the services in the cause of pisciculture, rendered by Sir Robert Officer and Mr Morton Allport, of Tasmania, deserved some recognition at their hands, and they therefore awarded to both these gentlemen the silver medal of the Society. Their bronze medal has also been presented to Captain Babot, of the *Hydaspes*, for his enterprize in bringing out sea turtle.

In conclusion, the Council are glad to state that the condition of the Society is sound and prosperous, and that they only require more liberal co-operation from the public to enable them, with the assistance of the small but efficient staff at the Royal Park, to produce great results in the cause of acclimatisation ; and would again inform their friends throughout the country, that donations of native animals or birds are always extremely useful, not only for the zoological collection at the Royal Park, but for purposes of exchange with other countries.

Since the last report the following gentlemen have been elected as members of Council, and their appointment requires to be confirmed at this meeting, viz., Charles Ryan, Esq., and Frederick Godfrey, Esq. In conformity with the rules, the following members retire from the Council, being the three who have attended the fewest meetings ; but are eligible for re-election:—The Hon. Dr. Dobson, T. J. Sumner, Esq., and John Steavenson, Esq. The balance sheets for the past year, audited by Mr. Rucker, public accountant, are laid before the meeting, by which it will be found that the total expenditure for the past year has been £1091 19s. 11d.

Mr. SAMUEL WILSON moved the adoption of the Report and Balance Sheet, and in so doing, said the Members would perhaps expect that he should give some account of the animals and birds belonging to the Society, of which he had charge at his station on the Wimmera. The Angora goats were now in the most thriving condition. When they arrived at his place they were in a delicate state, and had not, apparently, before been on pastures which suited them. One died on the first night of arrival, and many of them fell down from weakness when any one went near them. The ostriches during the past season had not done well: it seemed that heavy rains, such as had fallen this season, were not favorable to ostriches, although they were to stock generally; and that they throve best in a dry climate, or desert place. Only one of the female birds had produced seven young ones this season, but none of them had thriven. In the previous season one of the ostriches brought out twelve birds from thirteen eggs, and they all throve but one, which met with an accident. As regarded their management, it was most difficult to keep them in a state of domestication. When turned out of the paddock, they gradually got wilder, and as they ran faster than a horse, it was most difficult to get them in the yard again, to take their feathers from them. That operation had to be done at a certain season of the year, when the feathers were ripe, or, if not, they became bare and comparatively worthless. This year he had the greatest difficulty in trying to get the ostriches in the yard at the proper season, and the consequence was the feathers were of little value. He had some men out riding for many days trying to drive the birds; but they found it almost impossible to get them in at the right time. Now he had adopted another plan, and fed them near the yards, so that it was a comparatively easy matter to secure them; and when once in the yard it was not difficult to pluck the feathers off them. As their management was now understood, he thought they would increase rapidly, and that in future the feathers would be obtained more easily, and at the right time. The axis deer had spread to a very great extent; one herd of them had been seen at a distance of 30 miles to the south, and another herd about the same distance in a contrary direction; so that it might be considered they were now spread over an area of at least sixty miles. The deer might, therefore, be considered a complete success. The Murray cod, which were introduced into the Wimmera, had not yet increased to such an extent as to be of much service, and there had not been time to ascertain the state of the carp which were introduced into the same river. He might however say, that one of the carp was caught about two months after it was placed in the river, and it had grown considerably in that time.

Mr. F. R. Godfrey in seconding the adoption of the Report, said he wished to draw the attention of the Members of the Society to that portion of it which referred to the scheme proposed by the Hon. Secretary of the Society, Mr. Le Souef, for forming a depôt somewhere in the secluded ranges of the colony, where pheasants could be reared and allowed to go free as soon as fledged. He believed that it was only in this way that the acclimatisation of pheasants, and other valuable game birds, in large numbers, could be carried out; and he thought the Council had hitherto made a mistake by liberating birds near Melbourne, where they fell a prey to boys, hawks, and unsportsmanlike persons, who shot anything and everything they could. Mr. Godfrey said he had lately, with another Member of the Council and Mr. Le Souef, visited a place in the ranges, which, for reasons stated in the report, required to be kept secret, which was admirably adapted for pheasants and other game; and though none of the former were seen on the occasion of this visit, he and the other gentlemen had the satisfaction of seeing several guinea-fowl, which had been liberated with a number of pheasants some months before in the locality, and they were delighted to find them looking healthy, and in splendid plumage, and inferred, from the fact of the guinea-fowl being a more domesticated fowl than the pheasant, that the latter must also thrive, though it might be a year or two before they would be seen in numbers.

Mr. GODFREY also drew attention to the benefit which the Society had done, and might continue to do, in stocking reservoirs in various places with the English perch and other fish.

The Report was adopted unanimously.

A number of alterations in the rules, which had been made by the Council, were submitted and adopted.

The meeting then proceeded to the election of office-bearers, and Dr. Thomas Black was re-elected President of the Society.

DR. THOMAS BLACK returned thanks for the honor which had been conferred upon him, he referred to the very satisfactory position which the Society had now achieved, and to the certainty of its increasing value in the future. In the course of his remarks, he said Mr. Edward Wilson had been a very good friend to the Society, not only with his advice, but his hands had always been open when assistance was required. The Society were under a deep debt of gratitude to him, and also to Sir Henry Barkly, and other gentlemen of the same stamp, for the great assistance they had rendered to it.

Professor McCoy and Baron Von Mueller were re-elected Vice-presidents, and Dr. Joseph Black was appointed Hon. Treasurer in the place of Mr T. J. Sumner, to whom a vote of thanks was returned for his past services.

Messrs. F. R. Godfrey and Charles Ryan, who had been previously appointed Members of the Council, had their appointments confirmed, and Messrs. Samuel Wilson, W. Robertson, M.L.A., T. J. Sumner, and Dr. Dobson, M.L.C., were elected Members of the Council.

A vote of thanks for passed service was then passed to Dr. Pugh, who is about leaving the Colony for England.

Dr. Pugh, in acknowledging the vote, assured the Members that when he arrived in Europe he would do all in his power to further the objects of the Society, and would gladly try to carry out any of the wishes of the Members. He thought it was likely he would be able to be of more use to the Society in Europe than he could be here.

The Meeting then closed with a vote of thanks to the Chairman.

Account of Monies received and paid by the Acclimatisation Society of Victoria,

During the period 1st of January to 30th June, 1871.

RECEIPTS.

	£	s.	d.
Government Grant	400	0	0
Subcriptions and Donations	36	12	0
Proceeds of Sale of Stock	31	8	0
Money received from S. Sohn, New Caledonia ...	22	7	6
Refund from Dr. Ewing	3	10	0
Balance at Bank of Victoria 1st January £305 19 3			
Balance in Hon. Secretary's hands ... 3 0 1			
Amount advanced by him ... 1 4 0	310	3	4
	£801	0	10

AVAILABLE ASSETS.

	£	s.	d.
Balance at the Bank as above	258	14	2
Cash in the Collector's hands 30th June	6	3	0
	£264	17	2

PAYMENTS.

	£	s.	d.
Liabilities incurred *ante* 20th May, 1870	4	10	0
Purchase and Transport of Stock	57	12	0
Food and Forage	79	17	0
Wages	170	7	0
Office Expenses, Rent, &c.	64	4	7
Incidental Expenses, Printing, &c.... ...	71	19	5
Premises, &c.	45	10	10
Farming Implements, &c.	2	5	0
S. Sohn, dishonored Bill of Exchange, and Expenses...	44	0	0
Fishery Committee	5	0	0
Balance at Bank of Victoria, 30th June ...	258	14	2
	£804	0	10

LIABILITIES.

	£	s.	d.
Wages for the Month of June	23	13	0
Rent of Office to July 1st	13	0	0
S. House, Grain Account for June	9	18	5
T. B. Guest and Co., Dog Brend	2	11	0
C. Rosser, Meat for Animals	2	0	0
Water Rates	2	9	8
John Whiteman, Shoeing Horses	2	8	0
T. H. Miers, Dog Bread	1	15	0
A. A. C. Le Souef, Incidental Expenses ...	5	10	8
Sundry small accounts, (say)	5	0	0
	£68	5	9

Melbourne, 13th July, 1871.

T. J. SUMNER, Honorary Treasurer.

Audited and found correct. E. F. A. RUCKER, Auditor.

ALBERT A. C. Le SOUEF, Honorary Secretary.

Account of Monies received and paid by the Acclimatisation Society of Victoria,

During the period 1st July to 30th December, 1871.

RECEIPTS.

		£	s.	d.
Government Grant	...	500	0	0
Subscriptions and Donations	...	62	18	0
Proceeds of Sale of Stock	...	13	0	0
Balance at Bank of Victoria, 1st July ...	...	258	14	2
		£834	12	2

PAYMENTS.

		£	s.	d.
Purchase and Transport of Stock		90	5	6
Food and Forage		107	6	1
Wages		108	11	0
Office Expenses		62	4	11
Incidental Expenses		68	14	1
Premises		76	8	6
Farming Implements, &c.		18	10	0
Interest on Overdraft		1	19	2
A. A. C. Le Souef, Refund		1	4	0
Balance at the Bank, December 30th ...		230	7	8
Cash in the Hon. Secretary's hands ...		9	1	3
		£834	12	2

Audited and found correct, E. F. A. RUCKER, *Auditor.*

Melbourne, 25th January, 1872.

T. J. SUMNER, *Honorary Treasurer.*

ALBERT A. C. LE SOUEF, *Honorary Secretary.*

LIFE MEMBERS.

Aldworth & Co., Sandhurst £10 10 0
Armitage, George, Ballarat ... 10 10 0
Armstrong, W., Hexham .. 10 10 0
Barkly, His Excellency Sir H. 42 0 0
Bear, Hon. J. P., M.L.C. ... 21 0 0
Bear, Thomas H., Heidelberg 10 10 0
Black, Dr. Thomas, Melbourne
   Club 10 10 0
Black, W., Belfast 10 10 0
Borough Council of Sandhurst 10 10 0
Box, H., Little Collins-street
   West 10 10 0
Boyd & Currie, Collins-street
   West 10 10 0
Bright Bros., Messrs. & Co.,
   Flinders-lane 10 10 0
Brown, Lindsay, Garramadda,
   Wahgunyah 10 10 0
Canterbury, His Excellency,
   Viscount 10 10 0
Catto, J., Newbridge, Loddon 10 10 0
Chambers, H. J., St. Kilda ... Services
Cooper, Sir Daniel, London 37 2 0
Coppin, Geo. S. 10 10 0
Creswick, Borough Council of 10 10 0
Cumming, G., Mount Fyans 10 10 0
Cumming, W., Mount Fyans 10 10 0
Curr. E. M., Queen-street ... 10 10 0
Dalgetty & Co., Messrs., Little
   Collins-street 10 10 0
Docker, F. G., Wangaratta ... 10 10 0
Falconer, J. J., Bank Austra-
   lasia 20 0 0
Fellows, the Hon. T. H. ... 10 10 0
Firebrace, R. T. 10 10 0
Fussell, R. S. R.,'Fou Chou,
   50 dols. 11 0 10
Glass, R. J., Waiparella ... 10 10 0
Henty, S. G. 10 10 0
Hervey, The Hon. M. ... 10 10 0

Hoffmann, W., Bush Back,
   Essendon £25 0 0
Highett, Miss 10 10 0
Jamieson, Hugh 10 10 0
Jenner, Hon. C. J., M.L.C. 10 10 0
Jones, Lloyd, Avenel... ... 10 10 0
Joshua Bros., William-street 10 10 0
Landells, G. J., Lahore, India Services
Layard, C. P., Colombo ... Services
Layard, E. L., Cape Town ... Services
Learmonth, Thomas, Ercibdan-
   riley, Portland 10 10 0
Londesborough, The Right
   Honorable Lord, Carlton
   Gardens, London 37 10 0
Lyall, W. 10 10 0
Mackinnon, L., "Argus" Office, Services
Mackenzie, John 10 10 0
Mackintosh, Alexander ... 10 10 0
Marshall, Captain D. S. ... Services
Martin, Dr., Heidelberg ... 10 10 0
Matheson, J., Bank of Victori 21 0 0
McGill, A. 10 10 0
McGregor, Samuel, Belfast 10 10 0
McHattie, John, Phillip Island 10 10 0
McMullen, J., Union Bank ... 21 0 0
McKellar, Hon. T., M.L.C. 10 10 0
Molley, W. T., Hawthorn ... 10 10 0
Mueller, Baron Von, Botanic
   Gardens 10 10 0
Municipal Council of Ballarat
   West... ... ... 20 0 0
Murray, S., Dunrobin ... 10 10 0
Nicholson, Germain, Collins-
   street East 10 10 0
Officer, C. S., Mount Talbot 10 10 0
Power, Hou. Thomas H., Haw-
   thorn 10 10 0
Purchas, Albert, Kew ... Services
Ritchie, J., Streatham ... 10 10 0

LIFE MEMBERS—(*Continued*)—

Rostron, John R., Navarre	£10	10	0	
Rusden, G. W., Brighton ...	10	10	0	
Russell, A., Matuwalloch ..	10	10	0	
Rutledge, William, Belfast ...	10	10	0	
Salmon, J. E. S. and A. C. Bank	21	0	0	
Sargood, King and Sargood, Flinders-street East ...	10	10	0	
Shoobridge, E., Valleyfield, Tasmania	10	10	0	
Simpson, Robert, Lange Kal Kal	10	10	0	
Sladen, Hon. C., Birregurra	10	10	0	
Sloan, W. S., Fou Chou, 50 dols.	11	0	10	
Spowers, Allan, "Argus" Office	10	10	0	
Stanbridge, W. E., Daylesford	10	10	0	
Staughton, S. T., Little Collins-street West	10	10	0	
Stewart, J., Emmerdale, Streatham..	21	0	0	

Strachan, J., London Chartered Bank ... £21	0	0
Sumner, T. J., 24 Flinders-lane West	10	10	0
Taylor, Frederick, Melbourne Club	10	10	0
Taylor, W., Overnewton, Keilor	10	10	0
Templeton, Hugh, Fitzroy ...	Services
Ware, Joseph, Carramut ...	10	10	0
Wilson & Mackinnon, Collins-street East	42	0	0
Wilson, Edward, "Argus" Office	21	0	0
Wilson, Samuel, Wimmera ...	10	10	0
Winter, James, Toolamba, Murchison	10	10	0
Winter, Thomas, Winchelsea	10	10	0
Winter, S. P.'	10	10	0
Youl, James A., Clapham Park, London	Services

ANNUAL MEMBERS.

Anderson and Wright ...	£1	1	0	McNaughton, Love and Co.	£2	2	0
Banks Bros., Bell and Co. ...	2	2	0	McCoy, Professor, University	2	2	0
Briscoe and Co.	2	2	0	Michie, Hon. A., M.L.C., St. Kilda	2	2	0
Bligh and Harbottle	2	2	0	Moule, F. G., Brighton ...	2	2	0
Bindon, Judge...	2	2	0	McDougall, Mr., Carlton ...	1	1	0
Black, Dr. Joseph	2	2	0	Nutt, R. W., William-st. ...	1	1	0
Blair, James, Toorak... ...	1	1	0	Power, T. H.	2	2	0
Cumming, Hon. J., M.L.C., Toorak	2	2	0	Patterson, Ray, Palmer & Co.	2	2	0
Courtenay, E....	1	1	0	Pugh, Dr.	2	2	0
Clark, Walter	2	2	0	Russell, Hon. P., M.L.C. Brighton-road	2	2	0
Evans, Gowen, "Argus" office	2	2	0	Ryan & Hammond, Bourke-st.	2	2	0
Fanning, Nankivell and Co. ...	2	2	0	Richmond, James	1	1	0
Gray, Charles, Nareeb Nareeb	2	2	0	Stevenson, L. & Son, Flinders-lane	2	2	0
Godfrey, F. R., Mount Ridley	4	4	0	Sargood, Son and Co. ...	2	2	0
Grice, Richard, Flinders-lane	1	1	0	Sands and McDougall ...	2	2	0
Goldsborough, R. and Co., Bourke-street	2	2	0	Sloane, Wm. & Co., Collins-st.	2	2	0
His Excellency the Governer	10	0	0	Smale, A. W., Brighton ...	2	2	0
House, S. and Co.	2	2	0	Sprigg, George, St. Kilda ...	2	2	0
Haddon, F. W., "Argus" Office	2	2	0	Stawell Shire Council ...	5	0	0
Highett, William, M.L.C., Richmond	2	2	0	Steavenson, John, Brighton...	2	2	0
Joshua Brothers, William-st.	2	2	0	Skene, Hon. Wm., M.L.C. ...	2	2	0
Kilmore, Waltonians, Kilmore	5	0	0	Wilson, Edward, Kent, England	2	2	0

HONORARY MEMBERS.

Allport, Morton, Hobart Town
Beckx, Gustave, Flinders Lane West
Biagi, Guiseppe, William-street
Blanchard W., Collins-street West
Bouton, A., Youhoue, New Caledonia
Buckland, Dr. F., London
Castelnan, Comte de, Apsley Place
Chalmers, Dr., New Zealand
Cleeland, J., Albion Hotel, Bourke-st.
Cooper, Ricardo, Queen-street
Coste, Proffessor, Huningue
Damyon, James, Market-street
Drouyn, de Lhuys, Paris
Francis, Francis, London
Gillanders & Arbuthnot, Calcutta
Godfrey, Captain, J. B.
Graham, James, Little Collins-st. East
Grote, Arthur, Calcutta
Howitt, Ed.
Johnston, Clement, Crown Lands Office
Jones, Captain, Superb
Latham, General

Madden, Walter, Office of Mines
Mathieu, A., Yahoue, New Caledonia
Merryman, Captain, Essex
Michaelis, Moritz, Elizabeth-street
Michael, Major, Madras
McQueen, Captain, " Martha Birnie "
Mullick, Rajendo, Calcutta
Officer, Sir Robert, Hobart Town
Ploos Van Amsel, J. W., Collins-st. W.
Ramel, Monsieur, Paris
Rentsch, Samuel, Flinders-street East
Ridgers, Captain, " Sussex "
Robinson, J., Calcutta
Salt, Sir Titus, Saltaire, England
Scholstein, Adolp., Flinders-lane West
Sclater, Dr. P. L., London
Shinner, Captain " Northumberland "
Smith, Captain, " Dover Castle "
Squire, Surgeon, John, Dinapore
St. Hilaire, G., Bois de Boulogne, Paris
Were, J. B., Collins-street West
White, J. H., Collins-street West

SUPPLEMENTAL LIST OF MEMBERS,

To 9th July, 1872.

	£	s	d
Adam, John (Lawrence & Adam), Elizabeth-street	£1	1	0
Allfrey, Ernst. H., life member, Fernihurst	10	10	0
Allport, Curzon, Chancery-lane	2	2	0
Amess, Samuel, William-street	1	1	0
Anderson, A., Wallaloo ...	1	1	0
Anderson & Wright, Flinders-lane	1	1	0
Baines, E., Little Collins-st.	2	2	0
Banks Brothers, Bell, and Co., Flinders-lane	1	1	0
Barry, D. M., Brunswick ...	1	1	0
Barwise, John, Elizabeth-street	1	1	0
Batt, T., Yarra Flats	1	1	0
Bennet, T. K., Bourke-street	1	1	0
Black, J., Dr., Bourke-street	2	2	0
Blair, James, Toorak	1	1	0
Bligh & Harbottle, Flinders-lane	2	2	0
Borough Council, Portland ...	2	2	0
Bright, C. E., Flinders-lane ...	1	1	0
Briscoe & Co., Collins-street ...	1	1	0
Broadribb, K. E., Chancery-lane	2	2	0
Brown, Gavin G., Collins-st.	2	2	0
Burry, Leech & Co., Queen-st.	1	1	0
Campbell, F., Auchmore ...	1	1	0
Carter, E., Stephen-street ...	1	1	0
Charsley, Edward, Bank-place	1	1	0
Chomley, A. W., Temple Court	1	1	0
Clarke, W. & Co., Elizabeth-st.	1	1	0
Clarke, J. L., Elizabeth-street	1	1	0
Crooke, Dr., Gertrude-street...	1	1	0
Cumming, Hon. J., M.L.C., Toorak	2	2	0
Daly, John, Spring-street ...	1	1	0
Danks, John, Bourke-street ...	1	1	0
Davidson, James, Deniliquin	1	1	0
Dobson, Hon. Dr., M.L.C. ...	1	1	0
Doyle, Lawrence, Stephen-st.	1	1	0
Evans, G. E., "Argus" Office	2	2	0
Fanning, Nankivell, and Co., Collins-street	2	2	0
Fellows, Hon. T. H., Temple Ct.	1	1	0
Fergusson and Moore, Flinders-lane	£1	1	0
Fitch & French, Flinders-lane	1	1	0
Fleming, J. W., Brunswick ...	1	1	0
Ford, W. & Co., Swanston-st.	1	1	0
Foy, Mark, Smith-street ...	1	1	0
Foxcroft, J., Elizabeth-street...	1	1	0
Godfrey, F. R., Mount Ridley...	1	1	0
Goldsborough & Co., Bourke-st.	2	2	0
Graham, Hon. James, M.L.C., Little Collins-street ...	1	1	0
Grant, John, Collins-street ...	1	1	0
Gray, Charles, Nareeb Nareeb	2	2	0
Grice, Richard, Flinders-lane	1	1	0
Green, J. R., Gertrude-street	2	0	0
Greene, Molesworth, Mount Hope	1	1	0
Haddon, S. W. "Argus" Office	2	2	0
Haege, W., Queen-street ...	1	1	0
Harper, R. & Co., Flinders-lane	1	1	0
Hatton, S. W., Flemington ...	1	1	0
Henderson, T., Elizabeth-st....	1	1	0
Hepburne, B., Queen-street...	1	1	0
Highett, The Hon. W., M.L.C., Richmond	2	2	0
Holdsworth, J., Sandhurst ...	1	1	0
House, Samuel & Co., Queen-st.	2	2	0
Howitt, Dr. Godfrey, Caulfield	1	1	0
Hunt, Dr., Brunswick-street...	1	1	0
Ingamells, J., Royal Park ...	1	1	0
Inglis, Daniel, Flinders-street	1	1	0
Jacobs, F. and Co., Queen-st.	1	1	0
Johnston, E., Elizabeth-street	1	1	0
Keep, E., Elizabeth-street ...	1	1	0
Kerr, R., Collins-street ...	1	1	0
King, S. G., Hotham	2	2	0
Kinnear, Robt. H., Lower Moira	1	1	0
Kronheimer, J. & Co., Queen-st.	1	1	0
Lambert T., Lonsdale-street ...	1	1	0
Larnach, J., Kilmore Waltonians	2	12	6
Langhorne, Alfred, Laverton	1	1	0
Latham, E., Carlton	1	1	0
Lawrence, J. B. (Lawrence and Adam), Elizabeth-street...	1	1	0
Lee, B., Bourke-street... ...	2	2	0

	£	s	d
Lindley, A. B., Royal Park ...	£1	1	0
Lyster, W., life member, Spring-street	10	10	0
Lyster, A. B., Bourke-street...	1	1	0
Macknight, Chas. H., Dunmore	1	1	0
Manallack, T., Brunswick ...	1	1	0
Maplestone, H., Elizabeth-st.	1	1	0
Martin, P. J., Flinders-lane ...	1	1	0
Martin, T., Brunswick... ...	1	1	0
Martin, G. & Co., Market-st.	2	2	0
Maryborough Borough Council	5	0	0
Masterman, F. A., Brunswick-street	1	1	0
Matheson, J., Collins-street ..	1	1	0
M'Coy, Professor, University	1	1	0
McCulloch, Sellar & Co., Queen-street	2	2	0
McDougall, C., Brunswick	1	1	0
McEachern, A. & D., life members, Kangaroo	10	10	0
McKellar, The Hon. Thomas, M.L.C., Melbourne Club	10	0	0
McNaughton, Love and Co., Flinders-lane	2	2	0
Mitchell, the Hon. W. H. F., M.L.C., Melbourne Club	1	1	0
Moloney, Dr., Lonsdale-street	1	1	0
Moore and Co., Bourke-street	1	1	0
Moule, F. G., Market-street ...	1	1	0
Murphy, E. J., William-street	1	1	0
Nutt, R. W., Queen-street ...	1	1	0
Ogilvey, A. J., Queen-street ...	1	1	0
Oldfield, L., Royal Park ...	1	1	0
Overend, Best, Brunswick ...	1	1	0
Paterson, W., Collins-street ...	1	1	0
Paterson, Ray, Palmer & Co., Flinders-lane	2	2	0
Peterson, W. & Co., Queen-st.	1	1	0
Robertson, George, Elizabeth-street	£1	1	0
Robertson, W., M.L.A., Melbourne Club	2	2	0
Rocke, W. H., Collins-street	1	1	0
Rosser, E., Brunswick ...	1	1	0
Rosser, Charles, Brunswick ...	1	1	0
Rudd, A. P., Flemington ...	2	2	0
Russell, The Hon. P., M.L.C., Melbourne Club	1	1	0
Ryan & Hammond, Bourke-st.	2	2	0
Sanderson, J. & Co., William-st.	1	1	0
Sandridge Borough Council ...	3	3	0
Sands and McDougall, Collins-street	2	2	0
Stanford and Co., Bourke-st....	1	1	0
Sargood, Son & Co., Flinders-st.	2	2	0
Simson, Hon. R., M.L.C., Toorak	2	2	0
Skene, Hon. W., M.L.C., Toorak	2	2	0
Skinner, Judge, Windsor ...	2	2	0
Sloane, W. and Co., Collins-st.	2	2	0
Smale, A. W. Queen-street. ...	2	2	0
Smith, C. and J., Albert-street	1	1	0
Somner, W., Swanston-street	1	1	0
Sprigg, W. G., Brighton ...	1	1	0
Straw, T., Brunswick ...	1	1	0
Terry Alfred, Royal Park ...	1	1	0
Twentyman, T., Emerald Hill	1	1	0
Twentyman, R., Flinders-street	1	1	0
Venables, H. P., Education Office	1	1	0
Walker, P. N., Williams-street	1	1	0
Wilshin & Lighton, Williams-street	1	1	0
Wilson, E., "Argus" Office ...	2	2	0
Wilson, Dr. J. P., Craigieburn	1	1	0
Woods, J. & Son, Collingwood	1	1	0

DONATIONS.

	£	s	d
Cornwall, A., Brunswick ...	£0	10	0
Coward, James	1	0	0
Fairchild, J. R., Williams-st....	1	0	0
Firth, Henry, Brunswick ...	0	5	6
Frost, W., Benalla	1	0	0
Gordon & Gotch, Collins-street	1	1	0
Gratton, H. Gowangardie ...	1	1	0
Gunst, Dr., Collins-street ...	£1	0	0
Harrington, P. Victoria-street	1	0	0
Hoskin, T., Benalla	1	0	0
McKellar, James, Lima Station	1	0	0
McDonald, F., Solicitor, Benalla	1	0	0
Power, T. H., Collins-street ...	1	0	0
Turnbull, James, Emeu Plains	1	0	0

THE RULES AND OBJECTS

OF THE

Zoological & Acclimatisation Society

OF VICTORIA.

1. The objects of the Society shall be the introduction, acclimatisation, liberation, and domestication of innoxious animals and vegetables, whether useful or ornamental;— the perfection, propagation, and hybridisation of races newly introduced, or already domesticated;—the spread of indigenous animals, &c., from parts of the colonies where they are already known, to other localities where they are not known; the procuring, whether by purchase, gift, or exchange, of animals, &c.;—the transmission of animals, &c., from the colony to England and foreign parts, in exchange for others sent thence to the Society;—the collection and maintenance of zoological specimens, for exhibition or otherwise;—the holding of periodical meetings, and the publication of reports and transactions, for the purpose of spreading knowledge of acclimatisation, and inquiry into the causes of success or failure; the interchange of reports, &c., with kindred associations in other parts of the world, with the view, by correspondence and mutual good offices, of giving the widest possible scope to the project of acclimatisation;—the conferring rewards, honorary or intrinsically valuable, upon persons who may render valuable services to the cause of acclimatisation.

Objects of Society.

Membership. 2. A Subscriber of one guinea or upwards annually, which shall be payable in the month of January, shall be a Member of the Society; and contributors within one year of ten guineas or upwards shall be Life Members of the Society; and any person who may render special services to the Society, by contribution of stock or otherwise, shall be eligible for life membership, and may be elected as such by the Council, or by any annual general meeting.

Property vest in the Council 3. All the property of the Society shall vest in the Council for the time being, for the use, purposes, and benefit of the Society.

Executive Officers.

Council. 4. The Society shall be governed by a Council of eighteen Members, to include a President, two Vice-Presidents, and an Honorary Treasurer, who, with three other Members (viz., those who have attended the fewest meeting of the Council proportionately since their appointment) shall retire annually, but shall be eligible for re-election, subject to Rule 11. Provided that if any sum of money be voted to the Society by Act of Parliament, or trusts conferred upon the Council by the Government, then it shall be lawful for the Chief Secretary for the time being to appoint, if he consider it expedient, any number of gentlemen, not exceeding three, to act as members of the Council, and they shall have all the privileges as if otherwise duly elected,

Vacancy in Council, how supplied. 5. In case of a vacancy occurring by the death, resignation, or non-attendance of any member of the Council for a period of two months, without leave of the Council, the remaining Members shall, in due course, appoint another Member of the Society to be a Member of the Council in the place and stead of the Member who shall so resign or absent himself; but such new Member shall be nominated at an ordinary meeting of the Council prior to the meeting at which he is elected.

6. In case of a vacancy occurring by the death or re- Council to fill up Vacancies. signation of the President, Vice-President, or Hon. Treasurer, the Council may appoint from amongst themselves, or the other Members of the Society, a person to fill the vacancy so occurring, and the person elected shall hold office only until the next Annual Meeting ; but shall be eligible for re-election for the subsequent year. Provided that such vacancy shall not be filled up unless seven days' notice in writing shall have been sent to each Member of the Council, stating the vacancies which it is proposed to fill up.

7. No person shall be eligible as a Member of Council Elegibility of Members of Council. unless he be a subscriber to the funds of the Society of at least one guinea per annum ; and any member of Council whose subscription shall be in arrear for three months after his subscription is payable, shall cease to be a Member of Council : Provided that this rule shall not apply to persons who may have become life members of the Society, by a payment of ten guineas, or who may be honorary members of the Society ; and provided also, that a month's notice in writing shall be sent to the member before his place can be filled up.

8. The Council shall meet at least once a month, three Meetings of Council. Members to form a quorum, and transact the business of the Society.

9. The Council shall have the sole management of the Powers and duties of Council. affairs of the Society, and of the income and property thereof, for the uses, purposes, and benefit of the Society ; and shall have the sole and exclusive right of appointing paid servants, as a Manager or Secretary, Collector, and such other officers, clerks, and labourers, and at such salaries as they may deem necessary, and of removing them if they shall think fit, and shall prescribe their respective duties. And such Council shall have power to consider

and determine all matters, either directly or indirectly affecting the interests of the Society, and if they shall think fit so to do, shall bring the same under the notice of the Members of the Society at any general or special meeting ; and to make such bye-laws as they may deem necessary for the efficient management of the affairs, and the promotion of the objects of the Society, and for the conduct of the business of the Council: Provided the same are not repugnant to these rules ; to appoint one or more sub-committees, for any purpose contemplated by these rules; and generally to perform such acts as may be requisite to carry out the objects of the Society.

Branch Societies, &c. 10. The Society shall have power to associate itself with other Societies with similar objects, and to found Branch Societies.

Minutes of Proceedings. 11. Minutes shall be made, in books kept for the purpose, of all proceedings at general and special meetings of the Members, and minutes shall also be made of the proceedings of the Council at their general and special meetings, and of the names of the Members attendng the same, and such minutes shall be open to inspection by any Member of the Society at all reasonable times.

Moneys to be paid to Treasurer. 12. All subscriptions and other moneys received on account of the Society shall be paid to the Treasurer, or some person authorized by him in writing, who shall forthwith place the same in a bank, to be named by the Council, to the credit of the Society ; and no sum shall be paid on account of the Society until the same shall have been ordered by the Council, and such order be duly entered in the book of the proceedings of the Council; and all cheques shall be signed by the Treasurer as such, and be countersigned by the President, or one of the Vice-Presidents, or by the

Chairman of the meeting at which such payment is authorised.

13. An annual meeting shall be held in the month of February in each year, and the Council shall report their proceedings during the past year, and shall produce their accounts, duly audited, for publication; and the meeting shall elect by ballot the office-bearers for the ensuing year, and fill up any vacancy which may exist in the Council: provided that no person shall hold the office of President, Vice-President, or Treasurer, for two years successively. Annual Meeting.

14. The Council may, and upon receiving a requisition in writing, signed by twelve or more Members, shall convene a special meeting of the Members, to be held within fifteen days after the receipt of such requisition: Provided that such requisition, and the notices convening the meeting, shall specify the subject to be considered at such meeting, and that subject only shall be discussed at such meeting. Special Meetings of Members.

15. The Council, or any general meeting of the Society, may admit, as Honorary Members, any ladies or gentlemen who may have distinguished themselves in connection with the objects of the Society, and at such meeting any other business of the Society shall be transacted, of which one day's previous notice shall have been given to the Secretary by any Member desirous of bringing the same forward. Honorary Members.

16. No Medal of the Society shall be awarded to any person except by the vote of at least seven Members of Council present at a Council Meeting, and after notice of motion for awarding such Medal shall have been given at the next preceding meeting of the Council.

17. It shall be lawful for any annual or special meeting of the Society to alter, vary, or amend the rules; or to sub- Power to alter Rules.

stitute another for any of the same ; or to make any new rule which may be considered desirable ; if and after a notice specifying the nature of such alteration, variation, amend‑ ment, substitution, or new rule, shall have been given to the Secretary fifteen days before the holding of such meeting. And such alteration, variation, amendment, substitution, or new rule shall be valid if carried by a majority of not less than two-thirds of the Members present at such meeting.

LIST OF ANIMALS AND BIRDS

IN THE ROYAL PARK AND ZOOLOGICAL AND ACCLIMATISATION SOCIETY'S GARDENS, MELBOURNE.

3 Kangaroos
7 Brahmin cattle
8 Hog deer
5 Bairanga deer
7 Formosa deer
4 Sambur deer
1 Fallow deer
1 Nylghau
4 Mauritius deer
2 Japanese deer
4 Angora goats
1 Agouti
1 Madagascar sheep
1 Cape sheep
7 Monkeys
1 Wallaby
2 Kangaroo rats
1 Wombat
2 Echidna

1 Ceylon porcupine
1 Leopard
1 Native dog
1 English fox
3 Opossums
9 Emeus
40 English pheasants
30 Silver pheasants
9 Pea fowl
4 Jungle fowl
11 Egyptian geese
6 Geese
About 70 ducks
3 Crown goura pigeons
2 Ravens
1 Mooruke
4 Eagles
1 Native companion

2 Curassows
1 Kagus
2 Maori hens
2 Kiwi
4 Bleeding heart doves
2 Macaws
1 Blackbird
1 Jackdaw
1 English magpie
3 Owls

A number of native cockatoos and parrots of different varieties in the aviaries; and about the grounds large numbers of doves.

ANIMALS LIBERATED.

AT THE BOTANICAL GARDENS.

18 Canaries
18 Blackbirds
14 Thrushes

6 California quail
80 English wild ducks
35 Java sparrows

4 English robins
8 Turtle doves
50 Mainas

AT PHILLIP ISLAND.

10 Hares
5 Cape pheasnts
8 English pheasants
4 Indian pheasants
8 Ceylon partridges
5 Indian partridges

4 Chinese partridges
70 Chinese quail
23 Tasmanian quail
6 Starlings
10 Algerine sand grouse
6 Wild ducks

5 Pheasants
6 Skylarks
6 California quail
4 Thrushes
4 Blackbirds
1 Pair white swans

AT SANDSTONE AND CHURCHILL ISLANDS.

4 Pheasants | 4 Skylarks | 4 Thrushes

AT YARRA BEND.

6 Thrushes | 4 Skylarks

NEAR SYDNEY.

9 Thrushes | 4 Skylarks | 10 Blackbirds

AT SUGARLOAF HILL.

5 Ceylon elk | 3 Axis deer

AT WILSON'S PROMONTORY.

4 Axis deer

AT THE ROYAL PARK.

4 Hares	2 Thrushes	20 Siskin finches
20 Mainas	20 Greenfinches	6 Powi birds
6 Starlings	15 Yellowhammers	3 Partridges
60 English sparrows	200 Java sparrows	6 Pheasants
40 Chaffinches	6 Blackbirds	

AT PENTRIDGE.

40 English sparrows.

AT ST. KILDA.

20 Chinese sparrows.

AT BALLARAT.

5 English sparrows | 20 Java sparrows

AT BUNEEP.

13 Fallow deer.

AT CAPE LIPTRAP.

12 Hog Deer	4 Ceylon peafowls	4 Guinea fowl
	10 Pigeons	

AT AUCKLAND ISLANDS.

12 Goats	12 Rabbits	6 Fowls
3 Geese	3 Pigs	3 Ducks

AT WESTERNPORT.

7 Sambur deer.

AT THE WIMMERA.

35 Axis deer.

AT YERING.

5 Axis deer.

AT PLENTY RANGES.

10 Pheasants | 4 Jungle fowls | 7 Guinea fowls

ANIMALS SENT AWAY.

TO LONDON.

75 Kangaroos	26 Waterhens	40 Black ducks
5 Mountain ducks	4 Kangaroo rats	40 Teal
200 Murray codfish	10 Wombats	22 Wonga pigeons
22 Black swans	2 Cranes	31 Bronze-wing pigeons
20 Australian quail	7 Wood ducks	8 Swamp magpies
14 Eagle hawks	2 Kangaroo dogs	2 Iguanas
85 Magpies	3 Echidna	7 Land rails
4 Rosella parrots	26 Laughing jackasses	4 Sugar squirrels
8 King parrots	40 Shell parrots	3 Coots
8 Cockatoos	6 Mallee pheasants	5 Native companions
5 Dingos	36 Lowry parrots	Some Yarra fish
3 Talegallas	12 Oppossums	
1 Tasmanian devil	4 Emeus.	

TO PARIS.

20 Emeus	3 Curlews	8 Goatsuckers
30 Kangaroos	1 Native crane	2 Native companions
12 Black swans	8 Murray turtles	14 Rockhampton finches
3 Cape Barren geese	2 Wombats	1 Iguana
1 South Australian	17 Australian quail	4 Oppossums
wombat	4 Laughing jackasses	20 Black ducks
4 Native geese	2 Bronze-wing pigeons	20 Teal

TO ST. PETERSBURG.

3 Kangaroos	2 Laughing jackasses	3 Emeus
3 Black swans	2 Wallabies	

TO AMSTERDAM.

3 Water hens   1   6 Australian quail

TO ROTTERDAM.

2 Cape Barren geese   1   2 Water hens

TO HAMBURGH.

2 Wonga pigeons	2 Bronze-wing pigeons	2 Kangaroo rats
2 Black swans		

TO COLOGNE.

2 Black swans	2 Curlews	2 Water hens
2 Black geese		

TO COPENHAGEN.

2 Black swans

TO CALCUTTA.

24 Black swans	15 Rosella parrots	6 Bronze-wing pigeons
12 Emeus	10 Kangaroos	6 Laughing jackasses
2 Eagles	4 Opossums	20 Shell parrots
6 White cockatoos	1 Dingo	52 Magpies
7 King parrots	1 Wombat	

TO MAURITIUS.

2 Black swans	2 Eagle hawks	2 Laughing jackasses
1 Kangaroo	9 Fowls	4 Wallabies
2 Cape Barren geese	7 Magpies	

TO BOURBON.

8 Black swans

TO SICILY.

6 Black swans   1   14 Native ducks

TO RANGOON.

6 Black swans

TO JAVA.

2 Black swans   1   2 Cape Barren Geese   1   1 Kangaroo

TO BURTENZONG.

2 Black swans   1   2 Cape Barren geese   1   1 Kangaroo

TO SYDNEY.

5 Angora goats	6 English wild ducks	4 Larks
2 Brush kangaroos	1 Mallee hen	4 Starlings
2 Silver pheasants	10 Blackbirds	2 Ortolans
2 Canadian geese	10 Thrushes	A number of sparrows
2 Egyptian geese		

TO ADELAIDE.

10 Angora goats	2 Thrushes	3 Silver pheasants
2 Blackbirds	3 English pheasants	

TO HOBART TOWN.

1 Angora goat	2 Egyptian geese
9 Native bears	2 Hares
Wild ducks, Indian & English	A number of sparrows

TO NEW ZEALAND.

3 Thrushes	4 Opossums	Indian and English
6 Magpies	2 Brace of hares	wild ducks

TO FOO CHOW.

48 Wild rabbits	2 Kangaroo	2 Parrots

TO NEW CALEDONIA.

238 Sparrows		12 Laughing jackasses

AT MR. WILSON'S—LONGERENONG, WIMMERA.

17 Ostriches		55 Angora goats

LIBERATED IN THE BUSH IN 1870.

8 Hog deer	30 Pheasants	A number of doves
10 Pea Fowl	Several brace of hares	25 Skylarks
20 Guinea fowl		

A large number of hares were likewise distributed in 1870 in various parts of the country, and upwards of 100 Angora goats were disposed of in addition to those enumerated above.

LIBERATED IN THE BUSH IN 1871.

150 Guinea fowl	Several brace of hares
15 Pheasants	3 Deer

And 2400 trout fry placed in different streams.

A number of hares were likewise distributed in various parts of the country.

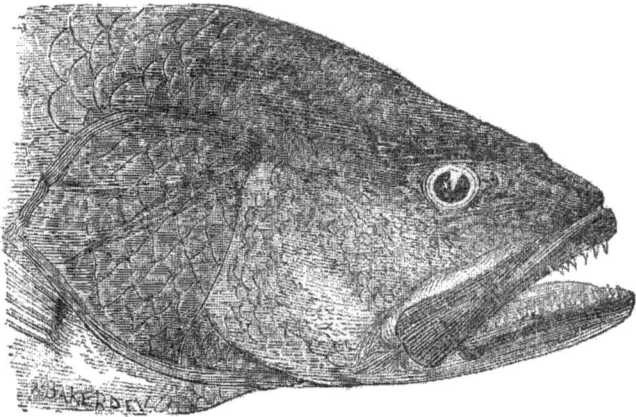

King Fish (*Sciæna Antarctica*).

Heads of Old (Male) Snappers (*Pagrus Unicolor*).

CONTRIBUTION

TO THE

ICHTHYOLOGY OF AUSTRALIA.

BY

COUNT F. DE CASTELNAU.

No. I.—THE MELBOURNE FISH MARKET.

My intention is, if circumstances allow me, to submit to the
public a succession of papers on the fishes of Australia. This
first one is devoted to the description of the different sorts I
have observed at Melbourne, alive or in a fresh state, during more
than a year, and which almost all come from the Fish Market.
The number of sorts (142) is very limited, compared with what
could be collected during the same period in other countries,
such as India or South America ; but, if many of the South
Australian forms indicate their *habitat* in a semi-tropical climate,
the diversity of species is not so great as in most regions equally
situated. This seems to be the rule with the Antarctic Seas, as
at the Cape of Good Hope, after several years' researches, I
could only obtain 157 sorts (with ossified skeletons or *Teleostei,*
Gunther), many of which came from distant parts, such as Lake
N'gami, Natal, &c. Since then, many sorts have been indicated
as from South Africa, and their number is so considerable in the
Catalogues of the British Museum as to make me, in many cases,
doubt of the exactness of the assigned locality. All the fishes of
Sir A. Smith's collection have been inscribed as coming from the
Cape sea, while I believe that many were obtained at very distant

localities. During several years, not only did I visit several times a day the Fish Market of Cape Town, but the Malay fishermen were most active in endeavouring to obtain specimens for me. Sir A. Smith himself, in his "Illustrations of South Australian Zoology," mentions a number of sorts of fishes much smaller even than the one I obtained myself (about 40); and Dr. Pappe, after ten years' study of the fishes of the Cape, only mentions 45 sorts of edible ones. (" *Synopsis of the Edible Fishes of the Cape of Good Hope.*" Cape Town, 1853.) As a general rule, I believe that the great Antarctic Sea will be found to contain less sorts of fishes than most others, and that this will also be the case with the rivers and lakes of the same regions. With few exceptions, the fishes of the southern parts of Australia are peculiar to the region they inhabit, as of 142 sorts (exclusive of a doubtful sort of *cyprinidæ*), 11 only are found in other regions, that is, 5 of the 123 sorts of *Teleostei*, and 6 of the 19 species of cartilaginous fishes. The five of the first are— 1. *Temnodon Saltator*, which is very widely spread over almost all the tropical and temperate seas of the globe. 2. *Thyrsites Atum*, found also at the Cape of Good Hope. 3. *Tetraodon Hispidus*, found in the Red Sea and all over the Indian Ocean. 4. *Diodon Spinosissimus*, from the Cape of Good Hope and the Indian Sea. 5. *Orthagoriscus Mola*, from the European seas. To this I ought, perhaps, to add *Mugil Waigiensis*, first discovered in New Guinea ; but this large island may be considered as belonging to the Australian zoological zona.

Amongst the cartillaginous fishes, we find *Sygæna Malleus, Galeus Canis, Rhina Squatina, Raya Oxyrhynchus,* and *Myliobates Aquila,* all found in the European seas ; and *Chimæra Antarctica,* from the Cape of Good Hope. It would seem as if the more the bones take a cartillaginous nature, the more the animal would be able to support the changes of climate, &c. ; but it must also be observed that some of these last sorts have not been sufficiently well compared with European specimens.

The fact that not one single true *Serranus* seems to inhabit the southern shores of Australia (*S. Rasor* being very distinct in general appearance) is also remarkable, as I had already observed the same fact at Table Bay; and here also, on the eastern coast, as at Natal and Algoa Bay, several sorts of real *Serranus* are found.

I certainly do not mean to give to these observations an exagge-rated importance, as I am well convinced that I have not yet seen one-half, perhaps not one-third, of the sorts that inhabit the Bass Straits, and even Hobson's Bay. Very little interest has been, till this time, felt in the Australian Colonies, on sub-jects of natural science, and I have found it impossible to get the fishermen to collect for me the sorts that are not usually considered as edible, and they almost always prefer throwing away specimens valuable for science, and for which they might obtain a remuneration larger than the one they get for eatable fishes, sooner than take the trouble of bringing them to the market. This indifference extends to all classes, and though the Acclima-tisation Society has requested, several times, in the public news-papers, persons desirous of helping it in the task of making better known the zoology of Victoria,, to send any specimens they may obtain, no answers have been received. It is singular to remark that not one of the Australian Colonies has a particular work on one single branch of its zoology, whereas every State of North America has a complete series of valuable works on each branch of that science. In this the Australian Democracy seems to be far behind its American sister. The only, very scanty, materials published on the fishes of Victoria consist—1st. Of a paper of W. Blandowski on the sorts he had collected in the interior of the Colony, and particularly in the Murray River. This paper was to be inserted in the " Transactions of the Philosophical Institute of Victoria," vol. 2, pages 124 to 132. It was accompanied by four plates, representing in a rough way nineteen sorts of fishes, many of which are unknown to me. A rather curious anecdote is told of this production : The author had, according to the custom of naturalists, dedicated several of the sorts to leading members of the Society ; but some of these gentlemen are said to have taken as an insult what was most probably intended as a compliment, and the letterpress and plates already engraved were withdrawn and destroyed before distribution. I must own that I cannot say much for the scientific value of the paper, but I have found in it a few observations on the habits of several sorts of the interior rivers.

2nd. Of a short notice on the fishes of Victoria in Professor M'Coy's Report on the Zoology of the Colony, in the " Intercolonial Exhibition Essays, 1866-1867." In this paper the learned author has endeavoured to give the scientific names of the common fishes of the market, and in this he has, in general, well succeeded. There are also to be found some interesting observations on several sorts in this essay.

3rd. A short paper by Dr. Gunther on a few Victorian sorts in the " Annals and Magazine of Natural History, 1863."

4rth. Several papers of Sir J. Richardson in the " Transactions of the Zoological Society" (vol. iii.); the Proceedings of the same, 1839-1840;" and in the " Annals and Magazine of Natural History, 1842-1843."

But if the materials on Australian fishes, published in works particularly devoted to them, are few, on the other hand all the publications made on the Scientific Expeditions sent by England, France, and other countries contain numerous descriptions and plates of Australian sorts, and Sir J. Richardson, in the " Ichthyology of the Voyage of the *Erebus* and *Terror*," has given a most valuable account of the sorts brought by that expedition from the Antarctic Seas. The work of this celebrated Ichthyologist forms the most valuable contribution to Australian Ichthyology ever published.

Of the general works on the science, two deserve a special notice. The first is the great " *Histoire Naturelle des Poissons*" of Cuvier and Valenciennes, which was left incomplete at its 22nd volume by the death of the first of its illustrious authors. This work is the base of the science, and not only recapitulates in an admirable manner all that had previously been published on it, but describes an immense number of new sorts. It is in this magnificent work that the great Cuvier gives the details of the system of which he had published the outlines in his " *Règne Animal*."

The second is Dr. Gunther's " Catalogue of the Fishes of the British Museum," complete in eight volumes. This work is one of the most remarkable productions of modern science, and places its author high amongst zoologists. Dr. Gunther follows Cuvier's system, but amends it considerably, and it must be owned that most of his changes are improvements on it, and in conformity with the natural arrangement of beings. The labour, patience, and science shown by the author are deserving of the greatest praise. After having said all the good I think of this great work, I must also submit a few critical observations on it. Many of Dr. Gunther's superior divisions are established only on anatomical characters, and I think this most objectionable, as it would exclude from the study of science all those who would not have at their entire disposition one of the large museums of Europe, and even the fortunate zoologists who are so situated can only, in comparatively few instances, sacrifice valuable specimens. I think that anatomical characters ought only to be used to confirm zoological ones.

Dr. Gunther, in most cases, prefers describing the colours from the discoloured specimens he has at his disposition sooner than adopting the description of travellers who have seen the sorts alive, and in many cases have made drawings from specimens so taken. For instance, *Phractocephalus Hemiliopterus* is described as a fish of obscure tinges, when he had my plate under his eyes, showing its beautiful colours, drawn from the living specimen.

He changes the names, derived from Greek or Latin, that he considers badly composed, and this I think useless, as it only increases synonymy unnecessarily. If men with the high literary acquirements of Lacepede and Cuvier have committed such mistakes, no one can expect to be exempt from them, and as names without any meaning are just as good, if not better, than those which pretend to have one. If a name is not well made, it is more simple, I think, to consider it as having no meaning at all, than to introduce a new one into the nomenclature.

Dr. Gunther divides the species admitted by his predecessors into two classes—those that he considers well characterized, and those that he regards as doubtful; he only gives descriptions of the first, which have almost all been seen by himself; and as to the others, it is necessary to resort to the original works, as amongst them a very large proportion have just as good a right to be maintained as those he admits. He must be approved of for rejecting, till further examination, all sorts established on figures and drawings only. Lacepede was the first to introduce into the science numerous sorts founded on these materials, and he went so far as to consider as sufficient documents rough paintings due to Chinese and Japanese draughtsmen. When he only used materials due to such men as Commerson, Forster, &c., he was pretty safe; but even then, it is well known that a naturalist, travelling in little known countries, is often so pressed for time as to necessarily neglect in his drawings many characters that will be found necessary when they will be submitted to the scrutiny of modern science. Putting these aside, there remains in his so-called *uncharacterized sorts*—an immense number that have been seen by his predecessors; and I think that when such authorities as Cuvier, Valenciennes, Richardson, Bleeker, Kaup, Ruppell, &c., admit them as distinct species, after having studied them, they are at least as much entitled to be believed as the zoologist who has not even seen them.

Taken, for example, the sorts brought back by myself from the central parts of South America, and deposited at the Garden of Plants of Paris, we find that Dr. Gunther considers many of them as identified with species of Cuvier and Valenciennes, when, in the Ichthyological part of my Travels, I give them as distinct. Perhaps the imperfection of my descriptions may have led him to believe in their identity; but it must be remembered that those specimens were all compared with Cuvier and Valenciennes' types, aside of which they are placed in the Museum, and that this examination was not only done by myself, but in many cases by Messrs. Valenciennes and Dumeril, and in all cases by Mr. Guichenot. On the other hand Dr. Gunther appears not to have examined the Parisian collection, which is certainly the most important in the world, on account of the immense quantity of typical specimens it contains.

I also think that Dr. Gunther carries too far the modern tendency of uniting sorts that were considered as distinct, and, misled by this principle, he has formed a certain number of artificial species which do not exist in nature. It is well known that in the class of fishes colours are, in general, subject to such alterations as not to afford, as a general rule, specific characters, as they do in almost all the other divisions of the animal kingdom, and that these characters must be looked for in the forms and sometimes in the distribution of bands, stripes, &c. In many cases, the learned doctor goes much further, and supposes even these forms to be subject to such variations as no specific characters would remain, and so, only to quote one example, to have the satisfaction of uniting the *gonorhynchus* of the Cape with those of Japan and of Australia, he is obliged to suppose a sort whose proportions vary according to age, which sort does not exist.

· I also think that Dr. Gunther shows too little attention to the geographical distribution of fishes. He delights in stating that a sort from the Northern Sea is found at the Cape of Good Hope ; that another from the coast of Senegal inhabits also the Antarctic Sea. Even fresh-water fishes, whose *habitat* had, till now, been considered as very limited, are submitted by him to the same process, and sorts from the rivers of Chili are united with those of Tasmania, or English sorts are said to be found in New Zealand. In many cases he asserts that they are not entirely similar, and even goes so far as to propose names for those *varieties*, but nevertheless they must be included under the same specific names. He seems to admit too easily new localities, and so, to give one example, the largest of all fresh-water fishes, the *Pirarucu* (sudis vastres), is said, on the authority of a dealer, to inhabit Bahia, without telling us what river of that locality is capable of feeding such a giant. The truth is, that it is restricted to the Amazonas and to its northern branches. It is also found in those of the rivers of Guyana, whose head waters, during a part of the year, or at least in floods, communicate with the branches I have just mentioned.

The old authors, such as Bloch, Lacepede, &c., never hesitated to state that a species inhabited Greenland and India ; but under the scrutiny of Cuvier and Valenciennes these sweeping assertions generally proved incorrect, and new ideas were introduced on the distribution of sorts in the waters of the world. But after having studied Dr. Gunther's work with the attention it so well deserves, one finds onself once more wandering in a complete sea of uncertainty, and it will take years of careful study to re-establish some rules in this part of geographical zoology. This I consider as the greatest fault in Dr. Gunther's most valuable work.

It is also to be regretted that the learned doctor does not add to his qualities a little more indulgence towards other naturalists, often his predecessors in the science. He has placed himself, by his works, quite high enough not to be quite so bitter towards those who have not, like himself, the privilege of never being mistaken. Even in speaking of Cuvier, the master of all modern naturalists, he cannot refrain from this habit of rude criticism, which so often becomes offensive. It is to be regretted that he has not, with so many other things, learned from the great man I have just mentioned to correct with urbanity the mistakes of others. If Cuvier was obliged to rectify a traveller or a little known naturalist, he would do it in such an indulgent way as to encourage him to pursue his labours ; and if he had to correct a man high in science, Linnæus for instance, he was always disposed to add that a little inattention was well excusable in the man of genius who had imposed on himself the task of describing the immensity of Nature. It is evident that Dr. Gunther's greatest delight is to find fault with everyone and with everything. When he mentions a plate, he must almost always add one of the following epithets :—" Not good." " Bad." " Very bad." And in many cases he has never seen the fish in question, and the drawing is due to one of those artists who, having devoted the labours of their lives to zoology, have become naturalists of no small merit themselves. His love for criticism is such as to make him point out mistakes that have been already corrected by the author himself. For example, in describing my *Holacanthus Formosus*, he says in a note that the number of the fins are entirely wrong as I have stated them, when, in the *Errata* of the work (" Fishes of South America "), in the Zoological part of my Expedition (p. 112), I myself corrected the mistake, and re-established the real numbers.

One of the greatest beauties of the study of Nature is generally considered to reside in the brotherly feeling it establishes between men of all nations, of all ages, of all ranks. It is the greatest boon of sufferance, and often the only consolation in misfortune ; but if it was to be followed in the spirit with which some modern naturalists seem to be imbued, it would soon change these kind and generous sentiments into feelings of spite, insult, and revenge. Instead of being a boon of peace and a comfort to men of quiet and studious habits, it would degenerate into a state of continual warfare, and few men of science would like to spend their lives ou such a field of battle.

To put an end to these remarks, I will only add that I think that when zoologists have long resided in a locality, aud have made its productions the object of a particular study, such as Ruppell, Bleeker, Day, &c , their opinion is of greater value than that of a man, whatever may he his scientific acquirements, who remains in his study in Europe. A visit to a fish market, in bringing under your eyes thousands of specimens of a sort, will certainly lead you to a more correct idea of its variations than ean be obtained by the residing zoologist, who only has at his disposition one, or in all cases, a very few specimens, having lost their colours, and more or less their form, by dessication or preservation in spirits.

The study of Ichthyology has been with me, for many years, the object of a particular predilection. When in my youth, I spent nearly five years in the United States and Canada. I collected a considerable number of fishes on the demand of Baron Cuvier. Later, when I was the Director of the Scientific Expedition sent by the King of the Freuch, Louis Philippe, to South America, I devoted much attention to this subject, and the specimens collected on my return, by the Amazonas River, are in the Parisian Museum ; but the greatest part of the vast collection I had formed during the first three years overlaud, from Rio Janeiro to Lima, was lost. A few of the dried specimens were saved, but all those put in spirits were destroyed, probably by the liquor becoming too weak, and also by the other incidents inherent to a two or three years' trip on the backs of mules and horses. When the Relation of this Expedition was published, after a few years' delay caused by the political events which had agitated my country, I reserved for myself the Ichthyological part of the work. Having, after the Revolution of 1848, been appointed French Consul at Bahia, I continued my researches in the northern parts of Brazil, and I was enabled to insert the results I obtained, by reason of the delay I have just explained, in the Relation of my Expedition. Sent afterwards to the Cape of Good Hope, where I remained three years, during which

I travelled over Caffraria and several of the most remote parts of the Colony, I not only actively collected all the fishes I could observe, but I wrote detailed descriptions, and made drawings of every sort, with their natural colours; but, charged by my Government to establish a French Consulate at Siam, I extracted, before I left the Cape Colony, a short notice from my manuscript, and sent it for publication in June, 1858, to my late friend, Professor August Dumeril. Different circumstances delayed, during my absence, the printing of my "*Mémoire Sur les Poissons de L'Afrique Australe*," which only appeared at the beginning of 1861. It is in his seventh volume (1868) that Dr. Gunther quotes for the first time this publication, and does it in his usual style. I must say that I still believe that the study, during several years, of the fishes of a distant region cannot be entirely useless to science. In India, I continued my ichthyological labours. At Bangkock I collected the sorts of the great Mainam River ; at Saigon, those of the Meklong ; and, during a more or less lengthened stay at Malacca, Sumatra Java, Ceylon, and Singapore, I described and sketched from nature over 750 sorts. On my return to Europe, I began to put in order my voluminous notes, but having been obliged, on account of sickness, to interrupt my work, I was, on my recovery, struck with a most disagreeable surprise, in discovering that my servant had, for more than one month, used the sheets of paper on which I had bestowed so much time and labour to light the fires, and other parts of my learned lucubrations were discovered in the last place in the world where an author would be proud of finding his works. Totally disheartened, I disposed of my collection and drawings in favour of Professor Lacordaire, of the Liege University, another of my old friends, who has also lately been swept away before he could complete his great work on the Coleoptera Insects, and once more I devoted the whole of my time to Entomological researches.

I had always since my arrival in the Colony, nine years ago, been struck by the want of a work on the fishes of Australia, and of Victoria in particular. In such a new country, vernacular names are far from possessing the same degree of fixity as they do in Europe ; and putting aside a dozen or two very common sorts, every fishmonger gives a different name to the same species. This increases very much the difficulties of study, and I thought it would be useful to condense in a paper what was known on the fishes of the Colony. The Acclimatisation Society, always desirous of promoting anything useful to the country, entered into these views, and that is the origin of the essay I now submit to the public. Before I finish this paper, I think it is useful to say a few words on a subject which has always much embarassed naturalists, and on which the diversity of their views is very great: I mean the question of what is a genus ?—what is a species ?

A genus is, for me, a more or less artificial collection of species offering some common characters; a few appear to constitue natural groups; but I think that in such cases it will generally be found that the missing links have not yet been discovered, or have entirely disappeared from the recent *fauna* of the globe. The genus, being an artificial division, is, of course, appreciated very differently by the various authors. All the so-called superior divisions are in the same case, and thus the *species* seems to me to be, of the zoological divisions, the only one to be found in nature. But even this, to be such, must be considered as a *constant variety;* that is, that as soon as a collection of specimens present the same characters, due to natural circumstances, they must be considered as forming a species. I believe that accidental or Geological phenomena, in driving a part of the individuals of a species to regions different from those they previously inhabited, will, with time, constitute a new species, as it is certain that those individuals, having to find a different way of living, and to be subjected to different temperatures, will deviate from the type, and constitute different sorts, or what is usually called, when this process is only beginning, *local varieties.* Types will retain their forms unchanged thousands of years when they remain in the same climate and in the same region, but they will deviate as soon as these circumstances are changed. I have observed elsewhere (Expedition to the Central Parts of South America) that the animals who can neither fly nor swim are almost all different on one side of the Amazonas to what they are on the other, and this has been even observed by the wild men who inhabit these regions, the Indians having often told me that all the animals on the northern side are different from those of the south. At the same time, the sorts are sometimes so nearly related as to make it certain that they once belonged to the same type. Still further, the large branches of that internal sea, such as the Madeira and the Negro, which are themselves mighty rivers, often produce the same zoological changes. This is particularly observable in the quadrumana and in the gallinaceous birds. The dispersion of the different sorts of *B achyurus* give a remarkable example of this fact. The immense range of the Andes has also produced similar effects, and sudden convulsions of nature, such as earthquakes, are known to have had the same consequences. By the same reason, the fresh-water fishes of the Amazonas and its mighty branches are, as a rule, of species different from those of the Parana and Paraguay, for all their head waters are sometimes only a mile or two distant one from the other; and if this rule presents exceptions, I consider that they are due to accidental inundations that may from time to time unite smaller branches of these mighty streams.

I submit these considerations with much humility, knowing with what animosity these questions are debated; but they are the result of a whole life spent in zoological investigations in all parts of the world. I have for many years studied nature in nature itself.

I cannot close these lines without expressing my best thanks to those who have assisted me. Sir Redmond Barry, to whom this Colony owes so much, granted me, by a most honourable exception, the loan of several Ichthyological books contained in the Public Library and missing in my own. Every naturalist knows that descriptions must be compared with specimens, and it is easy to understand how impossible it is to transport in a public establishment hundreds of preserved fishes which are often of large dimensions. I must also mention Professor McCoy, who did all in his power to assist me; Dr. Black and Mr Le Souef, the President and Secretary of the Acclimatisation Society, who are always ready to devote their time and experience to any undertaking they consider useful to the Colony; to Messrs. Livington Rooke, Morton Alport, and Waterhouse, who have most kindly sent me valuable specimens from Hobart Town and Adelaide; to Messrs. George Keesley and Thomas Christy, who have sent me specimens from the Edwards River, Riverina. Several of the leading fishmongers have kindly assisted me; but even their influence has been of little avail with the fishermen.

At the Cape of Good Hope, fish forms the principal article of the food of the population, and the poorer classes live almost entirely on it, its price being lower than in almost all other civilised countries. In Australia, on the contrary, its very high price makes it an object of luxury, almost entirely reserved for the tables of the wealthy. Till this day very little has been done to provide Melbourne with an efficient supply of this useful commodity, and high prices making the demand very limited, the fishermen have little inducement to send large quantities to the market. It would be much to be desired that the Government of the Colony should make some attempts towards giving to the working-classes a sufficient supply of this wholesome article of food.

It was the intention of the Acclimatisation Society to publish with this paper illustrations representing the different sorts of fishes observed, till this day, in Victoria, and mentioned in this paper; but great difficulties have been encountered, and it has been resolved to postpone to a more favourable opportunity the execution of this project. It is to be hoped that these plates will be published in the next Annual Report, at the same time as a supplement containing notices of all the new sorts that will most likely be obtained in the course of the year.

I think it useful to give here the characters of all the families of fishes found up till this day in Australia. These are extracted from Dr. Gunther's work. I thought it better to compile this part than to attempt to convey the same ideas in different words, which could never have been done in such a concise and correct way. In doing so, I follow the example of the learned zoologist, Mr. Gerard Krefft. ("Industrial Progress of New South Wales, 1871.")

Subclass I. TELEOSTEI.

" Fishes with ossified skeleton and completely separated vertebræ; the posterior extremity of the vertebral column either long, or covered with bony plates. Bulb of the aorta simple, with two opposite valves at the origin; branchiæ free.

Order I. ACANTHOPTERYOII.

" Part of the rays of the dorsal, anal, and ventral fins not articulated, forming spines. The inferior pharyngeal bones separated. Air-bladder, if present, without pneumatic duct.

BERYCIDÆ.

" Form of body oblong or rather elevated, compressed; eyes lateral, large; cleft of mouth extending on the sides of the muzzle, more or less oblique; villiform teeth in both the jaws, and generally on the palate. Eight or four branchiostegals. Opercular bones more or less armed. Scales ctenoid, seldom bony, or wanting. Ventral fins thoracic, with more than five soft rays; in one genus with less. Cæca pylorica in increased number.

" Tropical and temperate seas."

I have till now found no sorts of this family in the Melbourne waters, but several inhabit the Australian seas, particularly in those that bathe the northern shores of the Continent.

PERCIDÆ.

"Body generally oblong, and covered with ctenoid scales; lateral line continuous. Mouth in front of the snout, with lateral cleft, rarely at the lower side. Eye lateral. All or some of the opercles serrated or armed. Seven or six branchiostegals. Dentition complete; teeth pointed, in villiform bands, with or without canines; teeth either on the vomer, or on the vomer and palatine bones. No barbels. Cheek not cuirassed. Dorsal fin formed by a spinous portion and by a soft; ventrals thoracic, with one spine and five soft rays. Stomach cæcal; pyloric appendages generally in small number. Swim-bladder present, simple. Intestines little folded.

" Carnivorous fishes, inhabiting the fresh waters and seas of all parts of the globe."

They are numerous in Australia, particularly those of the fresh waters.

LATES.

Genus formed by Cuvier on a sort found in the Nile. One or two have since been found in the mouths of the great rivers of India.

LATES COLONORUM.

Lates colonorum, *Gunther, Ann. Nat. History*, 1863, xi. 114.

(*Gipps Land Perch.*)

D. 8—1/10. C. 17. A. 3/8. P. 15. l. l. 53. l. tr. 8/17.

Body ovale, rather high ; three times in total length ; head three and one-third in the same ; eye three and three-quarters in length of head, and equal to the snout ; the lower jaw longer than the upper one ; mouth extensible ; præoculer strongly serrated ; posterior limb of the præoperculum finely serrated, and having a light notch towards the inferior angle, from which the spines become very strong, the lower ones in particular, which are directed with their points forwards. The operculum has two points, the lower much larger than the other. The dorsals are continuous, the first having its first spine rather short, the second about twice its length, the third about equal to twice the length of the second, the fourth the longest of all ; the caudal is lightly emarginated. The spines of the anal are rather slender ; the first is the shortest, and the third the longest ; the lateral line extends to the base of the caudal.

The colour is of a dark green, becoming very light and greyish on the sides of the body, the lower parts of which are white. On the back, each scale has its centre of a bright silver colour, which shines like a diamond. Anterior parts of the head and mouth of a light purple ; operculum with green and red tinges ; fins of a yellowish grey ; the spines purple ; pectorals green. with the base more or less scarlet ; eye of a bright orange yellow

This fish is very common in the lakes of Gipps Land, and is often brought in great numbers by the steamers to the Melbourne market in winter. Its flesh is soft, and not savory. Medium length, 12 inches.

LATES SIMILIS.

This fish is very nearly allied to the precedent ; in fact, it is only by a very close examination that it can be distinguished from it. Its form and colours are similar, but the snout is shorter, and sensibly less than the diameter of the eye. The denticulations of the præoperculum are larger, and those of the lower limb are directed backwards. The second dorsal fin has only nine rays.

It is found with *L. colonorum*, but seems to be very scarce.

LATES ANTARCTICUS.
(*Sea Perch.*)

B. 7.   D. 8—1/10.   A. 3/8.   C. 16.   P. 14.   l. l. about 55. L. lat. 8/16.

Height, three and one-tenth in total length ; head three and two-thirds in same ; eye five and one-twelfth in length of head; and one and a-half in snout. General form oval, rather high. The upper parts of the head without scales; the lower jaw longer than the upper one; mouth extensible; præoperculum rather finely serrated; operculum equally serrated on its posterior edge, rounded at its angle; the spines becoming gradually stronger; those on the inferior edge larger, equal, and obliquely directed forward. In some specimens, the spines of the angle and the inferior ones are bifid, and there is sometimes an interval between them. The operculum is terminated by two spines; the lower one much longer than the other. The lateral line is sometimes rather sinuous. The first dorsal is formed of a first short spine, a second generally twice its length, a third much longer still, and the fourth the longest of all; the second dorsal has a rather strong and long spine, and the rays are large, the first being the longest, and the others decreasing as they extend backwards; caudal emarginated, with the lobes rather rounded; the anal with three rather slender spines, the first the shortest, and the third the longest; the rays have the same form as those of the anal; the spine of the ventrals is strong and short. The colour is silvery, with the back and upper parts of the head of a dark blue; dorsal and caudal blackish; ventrals and pectorals of a dark greenish grey; anal of a light grey.

This fish is not very common, and only appears now and then in the Melbourne market.

Nota.—The dried specimens are very much like those of *Lates Colonorum*, but the body is higher; the denticulations of the præorbital are proportionately finer, those of the præoperculum rather stronger on the posterior edge, and become longer in a more equal way. The colours are different, and the flesh of this sort is considered very savoury. It also becomes much larger, and generally attains about 16 inches.

LATES VICTORIÆ.

This sort is so very nearly allied to *Antarcticus* that I considered it, at first, as belonging to that species. It is only distinguished by the second spine of the operculum, which is formed of a bunch of spines, numbering four, and of which the two central ones are the largest. The lateral line has two very strong sinuosities—one opposite to the beginning of the first dorsal, and the other to its end. The anal, also, has only eight soft rays. The body is very silvery, with the back of a light green, showing on the living specimen seven or eight longitudinal lines, of a rather darker tinge ; the sides and belly have a rosy hue ; the sides of the head are rather purple ; the fins are of a purplish green ; the eye yellow. Length, 16 inches.

APOGON.

This genus extends its *habitat* over all the warm and temperate seas of the globe. In America alone its sorts appear to be very scarce, and I was the first to describe one from Brazils ; since then Dr. Gunther has made known another from the Pacific coast of South America. I have only observed one sort at Melbourne, and it appears to me not to have been previously described. It is certainly very distinct from Dr. Gunther's *Apogon Victoriæ*, which I have not yet seen.

APOGON GUNTHERI.

D. 7.—1/9. A. 1/7. P. 15. C. 21.

Upper profile very convex ; body very thick ; height contained a little over two and a-half times in total length ; head about two and two-thirds in the same ; eye very large, its diameter being one-third of the length of the head. Præoperculum with its first ridge entire, and the second rather strongly denticulated ; operculum with two spines ; scales large, ciliated on their external margin, numbering from 26 to 27 on the lateral line, and 11 or 12 on the transverse one. The spines of the first dorsal are as follow :—The first very short, the second more than twice its length, the third very large and very thick, arched, and at least double of the second—the following go on decreasing ; the second dorsal has a strong, straight spine, followed by the soft rays, which are one-third longer ; caudal rounded ; anal with two spines—the first short and arched, the second more than twice its length, and straight ; the soft rays like those of the dorsal ; the spine of the ventrals strong ; the pectorals rather large and rounded. The general colour is of a brownish pink, without spots or bands ; the sides of the head have a golden tinge ; the scales are covered with very minute black dots, except on their edge; the fins are pink, with their extremity of a blackish purple; eye of a dark purple brown, with an internal golden ring. Some specimens have the throat inflated.

Found rather often on the Melbourne market in the cold months. Average length, 4 inches.

ENOPLOSUS.

This very pretty fish was first observed by White, who, in his travels in New South Wales, describes it under the name of *Chœtodon Armatus*. Lacepede founded on it the genus *Enoplosus*, but left it as a sub-division of *Chœtodon*. Cuvier (*Règne Animal*) easily saw that its only connection with that genus was due to the distribution of its colours, and put it in, at its right place, in his family of the *Percoidœ*. Later, in his "Natural History of Fishes," he gives a good figure of it, but the blue tinge it is coloured with is not in conformity with nature. He also represents the eighth spine as forming part of the first dorsal; but it is always free in the numerous specimens 1 have seen, and situated between the first dorsal and the second. Dr. Gunthar only counts seven spines to the first dorsal, and does not mention this isolated one.

1. ENOPLOSUS ARMATUS.

Chætodon armatus, *White* (*Travels in New South Wales,* pl. 39).

Enoplosus armatus, *Cuvier; Lacepede.*

(*Bastard Dorey Fish.*)

D. 7-1—1/14. A. 3/14. P. 13. C. 17.

Of a silvery white; back of a brownish black; head with two and body with five broad brown transverse bands; those of the body generally alterning broad and narrow. The large dorsals are of a dark purple brown, with the spines of a whitish purple, marbled with dark tinges; caudal yellow, with its base and sides brown; anal and ventrals of a brownish black; pectorals pink; the posterior parts of the second dorsal and anal are often of a yellowish white; eye of a bright yellow, well marked with the brown band that crosses the head.

This sort is commonly seen in the Melbourne market, and is rather esteemed as food. It never attains very large dimensious. In the Australian winter the specimens are small, and do not measure more than from four to six inches; but in the warm months (December, January,) they are much larger, and some are nearly a foot long. The ground colour of those large specimens is of a fine reddish purple, and that of the fins red; the eye is yellow, with an external circle of an orange red. Those specimens were generally females, with well-developed eggs.

MICROPERCA.

Teeth numerous and sharp, disposed in several rows on both of the jaws and also on the palatines; no canines; tongue smooth; operculum and præoperculum not serrated, entire; the latter with two feeble points, of which the lower one is much larger than the other; the præorbital very finely serrated; two dorsals, slightly continuous—the first triangular, with eight spines; caudal rounded; anal with three spines; scales large. Form oval, rather high; head attenuated; body compressed; no scales on the upper part of the head nor on the snout.

This genus is nearly allied to *Psammoperca;* but the præoperculum without spines, and the absence of a scaly sheath at the dorsals, oblige me to separate it. Its general form is very similar to fig. 1 of pl. 57 of the fishes, *Erebus and Terror.*

MICROPERCA YARRÆ.

Height three times and a quarter in the total length; head four and one-fifth times in the same; eye four and a quarter in the length of the head. There are about 29 scales on the lateral line, and 12 on the transverse one; the first dorsal is situated rather backwards; it is formed of eight very strong spines—the first short, the second and third the longest, and nearly equal, the others becoming gradually shorter; the second dorsal has one long and straight spine, and eight soft rays; these go on increasing in length; the caudal has 17 rays; the anal has the same form as the second dorsal; its spines are strong; the first is short; the pectorals are small, and have 14 rays; the scales are large, rounded, and rather ciliated on their edge; the operculums are covered with similar but rather smaller scales; the mouth is rather protractile. The colours are subject to many variations; in some, the back is of a purple grey, and the belly and fins yellow; the centre of the scales is generally dark. In other specimens the back is green, and the belly white, with a black longitudinal spot on its lower part; the fins of an orange colour, bordered with black; the ventrals entirely of that colour; the body has more or less black spots; the eye is silvery.

This pretty little fish is found in the lower Yarra, where the water is brackish. Most of my specimens were obtained in Captain Sinnott's dock. The general length is about 2½ inches, but I have one which measures a little over 3.

CÆSIOPERCA.

Serranus, *Rich.;* anthias, *Gunther.*

The very pretty fish on which I propose forming this new genus is, in general form, very much like *Arripis*, and might at first sight be taken for a *Cæsio.* By its operculum and præoperculum being denticulated, and its palatines being armed with teeth, it must be placed with the *Percidæ;* but even the beauty and disposition of its colours convey the idea of a *Cæsio.* It would have been a *Centropristes* for Cuvier, if its head was not entirely covered with scales. Teeth very numerous, villiform, those of the inner row directed backwards; two very blunt and small canines on each jaw; a few sharp, arched teeth, larger than the others, on each side of the lower jaw; teeth on the palatine bones, disposed in a transverse line, in three groups; fins in their greatest part covered with small scales; one dorsal; operculum with two spines—the upper small, the other larger; dorsal with ten spines, and anal with three; all the parts of the head entirely covered with scales; those of the body moderate or rather large.

Dr. Gunther, in leaving provisionally this sort with his *Anthias,* states that it will probably form the type of a separate genus.

CÆSIOPERCA RASOR.

Serranus Rasor, *Rich.; Proceed. Zool. Society,* 1839, p. 95; *Trans. Zol. Soc.,* 1849, pl. 4, fig. 1.
Anthias Rasor, *Gunther; Catalogue* 1, p. 93.

D. 10—19/20. C. 15. A. 3/9. P. 13.

Height three and one-third in total length; head three and a half in the same; eye four times in the length of the head. L. lat. 56. L. tr. 5/18. Body oval, rather elongated ; pectorals large, having about the fourth of the total length of the fish ; caudal forked. The denticulations of the præoperculum very fine on its outer edge, but becoming much larger towards the angle ; the lower edge is also crenulated. The operculum is only distinctly denticulated on its inferior part ; præorbital strongly ciliated. The lateral line follows the curve of the back at about one-fifth of the height of the body. Scales rather large, and strongly ciliated on their external edge. The dorsal fin is covered with small scales to nearly two-thirds of its height ; the spines number ten, and are rather strong ; the first is the shortest, being about two-thirds the length of the second ; this is rather shorter than the third ; the fourth is the longest ; but all the following are very nearly equal to it. The soft rays form an exact continuation to the spines, but they are longer than the last of these, and go on increasing in length towards the posterior angle, which is rounded. Not only do the scales in this second part of the fin extend entirely over the lower part, but they do also on the membranes to nearly their end. The caudal fin is very strongly emarginated ; its rays are covered by the scales to much more than their first half ; the anal spines are slender ; the first is nearly two-thirds of the second, which is a little longer than the third ; the rays are rather long ; the posterior angle of the fin is rounded : small scales cover the almost totality of the membranes. Ventrals of moderate size ; their spine rather slender and straight ; the first ray is the longest, and the others become gradually shorter.

The body is of a pretty, light brown colour ; the back of a purplish light blue, with several rather broad, yellow, gilt longitudinal bands ; the two upper ones are irregular, and disappear a short time after the death of the fish ; the lower, which follows the lateral line, is more consistent, and extends from the end of the operculum to the centre of the base of the caudal. These bands extend over the sides of the head, and one in front of the eye. Each of the scales of the body has its edge of a light blue colour, and between the series of scales are very light yellow longitudinal lines. In the centre of the body, and in part covered by the extremity of the pectoral fin, is a black spot of a lozenge form, which covers, in its broadest part, three series of longitudinal scales and the same number of transverse ones. The dorsal has its scaly part of a light purple, and its extremity yellow ; the caudal is of a light blue, with rather transverse yellow spots ; the anal is also of a light blue, with the external part yellow, and numerous spots of the latter colour all over it ; its extreme edge is red; the pectorals are of a brownish red, and the ventrals pink ; eye yellow.

I have only seen one specimen of this sort, which was caught at Western Port in the first days of December.

The *Anthias Richardsonii* (Gunther, Proceedings Zoological Society, 1869, p. 429,) appears to me to be a simple variety of this fish, the only difference being that the black spot is situated a little further back than in *Rasor*.

ARRIPIS.

This genus was formed by Jenyns, in the " Zoology of the Beagle (1842)," on a sort of *Centropristes*, described by Cuvier and Valenciennes; but in 1847, Mr. Brisaut de Barneville published it again, under the name of *Homodon*. (" Revue Zool. de Guérin.")

Cuvier and Valenciennes describe, in their great work, three sorts, one of which (*Truttaceus*) they believe to be the *Perca Trutta* of Forster, and already described by themselves under that name in their second volume. Professor McCoy, in his " Notes on the Zoology of Victoria " (Intercolonial Exhibition, 1866), was the first to mention that two of Cuvier's sorts were only the the young and the adult of the same species, but I think that that learned naturalist is mistaken when he says that the *Centropristes georgianus*, C. & V.; *C. Salar*, Richard ; *C. Truttaceus*, C. & V.; and *Perca marginata* of the same, belong all to one species, and also when he says that the *arripis georgianus* is the *Salmon trout* of the Melbourne fishermen; this sort is their *Roughfy*. Their *salmon trout* is the *Centropristes truttaceus*, of which the adult is the *salmon* or *Centr. salar*. For what is of Forster's *Perca Trutta*, as that traveller, who found it on the coast of New Zealand, says that it is spotted with red, I think it very doubtful that it corresponds with any of the known Australian sorts.

The synonimy, thus rectified, will be as follows :—

ARRIPIS GEORGIANUS.

Centropristes georgianus, *Cuv. & Val.*, vii. 451.
Arripis georgianus, *Richard.; Gunther; Jenyns.*

(*The Roughfy.*)

There can be no doubt about this determination, as Cuvier
says that this sort has fourteen soft rays at the dorsal. The
numbers are :—

D. 9/14.   A. 3/10.   C. 17.   P. 15.

Grey on the back ; the other parts silvery ; slight and rather
irregular transverse gilt bands, which become dark on the upper
part of the body ; dorsal of a dirty yellow, with upper edge
obscure ; pectorals grey ; ventrals and anale white ; eye yellow.

The very fresh specimens have a general gilt tinge, and the
back green. I have seen during the hot months (December and
January) several specimens entirely of an uniform colour,
without spots.

This sort is very common all the year round, and always
remains small. When not fresh it is often poisonous ; it is
easily recognised by the roughness of its surface, caused by
its scales being strongly ciliated. The mouth is very extensible.

ARRIPIS TRUTTACEUS.

Centropristes ? truttaceus, *C. & V.*, iii. 50.
———— salar, *Richard* (*Voy. Erebus and Terror*,
p. 29, pl. 20).
———— tasmanicus, *Homb. & Jacquinot* (*Voyage de
Durville*, p. 40, pl. 4).
Arripis salar and truttaceus, *Gunther* (*Catal. Brit. Mus.*,
1, p. 253-254).

(*Salmon and Salmon-Trout.*)

D. 9/16-17.   A. 3/10.   P. 17.   C. 17.

The adult fish is the *salmon* of the Australian fishermen, and their
salmon-trout is the young. Its height is contained four and two-

third times in its total length; the head is three and three-fourth in the same; the eye five and one-third in the length of the head.

It is of a greenish lead colour, with the upper part of the head of a brilliant black; on the upper half of the body are numerous and irregular black spots. The operculum and the end of the pectorals are usually tinged with yellow. Its length is sometimes over 22 inches. This is the *arripis salar* of Richardson and Gunther.

The young specimens are the true *centr. truttaceus* of Cuvier; they are of an olive green on the upper parts; sides and lower parts of a silvery white. On the sides and upper surface extend three or four longitudinal lines of rather large, rounded, and golden spots numbering from 14 to 19 on each line. Dorsal transparent, bordered with black; caudal yellow, with its terminal part black; anal white, as are also the ventrals; pectorals yellow; the sides of the head and the eye of a bright yellow.

This is one of the most common of all Victorian fishes. The young only take the adult livery, when they are at least one foot long. During the cold months of the year, the adults are hardly ever seen, but they become common in the Australian summer. When not very fresh, this sort is also very dangerous; and, as Professor McCoy states, almost all the cases of fish poisoning are caused by it.

The genus *Arripis* is one of those curious beings who seem to have been created by Nature to puzzle the systematic zoologist. By its palatine teeth, it belongs to the *Percoïd* family; but its general form would otherwise cause it to be placed near or with *Cæsio*. The general appearance of the adult *truttaceus* is that of a *scomberoïd*, of which it has even the colours, but the young has the same *Cæsio* appearance I have just mentioned. The præoperculum is more radiated than serrated.

OLIGORUS.

This genus has been formed by Dr. Gunther on a species of *grystes* of Cuvier; but he adds to it a large New Zealand fish, evidently very different, and it ought to be characterised by having an operculum with a simple, smooth ridge.

OLIGORUS MACQUARIENSIS.

Grystes macquariensis, *Cuv. & Val., Richard.*
———- brisbanii, *Les.* (*Voy. de la Coquille*).
———- peelii, *Mitchell* (*Exped. Austral.*)

(Murray Cod.)

This fish is very plentiful in the Murray and in most of the rivers of New South Wales. The young ones are much more slender and elongated than the adult or old ones. It attains to a very large size, and is frequently over two feet long. I have seen one about three and a-half feet, and which was said to weigh over one hundred pounds.

Blandowski says that the *Murray Cod* forms the principal article of food of the natives who reside on the banks of the interior rivers. In winter, when the rivers overflow their banks, the natives spear them at night by fire light, while they are sleeping behind old logs. In the warm season, when the rivers are low or cease altogether to run, they spear them very easily. To do this they dive, head foremost, to the bottom of the river. It has been introduced into the Yarra by the Acclimatisation Society.

I find in all the authors that the dorsal fin is formed of fourteen soft rays; but this is not the case with any of the numerous specimens I have examined, and I find that some have fifteen, but most sixteen. Their colour is subject to considerable variations; it is generally of a dirty yellow green, becoming white on the belly; the upper parts covered with small, numerous, and irregular dark green spots, which often take the appearance of very irregular transverse lines. On the sides of the head and of the the operculum these lines are frequently well defined, and longitudinal. The fins are purple, with more or less of a scarlet hue.

The fishermen of the Murray and Goulburn, where this sort is very plentiful, send it to Echuca, from whence it is put alive into baskets. In dying by asphyxia, the body often becomes, in parts, of a splendid scarlet, and sometimes this tinge shows the impression of the wickers of which the baskets are made; this is particularly the case with those specimens which are on the bottom of the baskets.

Mr. Wilson has tried to naturalize the Murray Cod in the rivers of the Wimmera, but I believe without result. The Acclimatisation Society has been more successful in its endeavours to place it in the Yarra, and it seems to have considerably propagated in that river; for, although no large specimens have yet been found, small ones are seen rather frequently. The fish seem to go down towards the sea, as Captain Sinnott most kindly sent me a small specimen he caught in his dock, where the water is already brackish. It is a little less than three inches in length; its colour is of a light grey, and the upper part of the body is covered with small black spots; the dorsal and the base of the caudal are yellowish, and the extremity of the caudal rather dark.

The Murray Cod, as almost all the Australian fresh-water fish, is often marked with red spots, caused by intestinal worms.

NOTA.—A young specimen, obtained in January, 1872, and measuring six inches long, presented the following dimensions:— Height four times and two-thirds in total length; head three and one-third in the same; eye four and one-half in length of head. It was of a light lilac on the back, with the lower parts of a dirty white. On the sides and on the back were numerous irregular blotches of a dark purple.

DULES.

This genus was established by Cuvier and Valenciennes. The Australian sorts inhabit the rivers of the interior.

DULES AURATUS.

(*Murray Golden Perch.*)

D. 10/11. A. ⅘. P. 15. C. 17. L. 1. 76 (and 5 on Caudal). L. lat. 13/28.

Height three times and one-half in total length; head three and five-tenths in same; eye five and two-thirds in the length of the head; and one and a-half in length of snout. Head cavernous; teeth on the palatines; upper profile strongly convex on the back, the snout being elongate. Præorbital long, striated, and finely serrated. Head covered with scales, except on its upper surface; lower jaw longer than the upper one; præoperculum straight and equally serrated posteriorly, rounded and covered with much larger spines on its lower margin; these spines are flat, and separated in different series, those nearest to the mouth being directed forwards. The operculum is only and feebly serrated in its lower portion; it is ended posteriorly by two rather long spines, the first always simple, and the second the longest, and sometimes bifid. The supraseapula and caracoïd finely serrated.

The scales of the body small, and finely ciliated; the dorsal spines strong; the first being very short, and the fifth the longest of all; the soft portion of the dorsal much higher than the spiny one with its membranes covered to more than one-third of their length with minute scales; caudal rounded; the spines of the anal very strong, the second by far the strongest of the three; ventrals with a strong, straight spine; their first ray prolongated and bifid.

When fresh, this fish is adorned with most beautiful colours. The body is of a magnificent green; the sides are golden, as is also the upper portion of the body behind the dorsal. The head presents a beautiful mixture of green, purple, yellow, and scarlet, with fine golden tinges; the belly is white; the dorsal fin is of a purple green; the anal scarlet, with its base yellow and its end purple; the pectorals are scarlet at their base, and yellow in their second half; the eye is purple, with an interior white ring. These colours are subject to great variations, and the belly is sometimes red.

The young fish is much more elongate than the adult, and has little of the fine hues of the latter. The back is green, with the sides and belly yellow; the upper part of the head and the operculum are purple; the dorsal is grey, with its soft portion bordered with black; the caudal and anal similar; the spines of the latter are pink; the pectorals and ventrals are yellow.

This sort is much esteemed for the table. It often weighs five and sometimes seven pounds. It appears to be common in the Murray and in the other rivers of Riverina. I am in great doubt if it is not the *Dules Ambiguus* of Richardson and Gunther; but the numerous specimens I have examined have all one ray less at the anal, and also less scales on the lateral line. In Richardson's figure (*Erebus* and *Terror*, pl. xix.,) the lower præopercular spines are also much smaller and more regular.

DULES CHRISTYI.

D. 10—11 ?   C. 17.   A. $\frac{3}{9}$.

Height three times and one-fourth in total length; head four and one-sixth times in the same; orbit four and one-half in the length of the head, the latter very cavernous. The superior profile is very much elevated, almost gibbous behind the eye. The highest part of the body is at the base of the pectorals. The præoperculum is straight, finely and equally denticulated behind, with its angle rounded and slightly protuberant; the denticulations become gradually rather stronger in this part, and on the inferior edge they are still stronger, and present one or two interruptions. The operculum terminates with two flat, broad, serrated appendices, placed somewhat obliquely; the caracoïd presents a long series of denticulations. The teeth are very numerous, villiform; the vomer bears some teeth, but none are visible on the palatines; the lateral line follows the profile of the back; it runs over fifty-two series of scales; the transverse line numbers eight above it, and eighteen below. These scales are rather large, and ciliated on their edge. The dorsal is formed of ten spines, the fourth being the longest, and the first only about one-half of the second. I cannot ascertain with certainty the number of the soft rays, my specimen being deficient in this part. The caudal is rounded; the anal has three spines, of which the second is the longest. On the soft part of the dorsal, on the anal, and on the caudal, numerous scales are seen on the membranes, up to about one-third of their length. The spine of the ventrals is strong; the pectorals have about two-thirds the length of the head.

The upper parts of the body are of a brownish purple, and the lower white. The only specimen I have seen was kindly sent to me by Mr. Thomas Christy, from the Edwards River, near Deniliquin. It measured 14 inches long; when I received it, it had been some time preserved in salt, and I could not form a very good idea of its original colours. It is so much like *Murrayia Cyprinoïdes* in form that I should have thought it belonged to the same species, had it not been for the difference in the number of the spines of its first dorsal.

PRISTIPOMATIDÆ.

" Body compressed and oblong, covered with scales, the serrature of which is sometimes exceedingly fine and sometimes wanting. Lateral line continuous, not continued on the caudal fin. Mouth in front of the snout, with lateral cleft. Eye lateral, of moderate size. Five, six, or seven branchiostegals. Teeth in villiform bands, with pointed and conical canines in some of the genera; no molars or trenchant teeth in the jaws, generally no teeth on the palate; jaws toothless in two of the genera. No barbels. Cheek not cuirassed. One dorsal fin, formed by a spinous and soft portion of nearly equal development, the former of which either contains strong spines or is continuous with the latter; anal similarly developed as the soft dorsal; the lower rays of the pectorals branched; ventrals thoracic, with one spine and five soft rays. The bones of the head with a rudimentary or moderately developed muciferous system. Stomach cæcal; pyloric appendages in small or moderate number. Air-bladder present, more or less simple. Pseudobranchiæ well developed.

" Carnivorous fishes, without molar or trenchant teeth, inhabiting the seas of the temperate and tropical regions; a few entering fresh waters."

Those of Australia that I have to mention here are all from the rivers. They are very nearly allied to the sorts of *Dules* I have already described.

THERAPON NIGER.

(Murray Black Perch.)

D. 12/12.   A. ¾.   C. 17.   P. 15.   L. lat. 89.   L. tr. 14/28.

Height of the body three aud one-half times in the total
length; head four and two-thirds in the same; eye four
and one-third in the length of head. Superior profile considerably arched, much more so than the lower one; upper
surface of the head naked, the other parts covered with
scales; præorbital strongly denticulated; præoperculum with
its posterior edge rather emarginated, and covered with
very strong spines, particularly long on the rounded part,
and becoming much smaller on the lower edge, where they are
reduced to small denticulations; operculum terminated by two
bunches of flat spines, the first of two and the second of six; the
suprascapula and the caracoïd are very strongly denticulated.
The lateral line is very irregularly formed, passing sometimes in
the centre and sometimes on the edge of the scales; the numbers we have mentioned only relate to the numbers of transverse
series it crosses; it does also extend on the base of the caudal.
The dorsal is received in a longitudinal sulcate of the back; its
spines are strong; the three first are shorter than the others;
the membranes of the soft part have each a longitudinal patch
of scales placed near the rays, and extending to more than
one-third of the height of the fin. The caudal is emarginated;
it is covered at its base with scales of the same nature as those
of the body, and others, much more minute, cover the membranes
on all their first half. Anal with its spine large and striated; the
spine of the ventrals strong, striated, and longer than the half of
the length of the fin.

The back is grey, but appears dark on account of all the scales
having a rather broad, black margin; the lower part of the body
is of a dirty, yellowish white; the fins are grey; the posterior
part of the caudal black.

From the Murray River, but scarce. Length of specimen,
16½ inches. This sort must be nearly allied to the *Therapon
Unicolor* of Gunther (*Catalogue*).

THERAPON RICHARDSONI.

(Murray Silver Perch.)

D. 12/11-12. A. ⅜. C. 17. P. 16. L. l. about 65.
L. lat. 17/25.

Height of the body three times and eight-tenths in the total length
(to the central end of the caudal) ; head four and two-thirds in the
same length ; the eye four and one-seventh in the length of the
head. The superior profile strongly convex, and rather equally
arched ; the inferior almost straight ; general form elongate ; no
teeth to the palate ; præorbital very strongly serrated ; the præoperculum rounded, and armed with a series of long spines posteriorly, and of shorter ones below. The caracoïd is strongly
serrated at its posterior margin ; the operculum has two spines,
the lowest being the strongest. The upper part of the head is
naked, the rest scaly. The dorsal is received in a longitudinal
cavity of the back ; its fifth spine is longer than the precedents ;
the lateral line extends considerably on the base of the caudal,
which is also covered with scales. The caudal is slightly emarginate ; the spines of the anal are very strong, particularly the
second.

This species seems very nearly allied to *Therapon Ellipticus*,
Richardson *(Datnia);* but the number of the scales given by Dr.
Gunther seem very different. (L. lat. 85. L. trans. 17/31.)
Richardson's figure shows only about 52, which might agree with
our sort ; but he mentions nothing about them in his text
(Erebus and Terror).

This fish is very often brought to Melbourne from the Murray.
I have also a specimen from the neighborhood of Deniliquin ;
but the lower point of its operculum is flat and bifurcated ; this
may be accidental.

The general colour is of a greyish blue. The lower parts of
the body are of a dirty white : the sides shaded with yellow ;
each scale is bordered with black ; the head has a blueish
tinge, with the lips and the lower parts of the head rosy ; eye
yellow ; the first dorsal is dark, with the rays purple ; the second
has its lower half of a dirty yellow, and its exterior one black ;

the caudal is of the latter colour ; anal dark, with the rays purple ; ventrals white, with the rays rosy ; pectorals yellow at the base, and black on their interior half. Average length, 11 inches, but some are much larger.

MURRAYIA.

This new genus comes between *Dules* and *Therapon*.

The dorsal has eleven spines ; the operculum is denticulated in all its length ; there is a line of small teeth on the palatines, and the caudal is rounded. Scales minutely serrated ; head cavernous.

These fish inhabit the rivers of Riverina, and particularly the Murray, and are brought to the Melbourne market by the Echuca Railway. They are all considered good for the table, and are generally sold under the name of Murray Perch.

This genus must be very nearly allied to *Maequaria*, but the latter has no teeth in the jaws. I expect that the *Dules Viverrinus*, Krefft, " Proceedings Zoological Society, 1867," which I have not seen, belongs to this genus, as it has eleven spines at the dorsal ; it also comes from the Murray.

MURRAYIA GUNTHERI.

D 11/12. A. $\frac{3}{9}$. P. 16. C. 16. L. lat. 50 (and 5 on the Caudal). L. tr. $10\frac{1}{2}/18\frac{1}{2}$.

Height three and one-half times in length ; head three and two-thirds in same ; eye four and one-half in the length of the head. Upper profile very convex, the back being very much elevated behind the head, and almost gibbous ; lower profile much more regularly curved ; upper surface of the head naked ; the other parts covered with scales. Præorbital very finely denticulated ; præoperculum with its posterior margin rather emarginated, and finely serrated ; at its rounded part, these denticulations become much larger, and extend so on all the inferior margin. They present several small spaces devoid of them—one before the angle, one below it, and a few others on the lower edge. Operculum terminated by two very broad, flat, oblique appendices these are strongly serrated, and the space between them is very small ; all the posterior margin is finely serrated ; the superscapula and the caracoïd are also serrated. The lateral line is formed of a succession of small longitudinal ridges, extending on the middle of the scales; it extends on the caudal. The dorsal fin is large; its fifth spine is the longest; the membranes of the second portion are covered with scales to the fourth of the height of the fin. The caudal is rounded, and its membranes are covered with scales nearly up to the middle of their length; the anal is long, with its spines strong; the second is much longer han the first, and a little more so than the third; it is covered with scales at its base, as are also the pectorals. The ventrals are large, their first ray is prolongated in a filament, having about the fifth of the length of the fin; the spine is strong, and nearly two-thirds of the length of the rays.

The general colour is purple, becoming reddish on the lower parts. The upper surface of the head is green, and the sides of a rather brilliant purple; the lips and internal circle of the eye are of a flesh colour; all the scales of the body are bordered with a dark tinge; the dorsal fin is of a purplish green, with the spines purple; the caudal and anal purple; the ventrals are pink, with their external third black; the spine is purple; the pectorals yellow; eye brown.

From the Murray River; average length, 14 inches.

Nota.—I have a monstrous specimen of this sort which has an accidental spine on the left side of the third dorsal. The eye is red.

The smaller specimens are more elongate than the adult.

In one specimen, the soft rays of the dorsal number thirteen; in another those of the anal nine. I have received from Deniliquin, by Mr. Christy, a monstrous specimen of this sort, in which the ventrals are rudimentary, and only formed of one distorted spine and three rays. The second spine of the anal is also quite distorted, and there are eleven soft rays to the anal.

MURRAYIA CYPRINOIDES.

(*Murray Carp.*)

D. 11/13. A. 3/9. C. 17. P. 16. L. lat. 52. L. tr. 10½/18½.

Height of body three and one-third times in total length; head three and one-half in the same; eye five and a-half times in the length of the head.

Very much like the two precedents, but the body much highe and more gibbous on the back than even in *Guntheri*. The first ventral ray prolonged in a bifid filament.

The upper part of the body is green, with the border of the scales darker; lower parts of the body yellow; the lateral line dark; sides of the head purple; upper part of the pectorals pink, with their lower portion yellow. The dorsal, caudal, and anal are purple; the ventrals pink, with the spine white.

Sometimes common in the market, from ten to twelve inches long. From the Murray.

MURRAYIA BRAMOIDES.

(Murray Bream.)

D. 11/12. A. $\frac{3}{8}$. C. 17. P. 16. L. l. 52. L. tr. $9\frac{1}{2}/16\frac{1}{2}$.

Height four times in total length; head three and two-thirds in same; orbit three and eight-tenths in length of head. The body is rather short, similar to *Guntheri*. Head very cavernous; præoperculum straight on its back edge, and finely ciliated and serrulated. On the posterior angle, which is rounded, the denticulations become larger and blunt; those on the lower margin are directed forwards; there are several spaces devoid of denticulations between them. The inner edge of the operculum produces towards its angle a sort of rounded flap. The operculum is thinly serrated, and has two angles, the lower of which is a sort of flap divided into five flat spines. The præorbital is not strongly denticulated; the suprascapula is like a segment of a little round saw. The lateral line extends on the root of the caudal. The base of the spines is scaly; the longest spine of the dorsal is the fifth; the others grow shorter as they go backwards; the first is very small, the second longer, the third twice as long as the precedents, the fourth about one-third longer again, and not much shorter than the following. The spines of the anal are rather slender—the first much shorter than the others, the second being the longest; the spine of the ventrals is long, and rather slender; the first soft ray of the same fin is prolonged on a filament.

The general colour is of a dirty yellow. Each scale has an obscure border; head brown, with the lower parts reddish; fins dark, with the spines purple; pectorals and ventrals pink; eye yellow.

Scarce; Murray River. Average length, from 10 to 12 inches.

RIVERINA.

This genus is very nearly allied by its form to *Murrayia*, but the dorsal has twelve spines; no teeth on the palate.

RIVERINA FLUVIATILIS.

D. 12/11.   A. 3/8.   C. 18.   P. 16.   L. lat. 46, and 5 on the Caudal.   L. tr. $8\frac{1}{2}/16\frac{1}{2}$.

Height three and two-thirds in total length; the head three and six-tenths in the same. General form very much like *Murrayia Bramoides*. Posterior limb of the præoperculum straight, and finely serrated, the denticulations becoming much larger towards the angle and on the inferior edge. The two spines of the operculum are, the first bifid, and the second tridenticulated; the dorsal has its fifth spine sensibly longer than all the others; the twelfth is longer than the preceding one. The first anal spine is small; the second very thick, but not longer than the third, and blunt. The first ray of the pectorals prolongated in a rather long filament.

Same colours as *Murrayia Bramoides*, but the head of a more fleshy colour.

Murray. I have only seen one specimen.

MULLIDÆ.

"Body elongate, slightly compressed, covered with large scales, without or with an extremely fine serrature. Profile of the head more or less parabolic; hyal apparatus with two long barbels. Lateral line continuous. Mouth in front of the snout, with the cleft lateral and rather small. Eye lateral, of moderate size. Four branchiostegals; pseudobranchiæ. Dentition feeble, more or less complete. Two dorsal fins, remote from each other; anal similar to the second dorsal; ventrals with one spine and five rays. Air-bladder, if present, simple and of variable size; stomach siphonal.

"Inhabitants of nearly all the tropical seas, extending in Europe on to the coasts of the temperate region. Some species entering rivers."

UPENEICHTHYS.

Separated by Dr. Bleeker from *Upeneus*, on account of teeth being present on the vomer bones; but none on the palatine. One single sort known. .

UPENEICHTHYS POROSUS.

Upeneus porosus, *Cuv. & Val.*, v. iii. p. 455.

(*The Red Gurnet.*)

The colours are subject to much variation. In some the back is of a brownish purple; belly white, with some carmine blotches; a black longitudinal band on the side, which is broader behind, and does not generally attain the head. On the sides of the latter are two narrow and arched blue lines, which extend from the eye downwards. The fins are brown, marbled with light green; the spines purple; the anal, pectorals, and ventrals pink; the edge of the latter and the rays of the anal orange; barbels yellow; eye of the same colour, with an external circle orange. In other specimens the colours are lighter, and the back is grey. The adults are a foot long, and are entirely of a beautiful carmine colour, but they always have the black lateral streak and the blue lines of the head.

It is not very common, but considered one of the best table fishes.

SPARIDÆ.

"Body compressed and oblong, covered with scales, the serrature of which is exceedingly minute, and sometimes wanting. Tail not armed. Lateral line continuous, not continued on the caudal fin. Mouth in front of the snout, with lateral cleft. Eye lateral, of moderate size. Five, six or seven branchiostegals. Either trenchant teeth in front of the jaws, or lateral series of molar teeth; generally no teeth on the palate. One dorsal fin, formed by a spinous and soft portion of nearly equal development; anal with three spines; the lower rays of the pectorals generally branched, in one group simple; ventrals thoracic, with one spine and five rays. The bones of the head with a rudimentary muciferous system. Air-bladder present, often bifid posteriorly. Pseudobranchiæ well developed.

"Herbi- and carnivorous fishes, inhabiting the seas of the temperate and tropical regions; a few entering rivers."

MELANICHTHYS.

Temminck and Schlegel formed this genus, in their "Fauna Japonica," on a fish which had been described by Gray, under the name of *Girella;* but this latter had been used by Cuvier as the French name for *Julis,* and, for all it has been adopted by Dr. Gunther, I thought it was better to adopt the other to avoid the confusion that might otherwise result. The Australian sorts were first noticed by Richardson, who placed them with *Crenidens.*

The præoperculum is covered with scales, but the operculum is without any, except at its upper angle.

MELANICHTHYS TRICUSPIDATA.

Box tricuspidata, *Quoy et Gaim. Voy. de Freycinet Zool.*, p. 296.

Oblata tricuspidata, *Cuv. & Val.*, vii., p. 372.

Girella tricuspidata? *Gunther, Catal. Brit. Mus.*, v. 1, p. 428

Crenidens triglyphus? *Richardson, Erebus and Terror, Fishes*, p. 36, pl. 25, fig. 2.

(*Rock or Black Perch.*)

Almost black on the upper parts ; grey on the sides, and white below. On the anterior part of the head, and even on the operculum, there is a yellow tinge. Dorsal fin of an obscure olive grey, with the lower two-thirds of a dark red. Caudal obscure ; anal of a dark green, with the spines white ; ventrals of a dirty white ; pectorals sometimes of a light colour, and sometimes with their external half obscure ; eye yellow.

The fish that I consider to be Dr. Gunther's *Tricuspis* agrees much better with Richardson's figure of *Tephræops*, only the scales are not small, but of moderate size. They number 57 on the longitudinal line, and about 38 on the transverse one, of these 13 are above the lateral line. It is next to impossible to count with absolute certainty the very small ones of the extreme lower parts of the body.

The dorsal has 15 spines and 13 soft rays ; the caudal has 15 long rays and 4 shorter ones on each side ; the anal has 3 spines, of which the first is very small, and the others nearly equal ; the rays number 11 ; the pectorals have 16 rays.

Specimens of this sort sometimes show nine or ten very narrow, transverse, obscure bands. In the warm months, the colour of this fish seems to become much lighter ; and in December, 1 have seen many specimens almost white.

The teeth are very singular, being each three-lobed on the edge. These teeth form a continued series, but over them is another rather irregular and spaced one. In the inside of the mouth, these large teeth are succeeded by a deep groove, behind which are numerous rows of others, much smaller.

The *Black Perch* is esteemed as an article of food.

The usual size of this sort is from 12 to 15 inches long, but some specimens weigh up to six pounds and over.

I am not certain that *Girella Zonata*, Gunther (" Catal. Brit. Mus.," p. 429), is not one of the striped varieties.

MELANICHTHYS SIMPLEX. ?

Crenidens simplex? *Richard., Erebus and Terror, Fishes,* p. 120.

Girella simplex? *Gunther, Catal. Brit. Mus.,* p. 429.

This sort is entirely similar to the preceding in general appearance, and is confounded with it by the fishermen and fishmongers. Its only difference consists in its teeth, which are more irregular, and without any denticulations or lobes at their edge. I thought for some time that these were old specimens, whose teeth had been worn; but they are generally smaller than the specimens of *Triscuspidata*, still I very much doubt their forming a distinct species.

NOTA.—Dr. Gunther, in the second volume (1863) of the " Annals and Magazine of Natural History," p. 115, proposes a genus *Melambaphes*, to contain a Victorian fish, which is said to be the *Glyphisodon nigroris* of Cuvier and Valenciennes, but it is impossible for me to recognise this last sort. *Glyphisodon nigroris* was established on a specimen brought from Holland, and having been in the cabinet of the Stadtholder; its locality is unknown, but it is almost certainly from the Dutch East Indies, as were almost all the sorts coming from that Museum. The very few descriptive words given by the French ichthyologists do not permit to apply them in particular to any Australian species. Dr. Gunther adds that this sort is the *Black Perch* of the colonists (which is the fish I have just described), but there can be no doubt that this is Richardson's sort, and it cannot be Dr. Gunther's species, as he says that it has the cheeks and opercles covered with very small scales.

NEOTEPHRŒOPS.

Melanichthys or *Girella* is distinguished by its operculum without scales and the moderately-sized scales of its body; *Tephrœops* has also the same operculum, but its scales are very small. The new genus I propose, has the general form and small scales of the latter, but the operculum and præoperculum are covered with scales. The teeth are tri-lobed on the edge, disposed in one external series, behind which is the deep groove which I have mentioned, and behind this again are numerous series of smaller but similar ones.

NEOTEPHRŒOPS ZEBRA.

The height is about three and one-third times in the total length, and the head nearly five times in the same; the orbit is four and one-half times in the length of the head; this is entirely covered with small scales, except on its upper surface, which is naked, and covered with pores. Body oval; scales numbering about 79 on the longitudinal line, and about 61 on the transverse one; those of the back and of the lower parts of the belly are very small, and very difficult to count; the scales are all ciliated on their outer edge, and have concentric lines on their surface. The dorsal is formed of 14 spines and 13 rays; the caudal is rather emarginated, and has 15 long rays, with 4 shorter ones, on each side; the anal has three rather slender spines—the first much shorter than the others, which are almost equal; the branched rays number 12, and the pectorals 17.

The general colour is of a dark grey; the back almost black, with eight or nine transverse, black, and broad stripes; the fins have a dark, yellowish tinge, and the pectorals are of a lighter colour; the sides of the head are purple; the eye white and silvery.

Some specimens have fifteen rays at the dorsal.

This fish appears to be the *Crenidens Zebra* of Richardson ("*Erebus* and *Terror*," p. 70), described from a drawing taken at King George's Sound. The difference in the number of rays (D. 11/15) being probably due to a mistake of the draughtsman. I have several specimens of this sort from 4 to 7 inches long, and one of nearly 13.

PAGRUS.

Genus formed by Cuvier on large and beautiful fishes, a few of which are found in the Mediterranean, but most of which inhabit the Cape of Good Hope and the Chinese Seas. In many of the sorts, the old males are remarkable by a sort of gibbosity which grows over the forehead.

PAGRUS UNICOLOR.

Chrysophrys unicolor, *Quoy et Gaimard, Voyage de l'Uranie,* p. 299.

Pagrus unicolor and guttulatus, *Cuv. & Val.,* vi., p. 162, 160.

(*The Snapper.*)

The *Snapper* is one of the largest and handsomest of the fish of the Melbourne Market. It is found all the year round, but the specimens caught in the cold mouths of the year are generally small; in November and December it becomes much more abundant, and the very large specimens are common. It is a good article of food.

As I had already observed at the Cape of Good Hope, with respect to *Chrysophrys,* the specimens of this sort are subject to very remarkable changes in their form. The female has always a rather oval profile, and the young male has the same; but in this sex, age brings on the developement of a curious crest on the nape of the head, and of a protuberance which, in very old individuals, takes the appearance of an enormous nose, and gives to some of these individuals a most remarkable resemblance to the human face.

The *Snapper* is of a beautiful silvery pink, with the lower parts of the body white and silvery; dorsal pink, with sometimes white spots on the membranes. The caudal becomes blackish towards its end; all the fins are pink, with the exception of the anal and ventral, which are white.

The young specimens are covered with white and sometimes with blue spots, which disappear with age; these appear to be the *Pagrus Guttulatus* of Cuvier. Some old specimens take a beautiful red colour. This sort attains large proportions, and sometimes weighs up to fifty pounds.

CHRYSOPHRYS.

This genus of Cuvier only differs from *Pagrus* by the upper molar teeth, which are here in at least three series, when in *Pagrus* they are only in two.

CHRYSOPHRYS AUSTRALIS.

Chrysophrys australis, *Gunther, Catal. Brit. Mus.*, v. i. p. 191.

(*The Bream.*)

This fish is one of the most common in the Melbourne Market throughout all seasons of the year. It is esteemed as food, but never attains to a large size, the longest specimens being about 12 inches.

The Australian *Bream* is a sea fish, but often enters the rivers, and is common in the lower Yarra and also in the Gipps Land lakes.

Its colour is silvery; grey on the upper parts. There is a slight brown transverse band on the forehead; dorsal fin hyaline, bordered with black; caudal rather yellow, with a dark external border; anal sometimes yellow, other times dark; ventrals yellow, sometimes in part blue; pectorals yellow.

Dr. Gunther has been mistaken when he says (page 494) that this sort has *shining golden longitudinal streaks*. Nothing similar is seen in the fresh specimens.

SQUAMIPINNES.

"Body compressed and elevated, covered with scales, which are sometimes exceedingly finely ciliated, and sometimes smooth. Lateral line continuous, not continued on the caudal fin. Mouth in front of the snout, generally small, with lateral cleft. Eye lateral, of moderate size. Six or seven branchiostegals. Dentition formed by villiform or setiform bands, without canines or incisors; some of the genera with teeth on the palate. Dorsal fin formed by a spinous and soft portion of nearly equal development; anal with three or four spines, similarly developed as the soft dorsal, and both many-rayed. The vertical fins more or less densely covered with small scales; the spinous portions sometimes not scaly. The lower rays of the pectorals branched; ventrals thoracic, with one spine and five soft rays. Stomach cæcal; pyloric appendages, in moderate number; intestines generally with many convolutions. Air-bladder present, more or less simple. Pseudobranchiæ well developed.

"Mostly carnivorous fishes, inhabiting the seas between the tropics, especially of the Indian region ; a few entering rivers or spreading beyond the tropics."

I have not found any sorts of this family in the Straits of Bass nor in Hobson's Bay, but several are found on the coast of New South Wales and on the northern shores of Australia.

CIRRHITIDÆ.

" Body compressed and oblong, covered with cycloid scales; lateral line continuous. Mouth in front of the snout, with lateral cleft. Eye lateral, of moderate size. Cheeks not cuirassed. Generally six, sometimes five, in one genus three branchiostegals. Dentition more or less complete, composed of small pointed teeth, sometimes with the addition of canines. One dorsal fin, formed by a spinous and soft portion of nearly equal development. Anal with three spines, generally less developed than the soft dorsal. The lower rays of the pectoral fins simple and stout; ventrals thoracic, but remote from the root of the pectorals, with one spine and five rays.

" Carnivorous fishes, inhabiting the seas of the tropical regions of the southern temperate parts of the Pacific."

73

CHIRONEMUS.

This genus was established by Cuvier and Valenciennes, on a sort found at King George's Sound (*Georgianus*). These fish are very nearly allied to *Aplodactylus*, and are, in fact, only discernible from the latter by the presence of small teeth on the vomer; and it is remarkable that, the same as them also, they seem to be confined to the Antarctic Seas of the globe. Dr. Gunther changes the name of Cuvier's genus into *Haplodactylus;* but, as I have said previously, I think those rectifications ought not to be adopted, and that, when a name has been badly formed, it is better to consider it as having no meaning than to uselessly increase the scientific nomenclature.

CHIRONEMUS MARMORATUS.

Chironemus marmoratus, *Gunther, Catal. of the Fishes of the British Museum*, v. ii., p, 76.

(*Kelp Fish.*)

D. 15—1/17.   C. 15.   A. 3/7.   V. 1/5.   P. 15.

Height of body four and one-third in total length; head four and two-thirds in same; eye five and one-third in length of head. Incisors strongly tricuspid, disposed on the upper jaw in four, and on the lower one in three series; each series decrease in size; six simple pectoral rays in some specimens, and seven in others. Head rather thick; the lateral line follows the line of the back, at about one-third of the height of the body. First dorsal rather long, and joins the second by spines and membranes much lower than the anterior ones; the first spine low, not more than one-third of the second; this considerably shorter than the third, which, with the fourth, are longer than all the others, and these decrease in length as they extend backwards. The spine of the second dorsal is much longer than the last of the first, and about half as high as the soft rays, which follow it; the caudal is emarginated, the end of each lobe being pointed; the anal is narrow, but long and pointed; the first spines are small; the ventrals are long and pointed; the pectorals very large.

The general colour of the upper parts is brown. On the sides of the head there is a rosy tinge, and on the back a green one. The lower parts of the body are of a greyish white. The entire fish is variegated with irregular brown spots, forming numerous and irregular concentric lines. The eye is brown.

I found in the stomach a large quantity of seaweed. This fish appears rather scarce, and is only found during the hot months of the year (in September, November, and December,) on the Melbourne Market. The fishmongers say that it is not generally eaten; the flesh is dark, but was found good. The largest specimen I have seen of this handsome fish is 19 inches long. It is always found among the seaweed.

CHEILODACTYLUS.

This genus, which was formed by Lacepede, is almost entirely confined to the extreme southern parts of the globe, being from the south of Chili, the Cape of Good Hope, New Zealand, and Australia. Two sorts are rather common on the Melbourne Market, and are used as food of middling quality.

Dr. Gunther changes the name in *Chilodactylus*, but I, once more, do not consider these rectifications as desirable.

CHEILODACTYLUS MACROPTERUS.

Cichla macroptera, *Bloch.; Schneid.*, page 22.
Cheilodactylus macropterus, *Richard., Trans. Zool. Soc.*, v. iii.,
  p. 99 ; *Proceed. Zool. Soc.*, 1850, p. 62.

I have sometimes heard this fish called *Bastard Trumpeter* by the fishmongers. It is remarkable by its sixth pectoral ray, which is extended more than twice and sometimes three times the length of the others.

The colour is silvery, with the upper parts and the head of a light purple ; there is a black spot behind the upper part of the operculum ; the branchiostegal membrane is of a beautiful light blue ; the dorsal, caudal and anal are of a rather dirty yellow, with the spines purple ; the ventrals are white, and the pectorals yellow, with their interior rays white ; eye silvery, surrounded by a blue ring. The sides sometimes show some iridescent longitudinal streaks.

It is usually about a foot long, and very rarely attains 18 inches, and is found on all the southern coasts of Australia and New Zealand.

CHEILODACTYLUS NIGRICANS.

Cheilodactylus nigricans, *Richard., Proceed. Zool. Soc.*, 1850, page 63.

—————————.————— *Ann. and Mag. Nat. Hist.*, 1861, v. vii., p. 270.

—————————————·—· *Gunther, Catal.*, v. ii., p. 79.

(*The Butter Fish.*)

This is much more common than the other sorts on the Melbourne Market, and is found all the year round. The colour is of a blueish grey, covered with brown spots, which on the sides take the form of irregular longitudinal lines ; lower parts of the body of a dirty white ; the head has a copper tinge on its upper part, and a gilt one on its sides. There are generally two brown bands on the operculum. Eye yellow ; dorsal of an obscure olive colour, spotted with brown ; caudal and anal similar, with a narrow terminal white edge ; pectorals of a dark brown ; ventrals similar, with the part nearest to the body becoming white. In some specimens, the colour is darker, but the spots always exist. It is usually about a foot long, but sometimes it attains twenty-six inches ; in these very old ones the spots on the fins often disappear, but those of the body are permanent.

It is by mistake that the authors describe this fish as of an uniform blackish grey.

CHEILODACTYLUS GIBBOSUS.

Cheilodactylus gibbosus, *Richard., Transac. Zool. Soc.*, v. iii., p. 102 ; *Proceed. Zool. Soc.*, 1859, pl. 2, fig. 3.

D. 18—25. C. 15. A. 3—10. P. 13.

Height three and a-quarter times in total length ; head four and a-half times in same : eye three and eight-tenth times in length of head. The upper profile is rather short, and very gibbous over the head ; the mouth is extensible ; the teeth rather long for this genus ; the cheeks and the two opercles are covered with small scales. On the upper surface of the head there are on each side two large tubercles, the one situated over the anterior margin of the eye, and the other in front, just above the insertion of the lip. The lateral line follows the back, at about one-third the height of the fish at its insertion, and approximating more to the upper profile as it extends backwards; the scales number about 69 on this line, and 26 on the transverse row, 10 of which are above the lateral line. The dorsal fin has its three first spines much shorter than the others (the third being about three times as long as the first); the fourth is the longest of all, and about twice as long as the third, or six times the length of the first; the others go on decreasing gradually. The soft part of the fin is shorter than the other, and only about two-thirds its length, but it is higher; the first rays being one-third longer than the last spine; the base of the membranes of the soft rays is scaly. The caudal is very strongly emarginated, and bi-lobed; the upper lobe is larger than the lower one; the membranes are in part covered with scales; there are three short external rays on each side of the large ones; anal with three rather slender spines, the second more than twice the length of the first, and the third longer still; the first soft rays are about twice as long as any of the spines; the others go on increasing; the ventrals are rather long; the spine is slender, and about two-thirds the length of the first soft rays. The pectorals are large, formed of eight branched rays and of five simple ones; the second and third of these extend in a long filament, about three-fourths the total length of the branched rays; the first and fourth are much shorter, the fifth is shorter even than the branched rays.

The general colour is of a light purple, with the lips pink; the eye is yellow, with an external orange circle; the body is crossed by two very broad transverse bands, formed by the scales being, in the place they cover, largely bordered with black; the first extends from the root of the fourth dorsal spine to the base of the anal; the second begins behind the first soft rays of the dorsal, and attains the first soft one of the anal; the dorsal fin is purple, tinged with green; the transverse bands of the back extend sometimes on the corresponding membranes; the caudal is sometimes of a brownish red, and sometimes of a dark brown, showing a faint transverse reddish band; anal black, with the spine purple, and a reddish tinge on the first rays; ventrals black; pectorals also, but these have a narrow white border.

This fish appears in the warm months of the year (December and January). It is found in the sea weeds, and its usual length is about 12 inches.

LATRIS.

T̲his genus was established by Sir John Richardson, iu the third volume of the "Transactions of the Zoological Society," and in his account of the fishes brought to England by the Expedition of the *Erebus* and *Terror* he gives the figure of a second species, already named *Ciliaris* by Forster in his manuscript notes, which have been since published by Lichtenstein. Richardson also thinks that another of Forster's sorts, on which Bloch (edit. Schneider, page 341,) has established his *Cicla Lineata*, ought to be placed here. This latter seems to be very nearly allied to the second sort I describe, under the name of *Latris Forsteri;* but it is said that the sailors gave it the name of *Yellow Tail*, which could never have been applied to my sort; it was found in great quantities on the coast of New Zealand.

The different species of this genus are edible, and even considered great delicacies.

LATRIS HECATEIA.

Latrie hecatei, *Richard.*, *Proceed. of the Zool. Soc.*, 1839, p.¦99.
——————————— *Transac.* v. iii., p. 106, pl. 6, fig. 1.

(*Hobart Town Trumpeter.*)

Grey, with the back rather darker; three or four broad longitudinal bands extend all along the sides of the head and body; belly of a dirty white; the dorsal fin is of a dark colour, as well as the caudal; the other fins are generally of a dark yellow.

This sort is frequently found on the southern coast of Tasmania, and it has also been met with in Bass's Straits, and is accidentally caught in Hobson's Bay. Its name is derived from the singular noise it produces. It is said that some specimens are nearly three feet long; it is the dearest and most esteemed fish of the Melbourne Market. Large quantities are also brought salted from Tasmania.

LATRIS FORSTERI.

(*Bastard Trumpeter.*)

The height of the body is not quite three times in the total length; the head is four and a-half times in the same; the orbit is contained four and a-half times in the length of the head. The general form is almost a regular oval ; the top of the head and the snout have no scales, but all the other parts of the head are covered with them ; on the upper jaw, there is an external row of rather long, slender, conical and blunt teeth, and behind them several irregular rows of smaller, arched and more acute ones ; at the lower jaw, there is only the external row, and the teeth are placed at some distance one from the other. The lateral line is regular, extends to the base of the caudal, and covers about one hundred and twenty scales ; the dorsal fin is formed of sixteen spines, the longest of all being the fourth and the fifth ; the three first going on increasing as they are placed backwards, the last rays of the fin as short as the first. The second part of the dorsal is formed of one spine and forty rays ; this spine is much longer than the last of the spiny part, but much shorter than the first soft rays, which are even longer than the highest spines ; these rays go on decreasing to the end ; the anal has the same form as the soft dorsal ; it is formed of two spines and thirty-eight rays ; the caudal is very strongly bifurcated ; it has seventeen long rays and four shorter ones on each side ; the pectorals are about one-sixth of the total length of the body, and are formed of eighteen rays ; the ventrals are rather small ; they are placed considerably behind the pectorals, and are formed of one rather long but slender spine and of five branched rays, the first of which has one-third more than the spine.

The colours are beautiful. The head is yellow in front, and green behind the eyes, with the sides purple ; the mouth and the throat are of a fine pink ; the back is of a light purplish blue, with numerous narrow golden longitudinal bands, which extend to the root of the caudal, and of which two are broader than the others ; the lower parts of the body are of a whitish pink. The first dorsal has its membranes rosy, but they become darker in their upper part ; the second is of a fine red, with a black external margin ; the anal is similar ; the caudal is greyish in its first half, and black in its external portion ; the ventrals are rather dark, and the pectorals of a dirty yellow ; the eye of a fine orange yellow.

This fish is known under the name of *Bastard Trumpeter;* its flesh is said to be delicate. It is very rarely brought to the

Melbourne Market, but is said to be common on the Gipps Land coast. The specimen I am describing is about 17 inches long. I have also five small ones about 9 inches long, which are entirely similar, but have only thirty-three rays to the anal ; the dorsal is of a rather dull colour.

LATRIS BILINEATA.

This *Latris*, of which I have only seen one single specimen, is so very similar to the last that I hesitated to constitute it as a distinct species. The form is entirely the same ; the dorsal is formed of fifteen spines and forty-one rays ; the anal of two spines and thirty-five rays, but the fourth of these has a prolongated filament of about one-half its length.

The body is silvery, with the back blue ; this has two longitudinal and rather broad golden bands on the sides ; towards the middle of the height there is a longitudinal impression like a second lateral line ; the inside of the mouth and throat are black.

From Western Port. Length, 7 inches.

LATRIS INORNATA.

The profile is nearly oval ; the height is three and one-third times in the total length ; the head four and one-third in the same. The dorsal is higher in its spiny than in its soft part ; the first is formed of sixteen spines, the fifth, sixth, and seventh being the longest; the others grow shorter till they reach the second part, which is formed of one spine and forty rays ; these become smaller as they are inserted backwards ; the caudal is strongly bifurcated, of fifteen long rays ; the pectorals have nineteen rays.

The general colour is of a bluish silvery white, with the back and upper part of the head of a very dark blue, almost black. This colour extends to the lateral line, where it stops suddenly, without any graduation or shade ; this line has a yellow tinge. The first dorsal has its membranes of a greenish brown, with also a yellow tinge ; it has a rather narrow external black margin ; the second dorsal is rather red, and shows the same black border. The caudal is black, with an irregular transverse yellow margin, situated on its external portion ; the anal is white, with its base pink; a small black spot is seen on its anterior angle; the ventral is whitish, and the pectoral of a rather yellowish green, with the base dark; the eye silvery, with a bluish tinge. There is a black spot on the upper part of the operculum.

The only specimen I have seen was taken at Western Port, in the month of October; it measured six inches and a-half.

TRIGLIDÆ.

" Form of the body oblong, compressed, or sub-cylindrical; eyes generally lateral, the cleft of the mouth extending on the sides of the muzzle; sometimes of hideous aspect. Eyes directed upwards, and the cleft of the mouth subvertical. Dentition feeble; teeth in villiform bands; generally without canines. Some bones of the head armed; suborbital ring articulated with the præoperculum. Epidermoid productions very variable. Two separate dorsal fins, or two distinct portions of the dorsal fin. Anal fin similarly developed as the soft dorsal. Ventrals thoracic, often with less than five soft rays. Five to seven branchiostegals; pseudobranchiæ; air-bladder often absent.

" Carnivorous fishes, found in all seas, a few only entering fresh waters. Some inhabit exclusively the fresh waters of both the Arctic regions. All live at the bottom of the water, being bad swimmers; a few are able to raise themselves into the air."

CENTROPOGON.

The species, on which this genus was formed by Dr. Gunther, was first noticed by White, under the name of *Cottus Australis*, and placed afterwards by Cuvier and Valenciennes in their genus

Apistus ; but these naturalists formed on it a particular section, characterised by its being entirely covered with scales, and without any free rays.

CENTROPOGON AUSTRALIS.

Cottus australis, *White, Voyage N. S. Wales*, p. 266, pl. 52.
Apistus australis, *Cuv. & Val.*, v. iv., p. 399.
Sebastes pandus? *Richard., Erebus and Terror*, p. 70, pl. 41, fig, 3-4.

(*The Gurnet.*)

This is one of the most common fishes on the Melbourne Market, particularly during the cold months of the year.

The height of the body is about four times in the total length; the transverse diameter is contained about five times in the same, and the head three times and one-quarter. The diameter of the orbit is contained three and one-third times in the length of the head ; the mouth is extensible.

This fish is too well known to require a detailed description. The upper parts are generally brown, with the lower parts of the head and body scarlet ; dorsal green, with red spots ; caudal similar, with its posterior half black ; anal variegated with red, brown, and greenish white ; pectorals with their upper part obscure, and variegated with red, and the lower one white, but also spotted ; ventrals white. These colours are subject to much variation, and sometimes the upper parts are purple, and the lower almost white.

This sort is found on the western and southern coasts of Australia. Towards the north-east (Queensland), it gives way to another species very nearly allied to it (*Centrop. Marmoratum,* Gunther, " Proceed. Zool. Journ.," 1862, p. 190,) but which has the third spine of the dorsal proportionally short.

The largest specimens are about 16 or 17 inches long.

PENTAROGE.

This is another genus formed on a section of Cuvier and Valenciennes's genus *Apistus*, characterised by the absence of scales. Below the eye there is a long, arched, moveable spine, which, when extended, cuts like a sword ; the skin is remarkably loose on the body.

Apistus marmoratus, *Cuv. & Val.*, v. iv., p. 416; *Cuv., R. An. Illustré*, pl. 24, fig, 3.

Height three and one-fourth times in total length; breadth of body three and one-quarter times of the same; head three and one-fifth in entire length. The dorsal has thirteen spines and ten soft rays, but the last of the spines might be counted with the soft part; the third spine is the longest; the anal has three spines and six rays; the caudal has twelve rays; the pectoral eleven.

The colour is of a light olive on the upper and lateral parts, and white on the lower; the body is covered with large marmorated purple blotches, between which are numerous punctiform marks of the same colour; the dorsal, caudal, and anal are of the colour of the back, with similar spots; there is a broad purple band on the external part of the caudal and pectorals; the ventrals are white.

This sort is scarce at Melbourne. I have only seen three specimens—one three inches long, and the largest about seven. The eyes of the two smallest were purple, with an external series of small spots; the largest had its eyes yellow.

The specimens described by Cuvier and Valenciennes had been brought from Timor by the learned naturalist Péron; but this sort is found on all the western and southern shores of Australia.

PLATYCEPHALUS.

This is certainly a tropical form, though a few of the sorts extend to the coasts of Japan. Numerous species are found in Australia, and are known under the name of *Flat Heads*. They are more common in the cold than in the warm season.

PLATYCEPHALUS RICHARDSONI.

Height of body nine times in total length; breadth six times; head (to end of operculum) three and a-half times; orbit five times in the length of the head on the middle line, or six times to the end of the operculum. Head very flat, very broad, rounded in front, the transverse line before the eyes being only one and a-half times in the length of head, taken in its middle line; the lower jaw longer than the upper one; the upper surface is irregular, and presents longitudinal interrupted ridges; the præoperculum is armed towards its external angle with two very strong spines, the lower of these being something longer than the upper one; the orbit is round, and has a rather strong spine towards its anterior inner portion; the præorbital has a spine towards the angle of the mouth, and another one above this. The body is very inflated near the head, and goes tapering towards the tail; the lateral line covers about sixty scales, and is formed on each of them by a short ridge, which divides itself in two or three arborescent tubes; the total number of transverse lines of scales is about ninety. The first dorsal is formed of an isolated, short, but sharp spine, and of seven long slender spines, bearing membranes; the second is the longest and the seventh is laying on the back, and difficult to perceive. The second dorsal has fourteen rays, the first being the longest; the anal is similar; the caudal has twelve long rays and several shorter ones on each side; the pectorals have seventeen rays; the ventrals are about one-third longer than the pectorals, and have a rather long and slender spine, and five branched rays.

The general colour is of an olive brown, covered with numerous crimson spots; the sides are grey, but also spotted with crimson; the lower parts white; fins transparent, with the spines and rays of the dorsal spotted with brown; caudal, ventrals, and pectorals with transverse lines of orange, with crimson tinged spots; the posterior part of the caudal is black.

Rather scarce; 18 inches long.

PLATYCEPHALUS BASSENSIS.

Platycephalus bassensis, *Cuv. & Val.*, v. iv., p. 247.
——————— tasmanicus, *Richard.*, *Zool. Trans.*, v. iii., p. 23.
——————————————— *Erebus and Ter.*, *Fishes*,
p. 23, pl. xviii., v. 1-2.

(*The Common or Bass Flathead.*)

Height about eleven times in total length; head, to the centre of the posterior part, one and a-quarter times in total length, and from the extremity of the operculum one and a-half times in the same; the orbit of the eye is seven times in the greatest length of the head; the præorbital has only one point; the orbit none; the præopercular spines are large, the lower much longer than the upper one. The lateral line is marked on seventy-three scales, and the number of transverse lines is about one hundred and eight. The first dorsal is formed of a very small, isolated spine, and of some long ones, bearing membranes; the last is laying on the back, and thus six only are plainly visible. The second dorsal is formed of fourteen rays, as is also the anal; the first rays of the second dorsal are nearly as long as the first; caudal truncated, of twelve long rays and four shorter ones on each side; pectorals of seventeen rays; ventrals not much longer than the pectorals, but extending much further backwards. The teeth are very numerous, villiform, and all similar on both jaws; those of the palatines larger, and distant one from the other; the vomer teeth villiform in front, with the posterior ones larger and directed backwards.

The body is of a light lilac colour on the upper parts, covered with very small, obscure, rounded spots, which are much larger on the sides; fins transparent, with the rays of the dorsal, ventrals, and pectorals spotted with brown; the caudal has several transverse series of dark purple round spots, and a large blackish spot covers almost one-half of its extreme inferior part.

Very common on the Melbourne Market, particularly in the cold months. Length generally from 12 to 17 inches, but it is sometimes much larger.

Dr. Richardson, having received specimens of this fish from Tasmania, thought they were different from Cuvier's sort, and in this he has been followed by Dr. Gunther, but I have seen thousands of specimens from all parts of South-eastern Australia, and there is not the least doubt that they all belong to one sort.

PLATYCEPHALUS LÆVIGATUS.

Platycephalus lævigatus, *Cuv. & Val.*, v. iv., p. 243.

(*The Rock Flathead.*)

Height about eight times in total length; breadth about seven and a-half in same; head, to the end of operculum, four times in total length; orbit six and a-quarter times in head, to the extremity of the operculum. The body long, and almost cylindrical; head elongate, smooth; orbits without spines; the præorbital with a very feeble and blunt one ; the upper spine of the præoperculum longer than the second. The lateral line runs over about eighty-two scales, and the number of the transverse lines is about one hundred and twenty. The dorsal is formed of one small, isolated spine and of eight long ones, united by a large membrane ; the second dorsal and anal have fourteen rays ; the caudal thirteen long ones and several shorter ones on each side ; the pectorals are nearly as long as the ventrals, and are formed of eighteen rays. The teeth are very numerous, and all villiform on both jaws ; those of the vomer and palatines larger.

The general colour of the upper parts is a dark olive brown ; the lower parts being white and silvery ; on the sides of the body are numerous, round, brown and yellow spots. The lower parts of the head are of a reddish orange. Fins translucid, of a rather olive colour, with the spines and rays marbled with brown and orange ; anal rather rosy, with a brown spot on each ray ; the pectorals and ventrals are yellow, with transverse lines of round crimson spots. The colours of this species seem subject to considerable variations ; the very large specimens are often covered with large, elongate, marmorated blotches.

This sort is very common on the Melbourne Market, particularly in the cold months of the year. Its usual size is about 18 inches, but it sometimes attains nearly twice that size.

PLATYCEPHALUS PROXIMUS.

This sort is so very nearly allied to *Lævigatus*, in form and general aspect, as to have made me hesitate a considerable time before I separated it specifically. It differs from it by its head being considerably broader on its anterior part, and being, in front of the eyes, equal to a line drawn from the centre of the upper jaw to the posterior edge of the orbit, when in *Lævigatus* such a line would only attain two-thirds of the orbit. The eye is much larger and more oval, being nearly round in *Lævigatus*. The teeth are more numerous and finer ; those of the vomer all equal, and similar to a fine brush. The first dorsal is formed of one small free spine, and of only seven longer ones.

The colour is also rather different, being of a light purplish blue, with the lips and the sides of the head rosy ; the lower parts of the body are white, with some irregularly formed blackish spots on the sides; these have a general transverse form; the caudal is grey, and the other fins are white and diaphanous, with the upper half of the pectorals and the inner one of the dorsal almost black.

Scarce; seen only once on the Melbourne Market, in the month of October. Length, 16 inches.

PLATYCEPHALUS FUSCUS.

Platycephalus fuscus, *Cuv. & Val., Hist. des Poissons*, v. iv., p. 341.

———————————— *Quoy et Gaimard, Voyage de l'Astrolabe*, pl. 10, fig. 1.

(Grass Flathead.)

Height of body nine and a-half times in its total length; breadth five and two-thirds in same; head three and two-thirds in length of body; orbit five times and a-half in head to the line of the centre, or seven and a-half to the extremity of the operculum. Head broad and flat behind, conical and rather narrow in front; a transverse line drawn in front of the eyes, being contained twice in the length of the centre of the head, and once and three-fourths in its breadth at the operculum. The upper surface is rather smooth, and the elevated longitudinal lines interrupted; the orbits are rather oval, and have a strong tooth at their anterior inner portion; the præorbital has two strong teeth; the two spines of the præoperculum almost equal, but the lower one a little longer; the teeth are villiform, with the interior ones larger, and arched backwards on each side in front; on the palatines and on the vomer a line of strong, pointed, and hooked teeth; at the lower jaw the villiform teeth are less numerous, but there is an internal line of rather large and conical ones, placed a little apart one from the other. Body broad, going tapering towards the tail; the lateral line is formed as usual in this genus, and is marked on about sixty-four scales; the number of the transverse series is about one hundred. The first dorsal is formed of one short, isolated spine, and of eight long ones, united by the membrane; the last of these is partly hidden in the skin, so that only seven are plainly visible. The second dorsal is formed of fourteen rays, as is also the anal;

the caudal of twelve long rays and of several small ones on each side; pectorals rather large, formed of seventeen rays; ventrals very large, being a good third longer than the pectorals, formed of five rays and of a rather short spine.

The general colour is of a dark brownish blue, with the sides yellow, and the lower parts of a dirty white; the upper part of the head is green, as are also the fins; they are all marked with purple rounded spots; the caudal is black in its posterior portion, and more particularly on the lower part of it. In some specimens, the back is beautifully marbled with brown blotches.

This sort is found on seaweed bottoms. I have very little doubt that it is the *Platycephalus Fuscus*, but Cuvier and Valenciennes count one ray less to the second dorsal and to the anal.

NEOPLATYCEPHALUS.

Form of *Platycephalus*, but distinguished by the dentition; teeth very numerous, villiform, with other large canine and very sharp ones, widely separated, and placed between them at the lower jaw; at the upper one, these large teeth form a line on the palatines, and extend in a rather numerous bunch in front; those of the latter part are curved.

NEOPLATYCEPHALUS GRANDIS.

Height of the body about nine and a-half times in its total length; its breadth a little less than six times; head three and two-third times in total length; orbit seven and a-half times in length of head; this is broad posteriorly, almost conical; in front of the eyes, its breadth is one-half of its length, taken at its middle; the snout is rather angular in front; the upper surface of the head is smooth, and presents faint longitudinal uninterrupted lines; the præoperculum is armed towards its external angle with two strong spines, the lower being much longer than the upper one; in some specimens it is over twice its length. The orbit of the eye is oval, and has a nearly imperceptible point in front, at its upper part; the præorbital has two angles over the sides of the mouth; the lower jaw is considerably longer than the upper one. The body is inflated near the head, and goes tapering towards the tail; the lateral line runs over about sixty-two scales to the root of the caudal, on which it extends; it is formed on each scale of a short edge, which expands in several arborescent tubes; these are not visible on all the scales, and the number of transverse lines is about ninety-five. The dorsal is formed of one isolated and rather short spine, and of eight long, slender ones, supporting the membrane; the last is adherent to the skin, and seven only are plainly visible, the longest being the second. The second dorsal is formed of fourteen rays, as is also the anal; the caudal has eleven long ones, and several shorter on each side; the pectorals seventeen; the ventrals are twice as long as the pectorals, and have one slender spine and five rays.

The general colour is of a pink lilac, covered with numerous irregular orange spots; the sides yellow; the fins are transparent and rather grey; their spines and rays are marbled with orange; the caudal has four transverse lines of rather large, rounded, orange spots, and its end is black.

This sort is not common on the Melbourne Market. It attains large dimensions, my specimens measuring from 20 to 23 inches in length.

TRIGLA.

I have only observed one species of this genus on the Victorian coast; but it is said that *Kumu* of New Zealand is also found here, but I have not seen it.

TRIGLA POLYOMMATA.

Trigla polyommata, *Richard.*, *Proceed. Zool. Soc.*, 1839, page 96.

———————————— *Richard.*, *Trans.*, v. iii., page 87, pl. 5, fig. 2.

(*The Flying Gurnet.*)

This beautiful fish is of a most magnificent crimson pink, with orange tints; the lower parts are of a starry white with blue spots. The fins are of the colour of the back, with the rays more brilliant and of orange colour; the pectorals very large, and extending to the sixth ray of the anal, of a fine green with a purple external edge, and four or five transverse bands of dark blue. A large oblong double black spot, bordered with white, extends on the first half, near the external edge; the rays are purple; the anal is white: the eye silver colour.

One specimen had its pectorals of a light blue colour, spotted with yellow.

Without being common in the Melbourne Market, this fish appears in all seasons ; but often for months there are none to to be seen, and then several will be caught together, and always attract attention by their beautiful appearance.

It is said to be very good for eating.

Richardson's figure conveys a very poor idea of the extraordinary beauty of this fish, and Dr. Gunther's description a still worse one of its colors.

LEPIDOTRIGLA.

Separated by Dr. Gunther from *Trigla*, on account of the large size of its scales.

LEPIDOTRIGLA VANESSA.

Trigla vanessa, *Richard., Proceed. Zool. Soc.*, 1839, page 96.
———————— *Richard., Trans. Zool. Soc.*, v. iii., page 83.

plate 5.

(Small Gurnet.)

D. 11. A. 17. C. 11 (long rays). P. 10, and 3 free ones.

Height of body five and one-fifth in total length ; head three and one fifth in same; the lateral line formed of sixty-nine spiny scales ; caudal forcated, of a reddish pink colour, with belly white ; the first dorsal has a broad black spot rounded with white ; the pectorals are of a dark green, with a large bilobed black spot, edged with blue and white, placed at the end of its internal side.

The body is sometimes covered with small marmorated dark spots, but these are often missing. Eye yellow.

Seen several specimens in the months of July and August.

LEPIDOTRIGLA SPHYNX.

Trigla sphynx, *Cuv. & Val.*, v. iv., page 83.

1st D. 9.—2nd D. 14. A. 14.

Of a fine castaneous grey, with the sides of each scale rather dark ; a series of rather large rounded black spots on the back and on the lateral line ; the belly is white ; the first dorsal is pink, with a rather large rounded black spot on the external edge; it has a white ring round it; the second dorsal is white, with its edge rather yellow; its spines are marbled with yellow and brown; the caudal is rounded, of a grey colour, with five or six transverse lines of red spots; the anal has its first half white, and its external one of a bright yellow; the ventrals also yellow, with the rays orange; the pectorals are grey, with the rays pink and spotted with brown, their lower surface is black; the free rays are also spotted; eye yellow, spotted with brown, with an inner circle of a fine orange colour.

This sort seems to be very scarce, as I have only seen one specimen. It was in the month of July.

This fish was found many years ago, by the celebrated naturalist Péron, and was described by Cuvier and Valenciennes in their great work, but its locality was not known.

TRACHINIDÆ.

" Body elongate, low, naked, or covered with scales. Teeth in villiform bands, with pointed and conical canines in some of the genera; no molars or trenchant teeth. The infraorbital ring does not articulate with the præoperculum. One or two dorsal fins, the spinous portion being always much less developed and shorter than the soft; the anal similarly developed as the soft dorsal; ventrals with one spine and five rays. Gill-opening more or less wide; five, six, or seven branchiostegals; pseudobranchiæ. No prominent papilla near the anus. Air-bladder generally absent; pyloric appendages moderate in number or wanting.

" Carnivorous fishes, living at the bottom of the shores of nearly all the seas."

KATHETOSTOMA.

This genus was formed by Dr. Gunther on a sort of *Urano-scopus* of Bloch, remarkable by the total absence of scales.

KATHETOSTOMA LÆVE.

Uranoscopus lævis, *Bloch.*, *Schneid. system*, page 47, pl. 8.

—————————— *Cuv. & Val.*, v. iii., page 319.

—————————— *Gunther*, *Catalogue*, v. ii., page 231.

(Stone Lifter.)

Breadth of head two and a-half times in the length, to the base of the caudal; length of head, from the extremity of the upper jaw to the centre of the posterior part, four times in the same; the long spines of the shoulder straight or directed rather externally.

The general colour is of an uniform brown on the upper parts and white below. On the sides of the head, and on the line of separation between the brown and the white there is a reddish pink tinge; the fins are brown, with the end of the caudal and the edge of the pectorals pink; the anal is of this last colour. The eyes are red, spotted on their limb with black in very old specimens, and yellow in others; the lips are red.

It is rather common on the Melbourne Market, but is not generally eaten. I have a large specimen, which is nearly 18 inches in length, but this sort does not usually measure more than half that size.

I have seen several times small specimens not more than six to seven inches long, which may, perhaps, belong to a different species; they are not quite so broad, the breadth of their head being three times in the total length to the base of the caudal, and the long spines of the shoulder being longer in proportion, and directed rather inwards. The general colour of this variety is a greyish yellow, with two broad black transverse bands on the body; caudal black, bordered with pink, as are also the pectorals and the dorsal. Eye yellow.

Cuvier's specimen, which had been brought from Australia by Péron, belongs to this latter variety; Bloch's, which he describes from a drawing communicated to him by Latham, was, on the contrary, entirely brown.

The fins have D. 16. C. 10. A. 13. P. 17. V. 1/5.

PSEUDAPHRITIS.

The new specie I propose here is formed on a fish manifestly belonging to the *Trachinidæ* of Gunther, and to his group of *Trachinina*, but forming, on account of its eyes, placed obliquely at the upper part of the head, a passage to his *Uranoscopina*. The cleft of the mouth is rather oblique ; there are two dorsals ; ventrals jugular, with nine spines and five soft rays ; no canines. Almost all this would agree with *Aphritis*, but the scales are rather large ; the first dorsal has seven rays, and just in front of the anal there is a short fin composed of two spines.

PSEUDAPHRITIS BASSÜ.

General form of the body oblong, rather cylindrical, and elongate ; cleft of the mouth rather oblique, with the lower jaw longer than the upper one ; eye placed obliquely on the superior part of the sides of the head. Height of the body seven and one-third times in the total length ; head conical, four times in the same ; eye six and three-quarters in the length of head.

The lateral line runs straight all along the body, over fifty-nine scales ; the transverse line is formed of twenty scales, rather large and ciliated, of which six are over the lateral line. A longitudinal sulcate extends on the centre of the back from the posterior part of the head to the base of the dorsal ; the head is entirely covered with scales ; the præoperculum is entire ; the operculum is terminated by a broad flat point.

The first dorsal with one spine and seven rays ; it is rather high ; second dorsal inserted near the first ; it is formed of twenty rays ; the caudal is rather large, subtruncated, with the angles rather prolonged, and formed of twelve long rays ; anal similar to the second dorsal, formed of twenty-two rays, and in front are two small spines, rather curved. each supporting a small membrane, and adjoining the soft rays ; the first spine being longer than the other ; ventrals placed in front of the pectorals, and formed of one spine and five rays ; pectorals rather large, and formed of eighteen rays ; teeth very numerous on each jaw, cardiform, sharp ; others similar on the vomer and palatines.

The upper parts are brown, with a few very faint transverse broad green bands on the back; sides of the head purple; the colour is red in front of the eyes; lower parts white;

dorsal fins of the same colour and hyaline, with the rays marbled with yellow and brown; caudal yellow, with four or five transverse crimson bands; anal pink; ventrals yellowish; pectorals yellow, with several narrow crimson lines of spots; eye yellow.

Seen only once; taken in the Straits of Bass, and dedicated to the celebrated discoverer of that region.

SILLAGO.

Genus formed by Cuvier in the "Règne Animal," on a fish that Bloch had placed with *Sciæna* and Russel with *Sparus*. Forskal had made an *Atherina* of a sort he had found in the Red Sea. Cuvier placed this genus with his *Percidæ*, on account of the denticulations of its præopercule, and of the point that terminates its opercle, as also on account of the presence of teeth on the vomer; but Dr. Gunther has included it in the rather hetrogeneous family he calls *Trachinidæ*. It has certainly very little natural affinities with the group in which Cuvier had included it.

Most of the sorts inhabit the Indian Sea; others are said by Cuvier and Valenciennes to be found in Australia; but I have only observed two of them. *Bassensis*, which was found at Western Port by d'Urville's Expedition, has not yet come under my notice, and *Ciliata* was originally found at Cape York, but Dr. Gunther also records it from Tasmania and Sydney.

I cannot agree with this last author in considering *Bassensis* as a synonyme of *Maculata;* and as I have seen many thousand specimens of *Sillago* from Western Port, which all belonged to *Punctata*, I should be inclined to think it may be a variety of that sort, perhaps rather similar to the white one I describe below.

SILLAGO PUNCTATA.

Sillago punctata, *Cuv. & Val.*, v. iii., p. 413.

(The Whiting.)

Form very elongate; height of body eight times in total length; head five times in the same; orbit four and a-half times in the length of head. The dorsal has twelve spines at its first fin, and one with twenty-six rays at its second; the anal has one spine and twenty-two rays; the caudal is strongly bifurcated, and has seventeen long rays and four shorter ones on each side ; the pectorals have fourteen rays.

The upper parts are of a brownish grey ; the sides and lower parts are white; these latter are covered with numerous very small, irregularly placed, but rounded spots of an obscure brownish colour; fins rather olive colour; the caudal yellow; the anal and ventrals white; eyes silvery.

Very common on the Melbourne Market almost all the year round ; it is esteemed for the table. Average length, from 8 to 14 inches.

I have one specimen 9 inches long, of a white silvery colour, the back having only a greyish tinge ; the spots very minute, and in reduced number ; they were very little visible on the fresh specimen ; the muzzle is a little shorter, and more regularly convex ; the eye is a little larger than in the typical specimens.

SILLAGO MACULATA.

Sillago maculata, *Quoy et Gaimard, Exped. Freycinet Zool.,* pl. 53, fig. 2.

———-——— *Cuv. & Val., Poissons,* v. iii., p. 411.

The body is oval, much shorter than in *Punctata.* The first dorsal has eleven spines, and the second one spine and eighteen rays ; the caudal has seventeen long rays ; the anal two spines and nineteen rays ; the pectorals have sixteen.

The height is five times and a-half in the total length, and the head less than three times in the same.

The upper parts are of a light olive colour, marbled with rather large brown spots ; the lower parts are white ; on each side of the body is a rather broad longitudinal band ; the fins are diaphanous, with the rays spotted with orange ; the exterior portions of the dorsal and the caudal rather obscure ; the eye is silvery. Length, 6 inches.

Only seen once in September.

POLYNEMIDÆ.

" Body compressed and oblong, covered with scales, feebly ciliated or without serrature. Lateral line continuous, continued on the tail. Mouth at the lower side of the snout, with lateral cleft. Eye lateral, large. Seven branchiostegals ; pseudo-branchiæ. Villiform teeth on the jaws and on the palate. Two separate dorsals, the second, the caudal, and the anal fin more or less covered with minute scales. Several filliform appendages below the pectoral fin, entirely free, and articulated. Ventrals thoracic, with one spine and five rays. The bones of the head with the muciferous system well developed. Air-bladder varying in form and structure, and sometimes wanting.

"Tropical regions of the Atlantic ; East Indian seas to the Pacific. Entering rivers."

This family is represented by two sorts on the eastern coast of Australia, but none have yet been observed in the Victorian waters.

SPHYRÆNIDÆ.

" Body elongate, subcylindrical, covered with small cycloid scales ; lateral line continuous. Cleft of the mouth wide, armed with strong teeth. Eye lateral, of moderate size. Seven branchiostegals ; pseudobranchiæ and air-bladder present. Two dorsal fins, remote from each other ; anal similar to the second dorsal ; ventrals abdominal, composed of one spine and five rays.

" Carnivorous fishes, inhabiting the seas of the temperate and tropical regions."

SPHYRÆNA.

Though one sort of these fishes is found in the Mediterranean they may be considered as belonging more to the warm than to the temperate climates, the great majority of their sorts inhabiting below the tropics.

SPHYRÆNA NOVÆ-HOLLANDIÆ.

Sphyræna novæ-Hollandiæ, *Gunther, Catal.*, v. ii., p, 335.

(*The Pyke.*)

This sort is well described by Dr. Gunther, with the exception of the teeth, which are not those of the adult specimens, but of the young ones.

Teeth of the upper jaw small, equal, numbering thirty-eight or forty on each side ; two pair of fangs, of which the posterior are much the largest and strongest ; the palatines have three small teeth at their posterior part, and seven strong ones more forward ; these are very acute and conical, the third of them being often a little longer than the others. At the lower jaw there are, in front, a strong fang on each side, and a dozen straight, acute, canine teeth placed on each side ; they are distant one from the other, small in front, and becoming larger as they extend backwards.

The colour is of a slatey grey on the upper parts, with the sides and belly white ; the back and upper part of the head are sometimes almost black ; the sides of the head and sometimes the lateral line have a copper tinge ; the fins are of an olive green, changing to yellow in some parts ; eye silvery.

The fishmongers say that, some years ago, this fish used to be generally larger than now, and that it was quite common to get them over a yard long. It is only rarely that such specimens appear on the market. The *Pyke* is one of the best and most wholesome of the Melbourne fishes. I only find 126 to 129 scales on the lateral line.

NEOSPHYRÆNA.

This genus has entirely the general appearance of *Sphyræna*, but the ventrals are situated almost under the pectorals ; the second dorsal and the anal have a very large number of rays (over twenty) ; the head is entirely scaly ; the first dorsal is comparatively smaller, and the dentition is different.

The lower jaw is obtuse, and considerably longer than the other; on the upper one the teeth are small, almost equal, but the centre ones rather larger than the others, and are numerous. Behind this is a band of very numerous, villiform, and very small teeth ; this band is narrow in front and behind, but broad towards the centre of the jaw. In front, there are on each side two very large fangs, the posterior one much longer than the other ; on each palatine there is a single line of very small teeth, and some larger ones on the vomer. At the lower jaw, there is a line of very minute teeth, which does not extend in front, but is replaced in this part by rather large, acute ones, directed backwards ; towards the middle, and inserted behind the line I have mentioned, there are on each side two large fangs, apart one from the other. In some specimens there are three. The head is entirely scaly, and its upper part has no longitudinal sulcates ; the præoperculum is rounded, and finely ciliated on its margin ; the operculum terminates with a rather prolongated, obtuse, flat point. Scales rather large; they fall easily ; the lateral line is well marked, continuous ; the ventrals are united at their base ; they are formed of one spine and five rays.

NEOSPHYRÆNA MULTIRADIATA.

Body thick and rather short; contained about six and a-half times in the total length ; the head three and two-third times in same; the orbit four and two-third times in the length of the head. The snout is rather short; the distance between the extremity of the upper jaw to the anterior orbit being equal to the distance between the posterior edge of the same orbit and the extremity of the operculum ; head entirely scaly ; the lower jaw longer than the upper one by one-half the diameter of the eye ; the lateral line running over about seventy-five scales, which fall very easily ; the first dorsal is formed of five rays ; the second dorsal of from seventeen to twenty-one rays ; its anterior part much higher than its posterior one ; the caudal is emarginated, with sixteen rays ; the anal is longer than the dorsal, with twenty-eight rays ; the ventrals, placed almost below the pectorals, are formed of one very slender spine aud five rays ; the pectorals of sixteen rays ; the second dorsal is higher thau the first, its fourth, fifth, and sixth rays being the longest, and equal to the length of the snout ; the others become shorter as they go hackwards ; the anal is of the same form. The first dorsal is situated on a line that would cut the end of the pectorals ; the second is inserted at a distance from the first, equal to the space between the beginning of the first and the end of the operculum. The pectorals are a little longer than the ventrals.

The upper parts are of a slatey grey ; the lower white ; the eye is silvery ; the second dorsal and caudal are of an obscure yellow ; pectorals white, as are also the ventrals and anal ; sometimes a rather large, irregularly-rounded black spot on the upper lobe of the caudal, near its extremity

Commou in the months of May, June, and July ; it attains 2 feet in length. The fishermen sometimes call it *Skip Jack*, but that name is more particularly applied to *Temnodon Saltatar.* It is considered equal to *Sphyræna Novæ Hollandiæ* for the use of the table.

MEASUREMENTS.	*Inches.*
Total length	$15\frac{3}{8}$
From exty. of upper jaw to aut. edge of eye...	$1\frac{5}{8}\text{-}\frac{1}{2}$
————— lower ———————	2
Diameter of eye	$\frac{3}{4}$
Height from post. edge of eye to end of oper.	$1\frac{7}{8}$
——— to base of pectorals	$1\frac{5}{8}\text{-}\frac{1}{2}$
——————— of ventrals	$2\frac{1}{2}$
Height of head at centre of eye	$1\frac{5}{8}$
——— of body	$2\frac{3}{8}$
From extm. of upper jaw to root of 1st dorsal	5
————————————— of 2nd dorsal	$7\frac{3}{4}$
Length of 1st dorsal	$\frac{3}{4}\text{-}\frac{1}{2}$
——— of 2ud dorsal	$2\frac{1}{8}$
Height of 1st dorsal	$\frac{5}{8}\text{-}\frac{1}{2}$
——— of 2nd ———- at its base	$1\frac{3}{4}$
————————— at its extremity	$\frac{1}{2}\text{-}\frac{1}{2}$
Length of caudal in centre	1
——————— on the sides	$2\frac{1}{4}$
——— of pectorals	$1\frac{7}{8}$

	Inches.
Length of ventrals	1⅜
Distance of ventrals behind pectorals	⅝-¼
From extremity of lower jaw to ventrals	4¾
————————————— to anus	7⅛
————————————— to anal............	7⅝
From anus to base of anal	½
-————— to extremity of anal	4-1

Nota.—It would be more exact to say that the two first rays
of the second dorsal are not branched, and could be called spines
if they were not soft; the following (third) ray is much longer.

SCIÆNIDÆ.

" Body compressed and rather elongate, covered
with ctenoid scales. Lateral line continuous, and
often continued on the tail. Mouth in front of the
snout Eye lateral, of moderate size. Seven
branchiostegals. Teeth in villiform bands, with
canines in some of the genera; no molars or trenchant teeth in the jaws; no teeth on the palate.
Cheek not cuirassed; the opercles not, or feebly,
armed. Two dorsal fins, the soft one much more
developed than the spinous or the anal; the spines
of the first dorsal generally feeble and elevated.
The anal fin with two spines. All the rays of the
pectorals branched; ventrals thoracic, with one
spine and five soft rays. The bones of the head
with one spine and five soft rays; the bones of the
head with the muciferous system very developed.
Stomach cæcal; pyloric appendages in small or
moderate number. Air-bladder with branching

or very elongate appendages, sometimes absent. Pseudobranchiæ sometimes hidden."

It appears to me that this family is placed by Dr. Gunther too far from *Percidæ*, to which it is very nearly allied.

In speaking of this family Dr. Gunther says, "*not to be found in Australia* ; but in this, as it so often happens, nature does not submit herself to the laws imposed by naturalists. The presence of a large *Sciæna* in the Victorian seas was first announced by Professor M'Coy, in his " Notes on the Zoology of Victoria," in the Reports of the International Exhibition of Melbourne, 1866. He considers it as the same as the Mediterranean sort, *Sc. Aquila*. This might have been the case, as the species that abounds at the Cape of Good Hope, and on which Cuvier had formed his *Sciæna Hololepidota*, does not appear to differ specially from it, but on comparing a specimen of the Australian fish with the descriptions of Cuvier and Dr. Gunther, I find differences which will not allow me to adopt the opinion of the learned Professor of the Melbourne University. In fact it appears doubtful that it even belongs to the same genus. Dr. Gunther gives *Sciæna* as a character to have the upper jaw overlapping the other one, both jaws being equal; and in the Australian fish the lower jaw protrudes over the upper one. Cuvier attributes also to *Sciæna* the character of having the præoperculum serrated ; but in old individuals this disappears. Taking even for granted that the Australian fish belongs to *Sciæna*, we still find numerous differences with the European sort.

SCIÆNA.

SCIÆNA ANTARCTICA.

(*The King Fish*.)

Taking Cuvier's description, we find: 1st, that in the European sort the cleft of the mouth extends to below one-third of the eye: in *Antarctica* it ends before the eye. 2nd, that at the lower jaw there are numerous small teeth between the large ones : none exist in the Australian fish. 3rd, the diameter of the eye forms about one-sixth of the total length of the head : in *Antarctica* the orbit is only one-eighth, and the eye of the fresh specimen is contained nine and a quarter times in the same. 4th, that the diameter of the eye is only twice in the muzzle: in the Australian sort it is sensibly more. 5th, that the eye is near the superior profile of the head, and distant from the lower one by twice its diameter: in the new sort this last proportion is contained three times. 6th, that the European sort is, when fresh, of a silvery grey, rather brown on the back, and whitish below; that the first dorsal, the pectorals, and the ventral, were of a rather fine red, and the other fins of a reddish brown: in the Australian fish the upper parts were of a fine blue, changing to green; the sides and lower parts of a dirty white, rather silvery; the dorsal, anal, and ventrals reddish; the pectorals white, with their extremity dark; the præoperculum has no denticulations, but towards its angle there are some sinuosities or notches; this may depend on age.

The teeth on the upper jaw are of two sorts—1st, an external line of large conic ones; they are rather curved backwards, and placed at a considerable distance one from the other in rather an irregular way; they number about twelve on each side; those in front are the largest, and they become very small as they extend backwards. Behind these is a band of villiform teeth, formed of four or five very irregular series; these teeth are small, obtuse, and directed backwards; they are not so numerous in front as towards the posterior part of the mouth, but a few larger ones are seen in this part. At the lower jaw there is only the external line of large irregular teeth, fourteen or fifteen in number; at the anterior part there are two extra ones placed in front of the others; the inside of the mouth and the tongue are smooth.

The orbit is oblong, being one-fourth longer than its breadth.

The scales which cover the head are much smaller than those of the body; these are densely punctured, and have concentric lines; they are externally edged with a sort of a little Sciæna fringe. The lateral line runs over about sixty-eight scales, but their oblique disposition renders it difficult to count them with certainty. The head is four times in the total length; the eye yellow, with a narrow golden circle.

I have only seen one fresh specimen of this sort; it measured fifty-seven inches long, and twelve and one-fifth in height. The head alone weighed eighteen pounds; the first dorsal had nine spines, and the second dorsal one, and twenty-seven rays; the anal two spines and seven rays; the caudal seventeen long rays, and three shorter ones on each side; the pectorals seventeen rays.

This fish is very scarce, and sometimes two or three years elapse without one single specimen being caught; it is considered a great delicacy, and in consequence sells at a high price; the specimen I mention brought two pounds ten shillings. The remarkable edible qualities of this fish seem to be equal to those of the Mediterranean sort, which was considered by the Romans of the Middle Ages to be the most delicious of all food; and of which the learned Cuvier relates many curious anecdotes.

At the Cape of Good Hope, where *Aquila* is so common (at least Dr. Gunther considers that it belongs to the same sort), the young specimens only are eaten fresh, and the large ones, being hard and dry, are salted like cod, and exported to the Mauritius.

The Australian fish seems an accidental visitor in the Straits of Bass, as it appears exclusively in the cold months, and only very large specimens have ever been seen.

At the Cape of good Hope the young specimens are common in the warm months, and the large ones in the Antarctic winter.

TRICHIURIDÆ.

" Body elongate and compressed; naked or with minute scales; eye lateral; cleft of the mouth wide, with several strong teeth on the jaws, or on the palate; the spinous and the soft portions of the dorsal and the anal elongate and many rayed; tail sometimes with finlets; ventrals thoracic, some rudimentary, or entirely absent; no prominent papilla near the vent, gill-opening wide; seven or eight branchiostegals; pseudobranchiæ; an air-bladder; pyloric appendages in increased number; the abdominal and caudal portions of the vertebral column composed of numerous vertebræ.

" Inhabitants of the seas between the tropics, extending on to those of the temperate regions."

THYRSITES.

Formed by Cuvier and Valenciennes on a curious elongate fish. The sorts of this genus are not numerous; one is found in the Mediterranean Sea, and extends to Madeira, where a second sort is also met; another, *Lepidopoides*, inhabits the coast of Brazils; one the East Indies; and two are described as found in the Australian Seas. One of these is unknown to me (*Solandri*), the other is very common in the Straits of Bass, particularly during the cold months of the year; this sort is also found in great quantity at the Cape of Good Hope, where it bears the name of *Snoek*. In that Colony it appears in the beginning of August, becomes very abundant in September, and disappears a few months after; it is considered the best fish of the country.

THYRSITES ATUN.

Scomber atun, *Euphrasen, Vetensk. Acad.*, v. xii.

Thyrsites atun, *Cuv. & Val., Poissons*, v. viii., p. 196, pl. 219.

———— altivelis, *Richard., Proceed. Zool. Soc.*, 1839, p. 99.

(*The Barracuta.*)

The Australian fish appears to me to be entirely similar to the Cape specimens, and I don't doubt that this sort inhabits all the Antarctic Seas. It is of a dark silvery colour, with the upper parts of an obscure blue; eye yellow: the dorsal variegated with black and white.

Very common at certain seasons, and much esteemed as food.

The *Thirsites Altivelis* seems to have been established erroneously; in all the Australian specimens, I find the longest ray of the dorsal much lower than the body, and also only six *pinnulæ*. In some cases, particularly in old specimens, the last ray (or rays) of the second dorsal detaches itself from the others, and takes the appearance of a seventh

SCOMBRIDÆ.

"Body generally elongate, compressed, naked, or covered with scales of small or moderate (nomcina) size ; eye lateral. Dentition variable. The infraorbital bones do not articulate with the præopereulum. The spinous dorsal less developed than the soft or than the anal, either continous with or separate from, the soft portion, sometimes rudimentary or entirely absent. The soft dorsal and the anal sometimes divided posteriorly into finlets. Ventrals thoracic, sometimes rudimentary or entirely absent. No prominent papilla near the vent. Gill-opening wide ; generally seven branchiostegals. Pseudobranchiæ, and an air-bladder ; pylorie appendages generally in great number.

"Inhabitants of the high seas of nearly all the regions, many of the species having a very wide range."

THYNNUS.

Genus formed of a small number of large species, found in the temperate and warm seas. One alone appears in the Melbourne Market, and it has not been yet described, as far as I can ascertain.

THYNNUS MACCOYÜ.

(The Bonite.)

The height is four times in the total length ; head three and one-third in same ; the thickness of the body is contained one and two-third times in the length ; the body is short and thick. The lower jaw is rather longer than the other ; the orbit is not quite five times in the length of the head. The body is covered with very small scales, but along the back there is a line of larger ones, that extends downwards over the pectorals at about one-fifth the length of the body, and then stretches itself backwards to the full length of the above mentioned. This lateral line, from the posterior part of the space occupied by these large scales to the base of a ridge, which exists on each side at the posterior part of the body is margined by a succession of round scales, numbering about one hundred and eighty, and having each a longitudinal ridge or keel; the præoperculum is covered with irregular transverse lines, that are barely visible on the fresh specimens; the teeth are conical, rather curved backwards, sharp, and number from twenty-five to thirty on each side of both jaws. The first dorsal has thirteen or fourteen spines; it is high in front, and strongly emarginated, all the spines becoming smaller as they are inserted backwards; the second dorsal, which is separated by a short distance from the first, is composed of one spine and thirteen rays; the upper and lower *pinnulæ* number nine; the caudal is formed of eighteen long rays, and of a large number of shorter ones on each side; some of these are nearly as long as the full sized ones; the anal has the same form as the second dorsal, and has thirteen rays; the pectorals equal in length two-thirds of the head; they are received in a sort of a groove; they have thirty-two rays.

This fish is entirely of a blueish black, with brown tinges on the sides of the head. The first dorsal is of a general obscure colour, with the spines reddish; the other fins are brown, with a part blue; the *pinnulæ* of the last colour; eye silvery.

The flesh of this fish is not eaten, or at least is not esteemed as food. It is very scarce at Melbourne; those I saw appeared towards the end of November.

On the dried specimens there are two small ridges on the posterior part of the larger one we have mentioned, but they do not appear on the fresh ones.

My largest specimen is about twenty-three inches long.

SCOMBER.

The type of this genus is the common *Mackerel;* it used to contain a very considerable number of fishes, but it is to-day restricted to a very small number of species, all very nearly allied to the sort just mentioned. One species has been described by

Cuvier and Valenciennes as inhabiting King George's Sound, and a fish very nearly allied to it appears, but very rarely, on the Melbourne Market.

SCOMBER ANTARCTICUS.

(*The Mackerel.*)

Height of body five and a-quarter times in its total length; head four and a-quarter times in the same; orbit five and a-half times in the length of head. The first dorsal has eleven spines, the longest of which is the second, the last being very small and difficult to see; the second dorsal has one spine and eleven rays, of which the first is the longest, and the others go on decreasing, the four last being about equal amongst themselves and also to the spine; these cover five *pinnulæ*. The caudal has fifteen long rays and numerous shorter ones on each side; the lower *pinnulæ* are also five in number. The anal has the same form as the dorsal, and shows one spine and eleven rays; the pectoral has twenty rays. The membrane that covers, on each side, a part of the eye does not hide more than one-third of it. On the living specimen, the lower portion of the præoperculum appears entirely striated; but on the dried one it is smooth, and the interior edge seems to bear the marks of strong denticulations; the upper part of the præoperculum is covered with scales, and others, much larger and of a very elongate form, cover a space below the eye. The teeth are small, rather hooked, equal, and disposed on a line; at the upper jaw, they are only visible in front, and, after decreasing in size, disappear entirely on the sides; on the lower jaw, they are much more numerous and extend backwards; on each of the palatines there is also a line of numerous teeth, rather longer, more slender, and more arched than those of the jaws. There is no air-bladder.

The colour is of a dark greenish blue on the upper parts, and of a silvery white on the lower ones; the back is covered with black waving lines, very irregular, but having generally a transverse disposition. On the sides of the body is a longitudinal series of larger and rounded ones; all the lower parts are covered with little black dots, very numerous, and irregularly disposed. There are yellow tinges behind the eye and on the sides of the body, and the lower part of the sides of the head shows five indistinct colours. The first dorsal is greenish, with its external part rather darker; the second is yellow, as is also the last; the upper *pinnulæ* are black, and the lower white; the anal and ventrals are of the latter colour; the pectorals are almost black; the eye is silvery.

I have only seen one specimen of this fish on the Melbourne Market, in the month of September; it measured 13 inches.

This sort appears very distinct from *Scomber Australasicus* which has an air-bladder, and whose fins have—

Dorsal 9—1—12. Anal 2—11.

ZEUS.

The fish on which this genus was originally formed is known since the earliest ages, and the people on the shores of the Mediterranean give it the name of *Saint Peter's Fish.*

The first mention of an Australian species is due to Richardson (" *Erebus* and *Terror* "), but the only specimen he had seen was in such a bad state of preservation that he thought at first that it might belong to *Capros Australis* that he had himself previously described in the third volume of the " Zoological Transactions ;" but in a later part of the " Fishes of the *Erebus* and *Terror*," he states that he has been able to examine a more perfect specimen from Western Australia, and he maintains his *Zeus Australis.* Dr. Gunther, in the second volume of his Catalogue, considers this sort as the ordinary European one, and, without the least doubt occurring in his mind, states that this inhabits the Mediterranean, Atlantic, and Australian seas. The fact that it had never been observed out of Europe, or at least south of the Canary Islands, and that the different species found at Madeira and the Cape of Good Hope were specifically different from the European one, might perhaps have led a Zoologist to admit the probability of a specific difference in sorts whose *habitat* is so remote. The Madeira sort is the *Conchifer* of Lowe, and the South African one the *Capensis* of Cuvier and Valenciennes ; but it is true that these last authors say that Messrs. Webb and Berthelot have found the common sort at Teneriff.

ZEUS AUSTRALIS.

Zeus australis, *Riehard.*, *Erebus and Terror*, p. 36-136 pl. xxxv., fig. 1.

(*The John Dorey.*)

Height of body two and a-half times in total length ; head three times in the same ; orbit five times in the length of the head ; the lower jaw longer than the upper one, with the chin rather prominent. When the mouth is extended, the distance from the end of the lower jaw to the external angle of the orbit is contained three and a-half times in the total length ; the præoperculum forms a slight angle at about one-third of its length ; the operculum is prolonged in a flat, rounded angle, and in some specimens that part, being denudated of the skin, forms a strong bony point : the caudal portion of the operculum is covered with radiant striæ ; the body is covered with very minute scales. The lateral line is strongly rounded to nearly two-thirds of the body ; it from thence follows straight to the centre of the base of the caudal. Along the root of the spinous dorsal there is at the foot of each ray a spine, short, pointed, and directed backwards. Along the base of the second dorsal there are generally six, sometimes seven, plates, each bearing a strong, arched spine, directed posteriorly ; and on the four last there is another spine, placed at the base of the others, shorter, and directed externally. Along the soft anal there is also a series of plates, numbering seven or eight; all, except the first, bearing an extra spine, like those we have already mentioned. At the foot of each of the three last spines of the first anal there is a rather strong, single spine, and on the space between the root of the anal and of the ventrals there is a double series of nine spines. The first dorsal is formed of ten spines, the three or four first of which are arched, and the others straight ; the third and fourth are generally equal and longer than the others ; the membranes between the first and second is lower than the others, and emits a filament about as long as the first spine ; the membranes between the others also terminate in a filament ; those between the second and third, and the third and fourth, are considerably longer than twice the spine; the following are shorter. The second dorsal is formed of twenty-three soft rays; the caudal is truncated posteriorly of thirteen long rays, with one shorter one on each side.

The anal is divided in two; the first portion is formed of four strong straight spines; the membranes which unite these having each a pointed angle. The second anal is formed of twenty-two rays, it has the same form as its corresponding dorsal; the ventrals are large, being longer than the snout, when not extended; they are formed of a slender spine and of six rays; pectorals small, with fourteen rays.

The disposition of the colours is similar to that of the European sort: the general hue is a dark green, with yellow tinges on the sides of the head and body; the outer visible parts of the mouth are lilac colour; towards the centre of the fish there is a large rounded black blotch, surrounded by a wide circle, and below this the body is often variegated with purple and white. The first dorsal, caudal, first anal, and ventrals are green, with the spines or rays purple; the second dorsal and second anal are white and transparent, with their rays green; the pectorals of a light green; the eye yellow, with a purple tinge.

The *Dorey* is very rare on the Melbourne Market, and I have only seen three specimens of it, which were all taken in the month of August. It is considered a great delicacy.

Nota.—Professor M'Coy (*Report Intercolonial Exhib.*, 1866,) says that he has often caught in Hobson's Bay the *Cyttus Australis* of Richardson (*Capros*), which I have not yet met with.

HISTIOPTERUS.

This most singular genus was established in the "Fauna Japonica." Richardson, in his "Fishes of the *Erebus* and *Terror*," describes the Australian sort from a single head that had been brought from Tasmania.

HISTIOPTERUS RECURVIROSTRIS.

Histiopterus recurvirostris, *Richard.*, *Erebus* and *Terror*, page 34, pl. xxii.

(The Boar Fish or Bastard Dorey.)

The height is rather over three times and a-half in the total length; the head is three times and a-half in the same; the orbit is four and one-third times in the length of the head.

The general form is most singular ; the greatest height of the body is at the insertion of the head, and from this it goes on decreasing almost in a conical form to the base of the caudal ; the head is prolongated in a long muzzle, which is nearly half the length of the head ; this muzzle is scarcely broader at its base than at its extremity, and the nostrils are situated at its beginning. The chin is without asperities. The head is covered with bony plates, which are strongly striated, except on the cheeks ; in many places these *Striæ* are formed of punctures, and have a radiate disposition ; from a little under the eye the profile of the head ascends to the back by an oblique line, forming with the muzzle an angle of 45 degrees ; the teeth are very numerous, and are disposed on several lines, all nearly of the same form, but those in front being a little longer than the others, and sometimes slightly curved ; the series are also much more numerous in front than on the sides ; the suprascapula and the caracoïd are similarly striated ; the lateral line runs at about one-fourth of the height, and terminates at the centre of the tail ; it is very sinuous ; the body is covered with very fine scales, of which there are over one hundred and thirty on the lateral line.

The dorsal fin is composed of eight spines, the first of which is small, and measures about one-half of the diameter of the orbit ; it has no soft membrane ; the second has about twice the length of the first, and has a very narrow membrane not connected with the third spine ; this is very long, being over five times the length of the first ; it has a membrane which connects its base with the following spine, at about the height of the end of the first spine; this membrane is very narrow in the remainder of its length, and is free in its terminal part ; the fourth spine is the longest of all, and has about eight times the length of the first, or nearly one-third of the total length of the fish ; its membrane has the same form as the precedent, but the portion which is adherent to the next spine is about twice the height of the other ; this fourth spine is curved in rather a sinuous manner ; the fifth spine is considerably shorter than even the third, and is straight; this membrane has the same form as the other ; the sixth and seventh spines become shorter still ; the eighth and ninth equal to the seventh ; they are straight, and their membranes extend to about the following two-thirds of their length, and they have only a small free portion; all these spines are very acute, and strongly striated.

The second portion of the dorsal, which is joined to the first, begins with a spine nearly one-third longer than the two last of the first part, and is followed by fifteen soft rays; the first being one-third longer than the spine, and the second twice its length; these two rays are simple, the following are all branched, the third and fourth are the longest of all, but they are very little longer than the second; from these the fin, which has rather a triangular form, goes decreasing rapidly; the last ray having only one-sixth of the length of the third.

The caudal is rather large and slightly emarginated posteriorly; it is formed of seventeen rays, all branched except the two external ones; on each side of the base are three very short rays, almost entirely covered by the scales of the tail. The anal is formed of three spines, rather curved and sharp; the first is the shortest and the third the longest; this is about twice the length of the first. The membranes which join these spines are low, and have their ends free; the soft part of the ray has the same triangular form as the dorsal; it is formed of ten rays, the two first being the longest, and the others decreasing rapidly; the last is double; the ventrals are very large; their spine is very strong, compressed, striated, arched, and very pointed. The first soft ray is longer than those of the spine, and has three-fourths the length of the head; the four others go on decreasing. The pectorals are rather long; they are formed of eighteen rays, the first of which is very short, being less than one-third the length of the second, which itself is shorter than the following.

The upper parts are of a greyish blue, and the lower ones of a dirty white; a broad band, arched and black, extends from the anterior part of the dorsal fin to the posterior portion of the anal. The membranes of the fins are black, with the spines of a rosy colour; the pectorals are almost of the latter colour, with a yellowish tinge; the base of the ventrals is blue. There is often a second dorsal band in front of the one we have mentioned, and of the same form, but it does not attain the inferior part of the body. The colours of the head are sometimes very pretty, the upper part being of a dark brown, mixed with purple, and the sides pink. The operculum has a broad longitudinal band on the cheeks, of a fine white colour; the eye is yellow, with an external brown circle, often interrupted.

This fish is not very rare; and is esteemed as food. It appears now and then iu the Melbourne Market, in all seasons of the year. Average leugth, from 15 to 20 inches. I have several times found a large quantity of sand in its stomach.

I have, unfortunately, not been able to compare this sort with the Japanese species, the work iu which the latter is described not being obtainable iu Melbourne.

RICHARDSONIA.

The fish on which I propose to establish this new genus is very similar, iu general appearance, to *Histiopterus*, but its dentition is very different. Here, we have two different sorts of teeth—those on the sides of the mouth being true molars, short, thick, globular, disposed on four irregular lines on the upper jaw, and on three at the lower ; in front, there is a considerable number of other teeth, conical and pointed, disposed in a cluster on both jaws. The three first spines of the dorsal are very short, and the aual has only two spines.

RICHARDSONIA INSIGNIS.

D. 7—17. A. 2/10. C. 17. P. 18. V. 1/5.

The general form is almost exactly similar to the one of *Histiopterus*, but the body is more convex on the back, and the muzzle, formed by the auterior part of the head, is much shorter. The height of the body is a little less than the third of the total length ; the head is contained nearly three and two-third times in the length of the body; the orbit is coutained six and a-half times in the length of the head. The lips are very thick, and covered with tubercles ; the chin is also very rough ; the muzzle being very short, the slant upwards of the profile begins much nearer to the mouth, and the nostrils are situated on this snout ; the posterior edge of the præoperculum and the one of the operculum are serrated ; the edge of the first is also transversely striated ; the bony plates, that cover a great part of the head, are very deeply striated ; the *striæ* are disposed iu radiations, and not puuctated; the checks are covered with numerous, small, rouud scales, having each a tubercle in the centre. Suprascapula and caracoïd very strongly sulcated ; the scales of the body are very small and numerous ; they number about one hundred and ten on the lateral liue, which follows the profile of the back at about one-fourth of the height of the body ; this line is very sinuous ; it begins at the upper angle of the operculum, curves itself towards the back, presents several sinuosities, and extends towards the tail, but curls downwards before it reaches the root of the caudal ; it is formed of a series of small ridges. The dorsal fin begins by three short and isolated spines, which go on increasing in length ; the fourth spine is very long, compressed, and strong ; it ends in a filiform appendice, which makes it as long as the body of the fish is high ; its membrane is very narrow till a short distance from the body, where it extends to the following spine ; this (the fifth) has the same form as the precedent, but its filament is not so long ; its membrane extends to the following spine, at a greater height than the one of the fourth. These are followed by two more spines (making in all seven), which are shorter than the others, and the last has no filamentary appendice. The other part of the fin, composed of seventeen soft rays, is intimately connected with the other, and not sensibly higher ; the rays go on decreasing insensibly in height to the end. The caudal is large, slightly emarginated ; it is formed of seventeen long rays and of three shorter ones on each side ; these are in a great part covered with scales. The anal has one very small spine and one very large one, the latter being about eight times the length of the other, and very broad ; the soft rays are nine in number, the two first being a little longer than the second spine, and the others decreasing to the last. The ventrals have a very large, compressed, arched spine, having the form of a broad sword, and being two-thirds as long as the head, the first of the five soft rays is still a little longer than this spine. Pectorals rather large, of eighteen rays, the first not more than one-half the length of the second ; the total length of the fin is equal to the one of the ventral. All the spines are strongly striated.

The general colour of the fish is of a dirty green, with the head and the anterior part of the back tinged with purple ; the fins are of the latter colour, with the spines pink ; the caudal is posteriorly bordered with green ; eye brown.

I have only seen one specimen of this fish ; it was brought to the Melbourne Market in November, 1871, from Western Port, and the fishmongers said it was the first time they had seen it. Total length, 25 inches.

Nota.—Since writing the above, I have obtained a second specimen of this fish ; it is larger, and measures near 33 inches. It was taken in April, at Queenscliff. The three first short spines of the dorsal have membranes, which connect them.

The name of *Richardsonia* has already been given by Mr. Steindachner to a genus of fishes, which Mr. Gill had previously called *Retropinna*, and this name being, of course, adopted, the one of *Richardsonia* becomes disposable.

DIMENSIONS OF LARGEST SPECIMEN.

Inches.

Total length	$32\frac{5}{8}$
Greatest height	$9\frac{1}{4}$
Length of head	$4\frac{4}{8}$
———— from extm. of snout to ant. edge of orbit	5
Diameter of orbit	$1\frac{1}{8}$-$\frac{1}{2}$
Height of head at ant. edge of orbit	$4\frac{5}{8}$
———————— at centre of orbit	$5\frac{1}{2}$-$\frac{1}{2}$
———————— at posterior edge of orbit	$5\frac{1}{8}$
From post. edge of orbit to first dorsal spine	$4\frac{7}{8}$
—— base of first dorsal spine to base of fourth	$1\frac{3}{4}$-$\frac{1}{2}$
Total length of spinous dorsal	$5\frac{1}{4}$
—————— of soft dorsal	$9\frac{3}{4}$
Height of fourth spine	$3\frac{3}{4}$
From end of dorsal to base of caudal	4
Length of caudal at its centre	$2\frac{7}{8}$
——————— at its sides	6
From base of caudal to anal	$3\frac{5}{8}$-$\frac{1}{2}$
Total length of anal at its base	4
Height of the second spine of anal	$3\frac{3}{4}$
Breadth of same	$\frac{5}{8}$
Height of first branched ray of anal	$4\frac{7}{8}$
From anal to base of ventrals	5
Breadth of ventral at its base	$1\frac{1}{4}$-$\frac{1}{2}$
Length of ventral spine	$4\frac{1}{2}$
Breadth of same	$\frac{5}{8}$
From base of ventral to base of pectorals	4
Height of first branched ray	2-2
—————— of last	6
Greatest length of pectorals	$5\frac{1}{4}$
Shortest length of pectorals	$1\frac{3}{8}$-$\frac{1}{2}$

CARANGIDÆ.

" Body generally compressed, oblong, or elevated; covered with small scales or naked; eye lateral. Dentition variable. The infraorbital bones do not articulate with the præoperculum. The spinous dorsal less developed than the soft or than the anal, either continuous with, or separated from, the soft portion, sometimes rudimentary. The posterior rays of the dorsal and anal fins sometimes semi-detached. Ventrals thoracic, sometimes rudimentary or entirely absent. No prominent papilla near the vent. Gill-opening wide; generally seven branchiostegals and pseudobranchiæ. Air-bladder present; pyloric appendages generally in great number.

" Inhabitants of the seas of the temperate and tropical regions, many of the species having a very wide range."

Having followed the method of Dr. Gunther, I separate this family from *Scombridæ*, but I think the two ought to be united, as their only character is anatomic, and consists in the number of the vertebræ; the family of *Scombridæ* would then remain as it was established by Cuvier, with the exception of the *Trichiuridæ*, which form a most natural group.

SERIOLA.

The fish belonging to this genus are generally inhabitants of the tropical seas; but one sort is found in the Mediterranean, and one also on the eastern coast of Australia (Gigas, *Gunth.*) The following seems distinct :—

SERIOLA GRANDIS.

(The Yellow Tail.)

This remarkable sort plays a conspicuous figure in the Melbourne Market, particularly during the hottest months of the year. It often destroys the fishermen's nets; but on some occasions it is a cause of considerable profit, as on one occasion it is reported that one hundred and forty-two were caught at once, which, at the price of five shillings a piece, would make over £28 for a single haul. They often, in calm weather, come very near the shore; but, as soon as the sea becomes agitated, they fly with rapidity towards the deep water.

The body is of a regularly long oval form; its height is about four times in the total length; the head is about four and one-third times in the same; and the orbit seven and one-third in the length of the head. This orbit is oval, and directed obliquely. The lateral line is sinuous, and marked on about one hundred and forty-three scales, but the number of transverse lines of scales is near two hundred. The posterior part of the lateral line, from the end of the dorsal and anal backwards, is elevated in a sort of keel or ridge. The scales of the posterior part of the body are larger and longer than the others. The first dorsal is formed of six very short spines, united by very low membranes; the last is hardly visible. The second dorsal has one short spine and thirty-five branched rays; the caudal has eighteen long rays and four shorter ones on each side; the anal has one spine and twenty branched rays; the pectorals are formed of twenty-three rays. The second dorsal and the anal have their first branched rays much longer than the others, which go on shortening to the eighth, from which they preserve about the same size. The anal is similar, and also falciform.

The upper parts are of a dark blue, and the others of a silvery grey. On each side there is a longitudinal yellow band; the fins are of a yellowish grey; the caudal is yellow, with the internal part obscure. The pectorals are nearly black, with their edge yellow; parts of the mouth of a fleshy colour; eye yellow.

The average size in length is from 30 to 40 inches, but some are much larger, and they sometimes weigh up to ninety pounds. It is moderately esteemed as an article of food.

Nota.—This sort must be nearly allied to Gunther's *Seriola-gigas*, but appears to be quite distinct by the composition of its fins:—D. 8 1/24. A. 2 1/16.

CARANX.

The fish belonging to this genus abound in the tropical seas of both hemispheres, but in the temperate regions they are scarce. The Mediterranean has very few, and only one has been yet found on the southern coast of Australia, although several others are mentioned from the northern and western shores of that Continent.

CARANX GEORGIANUS.

Caranx georgianus, *Cuv. & Val.*, v. ix., p. 85.
———————— *Richard., Erebus and Terror, Fishes,*
p. 135, pl. lviii., fig. 1.

(*The Silver Bream.*)

In the numerous specimens I have seen, the second dorsal numbers sometimes twenty-six and sometimes twenty-seven soft rays. Cuvier and Valenciennes give them twenty-eight or twenty-nine. They also count twenty-four at the anal, and I only find twenty-two and twenty-three. It is evident that these branched rays are subject to considerable variations in their numbers.

The colours in the fresh specimens are very beautiful, the upper parts being sometimes of a light celestial blue, and sometimes of a beautiful purple ; the lower parts are of a silvery white, with bright iridescent tinges. Behind the operculum there is a black spot, and along the body extends a fine, longitudinal golden stripe. The dorsal fin is yellow, bordered with an obscure tinge ; the caudal is yellow or grey, and the other fins diaphanous ; the ventrals are rather pink.

In the old specimens the teeth are short, and many fall off. The eye is silvery.

This is a very common fish on the Melbourne Market, particularly in the cold months of the year. The large specimens are scarce. The average size is under 10 inches long, but some attain 23 and even 25 inches. It is considered good for the table, and appears to inhabit all the western and southern coast of New Holland.

TEMNODON.

Established by Cuvier on a fish remarkable by its first dorsal being very low, formed of eight feeble, continuous spines, but often difficult to see.

TEMNODON SALTATOR.

Temnodon saltator, *Cuv. & Val.*, v. ix., p. 225, pl. 260.
Scomber saltator, *Bl. Sch.*, p. 35.

(Skip Jack.)

This is one of the most common fish in the market; it is generally found at Melbourne of a small size, but I have seen one in September, which was 2½ feet in length.

Generally it is of a very bright silvery colour, with the upper parts of the body, head, and upper fins of a dark olive ; the lower fins being white ; the eye silvery or rather yellow.

This fish appears to be found in all the warm and temperate regions of the world, but it is not certain that several species are not mixed together. In some specimens I only see seven rays to the dorsal, and in a few the teeth are much more set apart than in others. I have also seen several times, at Melbourne, small specimens, called by the fishmongers *Snubgall*, which have the anterior part of the head shorter, and much more convex over the eye.

At the Cape of Good Hope, where it is very common, it is very often found of large dimensions. The young specimens are very brilliant, blue on the back, and green on the upper part of the head. The old ones are of a lead colour on the upper parts.

NEPTONEMUS.

Not one of the Australian fishes I have studied has caused such trouble to identify as this ; it is common on the Melbourne Market, and it is not likely, therefore, that it has escaped the attention of collectors and naturalists, but in the most modern authors I can find no description that can apply to it.

It has much resemblance to the genus *Trachynotus*, and also with *Psenes*, but it differs from the first in having no first dorsal spine directed forwards, nor its two first anal spines separated from the others. It agrees better with *Psenes*, but the limb of the præoperculum is striated and crenulated.

Dr. Gunther, in the second volume of his valuable catalogue, has established a genus *Neptonemus* amongst *Scombridæ*, to which he gives the following characters :—" Body oblong, compressed, covered with cycloïd scales of moderate size ; the cleft of the mouth of moderate width ; the snout obtusely conical ; præoperculer margin obtusely crenulated ; the first dorsal continuous, with some feeble spines ; the second dorsal and the anal are more developed, with a scaly sheath at the base ; no finlets ; anal spines indistinct : pectorals much longer than the ventrals ; a series of minute teeth in the jaws ; palate toothless ; branchiostegals six." One single sort from New Zealand (*Neptonemus Brama*).

In the second part of the " Proceedings of the Zoological Society for 1869," the same naturalist describes a second sort, under the name of *Dobula*, from Tasmania, and adds,—that on a further examination he finds that this genus belongs to the family of *Carangidæ*, and that there are two very small spines in front of, and at a short distance from the anal fin.

Almost all these characters applying to my sort, I have placed it in the genus *Neptonemus* ; but it cannot be the New Zealand sort, which has one spine and twenty-nine rays at the second dorsal, nor the Tasmanian one, which has—First dorsal 7. Second dorsal 1/40. Anal 2 1/23.

NEPTONEMUS ? TRAVALE.

(The Travale).

The body oblong, rather compressed, high, very curved over the eyes ; the greatest depth is at the insertion of the second dorsal, and is contained two and two-thirds in the total length ; the length of the head is not quite four times in the same ; the snout is short ; the eye large, placed at half the height of the head, and contained three and two-third times in its length ; the lower jaw is longer than the upper one ; the cleft of the mouth extends to the line of the anterior margin of the eye ; the nostrils nearer to the end of the snout than to the orbit ; upper part of the head naked ; cheeks and operculum scaly ; teeth numerous and fine, all equal, and disposea on a single line at each jaw; interior of the mouth and tongue smooth; the posterior edge of the præoperculum is emarginated, with its angle quite rounded; this edge is armed with a number of short acute spines, each of which extends on the præoperculum, and gives it the appearance of being radiated; the operculum extends in a long, obtuse, flat point over the base of the pectorals, and its lower limb is sometimes rather denticulated; six branchiostegals; the body is covered with rather small scales, which are marked with concentric lines, and fall very easily; the lateral line runs over about ninety-three scales, and follows the profile of the back at about one-fourth of its height, and extends to the centre of the base of the caudal. On the dry specimens its posterior part appears carinated; below this line there is a deep longitudinal sulcated line, which extends all along the body at half of its height, and has the appearance of a second lateral line; the first dorsal fin is very low, and begins over the insertion of the pectorals; it is formed of six small feeble spines, connected together by a very low membrane; the second dorsal is much higher; it is composed of two spines and thirty soft rays; the first spine is much shorter than the second, but considerably longer than any of the first dorsal; the first rays of the dorsal are nearly twice as long as the second spine, but the following decrease until the seventh or eigth, when the succeeding ones maintain about the same height; the total length of the second dorsal is contained two and one-third times in the total length of the body, and the distance from its end to the centre of the caudal is contained five and one-third times in the total length; the caudal is deeply formed, and has twenty-one long rays and several short ones on each side; the most external of these does not attain the extremity of the fin; the anal, having the same form as the second dorsal, is formed of two very small conical spines, and of two slender ones; the first is much shorter than the second, and this is only one-half of the following rays; these number twenty-one; this fin is much shorter than the second dorsal, and is contained more than four times the length of the body; the ventral fin is rather small; it is inserted a little behind the base of the pectorals, and the space behind it and the beginning of the anal is equal to the length of the latter, and is formed of a rather long, slender, straight spine, and of five rays; the pectoral is long, falciform, and formed of twenty-two rays; it extends to nearly the anus.

The general colour is of a blueish grey, with a copper tinge on the sides; the lower parts of the body are of a blueish white; the upper part of the head is of a copper-coloured brown; there is a broad purplish spot on the back, just behind the head; in this part the scales have a black margin; this spot extends laterally to the point of the operculum.; the lips are pink, as are also the root of the pieces of the operculum; the dorsal and caudal are rather obscure, with yellow tinge; the anal a little lighter colour; the ventrals of a rosy white; the pectorals are obscure, with their rays yellow; eye silvery. In some specimens the sides of the body are covered with very minute dark dots.

This fish is common on the Melbourne Market, particularly in the cold months of the year; it is used for food, and its average size is from 8 to 10 inches long; but I have one which measures 23 inches, and which only differs from the others by the absence of the sulcated line below the lateral one. The small spines of the operculum and præoperculum are worn out.

On the living specimens the body seems entirely covered with small tubercles, formed by the scales being very irregularly disposed. On the young ones the muscular fluxes are well marked on the sides of the body; the dark spot on the posterior part of the head is barely visible.

XIPHIIDÆ.

" Body elongate, compressed, naked, or covered with rudimentary dermal productions. Teeth none, or rudimentary. The upper jaw (ethmoid, vomer, and intermaxillaries,) much produced, sword shaped. One or two dorsal fins, without a distinctly spinous portion. Ventrals absent, or rudimentary and thoracic. Seven branchiostegals; pseudobranchiæ and air-bladder present. Pyloric appendages in great number.

" Mediterranean ; open seas between or near the tropics."

The Sword Fish (*Histiophorus Gladius*) is stated to occur at Port Jackson, but has not, to my knowledge, been seen in the southern seas of Australia.

GOBIIDÆ.

" Body elongate, low, naked, or scaly. Teeth generally small, sometimes with canines. The infraorbital ring does not articulate with the præoperculum. The two dorsal fins separated, or more or less united, the spinous portion being always the less developed, and composed of flexible spines; the anal similarly developed as the soft dorsal; ventrals with one spine and five rays; sometimes both ventrals united into a disk. Gill-opening more or less narrow, the gill-membranes being attached to the isthmus; four gills ; pseudobranchiæ. A prominent papilla near the vent. Air-bladder generally absent. Pyloric appendages.

" Carnivorous fishes, living at the bottom of the shores and of the fresh waters of the temperate and tropical regions. This family offers numerous instances of the fact that a part of the individuals of one and the same are entirely confined to fresh waters, whilst others live in the sea."

The principal genus of this group is *Gobius*, formed by Artedi; it comprises numerous species, generally of small size, and inhabiting all the temperate and tropical seas of the world.

GOBIUS BASSENSIS.

The anterior dorsal with six spines; scales large; no crest on the head; caudal fin very elongate, pointed. Body very elongate; its height contained seven and one-third times in the total length; head four and two-third times in the same; eye four and one-third times in length of head. Jaws about equal, the lower a little longer than the upper. Teeth on several rows at the lower jaw; no canines. No scales on the head nor on the nape of the neck; about thirty-eight scales on the lateral line; they are ciliated on their edge. Dorsals rather high, the second of eleven rays; caudal as long as the head, pointed, and formed of sixteen principal rays and of several others on each side; anal of eleven rays, which are, as those of the second dorsal, rather prolongated; pectorals about as long as the head, pointed, of fifteen rays, none of which are silk like.

The general colour is of a light grey, rather green on the back, and whitish on the belly. There are two longitudinal bands, which extend on the operculum, from behind the eye; the first strikes the upper edge of the root of the pectoral, and expands in a blotch; the other is placed lower; it is broader, and extends rather obliquely towards the lower side of the pectoral base. The two dorsals have a longitudinal narrow band, which runs at about one-third of their height from the back; the extreme edge of the second dorsal is yellow. The caudal has three or four transverse series of black spots, which only extend on its upper half; the two central rays are of an orange colour, ending in black; the anal and ventrals are white, without spots; the pectorals are also immaculate, but with a yellow tinge; the eye is silvery. On the lower side of the body, there is a longitudinal line of black blotches, which unite under the pectorals; some feeble, black transverse spots on the upper part of the body.

Only seen once, in February.

GOBIUS FRENATUS.

Gobius frenatus, *Gunther*, *Catal.*, v. iii., p. 39.

Anterior dorsal with six spines; scales numbering thirty-six on the lateral line; head without a crest; caudal fine, rather rounded, and sub-elongate. One canine tooth at each side of the lower jaw; no hard spines at the dorsal; body contained six and one-third times in total lengh (to the end of the caudal). First dorsal with six spines; the second with one and ten rays; anal also with one spine and ten rays.

Of a light green, with two irregular, longitudinal, black bands on the operculum, which curve downwards below the eye. There are some light blue spots on the operculum, and a double longitudinal series of similar points on the body. The dorsals are green, finely edged with black ; the caudal is the same with its base, reddish. The anal is of the colour of the body, but covered with very minute black dots ; the ventrals are green, with a large black blotch; the pectorals are olive green, with the black bands of the head marked on their base.

Hobson's Bay. Length, 2¾ inches.

GOBIUS PICTUS.

Form elongate. First dorsal with eight rays, of which the second is rather longer than the others, and the last much shorter; the second dorsal formed of one spine and ten soft rays, of which the first is not quite as long as the others ; caudal of twelve rays ; anal of one spine and nine rays. The fins are large. The height of the body is five and a-half times in the total length ; the head and operculum are covered with little, black dots. The lower jaw is longer than the superior; the scales of the upper part of the body are rather large, and brown on their edge.

The general colour is of a light lilac, with the inferior parts white. On the head are numerous, small, brown spots, and a dozen narrow, transverse, brown lines cover the back and extend on the sides. On the latter, there is a longitudinal line of black spots with terminals, and one (much larger) placed at the base of the caudal. On the latter, there are also two or three irregular black spots. The pectoral is yellow, and the ventrals white ; the eye is yellow, with an external red circle. The first dorsal is white, with two broad, longitudinal, brown bands ; the second dorsal is also white, diaphanous, with the spine brown, and the rays variegated with brownish red. This fin has a broad, transverse, terminal, brown band. The caudal has three transverse, broad, light red bands ; the anal is white.

Found at St. Kilda. Length of specimen, 4 inches.

GOBIUS PULCHELLUS.

Form elongate. Height of the body four and three-quarter times in the total length; head three and a-half times in same. The first dorsal is rounded, with six rays; the first shorter than the second, the third rather longer than the others, and the following go on decreasing; the second dorsal has twelve rays. In both, the rays are much longer than the membranes. The caudal is rounded, with twelve rays; anal with one spine and nine rays, formed like those of the dorsal; ventrals large, united, pointed, with their lower rays much longer than the others. Pectorals rather large, extending to nearly the end of the first dorsal, of fifteen rays. Scales large; about twenty-three of them on the lateral line; eye moderately large, placed on the upper surface of the head.

General colour of a light grey, with the edges of the scales brown; lower parts of the body opal and white; head marbled with white spots; operculum covered with very minute black dots; front part of the head rather yellow. Three large round black spots on each side of the body—one opposite to the beginning of the second dorsal, the other to its end, and the third at the root of the caudal. There are also some undefined, transverse, white stripes on the sides of the body. Dorsal hyaline, marbled with brown spots, a black spot covering nearly the exterior half of the first membrane. Second dorsal with its rays spotted with brown, and yellow at their end. Caudal with the rays also spotted with brown, the spots forming five or six transverse lines of that colour. Anal large, white, with the rays yellow at their base, and black to almost their full extent; ventrals black, with their base white; pectorals rather yellow, marbled with white; their rays covered with very small, black dots. Eye yellow, with orange spots on its exterior edge.

Length, two and one-third inches. From Western Port. It is nearly allied to *Gobius Pictus*.

ELEOTRIS.

Formed by Gronovius, but much better characterised by Cuvier. This genus has numerous representatives in all the warm seas of the world; it inhabits the fresh waters, but extends its *habitat* to the estuaries of large rivers. Richardson has described one sort from New Zealand; the following one appears in Dr. Gunter's first division (*Eleotris*, Bleeker); characterised by " Scales of moderate size, less than fifty in a longitudinal series; snout short, broad, flat, and depressed; the form of the head approaching that of *Ophicephalus*."

Amongst the eleven sorts contained in this division, there are only two which have seven spines at the dorsal; but it differs from both by the great size of its head, and also this being in great part without scales. The fish I describe here would, on account of the presence of teeth on the vomer, be a *Philypnus* for Cuvier and Valenciennes, but Dr. Gunther has not adopted this generic division.

ELEOTRIS NUDICEPS.

Height of body six times in the total length; head three and one-fourth times in the same; eye six and one-third times in length of head. Lower jaw considerably longer than the upper; head very large, very broad, being at its widest part one-half of its length. The mouth is very broad; the maxillary extends to the vertical from the centre of the eye; eyes considerably apart, the distance from one or other being nearly equal to the third of the length of the head. The teeth are very numerous, cardiform, those of the lower jaw larger than those of the other; they extend on the vomer and the palatines; the posterior part of the tongue is also covered with them. The head has no scales; its anterior part is very uneven, and its irregularities have the appearance of very minute scales; it presents several longitudinal ridges; but, from the transverse line running from the posterior edge of the eye to the end of the operculum, the skin is naked. Behind this begin very small scales, which extend to the base of the dorsal; the operculum and præoperculum are naked; the body is not so broad as the head. The scales are rather large, and number forty-seven on the longitudinal line; they are striated, and very finely ciliated on their edge. The first dorsal is rather rounded, of seven spines; the membrane of the last is attached to the body. The second is high, and formed of one spine and ten rays; they are all of the same length except the last, which is a little longer than the others. The caudal is long, rounded, and formed of fourteen long rays and of several others on each side almost as long; the anal is as high as the body, of one spine and ten rays; pectorals two-thirds as long as the head, and of eighteen rays.

The body is of a light olive green, with the lower parts of a blueish white; the head almost entirely black in the adult; the edge of the scales is rather obscure; the dorsals are generally green; the first has sometimes two series of reddish spots, and sometimes it is white, with two longitudinal broad bands, more or less carmine, the coloured part being covered with very minute black dots. The second dorsal has three or four longitudinal series of red dots, which sometimes unite, and form longitudinal bands. The caudal has numerous transverse series of small, red spots; the ventrals and anal white; eye gilt.

The young specimens have the head less inflated.

This fish is very common in the lower Yarra; they are very voracious, and have often in their broad mouth, and partly digested, fishes as large as themselves, and generally of their own species. Sometimes pieces of wood are found in the same way, and held fast by their teeth.

Mr. Krefft has described, in the "Proceedings of the Zoological Society," 1864, p. 183, four Australian sorts of *Eleotris*, one of which (*E. Grandiceps*) may be this. There is one ray less at the second dorsal and at the anal, but this may depend on the different ways of counting the last one. It is from the Clarence River. The principal reason for not uniting my sort with his is, that he says,—that the pectorals attain the base of the anal; while in my specimens they do not.

BATRACHIDÆ.

"Habitus cottoid; skin naked, or with small scales; the system of muciferous channels well developed. Teeth conical, small, or of moderate size. The spinous dorsal very short, the soft and the anal long. Ventrals jugular, with two soft rays;

pectorals not pediculated. Gill-opening a more or less vertical slit before the pectoral, rather narrow. Gills, three ; pseudobranchiæ absent ; an air-bladder.

"Carnivorous fishes, living on the bottom of the coasts of the tropical regions, several species advancing into the temperate seas."

No sorts have yet come under my notice.

PEDICULATI.

"Head and interior part of the body very large, without scales. Teeth in cardiform or villiform bands. The spinous dorsal either composed of a few, more or less, isolated spines, or entirely absent. Ventrals jugular, with four or five soft rays, absent in *Ceriatias ;* the carpal bones prolonged, forming a sort of arm for the pectorals. Gill-opening reduced to a small foramen, situated in or near the axil. Gills two and a-half, three, or three and a-half; pseudobranchiæ absent.

"Carnivorous fishes, inhabiting the seas of the temperate and tropical regions."

Several sorts of this family, particularly of the genus *Chiro-nectes,* are found in the Tasmanian and South Australian seas ; but I have not examined any in a fresh state.

129

BLENNIIDÆ.

"Body elongate, low, more or less cylindrical, naked, or covered with scales, which are generally small. The infraorbital ring does not articulate with the præoperculum. One, two, or three dorsal fins occupying nearly the whole of the back. The spinous portion, if distinct, being as much developed as the soft, or more ; sometimes the whole fin composed of spines, anal fin long ; ventrals jugular, composed of a few rays, and sometimes rudimentary or entirely absent. Air-bladder generally absent; pyloric appendages none.

" Carnivorous fishes, inhabiting the bottom of the shores of all regions ; several inhabiting fresh waters."

Sorts of these will certainly be found in the Straits of Bass.

CLINUS.

Formed by Cuvier, and containing a considerable number of rather small fishes, inhabiting almost all the seas of the world. I have only seen one sort in Victoria.

CLINUS DESPICILLATUS.

Clinus despicillatus, *Richard., Zool. Journ.,* 1839, p. 90.
——————————.— *Richard., Trans. Zool. Soc.,* v. iii., p. 128, pl. 6, fig. 2.

The fish I consider as belonging to this sort has its lateral line interrupted in its anterior part. The height is four and one-third times in the total length ; and the head four and one-fifth times in the same. The dorsal is formed of two fins, as in *Cristiceps,* but they are united by their membrane; the first is composed of three spines and the second of thirty-six, four or five of which are branched rays, but it is difficult to well indicate their number, as they seem to pass gradually one to the other; the caudal has twelve long rays; the anal twenty-six rays and two spines. The pectorals have twelve rays, and the ventrals three, the centre one much longer than the other two, and divided almost to its base.

The colour is subject to much variation; in one specimen, it is green, with the lower parts of the head and the belly yellow; the latter is covered with minute black points; the præoperculum presents numerous transverse lines, formed of red and black spots, which are disposed in rather a radiant way. On the back part of the second dorsal the rays are spotted with red; the caudal is yellow, with its rays marbled with red, and near its base are two rounded, brown-red spots; the anal is yellow, marbled with purple, and the prolonged parts of the rays are red. The ventrals and pectorals are yellow; the last has six or seven transverse lines of carmine spots; the lower portion of the operculum and the throat are covered with carmine points; the eye is green, spotted with black, and surrounded by an external white ring.

In other specimens the colour is brown, marbled with blotches of a rather darker colour. Over the eye, there is a small plumiform tentacle, of a green colour.

I have only seen few specimens of this fish, which appears to belong to *Cristiceps*, at least as much as does *Argentatus*.

CRISTICEPS.

Cuvier and Dr. Gunther separate from *Clinus*, and under the above name, the species which have a first dorsal fin separated from the second, and placed generally more forward than in the other sorts.

This is evidently an artificial character, and these species ought only to form a division in the genus *Clinus*. The greater number of the sorts are found in Australia. Several have been described by Cuvier, Valenciennes, and Dr. Gunther, but the only two I have seen at Melbourne appear different from all.

In his extraordinary tendency to consider, as belonging to the same species, fishes found in the most remote parts of the world,

Dr. Gunther places with the Mediterranean *Clinus Argentatus*, Cuv. & Val., specimens from Australia [having constantly twenty-three soft rays to the anal fin, instead of nineteen or twenty. Admitting, at the same time, that some zoologists may consider them as forming a distinct species, he proposes for them, in a note, the name of *Antinectes*. This naturalist must certainly entertain very particular ideas on the constitution of the species in Zoology.

CRISTICEPS MULTIFENESTRATUS.

Form elongate; length of body four and one-eighth in the total length; head four times in the total length; orbit of the eye four and five-sixths in the length of the head; there is a rather long and arborescent tentacle over the second, a very small simple one on the snout; scales very minute; the lower jaw is considerably longer than the upper one; first dorsal placed over the end of the præoperculum, formed of three spines; the two first are longer than the other one, and placed much nearer one to the other than to the third; the space between this fin and the second dorsal is equal to the transverse diameter of the eye. This dorsal is formed of thirty spines and four rays; it grows a little higher as it goes towards its extremity, which is rounded; the spines and rays are very strong; the caudal is rounded, formed of nine rays and a complex short one on each sort; the membranous dorsal extends to the end of the rays; the anal has the same form as the second dorsal; the rays are free at their end for nearly one-third of their length; there are two spines and twenty-three rays; the ventrals are formed of three rays, united in a membrane for more than one-third of their length; the central one is the longest; the pectorals have twelve rays, much longer than the membranes; the last ray of the dorsal is fixed by a membrane to the tail, but does not extend to the base of the caudal; the last of the anal is similar, but does not extend so far as the other.

This fish is of a handsome purple colour, with large black, rounded blotches, forming a line on the back and another on each side, the latter being the smallest. Between them are numerous short, irregular, white, interrupted longitudinal lines. The belly is of a lighter and rather pink colour, with large, white, oval blotches. The head is punctured with red, and has two irregular longitudinal lines on the præoperculum ; the second is rather oblique ; the lips are marbled with light brown, and on the sides of the head are five or six round blotches, of a fine silvery hue. The dorsals and anal are transparent, covered with purple-brown, opaque lines, forming a sort of trellis work ; the rays are brown, marbled with yellow ; those of the caudal are similar, and that fin is bordered with orange, as is also the soft part of the dorsal. The ventrals are striped yellow and purple ; the pectorals are dark ; the eye is pink, with an external series of red spots.

I have only seen two specimens of this sort; the largest measures 10½ inches.

This sort must have some resemblance to Forster's *Blennius Fenestratus*, but this is included by Cuvier and Dr. Gunther in the genus *Tripterygium*.

CRISTICEPS FORSTERI.

The body is very elevated in its anterior profile, and like gibbous over the head ; this bears a single, simple bifid filament over the eye. The height is contained four and a-half times in the total length ; the head four and one-third times in the same ; eye four and one-fourth times in the length of the head. The lips are thick and prominent. The first dorsal begins in front of the end of the operculum ; it is high, and formed of three spines. The second is separated from it by a small space, and is formed of twenty-nine spines and four rays ; these are rather higher than the spines ; the caudal is rounded, and formed of nine long rays ; the anal of twenty-six ; it is low at its anterior part, and goes on increasing towards its end, which is rounded; the rays are considerably longer than their membranes ; its last ray is fixed by a membrane to the tail, but at considerable distance from the base of the caudal ; the last one of the dorsal is similar, but extends a little further backwards ; the ventrals have two rays, the external short, the other long and bifurcated ; the pectorals have twelve rays.

The general colour is green, with the sides of the head and the anterior part of the lower side of the body of an ochre yellow ; the lips are purple, and the lower portion of the præoperculum carmine ; the dorsals, caudal and anal are green, with the spines and rays purple; the ventrals yellow, and the pectorals purple. Between the base of the pectorals and ventrals are two rounded white spots; several others, oblong and transparent ones, are seen on the fins. On the only specimen I have seen they are disposed as follows :—on the second dorsal a fenestrated, rounded spot between the fourth and fifth, the ninth, tenth, and eleventh, the twentieth and twenty-first, the twenty-sixth and twenty-seventh, and the thirty-second and thirty-third ones at the base of the caudal; on the anal one between the seventeenth and eighteenth, and the twentieth and twenty-first, one covering about all the twenty-third, twenty-fourth, and twenty-fifth, and between this and the last ray there are two, one placed over the other; near the base of the pectorals there is a transverse line, formed of three similar spots; eye green.

One single specimen .seen at Melbourne in the month of January; it was about six and a-half inches long.

ACANTHOCLINIDÆ.

"Body elongate, low, compressed; covered with small scales. One dorsal fin, occupying nearly the whole of the back, by far the greater part being composed of spines; anal fin long, with the number of the spines exceeding that of the rays; ventrals jugular, composed of a few rays. Dentition complete. Four gills, pseudobranchiæ. Air-bladder, none; pyloric appendages, none. Coasts of New Zealand. Carnivorous fishes."

TEUTHIDIDÆ.

"Body compressed and oblong, covered with very small scales. Lateral line continuous; tail not armed. Eye lateral, of moderate size. A single series of trenchant incisors in the jaws ; palate smooth. One dorsal fin, the spinous portion being the more developed; anal with seven spines. Ventral fins thoracic ; pseudobranchiæ well-developed.

" Herbivorous fishes, inhabiting the tropical seas of the East Indian region, and the western parts of the Pacific."

Several *Teuthis* are found in the Australian seas, but I have not yet been able to procure any.

ACRONURIDÆ.

" Body compressed, oblong or elevated, covered with minute scales. Lateral line continuous ; tail generally armed with one or more bony plates or spines, which are more developed with age, and frequently absent in very young individuals. Eye lateral, of moderate size. Mouth small; a single series of more or less compressed, sometimes denticulated, sometimes tapering, incisors in each jaw ; palate smooth. One dorsal fin, the spinous portion being less developed; anal with two or three spines ; ventral fins thoracic. Pseudobranchiæ well developed ; air-bladder present, forked posteriorly. Intestines with more or less numerous circumvolutions.

" Seas between the tropics. Herbivorous fishes."

Nota.—*Acanthurus* presents several sorts, particularly on the northern coasts of Australia, but it is not likely that any will be found extending their *habitat* so far south as the Victorian Sea.

NANDIDÆ.

" Body oblong, compressed, covered with scales.
Lateral line interrupted. Dorsal fin formed by a
spinous and a soft portion, the latter being the less
developed ; anal fin with three spines, and with its
soft portion similar to the soft dorsal. Ventral fins
thoracic, with one spine and four or five soft rays.
Dentition more or less complete, generally feeble.
Five or six branchiostegals ; gills, four or three and
a-half; pseudobranchiæ present in the marine,
absent or hidden in the fresh-water genera. An
air-bladder. No superbranchial organ.

" Carnivorous fishes."

I have observed no sorts of these fishes in Victoria, but *Plesiops*
cœruleo-lineatus and *Trachinops Tœniatus* are found on the Australian coast.

ATHERINIDÆ.

" Body more or less elongate, subcylindrical, and
covered with scales of moderate size ; lateral line
indistinct. Cleft of the mouth of moderate width,
with the dentition feeble. Eye lateral, well developed. Gill-opening wide ; four gills ; pseudobranchiæ ; five or six branchiostegals. Two dorsal
fins, the spine of the first feeble ; the second of
moderate length ; anal like the soft dorsal, or
rather longer. Ventral fins abdominal, with one
spine and five rays. Vertebræ very numerous in
the caudal and abdominal portions.

" Carnivorous fishes, inhabiting the seas of the temperate and tropical regions; several species entering or living in fresh water."

The species of *Atherina*, and particularly of *Atherinichthys*, seem to be rather numerous on the Australian coasts. I propose here a new genus, *Atherinosoma*, which, if it does really belong to the family, would, on account of its dentition, oblige me to modify its characters.

ATHERINICHTHYS.

Separated by Dr. Bleeker from *Atherinus* on account of the snout produced, and the cleft of the mouth not extending to the orbit. The general aspect is the same.

ATHERINICHTHYS MODESTA.

Height of body contained five and a-half times in the total length, or five times to the base of the caudal; head four and a-quarter times in the same; eye three times in the length of the head. Muzzle considerably shorter than the diamater of the eye; mouth extensible; scales large—about forty on the lateral line. The first dorsal of six spines; second of one spine and nine rays; anal of four spines and ten rays; caudal of nineteen rays.

The distance from the anterior root of the first caudal to the extremity of the snout is equal to that from its posterior edge to the beginning of the caudal; from the same anterior edge of the first dorsal to the anterior edge of the second the distance is equal to that between the anterior edge of the second and the base of the caudal; the height of the first dorsal is equal to the distance from the extremity of the snout to the centre of the eye; the caudal is strongly bilobed; the anal is inserted below the second dorsal, or a trifle in front of it, and the ventrals a little in advance of the first dorsal; the pectorals are considerably longer than the height of the dorsal; they have twelve rays. A rather broad, longitudinal, silvery band on the sides.

The general colour is of a light greyish green, with the edges of the scales rather brown or even black on the upper parts of the body ; the dorsals, caudal, and pectorals yellow; anal and ventrals white ; eye silvery.

Common in Hobson's Bay and the lower Yarra. Length from 2 to 3½ inches.

ATHERINICHTHYS PICTA.

Height of body six and a-half times in the total length, or five and a-half times to the base of the caudal; head four times in the total length ; eye three and one-fifth times in length of head. Body elongate ; scales large—about forty-four on the longitudinal series ; snout considerably shorter than the diameter of the eyes. 1st Dorsal 8; 2nd 10. A. 11. C. 17.

The two dorsals are placed like those of *Modesta;* the anal a little in front of the dorsal ; the ventrals under the first dorsal ; caudal long, more emarginated than bifurcated, the difference in length between the middle rays and the side ones not being over one-quarter of their length.

Of a pretty light green, with the lower parts of the body white and silvery. A broad, longitudinal, red band on each side ; fins diaphanous ; caudal yellow ; eye silvery ; a few very minute black points on the sides of the head.

Only seen once, at Capt. Sinnot's Dock, on the lower Yarra ; under 2 inches long.

ATHERINICHTHYS CEPHALOTES.

Height of body seven and one-third times in the total length ; head three and two-third times in the same, or three and one-fourth times to the root of the caudal ; eye three and one-third times in the length of the head ; this is very large ; the lower jaw considerably in advance of the upper one ; teeth in both jaws, those of the lower rather longer than the others; they are all arched and pointed. The mouth is large, but the cleft of the mouth does not extend to the orbit ; the maxillaries attain one-third of the orbit's length; the eye very large. The body is covered with very large scales ; these numbering forty-two or forty-three on the lateral line, which is distinctly marked. The body goes tapering towards the tail ; the first dorsal begins almost at the middle of the body, but a little nearer to the snout than to the base of the tail ; it is formed of seven feeble spines, of which the first is considerably shorter than the others. The second dorsal is situated at a considerable distance behind the first, this distance being contained three times in that to the extremity of the snout; it is formed of one feeble spine and eight rays. These two dorsals are well developed; the caudal is bifurcated, and formed of sixteen long rays and some short ones; the anal is inserted below the second dorsal, but it is much longer; it is formed of one spine and twelve rays; the ventrals are inserted a little in advance of the first dorsal. The pectorals are rather large, equal to the snout up to the anterior margin of the eye; they are formed of thirteen rays.

The back is of a light green, with the belly white, and a broad, longitudinal, silvery band on each side; the head is of a rather olive colour; the dorsals grey, the second of these has a yellow tinge on its external part; the caudal and pectorals are yellow, and the lower fins white.

On the living specimen, there was a rather large, round, black spot on the caudal, near its base; but it has entirely disappeared after having been preserved in spirits.

I have only seen one specimen, which was taken in the month of August. It is nearly 6 inches long.

Nota.—Since then, I have seen a second specimen, which had only a very faint trace of the caudal black spot.

ATHERINOSOMA.

General form of *Atherina*. Cleft of the mouth small, and not extending to the eye; longitudinal silvery band on the sides; but the teeth are large on each jaw, hooked, and placed on several rows. Also on the vomer and palatines there are numerous tuberculous teeth, which extend on all the upper surface of the interior of the mouth, and also on the tongue. The mouth is not, or at the utmost only slightly, extensible. Two dorsals.

This new form will render it necessary to rectify the characters of *Atherinidæ*, or to form for it a new family.

ATHERINOSOMA VORAX.

Height contained seven times in the entire length; head four and a-half times in the same; eye contained three and one-third times in the length of the head. The lower jaw is sensibly longer than the upper one; snout considerably shorter than the diameter of the eye; operculum and præoperculum entire. Body elongate, covered with large scales, numbering about thirty-six on the longitudinal line. First dorsal rather rounded, formed of six spines; its posterior membrane attached to the back. This fin is inserted nearer to the muzzle than to the root of the caudal. Second dorsal of one spine and nine rays; its length is equal to the distance from the muzzle to the posterior edge of the eye, and the space from its end to the base of the caudal is about one and a-half times the same distance. The height of this fin is about equal to that of the body at the point of its insertion. The caudal is strongly bifurcated, formed of seventeen long rays and of several others on the sides; the anal is formed of one spine and eight rays; it is inserted below the second dorsal; ventrals a little in front of the first dorsal, they are rather large, and composed of one spine and five rays. Pectorals of twelve rays. The upper part of the head is covered with large scales up to the centre of the eye; the anterior part with longitudinal lines.

I have only seen one specimen, caught at Cape Shanck by Dr. Howitt; it appears, after having been in spirits, of a light green, with the lower parts white and silvery; a broad longitudinal band, more brilliant, extends on the sides; upper fins and caudal yellow; anal and ventrals white. Length, 3 inches.

MUGILIDÆ.

"Body more or less oblong and compressed, covered with cycloid scales of moderate size; lateral line, none. Cleft of the mouth narrow, or of moderate width, without or with feeble teeth. Eye lateral, well developed. Gill-opening wide; four gills; pseudobranchiæ; five or six branchiostegals; two short dorsal fins, the anterior with four stiff spines; anal a little longer than the dorsal opposite; ventral fins with one spine and six rays, abdominal, suspended from the elongate carcoid bone. Number of vertebræ twenty-four.

" Fresh waters and coasts of all temperate and tropical regions. Feeds on soft organic substances, or very small animals."

I have only found one single sort of true *Mugil* in Victoria, but several others inhabit the eastern coast.

MUGIL.

As this genus is now restricted, I only know, as I have just said, of one sort in Victoria.

MUGIL WAIGIENSIS.

Mugil waigiensis, *Quoy & Gaim.*, *Exped. Freycinet, Fish.*, p. 337, pl. 59, fig. 2.

(Sand Mullet.)

Height four and two-third times in the total length; head four and eight-tenth times in the same; breadth of head one and a-half times in its length; orbit four and one-third times in the length of the head. Head very thick and very broad, entirely covered with large scales; teeth rather large for the genus, numerous, and disposed on a line on each jaw; scales large, numbering about thirty-seven on the longitudinal line, and twelve on the transverse one. Each scale has a longitudinal sulcate, which extends to about two-thirds of its uncovered part; the sides of the scales are lightly and longitudinally striated; their posterior part more strongly, and rather in a radiated disposition; their external edge has concentric lines. The first dorsal is formed of four spines, the three first being the longest, and joining each other at their base; the second dorsal is formed of one spine and eight branched rays; the caudal is strongly emarginated, of fourteen rays, of which the external ones, in particular, are in great part covered with small scales; the anal is formed of three spines and eight soft rays; the ventrals are situated on the line of the end of the pectorals; their spine is long; the pectorals have their first rays rather long, and their posterior edge is strongly emarginated below these ; their number is fifteen, with their first third, at least, covered with small scales.

The upper parts are of a very dark blue, and the lower of a dirty white; the lips are pink ; the eye yellow ; the sides of the head have a copper tinge ; the base of each scale of the body, being of a bright silver colour, gives the fish the appearance of having longitudinal lines ; the fins are yellow, with their base blue and their extremity black ; the ventrals are whitish.

This sort attains large dimensions. I have one specimen which is about 21 inches long. It is much esteemed as food.

AGONOSTOMA.

Genus formed by Dr. Gunther on the sorts of *Mugil*, which have an elongate muzzle and teeth on the vomer. The first of these mentioned by authors was observed by Forster, and called by him *Mugil Albula*. Cuvier and Valenciennes changed this name to *Mugil Forsteri*. Richardson (" Zoological Transactions") placed this sort in the genus *Dajaus*, of which it has most of the characteristics, and describes another sort under the name of *Diemensis*. It has been stated that the common *Mullet* of the Melbourne Fish Market was the *Agonostoma Forsteri;* but this is a New Zealand sort, and the fish alluded to belongs to *Diemensis*. I know that this is in conformity to the opinion of Dr. Gunther, who, in his Catalogue, unites the two sorts, but the difference in the numbers of the fine rays separates them clearly.

AGONOSTOMA DIEMENSIS.

Dajaus diemensis, *Richard., Zool. Trans.*, v. iii., p. 123.
——————————— ———— *Erebus and Terror, Fishes*, p. 37,
pl. 26, figs. 1, 2.

(The Mullet.)

Richardson gives the following numbers to the rays :—
D. 4—10. A. 3 /12. C. 14 5/4. P. 15. In most of the Melbourne specimens, 1 find one more branched ray to the anus, that is, thirteen ; but in a few I find also twelve.

The upper parts are of a greyish blue, with green tinges on the body, and brown on the head ; the lower parts of the body are silvery ; the upper and pectoral fins are light grey ; the caudal is yellow, bordered posteriorly with black ; the anal white ; there are very faint longitudinal lines on the sides ; eye gilt.

Very common all the year round ; they rarely exceed 12 or 13 inches. This is a sea sort, and *Forsteri* is said to inhabit the fresh waters of New Zealand.

AGONOSTOMA LACUSTRIS.

(*Lake Mullet.*)

Height five and a-half times in the total length ; head five times in the same ; orbit four and a-half times in the length of head. This latter is not so pointed as in *Tasmanicus ;* the teeth are deficient at the lower jaw, but very visible on the upper one, as also on the palatine and vomer. The præoperculum has four lines of rather large scales. The body is elongate, covered with rather large scales, of which sixty-two are on the longitudinal line and sixteen on the transverse one ; they do not fall so easily as in most *Mugilidæ ;* most of them have a very short longitudinal ridge, not extending over more than one-third of the visible portion of the scale, and forming fifteen longitudinal series ; they have radiated *striæ* on their posterior part, and their edge is slightly ciliated. The first dorsal is formed of four spines, of which the two first are joined at the base, and the third is a little more apart ; the second dorsal is composed of nine soft rays· The caudal has fourteen long rays and four short ones on each side ; it is rather strongly emarginated, the ends terminating in points ; the tail is covered with minute scales, which extend on the first part of the membranes, and even on the external rays. Anal with three spines and twelve rays—the first spine very short, the second one-half of the third ; the fin is strongly emarginated ; the spine of the ventrals is long and slender ; the pectorals have fourteen rays.

Of a greyish green on the upper parts ; white on the lower ; each scale with an obscure margin ; a reddish spot on the back part of the head ; the upper part of the head and lips of a dark violet colour ; fins greyish ; caudal with a black posterior margin ; eye of a very bright orange yellow.

Brought to the Melbourne Market from the Gipps Land lakes. Scarce.

TRICHONOTIDÆ.

"Body elongate, subcylindrical, covered with cycloid scales of moderate size. Eyes directed upwards. Teeth in villiform bands. The infraorbital ring does not articulate with the præoperculum. One long dorsal fin, with articulated, not branched rays, and without a distinct portion; anal long; ventrals jugular, with one spine and five rays. Gill-opening very wide, seven branchiostegals; pseudobranchiæ. No prominent papilla near the anus. Air-bladder and pyloric appendages absent. Caudal vertebræ much more numerous than those of the abdominal portion."

"Carnivorous fishes, living near the shores of the East Indian Archipelago and of New Zealand."

No sorts have yet been observed in the Victorian Sea.

GOBIESOCIDÆ.

"Body rather elongate, anteriorly depressed, naked. Teeth conical or compressed. A single dorsal fin on the tail without spinous portion; anal short; ventrals widely apart from each other, with one spine hidden in the skin and four (five) rays. A large adhesive apparatus between them, the posterior portion of which is suspended on the caracoid bones, which are partly free, in the axil of the pectoral fins. Three gills or three and a-half. Air-bladder absent.

Intestinal tract short; wide, without pyloric appendages.

" Carnivorous fishes. Most of the species live in the seas of the temperate regions of both hemispheres; two are known to inhabit seas between the tropics."

Several are described from Tasmania and Swan River; but I have not yet observed any at Melbourne.

CENTRISCIDÆ.

"Form of the body compressed, oblong or elevated; the anterior bones of the skull are much produced, and form a long tube, terminating in a narrow mouth. Teeth none. Body either covered with a cuirass or with non-confluent ossifications. Scales none, or small. Two dorsal fins; the spinous short, and with one of the spines strong; the soft and the anal of moderate extent. Ventral fins small, without spine, or rudimentary, abdominal. Branchiostegals three or four; air-bladder large; four gills and pseudobranchiæ. Pyloric appendages none; intestinal tract rather short.

" Mediterranean and northern shores of the Atlantic, eastern coasts of Africa, coasts of China, Japan and Australia."

Centriscus Humerosus inhabits Australia; but I have not seen it.

FISTULARIDÆ.

" Fishes of greatly elongate form; the anterior bones of the skull are much produced, and form a long tube, terminating in a narrow mouth. Teeth small. Parts of the skeleton and dermal productions form external mails. Scales none, or small. The spinous dorsal fin is either formed by feeble isolated spines, or entirely absent; the soft dorsal and anal of moderate length; ventral fins abdominal, composed of six rays, without spine ; they are separate from the pubic bones, which remain attached to the humeral arch. Branchiostegals five; air-bladder large ; four gills; pseudobranchiæ. Pyloric appendages in small number; intestinal tract short.

" Tropical parts of the Atlantic and of the Indian Ocean."

Fistularia Serrata inhabits Port Jackson and Northern Australia, but I do not think it extends to the southern coast of Australia. It is figured in " White's Voyage to New South Wales," pl. 64, fig. 2.

Order II.

ACANTHOPTERYGII PHARYNGOGNATHI.

"The inferior pharyngeal bones are coalesced, with or without a medium longitudinal suture. Part of the rays of the dorsal, anal and ventral fins not articulated, forming spines. Air-bladder without pneumatic duct."

POMACENTRIDÆ.

" Body compressed, more or less short, covered with ctenoid scales. Dentition feeble; palate smooth. The lateral line does not extend to the caudal fin, or it is interrupted. One dorsal fin, with the spinous as well developed as the soft, or more. Two, sometimes three, anal spines; the soft anal similar to the soft dorsal. Ventral fins thoracic, with one spine and five soft rays. Branchiostegals five, six, or seven; gills three and a half; pseudobranchiæ and air-bladder present. Pyloric appendages in small number. Intestinal tract of moderate length. Tropical seas."

GLYPHISODON.

Genus formed by Lacepede, but much better characterised by Cuvier. Dr. Gunther changes the name in *Glyphidodon;* but I do not think that these so-called rectifications can be admitted.

GLYPHISODON VICTORIÆ.

Glyphisodon victoriæ, *Gunther, An. and Mag. Nat. History,* v. ii., 1862, p. 116.

The height of the body is contained twice in the length, up to the end of the dorsal, and two and one-half in the total length. The head is four times in the same; the orbit is three and one-third in the length of the head, and it is not quite as long as the snout; teeth small, rather regularly placed; they are elongate and rather broader in the middle than at their extremity, which is rounded; the head is covered with scales, those of the operculum small, on six rows; a denudated space round the margin, covered with reticulations, which are transverse on the posterior edge, but become longitudinal below the angle; the operculum covered with scales, about one-fourth smaller than those of the middle of the body, but ciliated like them; the body is as thick as the length of the head; it shows twenty-eight scales on the longitudinal line, and several smaller ones near the root of the caudal; on the transverse series the lateral line runs over the fourth, and I count eight below it. The dorsal fin is formed of thirteen spines, but the soft rays vary from fifteen to seventeen; the first spine is short, the others nearly equal one to the other; the fourth is rather longer than the anterior ones, and the following are about equal to it; the soft dorsal is nearly twice as high as the spinous one; the caudal is very strongly bilobated, with the lobes rounded; it is formed of fourteen rays; the anal is rounded, and composed of two spines and of fifteen or sixteen rays; the second spine is about twice as long as the first; ventrals rather large, formed of one long spine and of five branched rays; they are nearly three-quarters as long as the head, and from their end to the base of the anal is a space equal to about one-half of their length; pectorals large, formed of nineteen rays. Almost all the spinous part of the dorsal, the three-quarters of the branched one and of the anal, and also the two-thirds of the caudal, are covered with small scales; these extend also on the base of the pectorals. The eye is yellow.

The colour is nearly black, with a purple tinge on the sides of the head and on the spines of the fins; the membranes of the dorsal have a yellow hue, but these colours seem subject to much variation, as one specimen, a female, was of a light purple colour, with the central parts of the body of a light brown, with the middle of the scales yellow; the belly was reddish; the fins yellow; a broad purplish white stripe extended round the operculum.

This is not a common sort on the Melbourne market, but a specimen appears now and then, particularly in the months of September, October, and November. It does not seem to have actually a vernacular name, but Dr. Gunther says it is called *Rock Perch*, which is not used now. I could not ascertain if it was fit for the table.

Length, 8 to 10 inches.

LABRIDÆ.

" Body oblong or elongate, covered with cycloid scales. The lateral line extends to the caudal, or is interrupted. One dorsal fin, with the spinous portion as well developed as, or more, than the soft; the soft anal similar to the soft dorsal. Ventral fins thoracic, with no spine and five short rays. Palate without teeth; only one lower pharyngeal line without medium suture. Branchiostegals, five or six; gills, three and a-half; pseudobranchiæ and air-bladder present. Pyloric appendages none; stomach without cæcal sac.

" Marine fishes, inhabiting the seas of the temperate and tropical regions."

LABRICHTHYS.

These fish were separated from *Labrus* by Dr. Bleeker. The sorts are numerous in the Australian waters, and most are remarkable for the beauty of their colours. Not being generally considered as good for food, it is very seldom that the fishermen send them to the market. The only three sorts I have, up to this time, observed, appear to be new, or, at least, none of the descriptions given by Cuvier, Richardson, or Dr. Gunther can apply to either. The *Parrot Fish*, as those *Labridæ* are commonly called, only appear in the warm months of the year; the first I saw was at the end of September. It is probable that the *Labrus Cyprinaceus* (White, New South Wales, p. 264, pl. 51, fig. 1,) belongs to this genus.

LABRICHTHYS BLEEKERI.

(*Parrot Fish.*)

The teeth are on a double line, particularly at the upper jaw. This would exclude these fish from *Labrichthys*, as Dr. Gunther, in the synopsis of the genera of *Labridæ*, gives to this genus, for a distinctive character, " teeth in the jaws in a single series;" but in the characters of the genus, a few pages further on, he says :— " Teeth in the jaws in a single series ; but there is sometimes an interior series of smaller teeth, destined to replace those in function " This only shows how artificial is this division. At the corner of the mouth there are two large posterior canine teeth ; those of the regular line are small behind, and grow gradually stronger as they are placed more forward ; in front, there is, on each side, a strong canine ; behind this line, there is another line of smaller and more blunt teeth. At the lower jaw, the teeth are disposed the same, but those of the inner series do not extend so far backwards. In the young specimens, and perhaps in the females, there are no posterior canine teeth at the angle of the mouth. The head is rough ; the opercles scaly ; on the cheeks, there are two series of scales, and all the surface is covered with irregular lines, which radiate from the eye ; the præoperculum is not serrated.

The height of the body is contained three and one-third times in the total length ; the head four times in the same ; eye four and one-third times in the length of the head. The general profile is oval, the highest place being at about the middle of the fish ; the dorsal scales do not extend on the base of the fin. The lateral line is continuous, following the upper profile till a little before the end of the dorsal, and then descending by an oblique line to the middle, which it follows up to the root of the caudal; it is formed of a succession of twenty-five long carinated lines, which expand in rather numerous but short arbuscles at their end. The transverse line numbers ten scales, the lateral line running over the third. Dorsal scaleless, formed of nine spines and eleven rays ; caudal rounded, of thirteen long rays; anal of three spines and ten soft rays ; ventrals of moderate size, pointed ; pectorals large, of thirteen rays.

Entirely of an obscure green on the upper parts, and of a dark blue on the lower ; a broad, black, longitudinal band extends from the posterior edge of the eye to the end of the operculum ; the cheeks are covered with little, irregular white spots ; the throat is purple, spotted with white ; all the scales of the body are bordered with carmine, but there is no trace of spots or bands. The fins are green, the spiny dorsal having red tinges, and the rays of the soft part are spotted with purple; these spots extend on the membranes; the fin is bordered with red. The caudal has its rays orauge, spotted with carmine; the anal has three longitudinal series of large, rounded, carmine spots; the ventrals are pink, aud the pectorals yellow; the eye is carmine, with concentric green lines.

I dedicated this sort to my old and celebrated friend, Dr. Bleeker, who not only showed me so much kinduess when I was at Batavia, but also has so much helped me for years in my Ichthyological studies in Iudia.

The length of this fish is, ou au average, from 10 to 12 inches.

LABRICHTHYS RICHARDSONI.

(*Parrot Fish.*)

Very much like the former, but a little broader. The teeth are the same, but there is only one canine at the corner of the jaw. The scales, composition of the fius, and lateral line are similar, the latter is formed of twenty-six tubes; the dorsal has nine spines and eleven soft rays; the caudal fourteen rays; the anal three spines and eleven rays; the pectorals thirteen rays.

The general colour is of a light blueish green, with a black spot on the extremity of the operculum, and two broad, transverse bands of the same colour—one extending from the third or fourth spine of the dorsal to the first soft ray of tho same; the second, which is often absent, is placed more backwards; the scales have no coloured margin; a few dark spots are usually seen between the fifth, sixth, and seventh spines of the dorsal; the fins are of the colour of the body, the caudal alone having a posterior orange margin; the eye is green, with an inner and outer crimson circle.

My largest specimen measures about 14 inches.

There are three series of scales ou the cheeks, and the entire surface is very rough; the dorsal scales do not extend on the base of the fin.

I consider as a variety of this sort a specimen which, with its general form and colour, had three faint transverse, obscure bands, and a longitudinal stripe extending from the angle of the mouth to the first transverse band passing below the eye; the caudal, ventral, and pectoral were yellow, with the fins orange;

the other fins were variegated with purple spots, and edged with crimson ; the eye was blue, with an inner and an external crimson circle.

On the dried specimens, appear sorts of longitudinal ridges, such as those that Dr. Richardson has represented in his plate of *L. Laticlavius.*

LABRICHTHYS VESTITA.

The height of the body is contained three and two-third times in the total length ; the head is three and three-fourth times in the same ; the orbit is seven times in the latter. The anterior part of the head is rather more rounded than in the two first sorts. There is only one long canine tooth on each side, but the dentition seems to vary considerably with age, as in a specimen 12 inches long, there is only one tooth at the corner of the mouth, but there are two, and in some places three, rows of teeth on the upper jaw ; on a specimen 17 inches long, there are two teeth at the corner of the mouth, and one line in all the anterior portion of the lower jaw. It is only on the sides that a line of small extra teeth are visible. On the cheeks, there are three or four irregular lines of rounded scales. The lateral line is of the same form as that of the preceding species ; it runs over twenty-six scales, and is formed of twenty-three long tubes, expanding posteriorly in very numerous, broad, and intricate arbuscles ; the transverse line is formed of fourteen scales. The dorsal is composed of nine spines and eleven rays ; it is nearly equal in all its length, the soft part being very little higher than the other. The dorsal scales do not extend over its base ; caudal rounded, of thirteen long rays, with another almost as long, and several short ones on each side. Anal with three spines and ten rays ; the first spine is about one-third shorter than the second, and this bears about the same proportion to the third ; the ventrals have one long and slender spine and five rays, the two first rather prolonged ; pectorals of thirteen rays.

The colour is of a reddish lilac, with two broad, transversal bands of a dark brown on the body—one situated just behind the extremity of the pectoral, and the other towards the middle of the soft dorsal. The middle of the head, from the jaws to the operculum, presents a beautiful blue tinge, which extends equally on the centre of the lower jaw; the spiny dorsal, the caudal, the pectorals, and ventrals are yellow; the soft dorsal and the anal are obscure, sometimes black with a blue tinge; the base of the pectoral is black. These colours are subject to some variation. When dry, the body presents the same feeble longitudinal ridges I have mentioned in another sort.

Seen several specimens, which were found in February; the longest measured 17 inches. The fishmongers say that this sort is very good for the table.

This may be the *Labrichthys Ephippium* of Gunther ("Ann and Mag. of Nat. History, 1863," p. 116), but it is certainly not the sort described by Cuvier under that name, and which is said to come from New Zealand.

NOTA.—The three sorts of *Labrichthys* I here describe can be distinguished in the following way :—

(*a.*) Two series of scales on the cheeks; no transverse bands.—
Bleekeri.

(*b.*) More than two; transverse bands on the body; ground colour, green.—*Richardsonii.*

——ground colour, reddish.—*Vestita*

I believe that the dentition is subject to great variations with age, and that the presence of one or two teeth at the angle of the mouth is sometimes due to the same cause.

ODAX.

Genus established by Cuvier and Valenciennes on several sorts which have the teeth solved together like the beak of a parrot, but differs from *Scarus*, which has also this character, by the scales of their body being small.

ODAX RICHARDSONII.

Odax richardsonii, *Gunther, Catal. Brit. Mus. Fishes,* vol. iv., p. 241.

Odax semifasciatus, *Richard., Proceed. Zool. Society.*

(The Stranger.)

Height of body five and two-third times in total length; head four times in same; orbit five and one-quarter times in length of head ; the longitudinal line passing through the centre of the eye, being exactly in the middle of the length of the head ; the anterior part of the head protruding in a long snout ; the upper lip much longer than the other ; the lateral line is not interrupted, and extends to the full length of the body ; it is arched upwards in its anterior part, over the pectorals ; it extends over about sixty-four scales. The dorsal is formed of thirty rays ; the latter eleven branched, the others being very soft, it is often very difficult to distinguish one from the other ; this dorsal is equal in all its length ; the caudal is rounded, and formed of twelve long rays ; the anal has the form of the dorsal, but much shorter, it is formed of twelve rays ; the pectoral of fifteen, and is of a rather rounded form. Authors generally attribute a larger number of rays to the dorsal (thirty-two) than I have mentioned, but I have seen many thousand specimens of this fish, and I have always found the same number.

The colours of this *Odax* are most changeable ; in fact, it is very difficult to find two specimens exactly alike ; it is sometimes of a beautiful green, sometimes blue, at other times red, and very often this ground colour is variegated with beautiful tinges, caused by the edges of the scales being yellow ; the body often shows from six to eight transverse obscure bands, that vanish before they reach the lower part, which is generally white ; there are often irregular longitudinal bands, sometimes yellow, sometimes blue, on the sides of the head and on the snout ; but often, also, the upper part of the head is of a dark green, with the sides silvery white, the latter showing irregular yellow spots. The fins are often hyaline, and without spots, but often also the dorsal and anal have numerous yellow or red irregular bands and spots ; in most specimens, black spots can be seen on the membranes of four or five of the posterior fins, commencing at the fifteenth or nineteenth ; the eye is of a beautiful yellow, sometimes bordered with green, sometimes with light blue.

The adult specimens measure from twelve to sixteen inches. This fish is very common all the year round in the Melbourne Market, and is moderately esteemed for food.

The *Odax Pullus*, Bl. &. Sch. (*Scarus*), is probably founded on one of the varieties of this sort. It was found in New Zealand by Forster, and in Western Port by Messrs. Quoy and Gaimard. Cuvier and Valenciennes (vol. xiv., p. 305,) state that it has thirty-four rays to the dorsal, but as all the thousands of *Strangers* that are brought from Western Port belong to the same sort, I cannot but think there is some mistake in these numbers.

I had taken this sort for the *Odax Semifasciatus* (Cuv. & Val., v. xiv., p. 299), and I see that Richardson has been of the same opinion; but Dr. Gunther, finding that it has its præoperculum entire, very properly distinguishes the Australian species from it; he also thinks that the *Pullus* of Cuvier and Valenciennes is not the one of Bloch, which was brought by Forster from New Zealand.

ODAX OBSCURUS.

Height of body a little over four and one-half times in the total length; length of head three and three-quarter times in same; eye four and three-quarter times in length of head.

The head is not protruded in so long a snout as in the first species, and a longitudinal line passing through the centre of the eye would be much nearer to the extremity of the muzzle than to that of the operculum; the profile of the head forms a rather long oval; the upper lip is rather longer than the other; the præoperculum is very finely denticulated; the lateral line extends to the base of the caudal, and is arched over the pectorals; it runs over about forty-five scales, these being much larger than those of *Richardsonii*.

Dorsal of twenty-eight rays; its height is equal in all its length; caudal rounded, of thirteen rays; anal of fifteen; pectorals rounded, of fourteen rays.

The general colour is almost black with a purplish tinge; the upper part of the head is of a lighter brown; on its sides are numerous, narrow, flexuous red lines running longitudinally; eye of a beautiful red, with a broad exteral blue circle; dorsal and anal of a light blue colour, covered with oblique scarlet lines; it has also a broad black border; the other fins black.

Only seen once at the Melbourne Market, in the month of December; but it is probable that the following only constitutes a variety of the same sort :—

Body of a grey colour, with a few irregular green spots on the back ; upper part of the head green, with the sides blue ; on these there are numerous longitudinal undulating narrow lines ; the posterior margin of the scales, on the sides of the body, are pink, as are also the throat and the fins ; the dorsal, caudal, anal, and ventrals have a rather broad black margin ; the three first are covered with irregular narrow spots, forming oblique lines on the dorsal and anal, and transverse ones on the caudal.

Seen several times in the Melbourne Market. In size never more than from 5 to 6 inches long.

Nota.—I should have taken this for *Balteatus*, if any of the specimens I have seen had shown any trace of the dark band from which the name of the sort has been derived.

OLISTHOPS.

Dr. Richardson formed this genus in the " Annals and Magazine of Natural History for 1850," and gave a figure of the sort he knew in the " Proceedings of the Zoological Society " of the same year. Dr. Gunther changed the name to *Olistherops ;* but I see no sort of use, nor even of right, in these so-called rectifications. The latter author characterises the genus thus :—" Head entirely naked ; scales of moderate size ; lateral line continuous ; snout of moderate extent ; dorsal spines numerous, flexible." All this agrees well with the fish I here describe ; but the sort known is represented as having a blueish streak along the upper and lower margins of the caudal, and along the upper margin of the pectoral, and may be different from mine.

OLISTHOPS CYANOMELAS.

Olisthops cyanomelas, *Richard., Ann. and Mag. Nat. Hist.,* 1851, p. 291.

Body elongate ; front part of the head rounded. Height of body five times in the total length ; head five and a-half times in the same ; orbit five times in the length of the head. Teeth like those of *Scarus,* soldered together, and forming a sort of parrot beak, on the edge of which the teeth are visible. Lateral line extending on the root of the caudal ; it is rather flexuous, and considerably rounded over the pectoral, running over about sixty scales ; these are of moderate size, and are covered with concentric lines. On the transverse line I find nineteen scales, on the seventh of which the lateral line passes. The anterior part of the latter forms on each scale a little ridge, which terminates posteriorly in a short, oblong line, recurved upwards. This is seen on the twelve or fourteen first scales only. The dorsal is high in front, depressed in the middle, with the soft portion high again ; it is composed of fifteen or sixteen spines and of eleven soft rays. The caudal is truncated, with its external angles prolongated ; it is formed of twelve long rays and of several short ones on each side ; the anal has one spine and from nine to twelve rays ; the ventrals are rather small ; the pectorals large, of thirteen rays.

The colours are subject to great variation. Some specimens are of a dark brilliant brown, with a rounded spot of a beautiful light blue on each side ; the lower parts are variegated with orange and blue ; the head is dark brown on its upper parts, of light blue on the sides, with longitudinal, narrow, and irregular orange lines ; these have a black border. Fins orange, with numerous light blue spots on the posterior part of the spiny portion of the dorsal ; on the soft portion of the same, and on all the other fins, are very numerous dark blue spots. On the upper part of the back, adjoining the head, is a broad, transverse, yellow spot ; eye yellow.

This description applies to three specimens I obtained in the month of June. One of them was shorter, and its upper profile was much more convex ; it was said by the fisherman to be a male. On the 10th of October, 1871, a large number of specimens made their appearance on the Melbourne Market ; their form was the same, but their colours generally very different. Some were entirely black, with a blue streak in front of the eye ; this was green, with an internal red circle ; the external rays of the caudal were strongly prolongated. Others were of a chocolate colour ; others of a livid yellow, and others, again, of a dark green.

I at first considered these as belonging to different sorts, and the difference in the numbers of the dorsal spines confirmed me in that opinion ; but, on examining numerous specimens, I found insensible passages from one to the other, and I believe they all belong to one very variable sort. On the dried specimens, a short sulcate is visible on each scale, and their union gives the appearance of longitudinal lines, which I did not observe on the fresh specimens.

The flesh of this sort is green, and it does not appear to be used as food, probably for that reason. It is rarely seen on the market, and does not appear to have any usual name. My largest specimen measures over 15 inches.

It is probable that this is the *Toobitooit* mentioned by Richardson, from a drawing—" *Erebus and Terror*, Fishes,' p. 134.

GERRIDÆ.

" Body compressed, elevated, or oblong, covered with sparoid scales. Lateral line continuous. Dorsal fin with spinous and soft portions equally developed, and with a scaly sheath along the base, which is separated by a groove from the other scales. Anal with three (two) spines, and with the soft portion similar to the soft dorsal. Ventral fins thoracic, with one spine and five soft rays. Teeth small, palate toothless. The lower pharyngeal bones are firmly united by a suture. Branchiostegals, six; gills, four; pseudobranchiæ present; glandular air bladder present. Stomach without cæcal sac; pyloric appendages, rudimentary. Oviparous.

" Tropical seas. "

Dr. Gunther, in the first volume of his " Catalogue," places *Gerres* in his *Pristipomatidæ*, where it seems to come very naturally ; but, in the fourth volume of the same work, he formed for it a family (*Gerridæ*), that he places near *Labridæ*, and immediately after the small family of *Embiotocidæ* of Agassiz.

GERRES.

Formed by Cuvier, and composed of rather numerous species, generally inhabiting the warm and tropical seas, one only having been found on the coast of North America, as far north as New York.

The great protractility of the mouth made the illustrious Cuvier place it in a family he had called *Menidæ*; but in my paper on the fishes of the Cape of Good Hope, written in 1861, I protested against this character being considered as of first importance, as it is to be found in sorts of almost all families.

The species I describe here partakes of the characters of *Ditrema*, by the large number of the anal rays, which in *Gerres* are not generally more than eight or nine.

GERRES MELBOURNENSIS.

The height of the body is contained two and a-half times in the total length, without the caudal ; the eye is very large, and only contained two and one-third times in the length of the head, when the mouth is not extended ; when it is, the distance from the extremity of the snout to the anterior margin of the eye is a little less than the diameter of the orbit. The teeth are numerous and villiform ; there are none on the vomer or palatine. The profile is very convex over the eye and the snout. When the mouth is not extended, it is rather bent downwards. The head is contained, in this state, four times in the total length, including the caudal ; the operculum is entire, as is also the præoperculum, and the præorbital. The scales are large, being only thirty-seven or thirty-eight on the lateral line ; this line is marked by a succession of short, elevated, oblique lines, and is strongly curved near the head. The spiny portion of the dorsal is much shorter than the soft one ; it is formed of nine rather feeble spines ; the first one is shorter than the following, which are about equal, the posterior ones being something longer than the others. The rays number sixteen ; the first are about of the same length as the last spines, but they become rather longer as they go backwards. The caudal is forked ; it is formed of eighteen long rays and of several shorter ones on each side ; anal with three spines, rather stronger than those of the dorsal; the first is the shortest, and the third the longest; the rays number seventeen, the first of which is longer than the third spine, and the others decrease slightly towards the tail. The ventrals are inserted a little behind the pectorals ; they are formed of a long slender spine and of five rays; the pectorals are arched; they are rather shorter than the head, and formed of fifteen rays, of which the first is short, and the third the longest of all, and extends further than the spines of the anal. The dorsal and anal are received in a low, scaly sheath; the longest spines of the dorsal are equal to the diameter of the eye; this same dimension is contained one and a-quarter times in the caudal at its centre, and twice on its sides.

General colour silvery; the upper parts are blue, and the sides have a copper tinge; there are faint longitudinal lines, due to the centre of the scales being rather obscure. The spinous dorsal is purple, and the soft part rather yellow; the caudal is of the latter colour; anal, pectorals, and ventrals, pink   eye yellow, the pupil rather angular.

Seen several specimens in the month of July.

Order III.—ANACANTHINI.

" Vertical and ventral fins (except in gadopsis) without spinous rays. The ventral fins, if present, are jugular or thoracic. Air-bladder, if present, without pneumatic duct.

GADOPSIDÆ.

" A small portion of the dorsal and anal fins is formed into true spines. Gadopsis Marmoratus.

" Fresh waters of Australia and Tasmania.

GADOPSIS.

This very singular fish has been separated from all others by Dr. Gunther as a distinct family.

The only sort yet described is the following :—

GADOPSIS MARMORATUS.

Gadopsis marmoratus, *Richard.*, *Ereb. and Ter.*, p. 122, pl. 59,

(The Black Fish.)

The *Black Fish*, well known to the colonists, is found in almost all the streams of South-Eastern Australia ; but it is not quite certain that it belongs to the sort described by Richardson, and which was brought from Tasmania ; at least the figure given by this author is much shorter than the specimens found in the Yarra River, and these have one dorsal spine more. D. 12—26. C. 16 (with six small rays on each side). A. 3—18. P. 17. V. 1 (bifid).

The height is six and a-half times in the total length ; the head four and a-half times in the same ; and the orbit five and a-half times in the length of the head. The teeth are very numerous, cardiform, and arched backwards. On the very old specimens, there are a few larger ones in front, having rather the appearance of canines.

It is of a dark olive colour, with the lower parts of a dirty yellow ; the back is covered with obscure blotches, which give the fish a black appearance ; the fins are almost black.

The largest specimens I have seen were 16½ inches long. I am not certain that the *Black Fish* of all the streams of the Colony belong to the same sort ; it is considered good food.

NOTA.—Mr. Merle, of Daylesford, has kindly sent me some specimens from the Loddon River. They are of a light green, with very few obscure blotches on the back ; the belly is white, and the sides of the head rosy. There are a few irregular obscure spots on the dorsal ; the eye is rather green. The dorsal has nine spines and twenty-seven rays, and the anal three spines and eighteen rays. The height of the body is contained five and two-third times in the total length. The largest of these specimens is a little over 6 inches long. The ventrals are evidently formed of two rays, united in a great part of their length ; but the fresh specimens of the common *Black Fish* of the Yarra have the same appearance.

GADIDÆ.

"Body more or less elongate, covered with small smooth scales. One, two, or three dorsal fins, occupying nearly the whole of the back; rays of the posterior dorsal well developed; one or two anal fins; caudal free from dorsal to anal, or if they are united, the dorsal with a separate anterior portion. Ventrals jugular, composed of several rays, or if they are reduced to a filament, the dorsal is divided into two. Gill opening wide; the gill-membranes generally not attached to the isthmus. Pseudobranchiæ none, glandular, rudimentary; an air-bladder and pyloric appendages generally present.

"Mostly inhabitants of the sea. Arctic and temperate regions."

PSEUDOPHYCIS.

The genus *Pseudophycis* was formed by Dr. Gunther on the *Lota Breviuscula* of Richardson ("*Erebus* and *Terror*"). This sort was found on the coast of New Zealand, and is very nearly allied to the fish I describe here. In fact, the only differences consist in the body, which is much shorter, and in the form of the ventrals, which, in Richardson's plate, are represented by a long bifid filament. This form of the ventrals does not admit of the fish I here describe being placed with it, and I should have to class it with *Lotella*, a genus established by Kaup, and characterised, in Dr. Gunther's Catalogue, as follows :—" Body of moderate length, covered with small scales ; a separate caudal ; two dorsal fins and one anal ; ventral fins with a flat base, and composed of several rays ; teeth in the upper jaw in a band, with an outer series of larger ones ; vomerine or palatine teeth, none ;

chin with a barbel." All this agrees well with my sort, except the teeth. It would appear to come very near to Forster's *Gadus Bacchus* (*Rubiginosus* Solander), but the composition of the fins is very different.

PSEUDOPHYCIS BARBATUS.

Pseudophycis barbatus, *Gunther*, *Ann. and Mag. of Nat. Hist.*, 1863, p. 116.

(*Rock Cod.*)

The height of the body is about three and a-half times in the total length, and the head four and two-third in the same; the orbit is very oval, and in its largest diameter is contained less than four times in the length of the head; this diameter is equal in length to the snout. The upper profile is regular, but the belly is rather inflated; the lower jaw is slightly longer than the other. The teeth are very numerous, in three or four rather irregular rows; they are all of the same form—slender, arched, acute, and all of about the same size; they are similar on both jaws; the chin bears a very short and slender barbel. The præoperculum is entire, and rounded; the operculum is terminated by a strong angle, and its posterior edge bears traces of radiated lines. The body is rather compressed, tapers posteriorly, is covered with small scales, which fall very easily; they number about one hundred and thirty on the longitudinal line. I find it very difficult, on my dry specimens, to count correctly those of the transverse lines, but I find thirteen over the lateral line, and more than twice as many below. The two dorsals are equal in height; their membranes are covered with scales on considerably more than one-half of their height; the first is formed of ten rays, the last of which is united with the second dorsal by a very low membrane; this latter is composed of fifty-one rays, and is rounded posteriorly; the caudal is also of this form, and composed of twenty-seven rays; the anal is similar to the second dorsal, but somewhat shorter; it has fifty-five or fifty-six rays. The pectorals are contained about twice in the length of the head, and are inserted a little behind the beginning of the first dorsal; they have twenty-two rays. The ventrals are placed before and below the end of the operculum; they are narrow, and formed of five rays, intimately joined, the external

one being prolongated in a filament ; taken from the extremity
of this latter, the fin is about one-half of the length of the head.
The space between the extremity of the lower jaw and the anus
is not quite as long as the anal fin.

The upper parts are of a light brown ; the head rather red ;
the lower parts of a whitish flesh colour, sometimes white ; the
fins are light brown, with a black terminal edge ; the pectorals
are sometimes almost white and transparent, and sometimes
rather dark.

My longest specimens are about 15 inches, and I do not think
it grows much larger. It is esteemed for food, and is very
common on the Melbourne Market, particularly during the cold
months of the year.

Dr. Gunther describes in the same work a *Lotella Collarias*
from Victoria, that I have not yet met with.

OPHIDIIDÆ.

"Body more or less elongate, naked or scaly.
Vertical fins generally united into one ; no separate
anterior dorsal or anal ; dorsal occupying the greater
portion of the back. Ventral fins rudimentary (reduced to a filament) or absent, jugular (except in
Brotulophis). Gill-openings wide ; the gill-membranes not attached to the isthmus. Pyloric appendages none, or in small number.

"Inhabitants of the seas of nearly all regions."

GENYPTERUS.

Genus established by Dr. Andrew Smith, in his "Illustrations of the Zoology of South Africa," under the name of
Xiphiurus, which, in my notice on the fishes of the Cape of
Good Hope, I adopted ; but Dr. Gunther, in the eleventh volume
of his Catalogue, finding it was pre-occupied, has very properly
changed the name to the appellation we now adopt.

The same author gives the genus the following characters :— "Body elongate, compressed, and covered with minute scales ; eye of moderate size ; vertical fins, continuous ; ventral fins replaced by a pair of bifid filaments (barbels) inserted below the glosshyal ; teeth in the jaws, on the vomer and on the palatine bones ; the outer series in the jaws, and the single series on the palates, contain strong teeth ; lower jaw received within the upper ; vent situated at some distance behind the pectoral ; seven or eight branchiostegals ; gill-opening wide ; gills, four, a slit behind the fourth ; pseudobranchiæ and air-bladder present ; pyloric appendages in small number (six).

GENYPTERUS AUSTRALIS.

(The Rock Ling.)

Height eight times in the total length, and one and a-half times in that of the body ; eye seven and a-half times in the head ; the barbels in the young specimens about one-third the length of the head, but in the old specimens one-half this length ; in the young the outer filament is much shorter than the inner half ; but in the large ones they are about equal.

The teeth of the jaws are on two series ; the outer ones are large, thick, conical, and wide apart one from the other ; the inner ones smaller, of the same form, but placed nearer one to the other, and sometimes two by two ; in the young specimens the teeth are more slender ; the inner ones in numerous series and arched. The lateral line is well marked on the full length of the body, except on its posterior eighth part ; it is formed of several lines placed near one another, and having a notch from distance to distance ; the number of these notches is about forty-seven ; at some of these there is a short oblong appendice. The scales are small ; the transversal lines numbering nearly three hundred ; the pectorals are all contained about two and a-half times in the length of the head.

The general colour is of a light lilac ; the belly is white ; the body is covered with large marbled blotches, irregular in form, but generally rounded ; on the back they are confluent, and they extend over the head. The eye is silvery. The dorsal and anal are dark and marbled like the body ; the extreme edge of the dorsal is white, and the one of the anal flesh colour ; pectorals spotted

The anus is situated a little nearer to the extremity of the mouth than to the end of the tail.

Very common in the Melbourne Market, particularly in the cold months of the year. Its flesh is considered very delicate. I think it must have been described, but I am unable to identify it with any known sort.

The figure of *Ophidium Maculatum*, given by Tschudi, *Faun. Peruv.*, p. 25, pl. 4, is so very similar to this fish, that I hesitate to separate the two ; but he represents the head as being without spots. The ventrals have been forgotten on the figure.

The *Ophidium Blacodes* that Forster found on the coast of New Zealand is also very nearly allied to it, and it is possible that all these fishes may belong to the same sort ; but Dr. Gunther says that the lateral line is scarcely visible, and disappears entirely in the middle of the body, which is not the case with the Melbourne fish.

The usual size is about 20 inches ; but I have a specimen which measures 27.

MACRURIDÆ.

" Body terminating in a long, compressed, tapering tail, covered with spiny keeled or striated scales. One short anterior dorsal, the second very long, continued to the end of the tail, and composed of very feeble rays ; anal of an extent similar to that of the second dorsal ; no caudal. Ventral fins thoracic or jugular, composed of several rays. Pseudobranchiæ none ; six or seven branchiostegals. Air-bladder present. Pyloric appendages numerous.

" Temperate parts of North Atlantic, Mediterranean, Japanese, and Australian Seas."

I have not observed any in Victoria.

PLEURONECTIDÆ.

"Body strongly compressed, flat, with one of the two sides, which is always turned upwards, coloured, whilst the other is colourless, and only sometimes spotted. Both eyes are placed on the coloured side; and although the bones are present on both sides of the skull, they are not equally developed or symmetrical. Dorsal and anal fins exceedingly long, without divisions. Gills, four; pseudobranehiæ well developed. Air-bladder, none.

"Carnivorous fishes, living on the sandy bottom of the coasts of all the regions; many ascend rivers."

RHOMBOSOLEA.

Genus established by Dr. Gunther, with the following characteristics:—Eyes on the right side, the lower in advance of the upper; the mouth unsymmetrical, narrower on the right side than on the left; the length of the left maxillary being less than one-third of that of the head; teeth on the blind side only, where they are villiform, forming bands; no vomerine or palatine teeth; most of the dorsal and anal rays branched; the dorsal fin commences on the foremost part of the snout; only one ventral, which is continuous with the anal; scales very small cycloid; lateral line straight; gill-openings narrow, the gill-membranes being broadly united below the throat; gill-rakers short and conical.

The following Melbourne fish enters evidently in this genus, but cannot be placed in any of the three species described by Dr. Gunther. In the sort I describe here, the dorsal extends to the end of the snout, but the number of its rays do not agree with any of the species mentioned by that author.

RHOMBOSOLEA BASSENSIS.

(*The Melbourne Sole.*)

The height of the body is two and a-half times in the total length; the head is nearly five times in the same; the space between the eyes is covered with scales, and is one-half the longitudinal diameter of the eye; the lower eye is considerably in advance of the upper; snout contained three and two-third times in the total length of the head; the eye five times in the same. The dorsal fin begins at the foremost extremity of the snout, and has seventy-five rays, the first twenty-five having a short prolongated filament; caudal quite free, formed of eighteen rays, thirteen of which only attain its extremity; anal of fifty-one rays; ventrals with seven rays, having short filamentary prolongations; the pectorals are one-half the length of the head, and are formed of twelve rays; the external fourth part of the rays being free of the membranes.

The operculum has a rather strong angle above the root of the pectorals; the lateral line is straight, and runs over about ninety lines of scales. The teeth on the right side are very few, irregular, and tuberculous, but on the blind side they are very numerous, on four or five very irregular lines; they are conical and sharp, and some are slightly curved; on the lower jaw the teeth are similar, but on four lines. The scales of the body are puncto-striated, and strongly ciliated, which makes the fish feel rough to the touch; the fin rays are entirely covered with scales.

The general colour is of a dark brown, marbled with black blotches, the sides of which are well shaded with the general colour; in the larger specimens this is sometimes entirely black.

The largest specimens attain one foot long.

It is found all the year, but more commonly during the cold months. It sometimes goes up the Yarra to Melbourne.

NOTA.—Professor M'Coy, in the "Intercolonial Exhibition Reports, 1866-67," says, that a true *Solea*, nearly allied to *S. Margaritifera*, is found in Hobson's Bay, and it is probable that he means this sort; but the distinctive character of *Solea* is that the upper eye is in advance of the lower one, and the contrary is here the case.

PLEURONECTES.

It is only with considerable doubt that I place in this genus the followiug sort, as the dorsal begins before the line of the eyes ; but in Dr. Guuther's divisiou of the *Pleuronectidœ*, it would be included in his second division :—" Cleft of the mouth narrow, with the dentition much more dcvcloped on the blind side than on the coloured." The lower eye is considerably in advance of the upper one ; and the dorsal does uot begiu on the foremost part of the snout.

PLEURONECTES ? VICTORIÆ.

(*The Melbourne Flounder*).

The height of the body is twice and one-third in the total length, or less than twice up to the base of the caudal ; head a little over four times in the total leugth ; eye five times in the length of head ; the space between the eyes narrow and scaleless ; the teeth are absent on the coloured side, but are rather long, slender, and numerous, particularly in young individuals ; on the other side they appear in part worn out iu the old ones ; the snout, up to the edge of the lower eye, is as long as the diameter of the latter ; the same diameter of the upper eye, is contained one and one-fourth times in the snout ; the operculum has an angle over the root of the pectorals ; the lateral line is straight, and runs over about eighty-five scales ; it is prolongated on the head, and emits a branch behind the operculum, which runs obliquely towards the dorsal, that it meets between the fifth and sixth dorsal ray ; the scales are small and rounded ; in the old specimens they are sensibly concave, particularly on the head and on the upper part of the body. The dorsal is much higher towards the middle of the body than in its other parts, it has fifty-six or fifty-seven rays, which are always longer than the membranes, and gives the upper edge an appearauce of being fringed ; the anterior ones are more prolongated, and the first of all is free, bifid, and only connected with the others by a very low mem-

branc ; the caudal is large, rather rounded, and formed of nineteen rays, of which thirteen only are long ones ; ventrals formed
of six rays, which are united to the anal by a membrane without
rays ; the anal is formed like the dorsal, and has forty-one or
forty-two rays ; the pectorals rather longer than the distance
from the end of the snout to the posterior margin of the eye,
and formed of eleven rays.

This fish is common on the Melbourne Market, but rarely
attains a foot in length. It is of an olive green, with large marbled blotches of a darker and brownish colour; the lower side
is white, with its pectorals rather pink ; the eye is black, with an
orange circle.

It is esteemed for the table.

NOTA.—Professor M'Coy considers this fish, " Intercolonial
Exhibition, 1866-67," as being the *Rhombosolea Flesoides* of
Dr. Gunther ; but the description of this specie, " Ann. and Mag.
of Natural History," 1863, p. 116, does not agree with it ; the
numbers of the rays are very different ; the bifurcation of the
lateral line is not mentioned ; the dorsal also seems to begin
too far behind to allow it to be placed with *Rhombosolea*.

Order IV.—PHYSOSTOMI.

" All the fin-rays articulated ; only the first of
the dorsal and pectoral fins is sometimes more or
less ossified. The ventral fins, if present, are
abdominal, without spine. Air-bladder, if present,
with a pneumatic duct.

SILURIDÆ.

" Skin naked, or with osseous scutes, but without
scales. Barbels always present ; maxillary bone
rudimentary, almost always forming the base of a
maxillary barbel. Margin of the upper jaw formed

by the inter-maxillaries only. Sub-opereulum absent. Air-bladder generally present, communicating with the organ of hearing by means of the auditory ossieles. Adipose fin present or absent. "Inhabitants of the fresh waters of all the temperate and tropical regions, some entering the salt water, but keeping near the coast."

COPIDOGLANIS.

This is the only sort of *Siluridæ* I have yet seen in Australia, but several others are described from the Northern Territory, and from New South Wales.

COPIDOGLANIS TANDANUS.

Plotosus tandanus, *Mitchell, Exped.*, v. i., p. 95, pl. 6, fig. 2.

Copidoglanis tandanus, *Gunther, Cat.*, v. p. 26.

(The Murray Catfish.)

The colours of this curious fish are subject to the greatest changes. Sometimes it is of an olive yellow, lighter on the lower parts. On the back are feeble marmorated spots, steel colour; head of a fine carmine colour, as also the barbels and pectorals; the first dorsal is of a dark olive at its base, and red in the other parts; the second dorsal is also of an obscure olive, bordered with red; the caudal and anal are dark green. In other specimens, the back is entirely of a brownish black, which extends on the sides, and the red tinges sometimes almost disappear; in others again, the general colour is almost white, and the head is often yellow. It is almost impossible to find two specimens entirely alike.

This sort appears to be common in the Murray and in the rivers of Riverina; it is brought to Melbourne, at times, principally in winter, by the Echuca Railway. It is considered good food, and attains two feet in length. The fishermen of the Murray distinguish three sorts—the white, the black, and the blue, but I think they only constitute varieties of colour.

HAPLOCHITONIDÆ.

" Body naked or scaly. Margin of the upper jaw formed by the intermaxillary; operculær apparatus complete. Barbels, none. Gill opening wide; pseudobranchiæ well developed. Air-bladder simple. Adipose fin present. Ovaries laminated ; the eggs fall into the cavity of the abdomen, there being no oviduet. Pylorie appendages, none.

" Fresh water fish, from the temperate parts of South America and South Australia, representing the Salmonoids of the Northern Hemisphere."

PROTOTROCTES.

Formed by Dr. Gunther on a very remarkable fish found in several rivers of Victoria and of North Tasmania.

PROTOTROCTES MARÆNA.

Prototroctes maræna, *Gunther*, *Catal.*, vol. v., p. 382.

(Yarra Herring.)

Having not yet seen this sort living, or in a fresh state, I only mention it here ; it exhales a very strong and particular smell. It used to be very common in the Yarra, but since the introduction into that river of the *Murray Cod*, it seems to have been almost destroyed by it. No specimens, are to my knowledge, now found near Melbourne, and it has become very scarce even in the upper parts of the river.

SCOPELIDÆ.

" Body naked or sealy. Margin of the upper jaw formed by the intermaxillary only ; opereular apparatus sometimes incompletely developed. Barbels none. Gill-opening very wide ; pseudobranchiæ well developed. Air-bladder, none ; adipose fin present. The eggs are enclosed in the sacs of the ovarium, and excluded by oviducts. Pyloric appendages few in number or absent. Intestinal tract very short."

AULOPUS.

Formed by Cuvier, in his "Règne Animal," on a curious Mediterranean fish, which, on account of its adipose dorsal fin, had been placed with *Salmo* by Bloch and others. Its characters give it much affinity with fishes of the most remote families. Dr. Gunther has placed it with his *Scopelidæ*. M. Valenciennes, Cuvier's learned colloborateur, having received from Teneriff the male and female of this sort, thought that they belonged to two different species ; but since then, it has been ascertained that the first mentioned sex is always adorned, in this genus, with dorsal filaments, which do not exist in the female. In the last volume that has ever been published of his great work on fishes, the French author describes a second sort from Australia, but it had been previously published by Dr. Richardson.

AULOPUS PURPURISSATUS.

Aulopus purpurissatus, *Richard.*, *Icon. Pisc.*, p. 6, pl. 2, fig. 3.
————— milesii, *Cuv. & Val.*, *Hist. des Pois.*, v. xxii., p. 519, fig. 650.

This sort is so very scarce at Melbourne as not to have received any particular name. At Sydney, it appears to be much more common, and is known as *Sergeant Baker*.

D. 1 /19. A. 13. V. 9. P. 11. C. 20 long rays.

Height of body five and two-third times in the total length ; the head is a little more than four times in the same ; the orbit is contained six times in the length of the head. The lower jaw is longer than the other ; the teeth very numerous, on, at least two lines, on the jaws, and other larger ones are on the palatine and the vomer. The ventral is very singularly conformed ; its four first rays are thick and bifid, but not branched; the first is even simple. The dorsal is large ; its spine is much shorter than the rays, and in the male the first of these prolongates in a very long filament ; this is bifid, the internal limb being much shorter than the outer one ; the adipose is covered with scales.

In a female specimen, I find a rather long filamentary appendice inserted on the posterior edge of the maxillary, over the angle. Having seen no other specimen of that sex, I do not know if this is accidental.

The colours of this fish are really magnificent. The upper parts are of a greyish blue, with fine red, orange, and yellow tinges on the sides of the head. On the back, extend rather numerous transverse blotches of a fine scarlet carmine ; these alternate with others which start from the lateral line, and extend towards the belly without attaining it. The dorsal is yellow, marbled with crimson ; the adipose are purple at the base, yellow in their middle, and bordered with red on their external edge. The caudal is yellow, spotted with the most beautiful crimson ; the anal is white, with orange bands ; pectorals yellow, with transversal red spots ; ventrals yellow, with purple spots, and the extremity of the rays are pink.

This description is taken from a female specimen caught in the month of May, 1871. In the same month, and a few days after, a male fish was brought to the market. The colours were less brilliant and darker ; the upper parts were almost entirely purple ; the caudal is of the last colour, with some marbled spots grey ; the lateral sides are of a rosy red; the long filament of the dorsal, and also the straight rays and their membranes, are of the same colour ; the remainder of the dorsal is white, with purple rounded blotches in considerable number ; the adipose is purple.

These are the only two specimens I have seen ; one was called by a fishmonger *Rock Gurnet*, and the other *Flying Gurnet*. The length of the longest is about 19½ inches, and the other about an inch shorter.

NOTA—Since this was written I have seen another specimen with the long dorsal filament; its colours were not brilliant.

SALMONIDÆ.

"Body covered with scales, head naked; barbels none. Margin of the upper jaw formed by the intermaxillaries laterally. Belly rounded. A small adipose fin behind the dorsal. Pyloric appendages generally numerous, rarely absent. Air-bladder large, simple; pseudobranchiæ present. The ova falls into the cavity of the abdomen before exclusion.

"Fresh waters of the temperate and Arctic regions of the Northern Hemisphere; many species periodically descending to the sea. One genus from New Zealand; two genera pelagic."

Only represented in the Australian seas by a sort of *Retropinna*, found in New Zealand, and, perhaps, a second in New South Wales (Krefft). This almost total absence of a family whose sorts abound in the fresh waters of South America, forms one of the most curious features of Australian ichthyology.

GALAXIDÆ.

"Body naked; barbels none. Margin of the upper jaw chiefly formed by the intermaxillaries, which are short and continued by a thick lip, behind which are the maxillaries. Belly rounded. Adipose fin none; dorsal opposite to anal. Pyloric appendages in small number. Air-bladder large, simple; pseudobranchiæ none. The ova fall into the cavity of the abdomen before exclusion.

"Fresh waters of the temperate zone of the Southern Hemisphere."

GALAXIAS.

Genus formed by Cuvier in his "Règne animal," on a sort brought from Tasmania by Péron and Lesueur. Since then, several other Australian species have been described by Richardson. This form inhabits also the extreme southern portion of the American Continent; and Dr. Gunther unites several of these American sorts with those of Australia, the propriety of which is very unlikely with fresh-water fishes.

It is to be remarked that Cuvier and Valenciennes, in describing their *Galaxias Fasciatus*, state that it is from New Zealand; but that the specimens were given to Messrs. Lesson and Garnot at Conception in Chili, by whalers, who had probably salted them for their food, and this may have led to some confusion.

It is said that some of the American sorts live amongst the seaweeds; the Australian fish inhabit the rivers, and those of the Yarra only extend their *habitat* a little below Melbourne, to the place where the water becomes brackish.

GALAXIAS OCELLATUS.

Galaxias ocellatus, *M'Coy, Inter. Exhibit. Essays*, 1866-67, page 14.

(*Yarra Trout.*)

This is very nearly allied to the Tasmanian sort *Truttaceus*, Cuvier. The body is short and thick for the genus; the head is convex over the eyes; the height of the body is contained five and one-third times in the total length; the head five and two-third times in the same. The dorsal has eleven rays, of which the first one is very short, the next two longer, but much shorter than the others; the caudal is entire and rounded, of fifteen long rays, with two or three shorter on each side; the anal is large, of fifteen rays, of which the first is very short; the ventrals are nearer to the anal than to the pectorals; they are formed of seven rays, and the pectorals of fourteen.

The body is of a light olive green, with the belly grey; it is covered with iridiated, round, ocellated black spots; the sides of the operculum have a golden tinge; the fins are of the general colour of the body; the pectorals are white; the eye is green, speckled with black.

River Yarra. Length, 6 inches.

GALAXIAS VERSICOLOR.

Body oval; head attenuated, and rather pointed. Height four and two-third times in the total leugth; head five and eight-tenths in the same ; eye four and one-third times in the length of the head. The lower jaw is a little louger thau the other; cleft of the mouth rather small ; the maxillary just attaining the vertical from the antorior margin of the eye. The fins are rather large ; the dorsal and anal begin opposite one auother ; the first has nine rays, and the second twelve ; the caudal is rather emar-ginated, with sixteen loug rays ; the pectoral is equal in length o the distance from the posterior margin of the eye to the end of the operculum ; it is formed of thirteen rays ; the ventrals are placed at an equal distance from the pectorals and the anal. The teeth are small on the upper jaw, but much larger, straight, pointed and rather distant one from the other on the lower ; those of the tongue are large, straight, and pointed.

The body is of a fine greeu ; the lower part of the head is grey, and the one of the body of an orauge yellow; the head and body are covered with very minute blue points. The fins are grey, with the rays white; the ventrals are also white; the fluxes form on the middle of the body traces of transverse obscure arched lines ; eye of the colour of gold.

Seen only one specimen, in a marsh near St. Kilda. Length, 5½ inches.

GALAXIAS ATTENUATUS.

Galaxias attenuatus, *Jenyns*, *Zool. Beagle, Fishes*, p. 121 pl. 22, fig. 5.

——————————— *Cuv. & Val.*, vol. xviii., p. 348.

Height of the body seven and six-eighth times in the total length; length of head, six and a-half times in same; eye five times in the length of the head. Body very elongate; rather cylindrical; jaws equal in length; cleft of the mouth rather small, not attaining the vertical from the frout of the eye. The lateral line is well marked and straight. From the beginning of the dorsal to the vertical of the centre of the eye, there is three times the distauce to the beginning of the caudal ; the dorsal has eleven rays; the caudal is emarginate, of sixteen rays; the anal is a little behind the dorsal, and has fourteen rays; the ventrals are inserted a little nearer to the anal than to the pectorals; they are rather large, and formed of seven rays; the pectorals are rather shorter than the ventrals, but longer than the distance from the posterior margin of the eye to the extremity of the operculum. The lower teeth are a little longer than the upper; on the tongue there are three or four large teeth in front, and a line on each side further backwards.

Of a light green colour, with the belly white; the head is purple; all along the body are numerous, minute, black points, disposed in transverse clusters. The fins are white; sometimes there is a transverse green blotch on the middle of the dorsal; base of the anal of the same colour; caudal, is green; the eye, silvery.

Very common in the lower Yarra; it attains 7 and 8 inches in length.

The specimens preserved in liquor, take a general brown appearance.

Nota.—I have given here the number of fin rays that I have usually found; but they seem to be subject to great variation, as in some specimens absolutely similar I find—D. 10. A. 15. In one, the number of the dorsal rays is much less still, (7); but I am not certain that it is entire.

GALAXIAS CYLINDRICUS.

Very nearly allied to *Attenuatus*, but still longer. The height of the body is contained ten and a-half times in the total length; the head is seven and a-quarter times in the same; the eye is four and a-half times in the length of the head. The lower jaw is rather longer than the other. The body is long and cylindrical. The dorsal is formed of ten rays —the first very short; the anal of from twelve to fourteen, the first of which is very short; the caudal is emarginated, of eighteen or nineteen long rays; the ventrals of seven rays; they are placed at an equal distance from the end of the mandibula to the base of the anal. Six very large hooked teeth on the front part of the tongue, and others, on each side, backwards.

The colours are the same as in *Attenuatus*; but when preserved in spirits, they become grey.

Lower Yarra. It attains the same size as the preceding.

GALAXIAS DELICATULUS.

D. 10. A. 19. C. 16.

Form elongate. The height of the body is six and eight-tenth times in the total length (to the middle of the caudal) ; the head is six and two-third times in the same length.

The head is of a light brownish red ; the body of a light yellow green above the lateral line, and is covered with faint, irregular, transversal spots, formed of very fine blue points. The lateral line itself is little marked on its anterior portion, but very distinct and of a yellowish colour on the other part of the body ; below this line, the colour is of a fine opal white ; the eye is silvery. The dorsal fin is of the colour of the back, but its terminal portion is lighter ; the caudal is of a yellowish green ; the pectorals, ventrals, and anal of a transparent white ; the caudal is feebly bilobed.

Yarra River ; 4 inches long.

GALAXIAS AMŒNUS.

D. 12. A. 14.

Form rather elongate. The height is five and two-third times in the total length (to the middle of the caudal) ; head four and one-third times in the same.

Of a light green colour ; a brown spot between the eyes, extending a little behind them ; the back covered with very minute black points, forming very indistinct, transverse, oblique lines, better marked on the posterior part. A considerable number of points, rather larger than the others, are disposed on the body, and form a double, but rather irregular, longitudinal line on the middle of the back. The lower side of the body is covered with the same punctuation and bands as the back, but the belly is of a rather dark blue, silvery colour ; the eye is of a dark green.

Yarra River. From 3 to 4 inches long.

SCOMBRESOCIDÆ.

"Body covered with scales; a series of keeled scales along each side of the belly. Margin of the upper jaw formed by the intermaxillaries mesially, and by the maxillaries laterally. Lower pharyngeals united into a small bone. Dorsal fin opposite the anal, belonging to the caudal portion of the vertebral column. Adipose fin none. Air-bladder generally present, simple, sometimes cellular, without pneumatic duct. Pseudobranchiæ hidden, glandular. Stomach not distinct from the intestine, which is quite straight, without appendages.

"Marine fishes of the temperate and tropical zones, many species entering or inhabiting fresh waters."

HEMIRAMPHUS.

This form may be considered as tropical, one sort alone extending its *habitat* to the Mediterranean Sea; several are found in Australia, but I have only observed one on the shores of Victoria.

HEMIRAMPHUS MELANOCHIR.

Hemiramphus melanochir, *Cuv. & Val.*, vol. xix., p. 41.
——————— intermedius, *Gunther, Catal.*, vol. vi., p. 260.
(The Gar Fish.)

The lower jaw, from its extremity to the point where it meets the upper one, is contained five times in the total length; the height of the body is about sixteen times in the same; and the head, to the extremity of the upper jaw, is five and two-third times in it; the orbit is contained about four times in the same distance. The upper mandible is long and obtuse; the teeth very numerous; the dorsal fin is long, and formed of seventeen rays; the anal has the same form and nineteen rays; the caudal, slightly emarginated, has fifteen long rays and three short ones on each side; the ventrals are rather small, and the pectorals rather long, and formed of thirteen rays.

The upper parts are of an olive grey, with a broad longitudinal, silvery band on the side; lower parts white The inferior mandible is black, with its extremity red; the eye is of a golden colour. Dorsal fin, obscure; caudal of a light olive, having some-times an obscure tinge on its posterior extremity; anal and ventrals of a light olive hue; pectorals in part black; and some-times covered by this colour, but in other specimens it only ex-tends over their posterior part.

This sort was first observed by Messrs. Quoy and Gaimard, at Western Port, during Captain d'Urville's Expedition. It is one of the commonest fishes in the Melbourne Market, during all seasons of the year, and is considered good food. It is equally common in Hobson's Bay as at Western Port, and young speci-mens are often found in the brackish waters of the lower Yarra. It rarely exceeds 14 inches.

A very young specimen, not more than an inch long, had its back green and a brown spot on the top of the head; the longi-tudinal band of the sides was of a most brilliant silver colour; the lower jaw was entirely black.

GONORHYNCHIDÆ.

" Head and body entirely covered with spiny scales; mouth with barbels. Margin of the upper jaw formed by the intermaxillary, which, although short, is continued downwards as a thick lip, situated in front of the maxillary. Adipose fin none; the dorsal fin is opposite to the ventrals, and short like the anal. Stomach simple, without blind sac; py-lorie appendages in small number. Pseudobranchiæ; air-bladder absent. Gill-openings narrow.

"Southern temperate parts of the Atlantic and Pacific; Japan."

GONORHYNCHUS.

The formation of this genus is due to Gronovius *(Zoophylacion)*, but the sort on which it was established was placed by Gmelin and Bloch with *Cyprinus*. It is to Cuvier, in the first edition of the " Règne Animal," that we owe the first modern notion of this fish; but he leaves it with his *Cyprinoidæ*. In the nineteenth volume of the " Histoire des Poissons," Mr. Valenciennes places it in the *Malacopterygii*, between *Chanos* and *Mormyrus*. Dr. Gunther, in his " Catalogue of the Fishes of the British Museum," formed for it a separate family *(Gonorhynchidæ)*, between *Scombresocidæ* and *Osteoglossidæ*. The typical species was from the Cape of Good Hope, but Dr. Richardson described and figured a second one from New Zealand and Western Australia, under the name of *Rynchana Greyii (Erebus* and *Terror)*. I believe, also, that my genus *Gnathendalia* " Memoire sur les Poissons de l'Afrique Australe," p. 56, comes very near to this genus, which was unknown to me at the time; but I have not the specimens with me; it was formed on a small fish I found in great numbers near the Moravian Mission of Gnadenthal, in the Cape of Good Hope colony. I considered it also to belong to the *Cyprinidæ*. In reference to this fish I beg to add, that it is on this subject that Dr. Gunther quotes, for the first time in 1868, my paper on the fishes of South Africa, written by me in 1858, and published in 1861, and he does it, of course, in an abusive way. Considering this sort as a *Cyprinidæ*, I tried, in a short notice, to distinguish it from the other groups then known. He pretends not to perceive that it is by a misprint that the river, which feeds it, is called Genadendal; " evidently,' says he, " meaning the well known Gnadenthal." It is likely that this locality is better known to me who have been there several times, than to Dr. Gunther; and the name given to the fish is a sufficient proof that the mistake belongs to the printer. As to the name itself, I gave it the French pronunciation in a French work. I must also add, that in the excellent map of South Africa, published by Henry Hall, the mountains where it is situated are called Geuadendal. No one, of course, expects any indulgence from Dr. Gunther on icthyological subjects, but on geographical ones he might be more lenient, as he could hardly attribute to others, the often repeated words *matta grosso,* river *capin,* &c., which have no meaning whatever, and are intended for *matto grosso* (great forest), *rio capim* (grass river), &c. All this could only show that I do not known German, nor Dr. Gunther Portuguese; and that nobody, not even the learned doctor, can be universal.

GONORHYNCHUS GREYI.

Rynehana greyi, *Richard., Erebus and Terror, Fishes,* p. 44, pl. 29, figs. 1-6.

Gonorhynchus greyi, *Cuv. & Val.,* vol. xix., p. 212.

(The Sand Eel.)

The upper parts of a light lilac, sometimes with marmorated tinges rather more obscure on the back; lower parts white; muzzle and the lower surface of the head pink; sides of the head of a golden tinge; all the fins of a yellowish white; dorsal with a large black spot near the end, the extreme edge remaining white; caudal with a broad black transverse band near its extremity; anal and ventrals with their end black; the eye is sometimes silvery, sometimes golden. A part of this organ is covered on each side by a membrane; the lower and pectoral fins have sometimes a blue tinge.

This fish is most remarkable by its general resemblance to a saurian reptile of the genus *Scincus.* It is often brought in all seasons to the Melbourne Market, where it is esteemed good for the table. It is found in clear quiet water, with a sandy bottom, and, according to the fishermen, it digs holes in the sand. The usual length is from eight to twelve inches; the largest specimen I have seen was a little under fourteen, and the smallest four inches and a quarter; I found this entire in a small shark.

Dr. Gunther unites the Australian sort with the one from the Cape of Good Hope, and also with another from Japan. To characterize this curious assemblage, he says (*Catalogue,* vol. vii., p. 374), " from an examination of these specimens I have arrived at the conclusion, that this species varies considerably in the depth of the body, and especially that young examples, are constantly less elongate than the adult." Having examined several hundred specimens in Melbourne, I may add, that there is no variation whatever in the proportions of the Australian specimens, and that the learned doctor might have come to a more simple and natural conclusion, if he had admitted that he was uniting, under the same name, several very distinct species.

OSTEOGLOSSIDÆ

" Body covered with large hard scales, composed of pieces like mosaic ; head scaleless, its integuments nearly entirely replaced by bone ; lateral line composed of wide openings of the mucus-duct. Margin of the upper jaw formed by the intermaxillaries mesially, and by the maxillaries laterally. The dorsal fin belongs to the caudal portion of the vertebral column, is opposite and very similar to the anal fin ; both approximate to the rounded caudal—with which they are abnormally confluent. Gill-openings wide ; pseudobranchiæ none ; air-bladder simple or cellular. Stomach without cæcal sac ; pyloric appendages two.

" Large fresh-water fishes of the tropics."

The genus *Osteoglossus*, which composes this family, was established by Vandelli, on a sort found in the Amazon River, and which I have also observed there ; another species inhabits Borneo and Sumatra ; and a third (Leichardti) has been found in Queensland, and described by Dr. Gunther. These are all tropical fishes, and it is not likely that this form will ever be found in the southern parts of Australia.

CLUPEIDÆ.

" Body covered with scales ; head naked ; barbels none. Abdomen frequently compressed into a serrated edge. Margin of the upper jaw formed by the intermaxillaries mesially and by the maxillaries laterally ; maxillaries composed of three, sometimes movable, pieces. Opercular apparatus complete. Adipose fin none. Dorsal not elongate; anal sometimes very long. Stomach with a blind sac; pyloric appendages numerous. Gill apparatus much developed, the gill-openings being generally very wide. Pseudobranchiæ large, except in Megalops. Air-bladder more or less simple.

" Inhabitants of all seas, many species entering fresh waters."

CHATOESSUS.

Formed by Valenciennes, on a small group of fishes, generally from the fresh waters of America and India, and often remarkable by the lowest ray of their dorsal being prolongated in a long filament.

CHATOESSUS EREBI.

Chatoessus Erebi, *Gunther, Cat. British Musuem,* vol. vii., page 207.

————— Comæ, *Richard., Erebus and Terror,* p. 61, pl. 38.

Clupea Thrissa (Kome) *Russel, Fishes, Corom.* ii., p. 76, pl. 196.

Richardson had considered this fish as belonging to the *Kome* of Russell, but Dr. Gunther has found it was distinct.

It is of a light silvery grey on the upper parts, with the edge of the scales rather obscure ; this is caused by the presence of numerous and very small black points; the lower parts are very brilliant, silvery, and iridated ; the top of the head is purple ; the dorsal of a fine grey, the others blueish; ventrals white ; the caudal bordered with an obscure tinge ; the sides of the head are rather yellow, as are also the eyes.

Very scarce in the Melbourne Market, and being very much

esteemed as food, it sells at a high price; I cannot discover if it has a common name.

The two or three specimens, I have seen, were found after very bad weather.

It appears also to be found in fresh water, being noticed by Blandowski amongst the sorts of the Murray River. He says the natives call it *Manur*; and adds, " leaps frequently out of the water, and is easily caught by its elongated ray in thin fine nets, laid by the natives horizontally on the water. The fish gets entangled in the twine, and cannot escape. It is most numerous in the Darling, but is also found above and below the junction of the Murray and Darling Rivers. In June and July it is considered a delicacy by the natives, and forms their principle food during these two months. The young women are not permitted to eat them, from a belief, that if they did all the fish in the river would die; but in reality, because it is thought to be an aphrodisiac, this fish being very fat and nourishing. It is also placed on the tops of graves, to point out the direction in which he lives who caused the death of the inmate; therefore this fish is much esteemed."

It is from ten to fourteen inches long.

I have not yet been able to obtain any specimens from the fresh waters, and I cannot say if it belongs to the sort which inhabits Hobson's Bay. The largest I have seen of the latter is thirteen inches long.

I find in the " Industrial Progress of New South Wales," 1871, page 770, that *Chateossus Erebi* is found in the north Australian rivers, the Murray, Clarence, Burnett, Fitzroy, &c., and that according to Mr. Masters, it is called *Bony Bream* by the Burnett settlers.

ENGRAULIS.

In following Dr. Gunther's division of this genus, this sort has to be placed amongst those that have none of their pectoral rays prolonged; the teeth in the jaws about equal in size; the origin of the dorsal fin in advance of that of the anal, and teeth in both jaws.

The known sorts are not numerous. All have very numerous rays to the anal.

ENGRAULIS ANTARCTICUS.

(*White Bait.*)

The height of body seven and one-quarter times in the total length; head four and one-quarter in the same; eye three and one-fifth in length of head; the muzzle considerably longer than the mandibula, and embracing it; the upper jaw presents a line of very minute and equal teeth, and the lower one has a similar line of still smaller ones. The dorsal is inserted at equal distance from the snout and the base of the caudal, it is as high as the body; of fifteen rays, the first much shorter than the others, but the second and fifth rather longer than the following; caudal strongly bifurcated; the lateral rays being about one-third longer than the height of the body; it is formed with twenty long rays, and five or six shorter ones on each side; anal rather lower than the dorsal, having twelve rays of which the first is short. From the posterior end of the anal the distance to the lateral root of the caudal is contained three times in the distance from its beginning to the end of the mandibula, and twice from the superior root of the caudal to the anterior one of the dorsal; the ventrals are rather smaller than the pectorals, and are formed of only one simple ray, and five branched ones; they are placed a little in advance of the dorsal; the pectorals are formed of fifteen rays.

The colour of the upper parts is of a light greyish green, with purple tinges; the head is brown; the lower parts are very silvery; there is a narrow, yellow, longitudinal streak from the upper part of the operculum to the base of the caudal, and below this extends a broad longitudinal, silvery, and very brilliant band, having sometimes a blue tinge; the operculum and throat are very iridescent; the fins are diaphanous; the caudal is yellow at its base, and obscure towards the extremity; eye silvery. After having been in the liquor the fish appears very silvery, with the upper parts of a dark blue.

Very common on the Melbourne Market during the whole year.

Dr. Gunther states that the common European anchovy *Engraulis Encrasicholus* is found in Australia; but this is only said to satisfy his usual tendency to unite, under the same species, fishes from all parts of the globe, and as he himself finds that Australian specimens present constant differential characters in the number of the rays, he forms with them a *named variety* (Antipodum). In following out this system, as the same ichthyologist has, also, in this genus *named Subgenera*, a single specimen would have two generic and two specific names, which would, I should think, be sufficient to disgust the most fervent student from zoological study.

In all cases *Antareticus* cannot be *Antipodum*, as Dr. Gunther says that it has no teeth at the lower jaw, nor a silvery band along the sides.

CLUPEA SAGAX.

Clupea sagax, *Jenyns, Beagle Fishes*, p. 134.
——————— *Gunther, Catal.*, vol. vii., p 443.
Alausa melanosticta, *Cuv. & Val.*, xx. p. 444.

Professor M'Coy has published the following interesting account of this fish " Intercolonial Exhibition," 1866-67 : " Of the family *Clupeidæ*, or herrings, there is only one of much importance in our seas. A specimen of this was first brought to me in August, 1864, from a small shoal then seen for the first time in Hobson's Bay, and quite unknown to the fishermen. It was supposed by the sender to be the *Yarra Herring*, or *Grayling*, gone out to sea; but on examination I found it was the *Clupea Melanosticta* of Temmink, or the species of *Pilchard*, so abundant on the shores of Japan. In the same month, in the succeeding year, they appeared in great abundance in the Bay, and were caught by thousands for the market. After remaining for a few weeks they disappeared until the same time in 1866, when they arrived in such countless thousands, that carts were filled with them by simply dipping them out of the sea with large baskets. Hundreds of tons of them were sent up the country to the inland markets, and through the city, for several weeks, they were sold for a few pence the bucketful while the captains of the ships entering the Bay reported having passed through closely packed shoals of them for miles. They may be now probably expected every year as a very important addition to the food fishes of the country. I imagine some alteration in the bed of the sea, from the earthquake disturbances north of Australia, about that time, may have facilitated or induced the extension of the shoals in such unusual quanties from Japan to our coasts. Duperrey (or Lesson and Garnot) found it in New Zealand, and Cuvier and Valenciennes referred their specimen to the genus *Alausa*. I find, however, that the authors of the "Histoire des Poissons" were in error, and Temmink in the right,—the former assigning five, and the latter seven gill-rays; and it has also a row of teeth on the tongue, as was correctly stated by Temmink, and erroneously denied by Cuvier and Valenciennes. The fish is therefore a *Meletta*, and not an *Alausa*, and should be referred to as the *Meletta Melanosticta* (Tem.)"

All that the Professor says about the extraordinary occurrence of the shoals of the fish is perfectly correct, and they have since that time made their appearance every year; but in 1871 a few only began to be seen on the 16th of November, and they became more abundant in December and January following, but at all times in much less numbers than those of other years, but I cannot agree with Professor M'Coy about the name of this fish, and it is impossible for me to see any teeth on its tongue; I therefore think that its genus was well named by Cuvier and Valenciennes. That it is not the *Melanosticta* of Schleg. is still more evident, as that sort has sixteen or seventeen rays to its anal, while the Australian fish has eighteen, and this is one of the characters of *Sagax*, which has also the round black spots on the sides. Dr. Gunther has well described and distinguished these two sorts, and if Professor M'Coy has not been mistaken in regard to the existence of lingual teeth, it would show that the two sorts appear in the waters of the southern parts of Australia.

According to Dr. Gunther, *Clupea Sagax* inhabits the western coast of America, from California to Chili, Japan, and New Zealand.

MELETTA.

This genus of Cuvier and Valenciennes, formed on sorts who have only teeth on the tongue, and none on the jaws, is not admitted by Dr. Gunther, who considers the dentition in this group of fishes as too rudimental to be taken as a generic character; but at the same time he takes it as his principal character of the division of the genus. If it is constant enough to furnish a safe guide for the recognition of the species, it seems difficult to understand how it has no generic value.

In the little fish I mention the upper jaw is shorter than the lower one; the abdomen is serrated from below the pectorals, or even a little in advance of their insertion; the anal fin has twenty rays; no teeth are visible on the jaws, nor on the palate, but some exist on the tongue; dorsal inserted a little behind the ventrals, which are well developed. A well-defined broad, silvery, longitudinal stripe runs on the sides.

The assemblage of these characters would place this sort in Dr. Gunther's genus, *Clupea;* but the situation of the dorsal fin in respect to the ventrals, is in opposition to all he says on this subject in his descriptions; Cuvier and Valenciennes, on the contrary, state, in speaking of *Meletta Vulgaris,* that the ventrals are rather in advance of the dorsal.

MELETTA NOVÆ-HOLLANDÆ.

Meletta Novæ-hollandiæ, *Cuv. & Val.*, vol. xx., p. 376.

(*The Smelt.*)

Height four and a-half times in the total length; head five and a-half in the same; eye as long as the snout, and contained three and a-half times in the head; the lower jaw longer than the upper; mouth extensible; no teeth on the palate; maxillary extending to below the front edge of the eye; body compressed; forty-six scales on the longitudinal line; sixteen rays to the dorsal; twenty to the anal; the caudal has nineteen rays, with five short ones on each side; the pectorals fourteen rays. The height of the first ray of the dorsal is equal to the distance from the end of the snout to the anterior edge of the eye; the other rays go on decreasing as they extend backwards, and the last are only one-half of the height of the first; the caudal is very strongly bifurcated, being twice as long on its sides as at its centre; the ventrals are as long as the dorsal, and a little shorter than the pectorals.

The general colour is of a light green, with a broad, well-marked, silvery streak on each side; the belly is white; the operculum and throat are silvery and iridescent; the dorsal and caudal are yellow, and the other fins translucid; the eye silvery.

This little fish is very abundant at times in the Melbourne Market; its length is about four inches.

The specimens studied by the French ichthyologists were brought from Sydney by Quoy and Gaymard, and I find in Mr. Gerard Krefft's very interesting "Report on Australian Vertebrata," (Intercolonial Exhibition, 1870), that at Sydney it bears the vernacular name of *Sprat*.

Nota.—There is no doubt that this is the *Meletta Novæ-Hollandæ* of Cuvier and Valenciennes, but it is very doubtful if it is the *Clupea Novæ-Hollandiæ* of Dr. Gunther, as this very accurate author not only describes the insertion of the ventrals as being below the anterior half of the dorsal fin; but also places it amongst the sorts having minute teeth on the palate.

SYMBRANCHIDÆ.

" Body elongate, naked or covered with minute scales; barbels none. Margin of the upper jaw formed by the intermaxillaries only, the well-developed maxillaries lying behind and parallel to them. Paired fins none. Vertical fins rudimentary, reduced to more or less distinct cutaneous folds. Vent situated at a great distance behind the head. Gill-openings confluent into one slit, situated on the ventral surface. Air-bladder none. Stomach cæcal sac or pyloric appendages. Ovaries with oviducts.

" Fresh waters and coasts of tropical America and Asia. Coasts of Western Australia and Tasmania."

Only represented in the Australia waters by *Chilobranchus Dor salis*, Richardson ; which I have not seen.

MURAENIDÆ.

"Body elongate, eylindrical or band shaped, naked or with rudimentary seales. Vent situated at a great distanee from the head. Ventral fin none. Vertieal fins, if present, eonfluent, or separated by the projeeting tip of the tail. Sides of the upper jaw formed by the tooth-bearing maxillaries, the fore part by the intermaxillary, whieh is more or less coaleseent with the vomer and ethmoid. Humeral arch not attached to the skull. Stomaeh with a blind sae; no pyloric appendages. Organs of reproduetion without efferent ducts.

"Inhabitants of the fresh waters and seas of the temperate and tropical regions."

ANGUILLA.

Eels, which constitnte this gonns, soem to be gonerally fonnd in the frosh waters of almost all climatos; bnt more particnlarly in those of the temperato conntrios.

The first notice of an eel in the New Zcaland-rivers was dne to J. E. Gray, in the appondico to Dioffonbach's travels to that island.

Dr. Richardson described, in 1848, under the name of *Australis*, another sort from Tasmania, which is said also to be fonnd in New Zcaland. In the fishes of the *Erebus* and *Terror*, he describes two other sorts, ono *Auecklandi*, from the Anckland Islands; and another, *Labrosa*, of which he did not know the precise locality. This latter is of a remarkable form, having its dorsal fin commencing rather noarer to the gill-opening than to the anns, and may very well be an inhabitant of the soa. The others are all from fresh waters. They may be distinguised thus ;—

(*A.*) Beginning of the dorsal considerably before the anus.

(*a.*) At about two inches, in a specimen of twenty inches long—*Dieffenbachii.*

(*b.*) At one inch, on a specimen of seventeen inches long—*Aucklandi.*

(*B.*) Beginning of the dorsal rather before the anus—*Australis.*

In the latter the pectorals are very small, and are much larger in *Aucklandi.* I must add that Dr. Gunther considers *Dieffenbachii* as the same as the European *Latirostris*; but it is evident that either this zoologist is mistaken, or that this eel has been imported to New Zealand, as several other European fishes have been to Australia.

Eels seem to extend over all the antarctic regions, and in my notice of the fishes of the Cape of Good Hope I mentioned a sort found in that part of South Africa.

ANGUILLA AUSTRALIS.

Anguilla Australis, *Richard., Zool. Trans.*, vol. iii., p. 157,
——————— *Richard., Erebus* and *Terror, Fishes,*
vol. i., p. 112, pl. 45.

THE EEL.

This is the common eel of the Yarra, and of several other streams of Victoria and Tasmania; but it appears doubtful whether it extends to New Zealand. Dr. Richardson has already pointed out some slight differences between the specimens from each locality.　.

This eel, though covered with minute scales, arranged in a lattice work way, is very smooth and slippery. The pectorals are not longer than the cleft of the mouth.

Its colours are very changeable; generally it is of a dark green, with the lower parts lighter and grey; sometimes it shows faint transverse spots or bands of a more obscure tinge. The dorsal and anal are often in a great part yellow.

It attains large dimensions.

ANGUILLA REINHARDTII.

Anguilla Reinhardtii, *Gunther*, vol. viii., p. 27.
——————— *Steindachner* (Gunther), *Ak Wiss. Wien,* 1867.

Very much like *Australis*, and generally confounded with it by the fishmongers. The differences consist in the following :— 1st, the body is thicker. 2nd, the tail is broader at its end. 3rd, the skin is much more rough. 4th, the pectorals are considerably larger, and the cleft of the mouth is not more than two-thirds their length. 5th. the dorsal begins on, or a little below the line of the anal, but there is sometimes a little difficulty, with all these fishes, to ascertain correctly where a fin begins. 6th, the teeth are shorter, thicker, and more blunt, particularly those situated towards the interior of the mouth. The lips are broader, more fleshy, and extend laterally ; the colour is almost black, with the lower parts of a dark grey ; the lips are of a reddish pink, and the eye is yellow with orange tinges.

From Western Port, and, I believe, also from the Mordialloc river. Average size from twenty to twenty-two inches.

CONGER.

Genus formed by Cuvier, but now restricted to three or four sorts, characterised by the absence of scales ; the dorsal fin commencing behind the base of the pectorals, and the jaws armed with an external series of closely set teeth.

CONGER WILSONI.

Gymnothorax wilsoni ? *Bloch ; Schneid.*, p. 529.

This sort attains very large dimensions, and its average size is from four to five feet long. It is sometimes found in Hobson's Bay, but appears to be much more frequent near Hobart Town, being often brought salted from that town to the Melbourne Market. The height is about twenty times in the length, and the distance from the anterior end to the opening of the gill is contained about eight times in the same. The head is elongate ; the teeth are all similar ; they are elongate, straight, blunt, and placed very near one another ; they form a small cluster in front of the jaws, the anterior ones being smaller than those placed backwards. Inside of this line of teeth, there is a sharp, crenulated and ossified ridge. The tongue is smooth. The lateral line is well marked to the end of the body ; it is rather curved over the pectorals, and, on the dry specimens, appears formed of a succession of notches. The dorsal fin begins behind the pectoral, at about a distance, from the end of this fin, equal to its own heighth; it is low, but extends all along the back, and has about three hundred and twenty rays, those of the posterior part being so crowded as to make it almost impossible to be accurately counted; the beginning of the anterior portion of the dorsal has no rays. The anal begins at a little before the half of the length of the body; it is formed of about two hundred and sixty rays, but these are subject to the same observation as the last ones of the dorsal. The pectorals are of about one-fourth of the length of the head, and formed of fifteen rays.

The general colour is of a shining brownish black, which degenerates in a greyish white on the belly. The lateral line is black, and there are large, marbled, pinkish white spots on the posterior parts of the body.

I have never heard of any other *Conger* being found in the southern part of Australia, and I do not know on what foundation it is stated that . *Conger Vulgaris* inhabits the coast of Tasmania.

CONGROMURÆNA.

Dr. Kaup separates from *Conger* this and some other sorts. The Australian fish is remarkable by its dentition. In this, the anterior teeth of the upper jaw are short, conic, and very acute; they are disposed in a cluster of a rather triangular form. On each side, behind them extend two rows of rounded molar teeth, and on the vomer are two other rows of the same form, but larger. There are also teeth on the palatines, but smaller, and disposed in four rows; those of the lower jaw are similar to those of the palatines. The anterior nostril has the form of a short tube, placed under the end of the snout; the tongue is smooth. The lower jaw is shorter than the upper one, and the cleft of the mouth extends to the centre of the eye; this latter is very large.

CONGROMURÆNA HABENATA.

Congrus Habenatus, *Richard., Erebus* and *Terror, Fishes.* p. 109, pl. 1., figs. 1-5.

The dorsal begins a little behind the insertion of the pectorals; it is formed of about one hundred and eighty rays, extends all round the posterior part of the body, and joins the anal, which is formed of about one hundred and twenty rays.

The height of the body is about eighteen times in its length; the muscular flakes are very visible, and form arched lines all along the body.

The upper parts of the body are of an olive green, with the belly of a blueish white; the sides are silvery, and the head is purple; the fins are olive green, the dorsal and anal having a black border.

I believe this sort to be the *Habenatus* of Richardson, and that the slight differences in the disposition of the teeth are caused by age, as his specimens seem to have been older than mine.

Total length ten inches.

Only seen once in the Melbourne Market, in the month of September. Dr. Richardson's specimen was from New Zealand.

PEGASIDÆ.

"Body entirely covered with bony plates, anchylosed on the trunk, and movable on the tail. Barbels none. The margin of the upper jaw is formed by the intermaxillaires and their eutaneous prolongation, which extends downwards to the extremity of the maxillaries. Gill-cover formed by a large plate, homologous to the operculum, præoperculum, and suboperculum; interoperculum a long fine bone, hidden below the gill-plate. One rudimentary branchiostegal. The gill-plate is united with the isthmus by a narrow membrane; gill-opening narrow in front of the base of the pectoral fin. Gills four, lamellated. Pseudobranchiæ and air-bladder absent; one short dorsal and anal fin, opposite to each other. Ventral fins present. Ovarian sacs closed. Indian Ocean and Australian seas."

Two sorts of *Pegasus,—Natans* and *Lancifer*, are found in Australia: the first in Queensland, and the second on the coast of Tasmania; but I have not yet seen either.

Order V.   LOPHOBRANCHII.

"The Gills are not laminated, but composed of rounded lobes, attached to the branchial arches. Gill-cover reduced to a large simple plate. Air-bladder simple, without pneumatic duct. A dernal skeleton, composed of numerous pieces arranged in segments, replaces more or less soft integuments. Muscular system not much developed. Snout produced. Mouth terminal, small, toothless, formed as in Acanthopterygians."

SYNGNATHIDÆ.

"Gill-openings reduced to a very small opening near the upper posterior angle of the gill-cover. One soft dorsal fin; no ventrals, and sometimes one or more of the other fins also absent.

"Chiefly marine fishes, occurring in all parts of the tropical and temperate regions; many species entering fresh waters."

HIPPOCAMPUS.

This name was given by Dr. Leach to the fish commonly known as *Sea Horse*, and has been adopted by all authors. It has since been restricted, and Dr. Gunther gives the genus the following characters:—"Trunk compressed, more or less elevated, composed of from ten to twelve rings; shields with more or less prominent tubercles or spines; occiput compressed into a crest, terminating at its superoposterior corner into a prominent knob (coronet). Supraorbital, temporal, and humeral regions, with prominences ; tail prehensible, finless ; pectoral fins. The males carry the eggs in a sac at the base of the tail, opening near the vent.

" Inhabitants of all seas of the temperate and tropical regions. they are pelagic fishes, which attach themselve to seaweeds, or other floating substances, and are liable to be carried by currents to great distances, consequently some specimens are spread over different parts of the globe. The species are difficult to distinguish, on account of the great amount of variation, to which the development of the tubercles, shape of shields, and length of snout, are subject ; the number of dorsal rays appear to be very constant."

All this is perfectly exact ; but I am not certain that the length of the snout, and form of the body shields, does vary so considerably in the same sort, at least I have seen no example of it, and the presence of filaments is, I believe, only to be observed in the males of a few sorts, except in *Phyllopteryx*, where they are constant in both sexes.

HIPPOCAMPUS NOVÆ-HOLLANDIÆ.

Hip. Novæ Hollandiæ, *Sitzgsber, Ak. Wiss. Wien.*, 1866 (Dr. Gunther)
——————————— *Gunther, Catal.*, vol. viii., p. 201.

Dorsal fins with seventeen rays ; the occipital coronet forms a little crown of five branches, leaving like a small cratere between them.

The body is yellow, covered with small red spots ; dorsal fin with a longitudinal brown narrow band ; the rays marbled brown and white ; back generally more or less marbled with brown.

HIPPOCAMPUS TRISTIS.

Same form as the preceding, but the tail shorter; dorsal fin with fourteen rays ; the shields of the body covered with transverse stripes ; the anterior abdominal crest of the body divided in points generally bifid.

Dorsal fin with a narrow longitudinal brown band, and the rays marbled with the same colour. No filaments,

One specimen.

HIPPOCAMPUS BREVICEPS

Hip. Breviceps, *Peters, Monatsber., Berlin,.* 1869, p. 710.

———————*Gunther, Catal.,* vol. viii., p. 200.

Dorsal fins with twenty two rays ; the tubercles are strong. The colour, during life, is of a light grey, with the inner parts yellow ; these are covered with small, dark, red dots ; the other parts of the body present numerous white spots, surrounded by a black circle ; the tail is ringed with yellow and brown ; the eye is yellow.

The male has numerous filaments on the upper part of the head and back they are simple, but inserted two by two ; their colour is black, and some of them are ended by a small yellow brush.   The egg pouch is of a fleshy pink, edged anteriorly with black.

Seen several specimens, but never over one inch long, when curled up.

NOTA.—Dr. Kaup's fig. 5, pl. 1, *Lophob.,* (*Hip. Japonicus*), has a remarkable resemblance with this sort.

PHYLLOPTERYX.

Formed by Dr. Kaup on some large Australian sorts, very remarkable by the long filaments that adorn their body.

PHYLLOPTERYX FOLIATUS.

Syngnathus Foliatus, *Shaw, Gen. Zool.,* vol. v., p. 456, pl. 180

——————— Tæniopterus, *Lacep. Ann. Mus.,* vol. iv, pl. 58

This singular fish is said by the fishermen to be scarce ; one of them told me that he had once found eighteen or twenty pairs in his net, but had often been several years without finding a single specimen.   I have not yet seen it alive, but according to a drawing made by Mr. Angus, and published by Dr. Gunther, " Proc. Zoological Society," 1865, its colours seem very beautiful ; but they are subject to considerable variations ; in some large specimens that I have just received from Hobart Town, through Mr. Lavington Roope, and which, having been only a few days in liquor, still maintain much of their brillancy, I find that the fish is of a fine carmine colour, covered with numerous oscellated white spots, which extend on the head, the snout, and the upper side of the tail; the anterior edge of the body is of a fine yellow ; the snout, back, and upper parts of the body are of a dark violet carmine ; the lower side of the tail is of a fine reddish brown ; the transverse violet bands of the anterior part of the body are still visible ; the fins are pink, with a large rounded black spot on the dorsal, which extends nearly to the edge ; the filaments are of a dark brown ; the operculum, and præopereulum are covered with fine radiated striæ.

It bears at Hobart Town the name of *Sea Dragon*.

SYNGNATHUS.

This genus used to contain the entire family ; but it has been very much restricted by Dr. Kaup : Dr. Gunther characterizes it thus—" Body with the ridges more or less distinct; the dorsal edge of the trunk not being continuous with that of the tail ; pectoral fins well developed ; caudal present ; dorsal fin opposite or near to vent,; humeral bones firmly united into the *breast ring ;* male with an egg pouch on the tail, the eggs being covered by cutaneous folds."

Inhabiting all the seas of the temperate and tropical regions.

SYNGNATHUS SEMISTRIATUS.

Syngnathus Semistriatus ? *Kaup*; *Loph.*, p. 48.

——————— Semifsaciatus ? *Gunther*, *Catal.*, vol. VIII, p. 462.

Lateral line interrupted ; the trunk is very arched, and contained four and a-half times in its length ; the snout, from its extremity to the anterior edge of the eye, is equal to the distance from the posterior edge of the eye to the end of the third body ring ; it is long, almost cylindrical, rather turned up ; head without ridges, but covered with strong convergent striæ ; these cover also the shields of the body. The head is contained one and two-third times in the trunk, and this, including the head, is one and one-third in the tail ; anus under the first third of the length of the dorsal ; this is large and formed of thirty-eight rays ; caudal fin very small as are also the pectorals ; the rings of the trunk number twenty and those of the tail forty-eight to fifty.

The general colour is of a light green, with the lower side of the head and the belly of a fine orange yellow; on the snout there are two white longitudinal stripes, edged with black, one placed laterally, and extending over the entire length; and the other on the upper part, and only on the second half of the snout; on the head there are also two similar stripes, one arched and extending from the posterior edge of the eye to the end of the operculum, on the upper part of the head, and the other similar but broader, and almost straight, extending on the side, in continuation to the one of the snout; the upper one extends on the back to the end of the trunk; below are numerous, very small, rounded white spots, surrounded by a black circle (they are more visible on the dried than on the living specimens); the dorsal has a greenish tinge; the eye is white, with a green mark on its upper edge.

I have only seen one specimen, in the month of September, it was eight and a-half inches long.

Nota.—I believe this to be the *Semistriatus* of Kaup; but the snout seems considerably longer.

UROCAMPUS.

Formed by Dr. Gunther on the following characters :—" Body elongate, compressed, with distinct longitudinal ridges; the upper edge of the trunk continuous with that of the tail; lateral line continuous with the lower caudal edge; tail elongate, quadrangular, tapering; pectoral and caudal fins developed; the dorsal is placed entirely on the tail, at a great distance behind the vent."

The only sort known is from Manchuria, but the Australian fish I here describe appears to me to belong to this genus.

UROCAMPUS CARINIROSTRIS.

Snout turned rather upwards, very short, being contained once and a-half in the diameter of the eye, and nearly three times in the length of the head; it is not abruptly separated from the forehead, and goes slanting to its extremity; the supraorbital ridges are very strong, and sometimes converge in front to form the medium ridge of the snout; in other specimens there is between them a rounded sharp ridge; there is a short spine at the anterior angle of the eye; the eyes are very prominent;

occiput and muchal shields with ridges ; operculum covered with strong radiated striæ, and almost carinated ; the pectorals are not much longer than the orbit, and not quite one-half of one of the body shields ; the snout is contained about seven times in the trunk ; the distance from the anus to the beginning of the dorsal is about equal to one-half its distance to the end of the snout; the body has three ridges, the upper one much more marked than the others ; the central one ending at the base of the tail ; each shield has two small longitudinal ridges, and is perpendicularly striated ; the osseous rings number nine on the body, seven more on the tail before the dorsal, which begins on the seventeenth, and extends over the three following; behind these are forty-five or forty-six others ; the caudal is very minute ; no anal; the tail is tapering and very thin, its ridges are much less marked than those of the body.

The general colour is a light green, with dark spots corresponding to the centre of the body rings ; eye of a golden hue. There is a rather indistinct black stripe on the side of the snout.

The length of my largest specimen is three and a-half inches. I have seen it rather commonly in the months of January and February ; taken with shrimps. Its motions are very active.

STIGMATOPHORA.

The most apparent characters of this genus of Dr. Kaup is the absence of a caudal fin, and the tail going tapering to its end.

Dr. Gunther characterizes it as follows :—" Body depressed, with the ridges obsolete, those of the trunk being continuous with those of the tail; shields covered with soft skin ; pectoral fin developed ; caudal absent; tail tapering to a very fine point ; dorsal very long; males with a caudal pouch, formed by cutaneous folds," Australia.

All this applies exactly to the species I have under examination, with the exception of the soft skin covering the shields ; I find them similar to the other *Syngnathidæ*.

STIGMATAPHORA NIGRA.

Stigmataphora Nigra., *Kaup, Lophob.*, p. 53.
——————————— *Gunther, Catal.*, vol. viii., p. 190.

The general form is very slender ; the height of the body being, in most specimens, contained about twenty-four times in the

total length, but in some the abdomen is rather inflated ; the snout
is long, slender, and nearly equal in all its length, except at its
extremity, where it is strongly turned upwards ; from the end of
the snout to the anterior edge of the eye, the distance is equal
to that between the posterior edge of that organ and the end of
the third segment of the body ; the head is contained a little
over six times in the total length, and the snout about ten times
in the same ; it is one and one-third longer than the remainder of
the head, and has some longitudinal ridges on its upper part.
Seen from the upper surface, the posterior edges of the snout
form on each side a point over the anterior edge of the eye,
which is deeply sunken ; the mouth is directed upwards ; the
operculum has a longitudinal ridge running rather obliquely ;
dorsal very long ; no caudal ; the pectorals are very short ; I
cannot distinguish any anal, and I find at its place the long cutaneous egg pouch in the males, and nothing in the others ; but as
all authors say they have one, it is likely that it exists,
though I could not discern it. The anal is below the
eighteenth segment of the body. I only find forty-two or
forty-three body-rings, but those of the posterior part of
the tail are so exceedingly minute as to leave some doubt in
this respect ; the body is depressed below, which gives
its section a triangular appearance; the body-ridges extend, on a
straight line, to the extremity of the tail ; the shields are finely
punctured, and perpendicularly striated ; the tail terminates
generally in a fine point, but in some specimens it is rather
blunt ; the operculum presents no ridge.

Colour of a light green ; the snout generally bears faint traces
of transverse bands rather darker than the ground colour ; the
whole body is covered with very minute red dots ; the edge of the
rings are rather dark ; in some specimens the longitudinal ridges
are of an orange red colour ; eyes green, strewed with black.

I have seen numerous specimens, caught in February with
shrimps ; their length varies from two to near four inches.

Nota. — Though this description does not in all points
correspond to *Nigra*, I believe that my specimens belong to
that sort.

Amongst the specimens of the *Nigra* I observe several similar to the others, but with enormous globular eyes; these are very prominent. I could not, up to the present, ascertain if they form a particular species.

Order VI. PLECTOGNATHI.

"Teleosteous fishes with rough scales, or with ossifications of the cutis in the form of scutes or spines; skin sometimes entirely naked. Skeleton incompletely ossified, with the vertebræ in small number. Gills pectinate; a narrow gill-opening in front of the pectoral fins. Mouth narrow; the bones of the upper jaw generally firmly united. A soft dorsal fin, belonging to the caudal portion of the vertical column, opposite to the anal; sometimes elements of a spinous dorsal besides. Ventral fins none, or reduced to spines. Air-bladder without pneumatic duct. Nearly all are marine fishes."

SCLERODERMI.

"Snout somewhat produced; jaws armed with distinct teeth in small number; skin with scutes or rough. The elements of a spinous dorsal and ventral fins generally present. Marine fishes of the temperate or tropical regions."

MONACANTHUS.

These fish being almost all confined to the tropical seas of the world it is remarkable to find that a considerable number of sorts have been observed in the most southern parts of Australia, but they only appear in the Straits of Bass in the warm months of the year (November, December, January, and February). They are not used for food, and the fishermen are in the habit of throwing them away whenever they catch them. It is probably due to this circumstance that I have yet only been able to obtain three of these sorts. They are all known under the name of *Leather Jackets*.

MONACANTHUS PERONII.

Monacanthus Peronii, *Hollard, Ann. Sc. Nat.*, 1854, vol. XI., p. 356, pl. 13, fig. 4.

————————————— *Gunther, Catal.*, viii., p. 249.

This sort enters in Dr. Gunther's division, characterized by " anal fin with less than forty rays ; dorsal spine with four series of barbels, the edges being equidistant, and armed with barbs." The upper profile is concave in front of the dorsal spine, and convex behind it ; the central profile is considerably distended. The body appears entirely granulated; these granulations are formed of minute tubercles ; towards the tail and near the anus they take a more spinous form. The dorsal spine is inserted over the centre of the eye ; its length is equal to one and a-half the transverse diameter of the orbit; it is straight and even a little curved outwards near its end; the barbs that extend on its edges are strong, particularly the external ones ; the second ray is contained four times in the length of the spine. The dorsal is formed of thirty-three rays, the caudal of twelve, the anal of thirty-two, and the pectorals of thirteen. The ventral spine is small, fixed, and armed with five or six rather strong spinelets.

The colour is of a dark brown, the back much lighter, and of a dirty yellow on the belly ; the lower parts are covered with very irregular brown spots; the dorsal and anal have an orange tinge.

Only seen one in April; length six and a-half inches.

MONACANTHUS FORSTERI.

The anterior upper profile, in front of the dorsal fin, is concave, and the posterior one convex ; the general form is elongated,- being contained two and one-third times in the total length ; the snout from its extremity to the anterior edge of the orbit is contained four and one-third times in the same length ; the lower profile is more convex than the upper one. The snout is produced; the dorsal spine is rather slender, short, and straight; it is contained once and one-fifth in the transverse diameter of the eye; it is inserted over the centre of the orbit, straight, or rather bent forwards, compressed, and quadrangular, the edges being equidistant, and armed with rather short barbels, directed downwards; there is no appearance of a short second ray. The second dorsal has thirty-four rays; the anal twenty-seven; the caudal is long, of twelve rays; the pectorals of thirteen; no ventral spine; the body is covered with very minute granulations, which become spinous on the tail. The four large anterior teeth are almost square.

The upper parts of the body are of a dark green, and the lower ones white; the whole is covered with very irregular black spots, particularly numerous on the sides; fins of a light greenish colour.

I have only seen a single specimen in the month of May; it was not quite three inches long.

It is not impossible that this should be *Balistes Scaber*, Forster, (*Bl. Shœn.*, p. 477); it evidently comes near *Peronii*, but its form is exactly like the one of *Alutarius Paragaudatus*, as represented by Richardson, "Erebus and Terror, Fishes," p. 66, pl. 39. (*Spilomelanurus*, Quoy and Gaim.)

MONACANTHUS PRASINUS.

This comes in the division characterised by—" anal fin with less than forty rays; the front ones much closer together than the hinder series," which constitutes, for Dr. Bleeker, his genus *Pseudomonacanthus*; the anterior profile is almost straight, the posterior one rather convex; the lower profile is regularly arched, when the pubic bone is not extended; the dorsal spine is inserted over the posterior third of the orbit; it is arched, and carries very strong barbs directed downwards; the back ones are much larger than the others; this spine is twice and a quarter as long as the diameter of the orbit, and is very strong; the inner ray is about one-third of the spine; the second dorsal has thirty-five and the anal thirty-four rays; the pectorals thirteen; the ventral spine is fixed and formed of a small net of spinelets, three of which, on each side, are much larger than the others, and curved; the height of the body is contained, when the pubic bone is extended, two and two-third times in the total length; the two front teeth are triangular and by their union form a pointed edge; the others are also pointed; the body is entirely covered with a very fine velvety granulation.

The colour is entirely of a light and rather brilliant green, darker on the back, rather yellow on the belly; the eyes and teeth are also green; the caudal of the same colour; second dorsal and anal transparent, rather dark on the edge.

Only seen once in the month of March; it is rather over two and a-half inches long, and has an oval form.

NOTA. None of the three sorts of *Monacanthus*, I here describe, have any particular spines or spots on the sides of the tail.

GYMNODONTES.

" Body more or less shortened. The bones of the upper and lower jaw are confluent, forming a beak with a trenchant edge, without teeth, with or without medium suture. A soft dorsal, caudal, and anal are developed,—approximate. No spinous dorsal. Pectoral fins, no ventrals.

" Marine fishes of the temperate and tropical regions. Some species confined to fresh water."

Group *TETRODONTINA*.

Tail and caudal fin distinct. Part of the œsophagus much extensible, and capable of being filled with air; no pelvic bone; air-bladder present.

TETRODON.

Found in all the warm or tropical seas of the world. They are, generally poisonous. I have observed two sorts on the shores of Hobson's Bay.

TETRODON HAMILTONI.

Tetrodon Hamiltoni, *Richard., Erebus & Terror*, p. 63, pl. 39.

(*Toad Fish.*)

The dorsal is formed of nine rays, and the caudal also of nine ; the anal of eight ; and the pectorals of fifteen. The body is covered with small pores, and is pretty smooth.

The upper parts are green, marbled with a darker tinge ; the lower white ; fins of a greenish yellow ; eye of a yellowish green, with an interior bright red line.

The usual size is from four to five inches, some adults measure up to nine. Very common. It sometimes goes up the river to Melbourne.

TETRODON HISPIDUS.

Tetrodon Hispidus, *Lin. Syst. Nat.*, vol. i., p. 411.

———————— *Lacep.* vol. i., p. 487, pl. 24, fig. 1.

———————— *Bloch*, pl. 142.

(*Toad Fish.*)

Dorsal of eleven rays ; caudal rather emarginated, of eleven rays ; anal of six ; pectorals of thirteen.

The entire body is covered with very minute spiny asperities upper parts of a greyish green, the lower of a pinky white ; numerous large irregular brown blotches on the upper part ; lips rosy ; dorsal white, with its internal half green ; caudal with a green tinge ; anal white ; pectorals of a light green, with a pink tinge on its external edge ; eye blue, with a lower brown external line.

ARACANA.

Separated from *Ostracion* by Grey, on the character of the carapace not being closed behind the anal fin. This is easily seen in preserved specimens, but does not appear externally in fresh ones. These fish are mostly Australian, and are adorned with beautiful colours.

ARACANA AMŒNA.

Carapace with five ridges, the abdomen forming an inferior one ; spines short, thick, conical, blunt, and not arched, placed one above the orbit, and directed externally ; two on each side of the back directed posteriorly ; below these are others much shorter

still, and which are only white striated tubercles: they are
placed, one on each side, towards the middle, and three on a line at
the beginning of the belly; one is under, and a little behind, the
root of the pectoral, and the two others near one another and more
backwards; the entire carapace is very rough, covered with
small tubercles, disposed in long quadrilaters, but not radiant;
the fins have eleven rays at the dorsal, ten at the caudal,
nine at the anal, eleven at the pectorals; the caudal fin is rounded
at its extremity; it is long, being equal to the length of the snout
from its extremity to the lower margin of the eye; the height
of the body is contained one and a-half times in its length, to the
base of the caudal, and the distance from the end of the snout to the
upper base of the pectoral is contained twice in the total length
of the body, including the caudal; the eye is contained two and
a-half times in the same distance; on the belly pentagonal shields
are well marked, they have an internal line and a small tubercle
in the centre; on this part (the belly) there is no other rugosities
or tubercles; the posterior part is not covered by the carapace,
and is smooth.

The upper and lateral parts of the body are of a dark purple,
covered with numerous white, narrow, longitudinal lines, running
all round the body: these are sometimes united two together
or are interrupted; on the cheeks they number four, having
between them five purple ones broader than the others; the
belly is of a beautiful uniform orange colour; the fins have
a light yellow tinge, without any spots; the eye is yellow.

The teeth are in small numbers, spaced, but rather large and
conic. I have seen two specimens of this beautiful little sort—
one caught in the cold and the other in the warm season; each
was two inches long. It is evidently nearly allied to *Ostracion
Auritus*, that I have received from Swan River, and which has
exactly the same colours, but appears different; I thought it might
be the young of that species, but I have lately received from Tasmania (Hobart Town), under the name of *Cow-fish*, a specimen of
Auritus, only two inches six-eighths long, in which the arched
spines are stronger even than those of the adult specimens, six
inches long; it is still nearer allied to *Ornata* (Gray), from
Adelaide, but it is also distinct from it by its spines, the anterior
profile of the head falling still more abruptly, &c.

DIODON.

This genus is found in all the tropical seas of the world; its body is covered with spines; the fish can swell itself out as a globe, and takes such an extraordinary appearance, that sailors and travellers are very apt to collect it, as an object of curiosity. There is no stronger proof of the semi-tropical nature of all the Australian seas than the frequent occurrence of these fishes in the most southern parts of this continent. Dr. Gunther limits this genus of Linnæus to the sorts who have "jaws without a medium suture, body covered with dermal ossifications, each with a pair of lateral roots, and with a stiff, moveable, and erectile spine; nasal tentacle simple, with a pair of lateral openings."

DIODON SPINOSISSIMUS.

Diodon Spinosissimus, *Cuvier, Mem. Mus.*, vol. iv., p. 34.

It is with great doubt I place under this name the present fish, but having at my disposal no means of comparison, I prefer not complicating still more the synonyma of a family which requires already a special study, but I believe the number of admitted species will, when this takes place, be very much increased. General appearance of *Diodon Histrix* of Bloch; nasal tentacle formed of a short simple tube, with a pair of lateral openings; mouth small, its opening being less than the diameter of the orbit; spines very numerous, long, slender, all of about equal length; the root of each has three ridges; the tail has no spine, but there is one rather stronger than the others on each side of the body at its base. Dorsal fin with twelve rays; caudal elongate, of eight rays; anal of the size of the dorsal, of twelve rays; pectorals of twenty-two.

The body is, on its upper half, of a light green; the lower one is white; on each side there are three faint black blotches of an irregular form; the spines and fins are of a light yellowish green, those of the lower parts are white; eye yellow; no spots on the fins.

I have two specimens, both about three and a-half inches long.

DIODON BLOCHII.
(*The Sea Hog.*)

This may prove to belong to one of the already described species, but I can identify it with none. General appearance of *Diodon Atinga* of Bloch, but spines much less numerous. The head is broad, and the mouth very wide ; nasal tantacle formed of a simple tube, with a pair of lateral openings ; the jaws are formed of numerous distinct teeth solved together, and forming numerous tubercles inside of the mouth, particularly at the lower jaw ; the opening of the mouth is about one and a-half the great diameter of the orbit, and the space from one eye to the other about twice that diameter ; in front there are five spines on the first row in front of the eyes ; they form in all eleven or twelve irregular transverse lines, they are very strong, particularly the posterior ones. The dorsal fin has thirteen rays, the caudal nine ; the anal is much larger than the dorsal, and has thirteen rays ; the pectorals are about as long as the space between the eyes, of nineteen rays. Each spine has two long roots and an anterior ridge.

The colour is of a rather light green on the back, with the lower parts white ; the lips are flesh colour, and the head purple ; the abdomen is rather rosy ; at the root of each spine there is a very faint dark brown spot, and on the posterior part of the body some purple blotches ; the fins are of a light green, without any spots, but their external portion is rather darker ; the eye is yellow, with its external part orange, and surrounded by a blue ring. The air-bladder is very large, rounded, and strongly bilobed. Six inches long ; rather common.

I should have taken this for the *D. Maculatus*, but Dr. Gunther gives it from sixteen to nineteen lines of spines ; perhaps it is the *Atopomycterus Bocagei*, of Steindachner, from Sydney, quoted by him as being probably the same sort.

CHILOMYCTERUS.

Separated by Dr. Kaup from *Diodon*, and characterised by Dr. Gunther as having " jaws without median suture, body covered with ossifications, all, or most of which, consist of three horizontal roots, and a stiff, erect, immoveable spine ; nasal tentacle simple with a pair of lateral openings." Nine or ten sorts are known from all the seas situated between the tropics; they have the general form of *Diodon*.

CHILOMYCTERUS JACULIFERUS.

Diodon Jaculiferus, *Cus. Mem. Mus.*, vol. vii., p. 3.

Chilomycterus Jaculiferus, *Gunther, Catal.*, vol. viii., p, 313.

(*The Globe.*)

My specimen agrees very well with Dr. Gunther's excellent description of this sort, but the spines are all about of equal length, and rather short; the posterior, if any, being the longest. I find the dorsal large, formed of sixteen rays; the caudal rounded posteriorly, of nine rays; the anal is much smaller than the dorsal, but is not complete in my specimen, and I only see the roots of six rays; the pectorals have twenty rays.

The colour is of a light green on the upper part, and white below; all the spines are white, but those of the back have a black rounded spot at their base; the fins are of a yellowish green, with the end of the dorsal and caudal darker; the anal is white; the eye was, on the living specimen, of a dark brown, with an internal yellow circle. This fish, when inflated, forms a perfect globe.

The specimen is four and a-half inches long. From Hobson's Bay The air-bladder is large, rounded, and strongly bifurcated.

Group *MOLINA*.

Body compressed, very short, not extensible by air; tail extremely short, truncate, vertical; fins confluent; no pelvic bone; air-bladder absent.

ORTHAGORISCUS.

The *Sun-fish* is sometimes found on the Victorian coast, and is considered by Dr. Gunther and Professor M'Coy as belonging to the European sort. The first also includes with *Orthagoriscus Mola* the sort described by me at the Cape of Good Hope under the name of *Pedalion Capensis.* He states that the remarkable nose-like hump it presents is the sign of old age, This is very possible, as a similar fact is known to exist in *Pagrus* and others ; but according to this my South African specimen, which weighed one hundred and fifty pounds, was an old adult ; and one caught off Western Port, in the beginning of September, weighing over four hundred, would only be a young one, as there was no indice of this excrescence. This requires some explanation.

The colour of the Australian fish was of a brownish red.

Sub-Class II. DIPNOI.

"Fishes with the skeleton partly cartilaginous, partly osseous; no occipital condyle. Bulbus arteriosus with two longitudinal valves; air-bladder double, lung-like, communicating by a duct and glottis with the hæmal side of the æsophagus, with a pulmonary vein. A narrow gill-opening on each side, with a rudimentary gill-cover; some of the branchial arches without gills; gills free, membranaceous. Nostrils double on each side. Intestine with a spiral valve. Optic nerves not decussating. Oviducts distinct. Ventral fins abdominal."

SIRENOIDEI.

"Body eel-shaped, covered with cycloid scales Vertical fins a continuous border to the compressed tapering tail. Pectoral and ventral fins subulate. A single maxillary dental plate is opposed to a single mandibular one. Scapular arch attached to the occiput. Vent not in the median line. No pseudobranchiæ.

"Fresh-water fishes of tropical Africa, America, and Australia."

No sort of *Sirenoidæ* has been yet found in the southern parts of Australia, and as those known are all from tropical regions, it is not very probable that any do inhabit them.

Mr. Krefft has made known a sort of *Ceratodus* (Fosteri), found in Queensland by Mr. Masters, which probably belongs to this family.

Dr. Guuther, with his usual urbanity, says that I have made some additions to the *synonymy* of the *Lepidosirens* in my work on the auimals of South America; I think that I have done something more, in making better known the singular dentition of those animals, in pointing out the curious anomaly they present in the want of symmetry of the position of the anus, which is not situated on the median line of the body, but ou its right side. The learned doctor declares also that my *Dissimilis* is the same as *Paradoxa*; but as of each there is only, if I am not mistaken, one specimen known (at least this was the case some few years ago), and as they are in very distant museums, I do not believe he has compared them; I even doubt very much if he has ever seen one or the other.

Sub-Class III.—GANOIDEI.

"Not yet discovered in Australia."

Sub-Class IV.—CHONDROPTERYGII.

"Skeleton cartilaginous; skull with sutures. Body with medial and paired fins, the hinder pair abdominal; caudal fin with produced upper lobe. Gills attached to the skin by the outer margin, with several intervening gill-openings; rarely one gill-opening only. No gill-cover. No air-bladder. Three series of valves, in the bulbus arteriosus. Intestine with a spiral valve. Optic nerves commissurally united, not decussating. Ovaries with few and large ova, which are impregnated, and, in some, developed internally. Embryo with deciduous external gills. Males with prehensile organs attached to the ventral fins."

Order I. HOLOCEPHALA.

" One external gill-opening only, covered by a fold of the skin, which encloses a rudimentary cartilaginous gill-cover; four branchial clefts within the gill-cavity. The maxillary and palatal apparatus coalescent with the skull."

CHIMÆRIDÆ.

"Form of the body elongate; pectoral fins free; anterior dorsal fin above the pectorals. Mouth inferior. Dental organs confluent into two pairs of laminæ in the upper jaw and into one pair in the lower. No spiracles. Males with a peculiar prehensile organ in the upper part of the snout. Skin naked in the adult."

CALLORHYNCHUS.

Formed by Gronovius on a most curious fish, whose rounded head has a snout ended in a cutaneous flap.

CALLORHYNCHUS ANTARCTICUS.

Chimæra Callorhynchus, *Lin. Syst. Nat.*, vol. i., p. 402.
Callorhynchus Antarcticus, *Cuv., Règ. Anim.*, vol. ii., p. 372.
Callorhynchus Tasmanius, *Richard., Trans. Zool. Society*, vol. iii., p. 696.

(Southern Chimera.)

This singular fish is common at the Cape of Good Hope, but appears very scarce in the Victorian sea, as I have only seen one specimen at one of the fishmonger's (Allen), in the month of March. Professor M'Coy says it is common near Portland, in the western part of the Colony, and it has also been found in Tasmania.

The colour is of a silvery grey, darker on the back, but without spots or bands.

Order II. PLAGIOSTOMATA.

" From five to seven gill-openings. Jaws distinct from skull."

Sub-order I. SELACHOIDEI.

"Gill-openings lateral. Body more or less cylindrical."

(SHARKS.)

CARCHARIIDÆ.

" The first dorsal fin opposite to the space between pectoral and ventral fins without spine ; an anal fin. Eye with a nictitating membrane. Mouth crescent-shaped, inferior."

I have found it, until now, almost impossible to induce the fishermen to bring to the market specimens of sharks, which are, unfortunately, but too common in Hobson's Bay. The only sorts I have been able to obtain are the following, but many more inhabit these waters. It is is curious that none of the handsomely spotted sorts, that are so common at the Cape of Good Hope, are found here.

ZYGÆNA.

Formed by Cuvier on curious sorts of sharks, having the head made like a hammer.

ZYGÆNA MALLEUS.

Zygæna, *Rondel.*, p. 389.

Squalus Zygæna, *Liss.*, *Syst. Nat.*, p. 399.

(*Hammer Shark.*)

This sort is found commonly in Hobson's Bay. I have had no opportunity of comparing it with European specimens, but Professor M'Coy considers it as similar.

GALEUS.

This genus is due to Cuvier, who established it in his magnificent work, the " Règne Animal."

GALEOUS CANIS.

Galeus Canis, *Rondelet.*, p. 377.

Squalus Galeus, *Lin.*, *Syst. Nat.*, vol. i., p. 397.

(*The Tope.*)

Common in Hobson's Bay, and appears similar to the European sort. It does not attain very large dimensions, and is entirely grey.

MUSTELUS.

Genus also due to Cuvier.

MUSTELUS ANTARCTICUS.

Mustelus Antarcticus, *Gunther*, *Catal.*, vol viii., p. 387.

(*Smooth Head.*)

This is also very common in Hobson's Bay ; it is entirely of a grey colour. Professor M'Coy had considered it as similar to the European *Must. Vulgaris*, but Dr. Gunther separates it on account of the origin of its dorsal fin being behind the inner posterior angle at the pectoral, when in *Vulgaris* it is nearly opposite to the middle of the inner margin of that fin.

These two last sharks are the most common sorts found in Hobson's Bay. They may be very easily distinguished by the teeth, which in *Galeus Canis* are sharp and serrated, and in *Mustelus* are disposed as a pavement.

CHARCHARIAS.

One sort is also stated by Professor M'Coy as having been recently found in Hobson's Bay.

CHARCHARIAS MELANOPTERUS.

Charcharias Melanopterus, *Quoy et Gaim.*, *Voy. de l' Uraine Zool.*, p. 194, pl. 43, figs. 1-2.

Professor M'Coy says that he has only seen one specimen, fifteen feet long.

LAMNIDÆ.

" The first dorsal opposite to the space between the pectoral and ventral fins, without spine; no anal fin. No nictitating membrane. Mouth crescent-shaped, inferior; nostrils not confluent with the mouth. Gill-openings generally wide. Spiracles none, or minute."

ODONTASPIS.

Genus of Agassiz, established in his work on the fossil fishes.

ODONTASPIS TAURUS.

Odontaspis Taurus, *Rafinesque, Muller & Henle*, p. 73, pl. 30.

Professor M'Coy says that this shark is common in the Victorian waters, but I have not yet obtained a specimen of it.

HEPTANCHUS.

Formed by Muller and Henle in their valuable work on the *Plagiostomidæ*. *Heptanchus Indicus* is said to be found in the Bay, but I can only repeat for this the same as I have stated for the precedent.

SCYLLIIDÆ.

"The first dorsal fins above or behind the ventrals, without spine; an anal fin. No membranæ nietitans. Spiraele always distinct. Mouth inferior. Teeth small, several series being generally in function."

I have received *Scyllium Maculatum* from Hobart Town, through Mr. Lavington Roop; but I have not seen it from the Victorian waters.

CESTRACIONTIDÆ.

"Two dorsal fins, with spines, the first opposite to the spaee between the peetorals and ventrals; the seeond in advanee of the anal. Nostrils and bueeal eavity eonfluent. Mouth rather narrow, the upper lip divided into seven lobes, the lower with a fold. Spiraeles small, below the posterior part of the eye. Gill-openings rather narrow. Dentition similar in both jaws, viz., small obtuse teeth in front, whieh in young individuals are pointed and provided with from three to five eups. The lateral teeth large, pad-like, twiee as broad as long, arranged in oblique series, one series being formed by mueh larger teeth than those on the other series.

"Pacific and East Indian Arehipelago."

CESTRACION.

Formed by Cuvier on a most singular shark, which can be easily recognised by its two dorsal fins having each a strong spine, and by its singular dentition in form of pavement, with the posterior teeth much larger. This genus has been called *Heterodontus* by Blainville.

CESTRACION PHILIPPI.

Squalus Philippi, *Bloch, Schn.*, p 134.
Port Jackson Shark, *Phillip, Voyage*, p. 283.

This sort does not attain very large dimensions, a specimen of three feet and a-half long being considered by the Hobson's Bay fishermen as being of rare occurrence. In one, of that size, the teeth are almost entirely obtuse; but in another of thirty-two inches long they are conic and pointed.

The upper parts are of a light brown, marbled with yellow, and the lower ones of a beautiful white; these fine yellow tinges extend along the sides and above the pectorals.

The colour is similar in all the specimens I have seen, and I believe that those with black bands, mentioned by Dr. Gunther, belong to a different sort, properly called *Zebra* by Mr. Gray (*Chondropterigii* of the British Museum), and which inhabits Japan and some parts of India.

Dr. Gunther describes a second Australian sort (*Galeatus*) of this genus, in which the anal fin reaches the root of the caudal; I have not seen it.

SPINACIDÆ.

"Two dorsal fins, no anal. Mouth but slightly arched; a long, deep, straight oblique groove on each side of the mouth. Spiracles present; Gill-openings narrow. Pectoral fins not notched at their origin."

Acanthias Vulgaris is found in Australia, but I have not seen it from Victoria.

PRISTIOPHORIDÆ.

"The rostral cartilage is produced into an exceedingly long flat laminæ, armed along each edge with a series of teeth (saw)."

PRISTIPHORUS.

Formed by Muller and Henle.

PRISTIPHORUS CIRRATUS.

Pristis Cirratus, *Latham, Trans. Lin. Soc.*, vol. ii., 1794, p. 281, pl. 26.

———————————, *Bloch, Schn.*, pl. 70 (the head only).

The saw, from its extremity to the anterior edge of the orbit, is contained four and one-third times in the total length of the fish; the distance between the tentacles and nostrils equals that between the nostrils and the fourth gill-opening; the fins are entirely covered with very minute scales, as is also the body.

The colour is entirely grey.

I have not seen this sort from Victoria, but I have received it from Hobart Town, through the kindness of Mr. Lavington Roop.

PRISTIPHORUS NUDIPINNIS.

Pristiphorus Nudipinnis, *Gunther, Catal.*, vol. viii., p. 42.

(Saw Fish.)

This sort is very nearly allied to the precedent, but has been most properly separated from it by Dr. Gunther. The saw is not so long, being contained four and three-quarter times in the total length; this saw is also broader at its base; the distance between the tentacle and nostril is considerably less than that between the nostril and the first gill-opening. A portion of the pectorals and of the dorsal is denudated of scales, but the extent of this portion is subject to considerable variation.

The colour is of a light grey, with the pectorals and ventrals reddish.

Common in Hobson's Bay.

RHINIDÆ.

"Spiracle wide behind the eyes. Nostrils with skinny flaps on the margin of the snout. Teeth conical, pointed, distant. Dorsal fins without spines on the tail; no anal.

"Temperate and tropical seas."

One single genus formed by Dumeril.

RHINA.

RHINA SQUATINA.

Squatina Bellon, *De Aquat*, p. 78.
Squalus Squatina, *Lin. Syst. Nat.*, vol. i., p, 396.

(Angel Shark.)

I have no means of comparing this fish with the European form, but it is admitted that they are similar.

The colour is of a light chesnut, with some rounded whitish spots on the pectorals and ventrals; the fins are bordered with pink ; the lower parts of the body are white, with a rosy tinge.

The colours are different from those of Bloch's plate ; but they agree well with Risso's description. These two authors state that the back is covered with large acute tubercles. In the smallest Australian specimens, the dorsal tubercles are very small, and similar to the others, of the upper surface of the body ; but in the larger ones, they are considerably larger, and at the base of the tail, in front of the first dorsal, they become arched spines. The teeth are on one single line, when Risso states that in the European fish they are on three ; but Bloch says that in his specimens (one foot long) the teeth are on three series at the upper jaw and on two on the lower, and adds that the lines of teeth increase with age, and this is probable, as my specimens are only seven to nine inches in length, and are evidently very young.

I have seen three specimens at the Melbourne Market in the months of November and December.

Sub-order II. BATOIDEI.

" Gill-openings ventral. In a few of the genera, which we place first, the habit is still that of the sharks; but the body is depressed; and in the typical genera the trunk, which is surrounded by the immensely developed pectoral fins, forms a broad flat disk, with a thin and slender tail. Spiracles always present. Five pairs of gill-openings. No anal fin; dorsal fins, if present, on the tail.

" Temperate and tropical seas; some species pelagic; some entering fresh waters or entirely limited to rivers within the tropics."

(RAYS.)

PRISTIDÆ.

" The snout is produced into an exceedingly long, flat lamina, armed with a series of strong teeth along each edge, (saw)."

RHINOBATIDÆ.

" Tail strong and long, with two well-developed dorsal fins; a caudal and a longitudinal fold on each side. Disk not excessively dilated, the rayed portion of the pectoral fins not being continued to the snout. No electric organ."

TRYGONORHINA.

Founded by Muller and Henle, on a sort found in the Straits of Bass, and which appears sometimes in the Melbourne Market.

TRYGONORHINA FASCIATA.

Trygonorhina Fasciata, *Muller and Henle*, p. 124, fig. 43.

(*The Fidler.*)

Body of a light brown, with the margin of the pectorals and the fins reddish; four or five irregular, transverse bands, appear on the back, but do not extend far on the pectorals; they are of a fine light blue, bordered with dark brown; lower parts of the body of a reddish white; eye yellow.

Its flesh is considered good for the table, but scarce.

TORPEDINIDÆ.

"The trunk is a broad, smooth disk; tail with rayed dorsal (absent in Tenicra) and caudal fins, and a longitudinal fold along each side. Anterior nasal valves confluent into a quadrangular lobe. An electric organ, composed of vertical hexagonal tubes between the pectoral fins and the head."

NARCINE.

Separated from *Torpedo* by Henle; it contains several tropical sorts, and one from the southern seas of Australia.

NARCINE TASMANIENSIS.

Narcine Tasmaniensis, *Richard., Proc. Zool. Soc.*, 1841, p. 22.

Elliptical; of a brownish purple; eye yellow.

Attains a large size, and I have seen, on the St. Kilda beach, a mutilated specimen, measuring over six feet in length. Found in Bass's Straits and in the Hobart Town sea.

RAJIDÆ.

" Disk broad, rhombic, generally with asperities or spines ; tail with a longitudinal fold on each side. The pectorals extend to the snout. No electric organ. No serrated caudal spine."

The only two sorts I have observed belong to the following genus :—

RAJA.

RAJA LEMPRIERI.

Raja Lemprieri, *Richard.*, *Erebus and Terror*, p. 34, pl. 23.

(*Thorn Back.*)

Snout short. The fish is of a fleshy colour, rather green on the back and the upper part of the tail, and of a reddish purple on the sides of the pectorals ; the spines seem to be subject to considerable variation ; on young specimens there is, on each side of the pectorals, two series of slender, arched, but very acute spines ; in the older ones, there is only one series of these ; but on the contrary, those of the tail of the young specimens are only disposed on one line on the middle of its upper part, when in the larger specimens they form three series on the upper part of this organ. In dried specimens, the lateral part of the pectorals, and also the portion situated on the sides of the snout, appear of a light yellow colour, as they are represented on Richardson's plate.

Common.

RAJA OXYRHYNCHUS.

Raja Oxyrhynchus, *Lyn. Syst. Nat.*, vol. i., p. 395.

(*Common Ray.*)

The snout long ; body entirely covered with asperities, which are more considerable on the snout, where they form small triangular points ; on the lower surface of this part of the edges of the ventrals, up to the height of the eyes, these points are considerable and crowded. The anterior profile is deeply concave ; the angle of the pectorals is rather pointed; there are no spines round the eyes, but a series of three or four is seen on each side of the back, and ends before the insertion of the ventrals ; the tail is armed with three series of strong tuberculous spines, and one or two are seen on the middle of the back behind the head. The teeth are rather large, like pavement, and numerous.

The general colour is of a greyish purple, with the sides reddish ; all the body is covered with rounded white spots. This sort is very common in the market, and is esteemed for the table.

It is always with doubt that I admit that a fish from the Antarctic Seas is specifically similar to an European one, more so as I have no specimens of the latter region for comparison ; but the descriptions and figures of *Oxyrhynchus*, that I have at my disposal, agree so well with the Australian fish that I should not be justified in separating them. I think, also, that *Raja Nasuta* of Muller and Henle, which is established on a figure drawn in New Zealand by Solander, will prove to belong to this species.

The egg is large, of the usual form in *Rays*, of a silky green. In a large female I found one large egg on each side, and numerous small ones.

MYLIOBATIDÆ.

" The disk is very broad in consequence of the great development of the pectoral fins, which, however, leave the sides of the head free, and reappear at the extremity of the snout as a pair of detached (cephalic) fins."

MYLIOBATIS.

Genus formed by Cuvier, and containing nine or ten sorts, of which two are found in the South Australian Seas.

MYLIOBATIS AQUILA.

Raja Aquila, *Lin.*, *Syst. Nat.*, vol. i., p. 396.

Coloration of a dark green, almost uniform.

Often found by the fisherman in Hobson's Bay, but never brought to the Market; it seems not to differ from the Mediterranean specimens.

MYLIOBATIS NIEUHOFII.

Raja Nieuhofii, *Bloch, Schneid.*, p. 364.

Body of a fine light brown yellow; with four or five transverse bands of a beautiful blue; these bands are irregular and interrupted; the tail and ventrals have a greenish hue.

Only seen once at the Melbourne Market, in the month of October, and the specimen was most kindly sent to me by Dr. T. Black. I had previously seen several specimens from Singapore and Malacca.

Sub-class V.   CYCLOLTOMATA.

" Skeleton cartilaginous and metochordal, without ribs, and without real jaws. Skull not separate from the vertebral column. No limbs. Gills in form of fixed sacs, without branchial arches, six or seven in number of each side. One nasal aperture only. Heart without brilbus arteriosus. Mouth anterior, surrounded by a circular or sub-circular lip, suctorial. Alimentary anal straight, simple without cæcal appendages pancreas, or spleen. Generative outlet peritoneal. Vertical fins rayed.

PETROMYZONTIDÆ.

" Body eel-shaped, naked. Subject to a metamorphosis. In the perfect stage with a suctorial mouth, armed with teeth, simple or multicuspid, horny, sitting on a soft papilla. Maxillary, mandibulary, lingual, and suctorial teeth may be dis-

tinguished. Eyes present (in native animals).
External nasal aperture in the middle of the upper
side of the head. The nasal duct terminates without perforating the palate. Seven branchial sacs
and apertures on each side behind the head. The
inner branchial ducts terminate in a separate common tube. Intestines with a spiral valve. Eggs
small. The larvæ without teeth, and with a single
continuous vertical fin.

" Inhabitants of the fresh waters and coasts of
the temperate regions of both hemispheres. Suck
themselves fast to other fish, and live by scraping
off their flesh."

I find the greatest difficulty in the determination of the Victorian fishes of this family ; there are two types, one of which
has the second dorsal united with the caudal, and the other which
has it separate ; but the most important character, the dentition,
seems to be subject to the most extraordinary variations ; in fact,
I cannot find it exactly similar in two specimens. The teeth
have horny coverings, which are very apt to fall, and this changes
entirely the appearance of the mouth. The one having the
second dorsal separated from the caudal is a *Geotria* for Dr.
Gunther.

GEOTRIA.

GEOTRIA AUSTRALIS ?

Geotria Australis ? *Gray, Proc. Zool. Soc.*, 1851, *Chondrop.*,
p. 142, pl. 2.

Formed by Dr. Gray on a most singular Australian sort,
but Dr. Gunther unites with it the genus *Velasia*, of the
same author, from Chili, in which there is no trace of a
pouch. The mouth is rounded, but rather angular, with
the lateral lobes broad ; it is fringed all round. The
maxillary lamina is formed of four teeth, the exterior of
which are flat lobes, and the two interior ones, long, conical

pointed teeth. The mandibulary lamina is large, and forms a transverse crescent ridge, like the teeth of a *Scarus*, and showing at its edge faint traces of teeth. I believe it is not externally visible in the living specimens. Suctorial teeth in numerous transverse series, those situated backwards larger than the others; lingual teeth, two in number, straight, strong, and conical. Seven branchial openings, large, round, and bordered. The distance between the two dorsals and the base of the caudal is a little more than the diameter of the mouth, and this is equal to half the distance from the end of the snout to the anterior edge of the eye. The caudal fin is discoid, and rounded at its extremity.

The colour is of a dark blue on the back, and silvery on the sides and belly; on the middle of the back, a little before the insertion of the first dorsal, begins a space of a brilliant green, which extends to the tail; fins red, bordered with black.

Found in the Saltwater River. The following are its dimensions:—

	Inches.
Total length	$20\frac{1}{2}$
Circumference of the middle of body	$2\frac{5}{8}$
From muzzle to centre of eye	$1\frac{1}{8}$
———— to first branchiostegal opening	$1\frac{1}{2}$
———— to last ————	$3\frac{1}{8}$
———— to beginning of first dorsal	$12\frac{7}{8}$
Length of first dorsal	$1\frac{3}{4}$
From first dorsal to beginning of second	$1\frac{5}{8}$
Length of second dorsal	$1\frac{7}{8}$
From second dorsal to beginning of caudal	$\frac{7}{8}$
From beginning of caudal to end of body	$1\frac{1}{4}$
From end of body to anus	$5\frac{1}{4}$

A very young individual, only three inches long, has exactly the same form, the same dimensions, and the same dentition.

Mr. F. G. Waterhouse has kindly sent me, from the Torrens River, Adelaide, a specimen of the only sort said to inhabit those waters, and which I felt a great desire to examine, as the typical specimen of *Geotria* was said to have come from that Colony. This specimen is exactly like the one from the Saltwater River, only ome of the suctatorial teeth are long and sharp, and this is caused by their having preserved their horny coverings. It has no trace of the gutteral pouch, and so I believe that this is accidental, or rather belongs to a particular state of some specimens, perhaps to the old individuals of one sex. The only dental difference between *Geotria and Mordax* seems to be the presence in the latter of the two groups of three long teeth in the maxillary. Nothing shows better the remarkable knowledge that Dr. Gunther possesses of fish than his not having taken the extraordinary gular sac as a generic character; but I cannot consider the specimens which do not possess it to be young, as the length of the one I have described here is a little more considerable than that of the type in the British Museum (twenty inches).

In the list of the *Chondropterygii* of the British Museum it is said that the type, which was given to that institution by Mr. Pain, was from a river *Inkar Pinki*, in South Australia, but there must be some confusion, as that gentleman tells me that he picked it up on the Brighton beach, Hobson's Bay.

MORDACIA.

Formed by Gray on a *Lamprey* from Tasmania, which has appeared to Dr. Gunther to be similar to one from Chili. There is no doubt that the two belong to the same genus, but it is very improbable that they should be specifically similar.

MORDACIA MORDAX.

Petromyzon Mordax, *Richard, Loc. Cit.*, p. 62, pl. 38, fig. 3.
Mordacia Mordax, *Gray, Chondropterygii of the Brit. Mus.*,
p. 142
——————— *Gunther, Catal.*, vol. viii., p. 508.

.   (*The Lamprey*.)

The mouth is elleptical; the lateral lobes not broad nor fringed; mandibulary lamina not visible externally, but bearing seven to nine acute conical cusps, which, when the horny coverings fall, have the appearance of tubercles. On the maxillary is, on each side, a group of three conical, acute teeth, directed backwards, and placed one in front and two behind; suctatorial teeth forming a circle round the lips; they are small, and number at least twenty; behind them is a series of much larger ones, very broad at their base, and very acute; in front, three of them are disposed in a triangle; the others emit a sort of transverse ridge which on the sides bears on other teeth, so as to be bifid in this part ; those placed at the lower part of the mouth are even bifid. Lingual teeth formed of two large ones ; canines very strongly serrated, even denticulated, at their under side, which is arched. The head has a rather pointed appearance, which is caused by the lips not falling, as in *Geotria ;* the eye is small; the branchial openings are much less distinct, being placed under a fold of the skin ; they number seven. The first dorsal is rather triangular, and situated at a considerable distance from the second, which is high at its beginning, and lowers considerably before it joins the caudal ; this last is rather pointed.

The colour is of a bluish grey, darker on the back ; the head is yellowish ; the eye silvery ; the first dorsal is grey ; the second is bordered with pink, and has its posterior part black ; the caudal is of that last colour, but has a pink margin.

These fish are commonly found in the Yarra at its lower part ; they are considered good food. Their motions are very rapid ; they are very voracious, and pursue any object in the water, and they adhere to it with an extraordinary and ferocious tenacity.

Dr. Gray's figure (*Chondropt.*) is copied from Richardson's, which, as Dr. Gunther has already observed, is not correct in showing the dentition. I thought at first that the bifid, and sometimes trifid, teeth of the Victorian specimens would constitute them into a separate species, but the coverings of the teeth fall off so frequently in the specimens preserved in spirits, and change so much the appearance of these organs, that, after examining many specimens, I believe they all belong to the same sort.

The average length is from fifteen to seventeen inches. I have taken on one the following measurements :—

	Inches.
Total length	15¼
From the end of snout to anterior edge of eye......	1
Diameter of eye	1-7
Circumference	2⅛
From end of snout to first dorsal	6½
Length of first dorsal	6½
From end of first dorsal to base of second	1¾
From base of second to extremity of caudal........	3¾
Height of second dorsal at its base	¾

The difference in the form of the lingual teeth indicated by the authors do not exist in *Geotria*, and in *Mordacia* they are similar, being, when seen in front, like two small horns, and, when sideways, having the appearance of serrated arches.

NOTA.—I consider as belonging to the *Ammocœtes* type, or larval stage, a singular little *Petromyzonid*, which was found in the Yarra. The body is eel-shaped, naked, cylindrical, and elongate, being twenty-three times as long as high ; it is entirely divided in annular rings, which appearance seems due to the muscular flakes being very visible through the smooth skin. I can see no teeth ; the upper lip is flat, and considerably prolongated over the buccal aperture ; it is truncated in front, and this part, seen upperly, is rather bifurcated. The lateral line is well marked in all the length of the body ; there is only one dorsal, which begins at about two-thirds of the length of the body, and is joined with the caudal and the anal ; the latter is considerably shorter than the dorsal ; these fins are all equal in their length ; no eye visible. The skin of the throat is rather extensible ; the prolongation of the upper lip over the lower is equal to the height of the body ; the tail is pointed.

The colour is of a light green, with the belly white ; on the back extends a narrow longitudinal line ; the head and throat are pink, and the fins of the same colour. Total length, four and three-eighth inches.

I should have thought this might be the first state of *Geotria*, but we have just seen that I had a still smaller specimen of this, which has entirely the form of the adult. In this state of things, I propose giving provisionally to this the name of *Yarra Singularis*.

In a dried state, the prolongated part of the head is apt to bend upwards, which gives the fish rather the appearance of a *Syngnathus*. The branchial apparatus are visible ; the body is remarkably soft, which makes it very difficult to examine it ; no barbels round the mouth.

It was found in Captain Sinnot's dock, on the lower Yarra, in brackish water.

NEOMORDACIA.

I propose giving this name to a very small lamprey, which has no first dorsal, or rather has only one dorsal, separate and rather distant from the caudal; this forms a broad oval, and is angulous at its extremity. Form of *Mordacia*.

NEOMORDACIA HOWITTII.

Height of body about nineteen times in its total length; the length of the snout, up to the external edge of the eye, a little longer than the height of the body; the head is not inflated, and follows on to the snout by an arched line, and on the body by a straight one; the dentition is very difficult to be distinctly seen with the weak magnifying power I possess, but I observe a row of strong conical and pointed teeth placed round the mouth, and wide apart; a few teeth on each side larger than the others, and inserted forwards. I can only say that there are others further back, and a few appear tricuspid; there are a few fringes round the mouth; the branchiostegal apertures are seven; they are round, and begin at a short distance from the eye, which is large.

The first half of the body and the head are like reticulated, and covered with irregular excavations; the middle of the body is smooth, but the posterior part is again similar to the anterior.

Very different from the other lampreys. This has a hard body, and being incrustated with sand, I do not doubt but that it lives in perforated holes on the sea shore.

It is of a dark blue on the upper parts, and silvery below; the caudal fin is red, and the eye yellow; the muzzle black. The only specimen I have seen is about three inches long; it was found at Cape Shanck by my old and highly esteemed friend, Dr. Howitt.

, MYSCINIDÆ.

"Body eel-shaped, naked, the single nasal aperture is above the mouth, quite at the extremity of the head, which is provided with four pairs of barbels. Mouth without lips. Nasal duct with cartilaginous rings penetrating the palate. Median tooth on the palate, and two comb-like series of teeth on the tongue. Branchial apertures at a great distance from the head. The inner branchial ducts lead into the œsophagus. A series of mucous sacs along each side of the abdomen. Intestine without spiral valve. Eggs large with a horny ease provided, with threads for an adhension.

" Inhabitants of the seas of the temperate regions of both hemispheres ; burrow into other fishes, and feed on their flesh." (Gunther.)

Bdellostoma Cirrhatum (Bloch., Schneid., p. 582,) was found by Forster in New Zealand.

Sub-Class VI.   LEPTOCARDII.

" Skeleton membrane, cartilaginous and notochordal, ribless, no brain. Pulsating sinues in place of heart. Blood colourless. Respiratory cavity confluent with the abdominal cavity; branchial clefts in great number, the water being expelled by an opening in front of the vent. Jaws none."

CIRROSTOMI.

" Body elongate, compressed, sealeless, limbless. Mouth a longitudinal fissure, with subrigid cirri on each side, inferior. Vent at a short distance from the extremity of the tail. A low rayless fin-like fold runs along the back, round the tail, past the vent, to the respiratory aperture. Eye rudimentary. Liver reduced to a blind sack of the simple intestine. One genus only, occupying the lowest scale in the class of vertebrata.

" Found imbedded in sand on many coasts of the temperate regions of both hemispheres."

A sort of *Branchiostoma* was discovered by the Expedition of the *Harold* in Bass's Straits, at a depth of from ten to twelve fathoms. Dr. Gunther considers it similar to the European sort (*Limax Lanceolatus Pallas*). I have not seen it.

APPENDICE.

CYPRINIDÆ.

This family, so widely represented in India, has not, till this, appeared to be indigenous to Australia; but several sorts have been introduced, and one seems likely to prove indigenous.

1. CORASSIUS VULGARIS, known as the *Prussian Carp*, has very well succeeded throughout the country. The specimens I have seen are absolutely similar to the European type.

2. CORASSIUS AURATUS—the *Gold Fish*. It presents a particular race, that I have thought proper to describe here.

CORASSIUS AURATUS. VAR.

Cyprinus Auratus, *Lin.*, *Bloch.*
Corassius Auratus, *Bleeker*, *Gunther.*

D. 3/17. A. 3/6. C. 19 long rays, and 4 small on each side.
P. 1/15. V. 1/8.

Height of the body twice and six-tenths of the total length to the middle of the open caudal; head four times in the same length. The body is broad, very much like the figure of *Cyp. Corassius*, given by Cuv. and Val.; the eye is one and two-third times in the snout, and a little over three times in the length of the head; the lateral line is rather arched, and extends over twenty-eight scales; these are large, with their external edge rather sinuous and reborded; they are in lines of eight over the lateral line (this line passing over the eighth), and seven below; the dorsal fin is very high, being nearly as broad as the portion of the back over the lateral line; it is formed of three spines, the first very minute, the second about four times, and the third nearly five times longer; this third spine is slender, curved, and has very strong teeth on its posterior part; the soft rays number seventeen, and are slender; the caudal, taken from its centre, is one-sixth of the total height ; it is strongly bilobed ; the anus is rather long but narrow ; it is formed of three spines and six soft rays ; the first spine is very minute, the second about three times its length, and the third about four times as long as the second ; this third is slender, and has some very feeble denticulations on its inner side ; the pectorals are contained one and one-half times in the length of the head ; it has a first hard ray and fifteen soft; the ventrals have one spine and eight soft rays, the spine being about two-thirds of the length of the first soft ray.

The general colour is of a beautiful yellow brown, with golden tinges ; it degenerates into a brilliant white on the belly, the edge of which is rather yellow ; the pectoral is bordered superiorly with black ; the caudal tinged with red. The mouth has no teeth, and there are no barbels ; the operculum and scales are covered with fine concentrical striæ ; the eye is of a pale yellow ; the mouth is extensible ; the eye of moderate size ; the second portion of the air-bladder is very elongate, and about two and one-half times as long as the other.

I have only seen one specimen in the Melbourne Market. It had been found in the Mordialoc River; but several others were sent to the Acclimatisation Society from Sydney, and there is no doubt that it is an introduced fish, but I do not know from what country it came direct.

Apart from this variety, which seems remarkably constant, the common Chinese *Auratus* is very widely spread in Melbourne, and presents all its usual beautiful colours.

3.—NEOCORASSIUS.

This is the only *Cyprinoid* sort on which I have considerable doubts as to its having been imported. The two specimens I have seen of it were caught in the Saltwater River, at Footscray, during the cold weather. The first was found a year ago, and I was so convinced that no fish of this family was to be found in Australia, that I thought it belonged to some imported sort of *Corassius*, of which it has the general appearance ; but a second specimen having been recently found in the same locality, I examined it with more care, and I find it impossible to place it in any of the groups mentioned by Dr. Gunther, or any other author. I cannot, on the fresh specimen, find any trace of teeth whatever; but by its anal fin being very short, formed of six branched rays, its lateral line running along the medium line of the tail; its dorsal fin with a strongly serrated spine, situated a little behind the ventrals, its abdomen compressed into a sharp ridge behind the ventrals, and the absence of barbels, it seems to come very near to Dr. Bleeker's genus, *Rohteicthys*; but the very large scales which cover its body make it distinct from this Indian genus, and its enormously developed belly gives it a very particular appearance.

I have just said that on the fresh specimens there is to trace whatever of teeth; but on the dried one there is visible on each side of the palate a very large horny tubercular one, having the form of a sugar loaf; but this seems only to have appeared through the skin by the effect of dessication.

NEOCARASSUIS VENTRICOSUS.

The body is very high, very thick, and the lower profile remarkably rounded and convex; the mouth is rather extensible. The height of the body is contained two and one-third times in the total length; head four and a-half times in the same; orbit four and four-tenth times in the length of head. No barbels; head without scales, except under the eye. The scales on the infraorbital are very large, in small number, radiated, and serrated on their edge; operculum covered with arched, convergent striæ; scales of the body very large—thirty on the lateral line, fifteen on the oblique one, of which seven are over the lateral line (which runs over the eighth); they are covered with fine concentric striæ; they appear, when seen through a lens, finely serrated. The lateral line is always straight, rather elevated near the head, and runs over the middle of the tail; it is formed of a succession of elevated ridges, which only extend over the two first thirds of the scale, and end (on the living specimen) by a rounded point of an obscure colour. The first dorsal is formed of four spines, of which the first is very small, the second rather longer, the third nearly three times as long as the second, and the fourth very long, rather strong, with numerous spinelets on its inner side; it is four times longer than the third. The rays number seventeen, and the first are longer than the longest spines, but they decrease in height as they extend backwards. The caudal is emarginated, slightly bilobed, formed of nineteen long rays and of three or four small ones on each side. The external rays are about one-third longer than the centre ones. Anal short, contained nearly nine times in the total length, caudal included, and formed of two spines, of which the first is small, and the second five times longer ; it is compressed, very strongly serrated on its inner side, and of six rays ; the first of these is longer than the rays, and the last considerably shorter. The ventrals are formed of one rather long and slender spine, and of nine rays ; the pectorals are inserted very low, much below the angle of the mouth, and have nineteen rays ; they are a little shorter than the distance from the anterior edge of the orbit to the end of the operculum ; the ventrals have one long, slender spine, and seven rays rather longer than the spine, which is neither notched nor serrated.

The colour of the first specimen was of a light gilt green on the upper and lateral parts, and of a silvery white below ; the base of the scales very brilliant ; the eye silvery ; the throat and anterior part of the belly very brilliant and iridescent ; the dorsal, caudal, and anal were of a greyish green ; the ventrals white ; the pectorals white at their base, and green in the remainder of their length.

The natatorial bladder is large, formed of two parts—the first about two-thirds as long as the other, but broader ; it is rather bilobed in front ; the second portion is oblong, and rounded at its extremity.

The second specimen was entirely of a beautiful red colour, with golden tinges on the sides of the head and body, very much like *Cyprinus Auratus.*

	Inches.
Length of first specimen	9¾
Height of body	3⅝
Length of dorsal	3½
———— of pectoral	1¾-½
———— of anal	1½

This second specimen—the one of a red colour—has a far more irregular form than the first, the back, behind the head, being very gibbous, and the lower profile still more inflated. Its length is eleven inches, and its height five and a-quarter.

LIST OF VICTORIAN FISHES

DESCRIBED OR MENTIONED IN THIS WORK.

CONTRIBUTION

TO THE

ICHTHYOLOGY OF AUSTRALIA.

II.—NOTE ON SOME SOUTH AUSTRALIAN FISHES.

I have received from Mr. Waterhouse, the able and indefatigable Curator of the South Australian Museum, a most interesting series of small fishes, collected by himself in the St. Vincent's Gulf, by means of a trawl. A considerable number appear new, and others are only imperfectly known. I intend, in the next volume of the publications of this Society, to give a full account of them, but I think it is only doing justice to Mr. Waterhouse to give here a list of the species, and a short diagnostic of his new discoveries. I just follow the order of his invoices :—

1. *Hippocampus Breviceps.*—Peters.

2. *Phillopteryx Elongatus.*—Cast.

   Differs from *Foliatus* by its being of a smaller size ; the body much more elongate in both sexes; its foliated appendices much shorter, broader, and of an oval form.

3. *Syngnathus Pœcilolæmus.*—Peters.

4. *Leptoichthys Fistularius.*—Kaup.

5. *Stigmatophora Argus.*—Richard.

6. *Syngnathus Curtirostris.*—Cast.

   The snout is contained three times in the length of the head. Of a dark brown colour, with silvery spots on the head and anterior part of the body.

7. *Stigmatophora Olivacea.*— Cast.

Snout at least twice as long as the remaining part of the
head ; opereulum without a longitudinal ridge ; vent below
the middle of the dorsal fin ; egg-pouch extending over
thirteen rings ; body rings, nineteen. Entirely of an olive
colour.

8. *Aploactisoma.*—Cast.

This new genus is nearly allied to Richardson's *Aploactis*,
but differs from it by the presence of teeth on the palatine
bones, and the composition of the fins.

Aplo. Schomburgki.—Cast.

1st D., 5 ; 2nd D., 8/15. Dark brown, marbled with black ;
a spot of the last colour at the end of the dorsal.

9. *Patœcus Waterhousii.*—Cast.

The pectoral fin rather longer than the head, only extending
to the anus ; dorsal with thirty spines, the first sensibly
longer than the others, and with its membrane deeply
emarginated ; caudal with the fifth, sixth, and seventh
rays considerably prolongated ; anal with ten rays, the posterior ones being prolongated and pointed ; mouth surrounded
by several series of bifid papillæ. Brown, marbled with
white.

10. *Apistes Marmoratus.*—Cuv. and Val.

11. *Glyptauchen Panduratus.*—Richard.

12. *Christiceps Splendens.*—Cast.

Upper profile very convex ; first dorsal high, of three rays ;
the second of twenty-eight spines and six rays ; the anal has
two spines and twenty-three rays. Carmine colour, with
the head and fins orange.

13. *Chironectes Filamentosus.*— Cast.

Comes near *Marmoratus*. On the head, a long, thin, tenta-
culated spine, having on each side a slender, filiform, bifid
tentacle ; on the back, there is another long spine, ending,
like the other, in a tubereulous knob, and bearing tentacles.
D., 13 ; A., 8. Light brown, with black blotches ; lower
parts of the body covered with long fleshy appendices.

14. *Monacanthus Perulifer.*—Cast.

Anal fin with twenty-seven rays; dorsal spine with four series of barbs; the front series much closer together than the posterior series, and formed of small barbs. General appearance of *Granulatus.*

15. *Vincentia.*—Cast.

General characters of *Chilodipterus,* but no canines; differs from *Pomatomus* by its general high form; its two dorsals are inserted one very near the other; the anterior part of the body is considerably developed; eyes large; two dorsals; the cleft of the mouth oblique; no teeth on the palatine bones, and no spines to the operculum. General appearance of *Apogon.*

Vin. Waterhousii.—Cast.

Reddish colour.

16. *Cheilinus Aurantiacus.*—Cast.

D. 9/11.   A. 3/10.   P. 11.

Twenty-three scales on the longitudinal line, and ten on the transverse, three of which are above the lateral line. Of a beautiful orange colour; the dorsal and anal with a broad external black band, and a series of feeble, obscure spots near the body.

17. *Gerres? Melbournensis.*—Cast.

18. *Odax.* Three sorts:—

O. Radiatus.—Quoy and Gaim.

O. Frenatus.—Gunther.

O. Richardsonii.—Gunther.

19. *Upeneichthys Porosus.*—Cuv. and Val.

20-22. *Heteroscarus.*

I propose separating from *Scarus,* under this name, fishes having the upper jaw longer than the other; teeth soldered together, with a median suture in front at the upper jaw; scales large; fourteen or fifteen stiff dorsal spines, the three first prolongated in form of filaments; head naked, porous; cheeks covered with scales, difficult to perceive, and seemingly soldered together; operculum with several rows of large scales; lateral line continuous.

Heteroscarus Filamentosus.—Cast.

The three first dorsal spines prolongated in long filaments. D., 15/11; A., 2/12.

Heteroscarus Modestus.—Cast.

The first dorsal spines less prolongated. D., 14/10; A., 2/11.

21. *Platycephalus Inops ?*—Jenyns.

Accords well with the description, with the exception of the colour of ventrals and anal, which are of a light yellow, covered, like the other fins, with black punctiform spots.

23. *Enoplosus Armatus.*—White.

All the specimens are of a remarkably bright colour, and the cross-bands extend more on the second dorsal and on the anal than on the Melbourne specimens.

24. *Diodon Spinosissimus ?*—Cuv.

25. *Aracana Ornata.*—Gray.

26. *Ophiclinus.*—Cast.

This new genus is characterised by—Body very elongate; mouth opening upwards; snout having two short filaments; ventral fins inserted in front of the pectorals, being formed of one short and two long filaments; dorsal composed of numerous spines and two rays, which are situated posteriorly; it has no anterior detached portion, and is, as the anal, attached to the caudal; the anal has no spines; lateral line only marked on the extreme anterior part of the body; teeth very numerous, short, very thick, crowded on all the bones of the palate, and also on very numerous rows on the lower jaw.

Ophicl. Antarcticus.—Cast.

Dorsal with sixty-three spines and two rays; anal with thirty-nine rays. Of a brownish red, with the lower parts lighter.

27. *Heteroclinus.*—Cast.

This new genus is characterised by—Body sub-elongate; mouth opening upwards; snout without tentacles; ventral fins inserted in front of the pectorals, formed of one short and two long filaments; dorsals two, the first of three spines; the second of twenty-eight spines and three rays, placed posteriorly; it is attached to the tail; lateral line only marked on the extreme anterior part of the body; teeth short, blunt, thick; crowded on both jaws, with an external line of more slender and sharper ones; very numerous on all the palatine bones.

Heter. Adelaidæ,—Cast.

Of a reddish brown, with the lower parts of a yellowish white; an irregular black band on the side.

ERRATA.

Page 33, line 26, instead of: and *as* names without meaning, &c., read: and names without meaning, &c.

„ 37, „ 19, instead of: I spent nearly five years in the United States and Canada. I collected a considerable, &c., read: I spent nearly five years in the United States and Canada, I collected, &c.

„ 40, „ 37, instead of: Livington Rooke, read: Lavington Roope.

„ 92, „ 2, instead of: the new *species* I propose here, &c., read: the new *genus* I propose here, &c.

„ 129, „ 16, instead of: sorts of these will, &c., read: sorts of *Blennius* will certainly, &c.

OBSERVATIONS.

My genus *Neotephræps* may be identical with Dr. Gunther's genus *Melambaphes.*

Trigla Polyommata is the type of a genus, *Hoplonotus*, Guichenot, " Ann. de la Société Linnéenne de Maine et Loire," vol. xix.

I have just received, through the kindness of Mr. George Kissley, a specimen of the Murray Chatæssus, and I find it identical with *Erebi.*

SELECT PLANTS

(EXCLUSIVE OF TIMBER TREES)

READILY ELIGIBLE FOR

VICTORIAN INDUSTRIAL CULTURE,

with indications of their native countries and some of their uses.

AN ENUMERATION OFFERED BY

BARON FERD. VON MUELLER,

C.M.G., M.D., Ph.D., F.R.S., F.L.S., F.R.G.S., C.M.Z.S., F.R.B.S.,
Commander of the Order of St. Jago., and of the Order of Isabella Cath.,
Vice-President of the Acclimatisation Society of Victoria.

WHEN offering an Appendix to the Acclimatisation Society's Report of last year, in the enumeration of timber trees desirable for a country of our clime, my willingness was expressed to extend the notes, then offered, also to other plants of prominent utilitarian value So considerate was the reception, which the former Appendix experienced, that I am induced already to redeem my promise of extending these data; and I do this with all the more readiness, as the rapid progress of tillage almost throughout our Colonial dominion is causing more and more a desire for the general and particular indication of such plants, which a colder clime excludes from the northern countries, where most of us spent our youth. Within the pages, allotted to this communication, the notes offered could only be indicative. Hence this list is merely intended to facilitate the choice of selection. More extensive information must be sought in special works, to which, through the English language, access is given by the literature of Britain and North America. Thus the colonist, who wishes to pursue an altered path of husbandry, by adopting some new foreign plants for his culture, can follow up easily enough the enquiry, to which he may be led by the indications now submitted.

The writer found himself surrounded by some difficulty of drawing the line of demarcation between the plants admissible into this list and those which should be excluded, because the final importance of any particular species, for a particular want, locality or treatment, cannot be fully foretold. Moreover, the field is so ample from which our plants for novel culture may be gathered, that only the first instalment of a suggestive and abridged index could be presented on this occasion; but it may be supplemented, as well as the former notes on timber trees, should friendly consideration recognize the spirit, in which these suggestions are offered. As an instance of the difficulty to adduce what is most desirable for an enumeration, such as the present, it may be mentioned, that many species of the thousands of foreign grasses would be highly eligible here, either for naturalization or for cultural purposes. A few, however, could only be singled out for the present purpose, and this with no other view than leading the occupants of our soil onward in some new direction for their pastoral or agrarian pursuits.

The plants, which appear to be of primary importance for our rural wants, have been designated in this list with an asterisk. Of these, indeed, many are long since secured by the efforts of numerous colonists and their friends abroad, who strove to enrich our cultural resources; and in these efforts the writer, so far as his public or private means did permit, has ever endeavoured to share. But although such plants are introduced, they are not in all instances as yet widely diffused, nor in many localities tested. Also, for the sake of completeness, ordinary culture plants appear in this index, as the opportunity seemed an apt one, to offer a few passing remarks on their value. The claims of this contribution on originality must necessarily be very limited. What for ages has engaged the reflection of thousands cannot present absolutely or largely a new field of research. So

It is especially with the means and objects of ordinary culture of fields. To gather, therefore, from a widely-scattered literature that, which might be here instructive or suggestive, was mainly my task, though those gatherings may prove insignificant. Likely also such enumerations, in a very condensed form, will promote our communications for rural interchanges, both cis- and trans-equatorial, though mainly with the countries of the Northern Hemisphere, which predominantly, if not almost exclusively, provided all the vegetable substances, which enter into the main requisites of our daily life. Lists like the present may aid also in naming the plants and their products with scientific correctness in establishments of economic horticulture, or in technologic or other educational collections. In grouping, at the close of this tract, the genera of the plants enumerated, according to the products which they yield, facility is afforded for tracing out any particular series of plants, about which special economic information may be sought, or which may prominently engage at any time the attention of the cultivator, the manufacturer, or the artisan.

Melbourne Botanic Garden, April, 1872.

Acacia Farnesiana, Willd.

Dioscorides's small Acacia. Indigenous to South Asia; found westward as far as Japan; a native also of the warmer parts of Australia, as far south as the Darling River; found spontaneously in tropical and sub-tropical America, but apparently not in tropical Africa. Professor Fraas has recognised in this Acacia the ancient plant. The scented flowers are much sought after for perfumery. This bush may also be utilized as a hedge plant, and a kind of Gum Arabic may be obtained from it.

Achillea Millefolium, L.

Yarrow or Millfoil. Europe, Northern Asia and North America. A perennial medicinal herb of considerable astringency, pervaded with essential oil, containing also a

bitter principle (Achillein) and a peculiar acid, which takes
its name from the generic appellation of the plant.

Aconitum Napellus, L.

The Monk's Hood. In the colder, especially mountainous
parts of Europe and Northern Asia. A powerful medicinal
plant of perennial growth, but sometimes only of biennial
duration, variable in its forms. It was first introduced into
Australia, together with a number of other Aconits, by the
writer of this communication. All the species possess more
or less modified medicinal qualities, as well in their herb as
in their root ; but so dangerously powerful are they, that
the plants can only be administered by the exercise of legiti-
mate medical practice. Napellus root, according to Professor
Wittstein, contains three alkaloids : Aconitin, Napellin and
Narcotin. The foliage contains also a highly acrid, volatile
principle, perhaps chemically not unlike that of many other
Ranunculaceæ. Aconitin, one of the most potent of any
of the medicinal substances in existence, can likewise be
obtained from the Nepalese Aconitum ferox, and probably
from several other species of the genus.

Acorus Calamus, L.

The Sweet Flag. Europe, Middle and North Asia, North
America. A perennial pond or lake plant. The somewhat
aromatic root is used as a stomachic, and also in the preparation of confectionery, in the distillation of gin, and in
the brewing of some kinds of beer. The flavor of the
root depends mainly on a peculiar volatile oil.

Actæa spicata, L.

The Baneberry. On forest mountains, mainly in limestone
soil of Europe, North Asia and North America. A perennial medicinal herb. Its virtue depends on peculiar acrid
and bitter, as well as tonic principles. In North America,
this species, and likewise A. alba, are also praised as effica-
cious antidotes against ophidian poisons.

Adesmia balsamica, Bertero.

The Jarilla of Chili. A small shrub, remarkable for exuding
a fragrant balsam of some technic value.

Æschynomene aspera, L.

The Solah of tropical Asia. A large perennial erect or floating swamp plant, probably hardy in the warmer tracts of our Colony. Introduced from the Botanic Garden of Melbourne into the tropical parts of Australia. The pith-hats are made from the young stems of this plant. The Solah is of less importance for cultivation than for naturalisation.

Agave Americana, L.

The gigantic Aloe of Central America. It comes here into flower in about ten years. The pithy stem can be utilized for some of the purposes, for which cork is usually employed, for instance, to form the bottom of insect-cases. The honey-sucking birds and the bees are very fond of the flowers of this prodigious plant. The leaves of this and some other Agaves, such as A. Mexicana, furnish the strong Pita-fibre, which is adapted for ropes, and even for beautiful textile fabrics. The sap can be converted into alcohol. Where space and circumstances admit of it, impenetrable hedges may be raised in the course of some years from Agaves.

Agrostis alba, L.

The Fiorin or White Bent-Grass. Europe, North and Middle Asia, North Africa, North America. Perennial, showing a predilection for moisture. It is valuable as an admixture to many other grasses, as it becomes available at the season, when some of them fail. Sinclair regards it as a pasture grass inferior to Festuca pratensis and Dactylis glomerata, but superior to Alopecurus pratensis. The variety with long suckers is best adapted for sandy pastures, and helps to bind shifting sand on the sea coast, or broken soil on river banks.

Aletris farinosa, L.

The Colic root of the woodlands of North America. This pretty herb is of extreme bitterness, and can be medicinally administered as a tonic.

Alkanna tinctoria, Tausch.

On sandy places around the Mediterranean Sea. It yields the Alkanna root, used for dyeing oleaginous and other substances. It might be naturalized.

Allium Schœnoprasum, L.

The Chives. Europe, Northern Asia and North America. Available for salads and condiments. This species of Allium seems not yet so generally adopted in our culinary cultivation as Allium Ascalonicum (the Shallot), A. Cepa (the ordinary Onion), A. fistulosum (the Welsh Onion), A. Porrum (the Leek), or A. sativum (the Garlick). A. Scorodoprasum, or the Sand Leek of Europe and North Africa, resembles both Garlick and Shallot.

Aloe ferox, Mill.

South Africa. This species yields the best Cape Aloe, as observed by Dr. Pappe. The simply inspissated juice of the leaves of the various species of this genus constitutes the Aloe drug. It is best obtained by using neither heat nor pressure for extracting the sap. By re-dissolving the aqueous part in cold water, and reducing the liquid through boiling to dryness, the Extract of Aloes is prepared. All species are highly valuable in our Colony, where they are hardy, and can be used, irrespective of their medicinal importance, to beautify any rocky or otherwise arid spot.

Aloe linguiformis, Miller.

South Africa. According to Thunberg, from this species the purest gum-resin is obtained.

Aloe plicatilis, Mill.

South Africa. The drug of this species acts milder than that of A. ferox.

Aloe purpurascens, Haworth.

South Africa. Again one of the plants, which furnishes the Cape Aloe of commerce.

Aloe socotrina, L,.

Hills of the Island of Socotra. Also cultivated in Barbadoes and elsewhere, thus yielding the Socotrin Aloe.

Aloe spicata, Thunberg.

South Africa. This aloe provides Cape Aloe. It is an exceedingly handsome plant.

Aloe vulgaris, Lamarck.

The Yellow-flowered Aloe. Countries around the Mediterranean Sea, also Canary Islands, on the sandy or rocky sea coast. Such places could also here readily be utilized for this and allied plants. Dr. Sibthorp identified this species with the 'Αλόη of Dioscorides; hence it is not probable, that A. vulgaris is simultaneously also of American origin, although it is cultivated in the Antilles, and furnishes from thence the main supply of the Barbadoes Aloe. In East India this species is also seemingly only existing in a cultivated state. Haworth found the leaves of this and of A. striata softer and more succulent than those of any other aloe. It is said to be the only species with yellow flowers among those early known. It is also this species only, which Professor Willkomm and Professor Parlatore record as truly wild in Spain and Italy.

Aloe Zeyheri, Harvey.

South Africa. A magnificent, very tall species, doubtless valuable like the rest.

Alopecurus pratensis, L.

Meadow Foxtail Grass. Europe, North Africa, North and Middle Asia. One of the best of perennial pasture grasses. Though so extensively cultivated for years in our Colony, it is mentioned, for completeness' sake, in this list. It attains to its full perfection only after a few years of growth, as noticed by Sinclair. For this reason, it is not equal to Dactylis glomerata for the purpose of changing crops. Otherwise it is more nutritious than the latter, although the annual return in Britain proved less. Sheep thrive well on it. Sinclair and others found that this grass, when exclusively combined with white clover, will support from the second season five ewes and five lambs on an acre of sandy loam. But this grass, to thrive well, needs land not altogether dry. In all permanent artificial pastures, this

Alopecurus should form one of the principal ingredients, because it is so lasting and nutritive. In our Alpine regions it would also prove prolific, and might convert many places there gradually into summer-runs. It is early flowering, and likes the presence of lime in the soil.

Alstonia constricta, F. v. M.

Warmer parts of East Australia, particularly in the dry inland districts. The bark of this small tree is aromatic-bitter, and regarded as valuable in ague, also as a general tonic.

Alstrœmeria pallida, Graham.

Chili. Palatable starch can be obtained from the root of this plant, which, for its loveliness alone, deserves a place in any garden. The tubers of others of the numerous Alstrœmerias can doubtless be utilized in a similar technic manner.

Althæa officinalis, L.

The Real Marsh-Mallow. Europe, North Africa, North and Middle Asia. A tall perennial herb, with handsome flowers. The mucilaginous root and also the foliage are used for medicinal purposes. The plant succeeds best on damp, somewhat saline soil.

Amelanchier Botryapium, Candolle.

The Grape-Pear of North America. This fruit tree attains a height of 30 feet. The purplish fruits are small, but of pleasant taste, and ripen early in the season. This bush or tree will live in sandsoil; but it is one of those hardy kinds particularly eligible for our Alps.

Amygdalus communis, L.

The Almond Tree. Countries around the Mediterranean Sea and Orient. Both the sweet and bitter Almond are derived from this species. Their uses, and the value of the highly palatable oil, obtained by pressure from them, are well known. This oil can well be chosen as a means of providing a pleasant substitute for milk during sea voyages, &c., by mixing, when required, with it half its weight of powdered gum arabic, and adding then successively, while quickly agitating in a stone mortar, about double the quantity of water. Thus a palatable and wholesome sort of cream for tea or coffee is obtained at any moment. There exist hard and soft shelied varieties of both the sweet and bitter Almond. In time, they should form an important article of our exports. Almonds can even be grown on sea shores. The crystalline Amygdalin can best be prepared from bitter Almonds, through removing the oil by pressure, then subjecting them to distillation with alcohol, and finally precipitating with Æther. The volatile bitter Almond oil—a very dangerous substance—is obtained by aqueous distillation. Dissolved in alocohol, it forms the Essence of Almonds. This can also be prepared from peach kernels.

Anacyclus Pyrethrum, Candolle.

Countries near the Mediterranean Sea. The root is used medicinally.

Andropogon avenaceus, Michaux.

(Sorghum avenaceum, Chapman.)

North and Central America. This tall perennial grass lives in dry, sandy soil, and should here be tried for growth of fodder.

Andropogon bicolor, Roxburgh.

Warmer parts of Asia. One of the annual tall Sorghums· It ripens its seeds in three or four months from the time of sowing, the produce in good soil being often upwards of one hundredfold. It is a wholesome grain.

Andropogon Calamus, Royle.

Central India. The Sweet Calamus of the Ancients. From this species the Gingergrass-oil of Nemaur is distilled, an article much used in perfumery.

Andropogon cernuus, Roxb. *(Sorghum cernuum, Willd.)*

One of the Guinea Corns. India, where it is much cultivated, and so also in other tropical countries. It is perennial, and forms the "staff' of life of the mountaineers" beyond Bengal. It reaches a height of 15 feet, with leaves over 3 feet long. The thick stems are rooting at the lower joints, and cattle are very fond of them. The grain is white. The specific limits of the various Sorghums are not well ascertained.

Andropogon citratus, Candolle.

The Lemon Grass of India. It yields an essential oil for perfumery; besides it is occasionally used for tea. This applies as well to Andropogon Nardus, L., and some allied grasses.

Andropogon Haleppensis, Sibthorp.

South Europe, Orient. A rich perennial grass, cultivated often under the name of Cuba Grass.

Andropogon Ivarancusa, Roxb.

One of the fragrant grasses of North India, much used like A. Shœnanthus.

Andropogon Martini, Roxb. *(A. flexuosus,* Nees.)

On the mountains of India. The fragrant Citronella Oil is distilled in Ceylon and elsewhere from the leaves of this species. General Martin observed, that cattle are voraciously fond of this grass; but it imparts its fragrance to meat and milk.

Andropogon muricatus, Retz.

India. A Swamp-grass, with delightfully fragrant roots.

Andropogon nutans, L. *(Sorghum nutans,* Gray.)

North America. A tall, nutritious, perennial grass, content with dry and barren soil.

Andropogon saccharatus, Roxb. *(Sorghum saccharatum,* Pers.)

Tropical Asia. The Broom-Corn. A tall annual species, splendid as a fodder grass. From the saccharine juice sugar is obtainable. A sample of such, prepared from plants of the Melbourne Botanic Garden, was shown at the Exhibition of 1862. This Sorghum furnishes also material for a well-known kind of brooms. A variety or a closely allied species yields the Caffir Corn *(A. Caffrorum,* Kunth). The plant can be advantageously utilized for preparing treacle. For this purpose, the sap is expressed at the time of flowering, and simply evaporated; the yield is about 100 gallons from the acre. In 1860, nearly seven millions of gallons of sorghum treacle were produced in the United States.

Andropogon Shœnanthus, L.

Deserts of Arabia. A scented grass, allied to the Indian oil-yielding Andropogons. A similar species occurs in arid places of the interior of North Australia.

Andropogon Sorghum, Brotero. (*Sorghum vulgare*, Persoon.)

The large Indian Millet or Guinea Corn, or the Durra. Warmer parts of Asia. A tall annual plant. The grains can be converted into bread, porridge and other preparations of food. It is a very prolific corn and to us particularly valuable for green fodder. Many others of the numerous species of Andropogon, from both hemispheres, deserve our attention.

Anemone Pulsatilla, L.

Europe and Northern Asia. On limestone soil. This pretty perennial herb is of some medicinal importance.

Anona Cherimolia, Miller.

Tropical and sub-tropical South America. This shrub or tree might be tried in the frostless lower valleys of East Gipps Land, where humidity and rich soil will also prove favourable to its growth. It yields the Cherimoyer fruit. The flowers are very fragrant.

Anthemis nobilis, L.

The true Camomile. Middle and South Europe, North Africa. A well-known medicinal plant, here frequently used as edgings for garden plots. Flowers in their normal state are preferable for medicinal use to those, in which the ray-flowers are produced in increased numbers. They contain a peculiar volatile oil and two acids similar to Angelica and Valeriana acid.

Anthemis tinctoria, L.

Middle and South Europe, Orient. An annual herb. The flowers contain a yellow dye.

Anthistiria ciliata, L. fil. (*Anthistiria Australis*, R. Brown.)

The well-known Kangaroo Grass, not confined to Australia, but stretching through Southern Asia also, and through the whole of Africa. It is mentioned here, because its growth should be encouraged by every means. There are several species of Anthistiria deserving introduction and naturalisation in our Colony.

Anthoxanthum odoratum, L.

The Scented Vernal Grass. Europe, North and Middle Asia, North Africa. A perennial, not of great value as a fattening grass, yet always desired for the flavor, which it imparts to hay. Perhaps for this purpose the scented Andropogons might serve here also. On deep and moist soils it attains its greatest perfection. It is much used for mixing among permanent grasses on pastures, where it will continue long in season. It would live well in our Alps. The lamellar-crystalline Cumarin is the principle, on which the odor of Anthoxanthemum depends.

Apios tuberosa, Moench.

North America. A climber, with somewhat milky juice. The mealy tubers are edible.

Apium graveolens, L.

The Celery. Europe, North Africa, North and Middle Asia. It is here merely inserted with a view of pointing out, that it might be readily naturalized on our sea shores.

Apium prosʼratum, La Billardiere.

The Australian Celery. Extra-tropical Australia, New Zealand, extra-tropical South America. This also can be utilized as a culinary vegetable.

Apocynum cannabinum, L.

On river banks in North America. This is recorded among plants yielding a textile fibre.

Arachis hypogaea, L.

The Earth-nut, Pea-nut or Ground-nut. Brazil. The seeds of this annual herb are consumed in a roasted state, or used for pressing from them a palatable oil. The plant is a very productive one, and yields a very quick return. It ranks also as a valuable fodder herb. A light somewhat calcareous soil is best fitted for its growth. On such soil, 50 bushels may be obtained from the acre.

Archangelica officinalis, Hoffmann.

Aretic zone and mountain regions of Europe. The stalks are used for confectionery; the roots arc of medicinal use. Only in our Alps would this herb fully establish its value. The root is biennial and used in the distillation of some cordials.

Arctostaphylos uva ursi, Sprengel.

Alpine and Arctic Europe, North Asia and North America. A medicinal small shrub, which here could best be reared in the heath-moors of our Alpine regions.

Argania Sideroxylon, Roem. and Schult.

The Argan-tree. Western Barbary, on dry hills. Its growth is here found to be slow; but it is a tree of longevity. Though comparatively low in stature, its foliage occasionally spreads to a circumference of 220 feet. It sends out suckers from the root. The fruits serve as food for cattle in Morocco.; but here the kernels would be more likely to be utilized by pressing the oil from them.

Aristolochia Serpentaria, L.

The Snake-root of North America. The root of this trailing herb is valuable in medicine; it contains a peculiar volatile oil. Several other Aristolochiæ deserve culture for medicinal purposes, for instance,—Aristolochia ovalifolia (Guaco), and A. anguicida, from the mountains of Central America, should they prove hardy.

Arnica montana, L.

Colder parts of Europe. This pretty herb is perennial, and of medicinal value. It is eligible for our sub-alpine regions. The active principles are:—Arnicin, volatile oil, eupron and capryl acid.

Arracacha xanthorrhiza, Bancroft.

Mountain regions of Central America. An umbelliferous herb. The roots are nutritious and palatable. There are yellow, purple and pale varieties.

Artemisia Absinthium, L.

The Wormwood. Europe, North and Middle Asia, and North Africa. A perennial herb, valuable as a tonic and anthelminthic. Several other species of Artemisia deserve cultivation for medicinal purposes. Active principles :— Absinthin, an oily substance, indurating to a crystalline mass ; a volatile oil peculiar to the species.

Artemisia Dracunculus, L.

The Tarragon or Estragon. North Asia. A perennial herb, used as a condiment. Its flavour rests on two volatile oils, one of them peculiar to the plant.

Arundinaria falcata, Nees.

Nepaul. One of the hardiest kinds of the Bamboo tribe. It rises to the height of 20 feet, the canes attaining a diameter of 4 inches.

Arundinaria macrosperma, Michaux.

Southern States of North America,—particularly on the Missisippi. This Bamboo-like reed forms there the eane-brakes. It requires to be replanted after flowering in the course of years. Height 20 feet.

Arundo Donax, L.

The tall evergreen lasting Bamboo-reed of South Europe and North Africa. It is one of the most important plants of its class for quickly producing a peculiar scenic effect in picturesque plantations, also for intercepting at once the view to unsightly objects, and for giving early shelter. The canes can be used for fishing-rods.

Arundo Pliniana, Turr.

On the Mediterranean and Adriatic Seas. A smaller plant than A. Donax, with more slender stems and narrower leaves, but similarly evergreen, and resembling the Donax reed also in its roots.

Arundo saccharoides, F. v. M.

(Gynerium saccharoides, Humboldt.)

Northern parts of South America. This species is here not yet introduced ; but it is likely to prove hardy. Like the following, it is conspicuously magnificent.

Arundo Sellowiana, Schultes. (*Arundo dioica,* Spreng. *non* Louriero. *Gynerium argenteum,* Nees.)

The Pampas Grass of Uruguay, Paraguay and the La Plata State. A grand autumnal flowering reed, with gorgeous feathery panicles. As an industrial plant it deserves here a place, because paper can be prepared from its leaves.

Asparagus officinalis, L.

Europe, North Africa, North Asia. The well-known Asparagus plant, which, if naturalized on our coast, would aid in binding the sand. The foliage contains Inosit-Sugar ; the shoots contain Asparagin.

Astragalus Cephalonicus, Fischer. (*A. aristatus,* Sibthorp.)

Cephalonia. A small shrub, yielding a good tragacanth ; and so probably, also, the true A. aristatus of l'Heritier is producing it.

Artragalus Creticus, La Marck.

Candia and Greece. A small bush, exuding the ordinary vermicular Tragacanth. The pale is preferable to the brown sort.

Astragalus gummifer, La Billard.

Syria and Persia. This shrub also yields a good kind of Tragacanth.

Astragalus strabiliferus, Royle.

Asiatic Turkey. The brown Tragacanth is collected from this species.

Astragalus verus, Olivier.

Asiatic Turkey and Persia. This shrub furnishes the Takalor or Smyrna Tragacanth, or it is derived from an allied species.

Atriplex hortensis, L.

North and Middle Asia. The Arroche. An annual Spinage plant.

Atropa Belladonna, L.

The Deadly Nightshade. South and Middle Europe and Western Asia. A most important perennial medicinal herb.

The highly powerful Atropin is derived from it, besides another alkaloid, the Belladonnin.

Avena fatua, L.

Wild Oat. Europe, North Africa, North and Middle Asia, eastward as far as Japan. The experiments of Professor Buckman indicate, that our ordinary Culture-Oat (*Avena sativa*, L.) is descended from this plant.

Avena flavescens, L. (*Trisetum flavescens*, Beauv.)

Yellowish Oat Grass. Europe, North Africa, Middle and North Asia, eastward as far as Japan. One of the best of perennial meadow-grasses, living on dry soil; fitted also for our Alps.

Avena pratensis, L.

Meadow Oat Grass. Europe, North Asia. It thrives well on dry, clayey soil; it produces a sweet fodder, but not in so great proportion as several other less nutritious grasses. It is perennial, and well adapted for our snowy mountains, where it would readily establish itself, even on heathy moors.

Avena pubescens, L.

Downy Oat-Grass. Europe, North and Middle Asia. A sweet perennial grass, requiring dry but good soil, containing lime. It is nutritious and prolific. Several good Oat-grasses are peculiar to North America and other parts of the globe. Their relative value as fodder-grasses is in many cases not exactly known, nor does the limit assigned to this little treatise allow of their being enumerated on this occasion.

Bactris Gasipæs, Humboldt. (*Guilielma speciosa*, Mart.)

The Peach Palm of the Amazon River, ascending to the warm-temperate regions of the Andes. Stems clustered, attaining a height of 90 feet. Dr. Spruce describes the large bunches of fruits as possessing a thick, firm and mealy pericarp, which, when cooked, has a flavor between Potato and Chesnut, but superior to either. To us, however, this palm would be mainly an object of grandeur. It is likely to endure our clime in the fern-tree gullies.

Bambusa arundinacea, Roxb.

The Thorny Bamboo of India. It requires rich, moist soil, and delights on river banks. It is of less height than Bambusa vulgaris; it also sends up from the root numerous stems, but with bending branches, thorny at the joints. The seeds of this and some other Bamboos are useful as food for fowls.

Bambusa attenuata, Thwaites.

The Hardy Bamboo of Ceylon, there growing on the mountains at elevations between 4000 to 6000 feet. It attains a height of 25 feet.

Bambusa elegantissima, Hasskarl.

Java, on mountains about 4000 feet high. Very tall and exceedingly slender; the upper branches pendulous. A hardy species.

Bambusa monadelpha. (*Dendrocalamus monadelphus,* Thwaites.)

Ceylon, on mountains from 4000 to 6000 feet high. A dwarf but handsome Bamboo, reaching only a height of 12 feet.

Bambusa spinosa, Roxb.

Bengal. A Bamboo of considerable height. The central cavity of the canes is of less width than in most other species, thus the strength for many technic purposes is increased.

Bambusa stricta, Roxb. (*Dendrocalamus strictus,* Nees.)

India, particularly Bengal. Grows on drier ground than B. arundinacea. It is also smaller, and quite straight. Its strength and solidity renders it fit for many select technic purposes.

Bambusa verticillata, Blume.

The Whorled Bamboo of Java.

Bambusa vulgaris, Wendland.

The large unarmed Bamboo of Bengal. It attains a height of 70 feet, and stems may attain even a length of 40 feet in one season, though the growth is slower in our clime. It has proved to be capable of resisting the occasional night frost of the lowlands of Victoria. It is the best for building Bamboo-Houses. Immersion in water for some time renders the cane still firmer. To the series of large thornless Bamboos belong also Bambusa Tulda and Bambusa Balcooa of India, and Bambusa Thouarsii from Madagascar and Bourbou. These Bamboos are much used for various kinds of furniture, mats, implements and other articles. There are many other kinds of Bamboo eligible among the species from China, Japan, India, tropical America, and perhaps tropical Africa. One occurs in Arnhem's Land.

Barosma serratifolia, Willd.

South Africa. This shrub supplies the medicinal Bucco-leaves. B. crenulata, Hook. (Diosma crenulata, L.), is only a variety of this species. Active principles—A peculiar volatile oil, a peculiar resin, and a crystalline substance called Diosmin.

Beta vulgaris, L.*

The Beet or Mangold Root. Middle and South Europe, Middle Asia, North Africa. This well-known perennial or biennial herb ought to engage the general and extensive attention of our farming population. The herb is most valuable as a palatable and nutritious spinage; the root is of importance not only as a culinary vegetable, but, as well known, also for its content of sugar, fit to be crystallised. That of Beet, indeed, is now almost exclusively consumed in Russia, Germany, Austria, France, Sweden and Belgium; and these countries not only produce the Beet Sugar, but also export it largely to the neighbouring States. The white Sicilian Beet is mainly used for salads, spinage and soups. The thick-ribbed variety serves like Asparagus or Seakale, dressed like Rhubarb. Cereal soil, particularly such as is fit for Barley, is generally adapted also for the culture of Beet. The rearing of the root, and the manufacture of the sugar, can be studied from manifold works; one has been compiled by Mr. N. Levy, of this city. A deeply stirred, drained soil, rich in lime, brings the saccharine variety of Beet to the greatest perfection. The Imperial Beet yields from 12 to 20 per cent. sugar. The Castelnau-derry, the Magdeburg, the Siberian Whiterib and the Vilmorin Beet are other varieties rich in sugar. About

5 lbs. of seeds are required for an acre. In rotation of crops, the Beet takes its place best between Barley and Oats. In Middle Europe the yield averages 14 tons of Sugar Beet to the acre, and as many hundred weight of raw sugar. The mercantile value of the root, at our distilleries, ranged from 20s. to 30s. per ton. In our clime, the Beet harvest can be extended over a far longer time of the year than in Middle Europe. The extraction of the sap is effected generally by hydraulic pressure. The juice is purified with lime and animal coal. Excess of lime is removed by carbonic acid, and the purified and decolorized juice is evaporated in vacuum pans, with a view to preventing the extensive conversion of the crystallisable sugar into treacle. The production of Beet sugar needs far less labor than that of cane sugar, and the harvest is obtained in so short a time as eight months. Beet has shown itself subject neither to alarming diseases nor to extensive attacks of insects. Beet is grown in extra-tropical zones like ours, while the sugar-cane is a plant confined to tropical and sub-tropical latitudes. Beet culture, by directly or indirectly restoring the refuge, ameliorates the soil to such an extent, that in some parts of Germany land, so utilized, has risen to fourfold its former value. Beet, furthermore, affords one of the most fattening stable fodders; and thus again an ample supply of manure. In Middle Europe now about one-sixth of all the arable land is devoted to Beet, yet the produce of cereals has not become reduced, while the rearing of fattened cattle has increased. Notwithstanding a heavy tax on the Beet-sugar factories in Europe, the industry has proved prosperous, and assumes greater and greater dimensions. In 1865, the sugar consumption of Europe amounted to 31,676,497 cwt., one-third of which had been locally supplied by the Beet, from over one thousand beet-sugar factories. Treacle obtained from beet is distilled for alcohol. For establishing remunerative factories on a large and paying scale, it has been suggested that farmers' companies might be formed. For ascertaining the percentage of sugar in Beet, saccharometers are used. In Germany, some scientific periodicals are exclusively devoted to the fostering of this industry.

Boehmeria nivea, Gaudichaud.*

The Ramee or Rheea. Southern Asia, as far east as Japan. This bush furnishes the strong and beautiful fibre woven into the fabric, which inappropriately is called grass-cloth. The bark is softened by hot water or steam, and then separable into its tender fibres. The best is obtained from the young shoots; it is glossy, tough and lasting, combining to some extent the appearance of silk with the strength of flax. The ordinary market value of the fibre is about £40 per ton; but Dr. Royle mentions that it has realized, at times, £120. The seeds are sown on manured or otherwise rich and friable soil. In the third year, or under very favorable circumstances even earlier, it yields its crops, as many as three annually. The produce of an acre has been estimated at 2 tons of fibre. This latter, since Kaempfer's time, has been known to be extensively used for ropes and cordage in Japan. Our rich and warmest forest valleys seem best adapted for the Ramee, as occasional irrigation can be also there applied. In the open grounds of Victoria it suffers from the night frosts, although this does not materially injure the plant, which sends up fresh shoots, fit for fibre, during the hot season. The plant has been cultivated and distributed since 1854, in the Botanic Garden of Melbourne, where it is readily propagated from cuttings, the seeds ripening rarely there. Cordage of this Boehmeria is three times as strong as that of hemp. Other species require to be tested, among them the one which was recently discovered in Lord Home's Island, namely Boehmeria calophleba.

Boronia megastigma, Nees.

In West Australia on margins of swamps. This remarkable bush is recorded here as an emblem of mourning, its external blackish flowers rendering it especially eligible for graves. Industrially it interests us on account of its powerfully fragrant blossoms, for the sake of which this bush will deserve to be cultivated. The scent might be extracted by Mr. Bosisto's process.

Borrago officinalis, L.

South Europe, Orient. An annual herb, occasionally used for medicinal purposes or as an admixture to salad.

Brabejum stellatifolium, L.

South Africa. The nuts of this shrub are edible, resembling those of our Macadamia ternifolia, to which also in foliage and flowers Brabejum is closely allied. The nuts are also similar to those of the Chilian Guevina Avellana.

Brassica alba, Visiani. *(Sinapis alba, L.)*

White Mustard. Europe, North Africa, North and Middle Asia. An annual. The seeds are less pungent than those of the Black Mustard, but used in a similar manner. The young leaves of both are useful as a culinary and anti-scorbutic salad. Dr. Masters enumerates Brassica Chinensis, B. dichotoma, B. Pekinensis, B. ramosa and B. glauca among the Mustards, which undergo cultivation in various parts of Asia, either for the fixed oil of their seeds or for their herbage. From 15 lbs. to 20 lbs. of seeds of the White Mustard are required for an acre. In the climate of California, similar to ours, 1400 lbs. of seeds have been gathered from an acre.

Brassica nigra, Koch. *(Sinapis nigra, L.)*

The Black Mustard. Europe, North Africa, Middle Asia. An annual. The seeds, simply crushed and then sifted, constitute the Mustard of commerce. For medicinal purposes the seeds of this species are preferable for sinapism and other purposes. In rich soil this plant is very prolific; and in our forest-valleys it is likely to remain free from the attack of aphis. Chemical constituents : A peculiar fixed oil, crystalline sinapin, the fatty sinapisin, Myron-acid and Myrosin.

Brassica oleracea, L.

An annual or biennial coast plant, indigenous to various parts of Europe. It is mentioned here with a view of showing, that it might be naturalized on our rocky and sandy sea shores. From the wild plant of the coast originated various kinds of Cabbages, Broccoli, Cauliflower, Brussel Sprouts,

Kail, Kohlrabi, &c. Other races of this species are collectively represented by Brassica Rapa, L. *(B. campestris,* L.), the Wild Navew, yielding most of the varieties of Turnips, some with other cultivated forms transferred to us from ancient times. Again other varieties are comprehended within Brassica Napus, L., such as the Swedish and Teltower Turnips, while the Rape seed, so important for its oil (Colza), is also derived from a form of B. Napus. The Rape should be produced here as an agrarian produce, giving a rapid return, wherever it should remain free of aphis. The hardier turnips could be produced on our highest Alps, as they are grown still within the Arctic circle, and, according to Dr. J. Hooker, at a height of 15,000 feet in the Himalaya mountains.

Butomus umbellatus, L.

The Flowering Rush. Europe, North and Middle Asia. This elegant perennial water-plant is mentioned here more for its value in embellishing our lakes and watercourses than for the sake of its roots. The latter, when roasted, are edible. The plant would live in our subalpine rivulets.

Bromus unioloides, Humboldt.* (*B. Schraderi,* Kunth.)

Here called the Prairie Grass. From Central America it has spread over many parts of the globe. The writer saw it disseminated in the mountains of St. Vincent's Gulf as early as 1847. It is one of the richest of all grasses, grows continously and spreads readily from seeds, particularly on fertile and somewhat humid soil, and has proved as a lasting and nutritious fodder-grass or pasture-grass one of our best acquisitions.

Broussonetia papyrifera, Ventenat.

The Paper Mulberry. Islands of the Pacific Ocean, China, Japan, perhaps only truly indigenous in the last-named country. The bast of this tree or shrub can be converted into very strong paper. It can also be used as a textile fabric ; furthermore the fabrics made from it can be dressed with linseed oil for waterproof coverings. In cultivation the plant is kept like an osier. The leaves cannot be used

for silkworms. European fabrics have largely superseded the clothing made of this plant in the South Sea
Islands.

Caesalpinia Gilliesii, Wallich. (*Poinciana Gilliesii,* Hooker.)
La Plata States. This beautiful hardy bush can be utilized
for hedges.

Cajanus Indicus, Candolle.
The Catjang ; in Assam, called Gelooa-mah. A shrubby
plant of India, probably available for profitable culture and
naturalization in the warmer parts of our Colony. It sustains itself on dry ground, and yields the pulse known as
Dhal, Urhur and Congo-pea. The plant lasts for about
three years. Several species of Cajanus of the Atylosia
section, indigenous to the warmer parts of Australia, might
be tested here for the sake of the economic value of their
seeds. The insect, active in the formation of lac, lives
extensively on the Cajanus, according to Mr. T. D. Brewster
of Assam. Silkworms live also on it.

Calamus montanus, T. Anderson.
Himalaya, up to 6000 feet. A hardy climbing palm. The
aged canes are naked. " The light but strong suspension-
bridges, by which the large rivers of Sikkim are crossed, are
constructed of this palm. It supplies material for the
strongest ropes for dragging logs of wood from the forests.
The most durable baskets and the cane-work of chairs are
manufactured from the slit stems. Walking-sticks and
riding-canes made of this species are exported from Sikkim
in considerable quantity." Many other Calami serve similar
purposes, but probably few or perhaps none are equally
hardy.

Camelina sativa, Crantz.
Middle and South Europe, temperate Asia. An annual
herb, cultivated for the sake of its fibre and the oil of its
seeds. It is readily grown after corn crops, yields richly
even on poor soil and is not attacked by aphis. Mr. W.
Taylor obtained 32 bushels of seeds from an acre, and from
these 540 lbs. of oil. The return is within a few months.

Canna Achiras, Gillies.

Mendoza. One of the few extra-tropic Cannas, eligible for Arrow-root culture.

Canna coccinea, Roscoe.

West India. Yields with some other Cannas the particular Arrow-root, called " Tous les mois."

Canna edulis, Edwards.

The Adeira of Peru. One of the hardiest of Arrow-root plants, and thus well adapted for our clime. Seeds, even if many years old, will germinate. This species has yielded excellent starch at Melbourne. Western Port, Lake Welling-ton, Ballarat and other localities, from plants supplied at the Botanic Garden. The Rev. Mr. Hagenauer, of the Gipps Land Aboriginal Mission station, obtained 220 lbs. of Arrow-root from one-eighth of an acre of this Canna. The gathering of the roots is effected about April. The plants can be set out in ordinary ploughed land. Captain James Hall, of Hastings, prepared also largely the starch from this root. Starch grains remarkably large.

Canna flaccida, Roscoe.

Carolina. Probably also available for Arrow-root, though in first instance like many congeners chosen only for orna-mental culture.

Canna glauca, Linne.

One of the West Indian Arrow-root Cannas.

Cannabis sativa, L.*

The Hemp-plant ; indigenous to various parts of Asia, as far west as Turkey and as far east as Japan. Cultivated for its fibre since ancient times. Particularly in hot climes it exudes the " Churras," a resinous substance of narcotic intoxicating property. The foliage contains also a volatile oil, which the seeds yield by pressure—the well-known fixed Hemp-oil. The staminiferous plant is pulled for obtaining the fibre in its best state immediately after flowering ; the seeding plant is gathered for fibre at a later stage of growth. Good soil, well drained, never absolutely dry, is needed for successful Hemp culture. Hemp is one of the plants yielding a full and quick return within the season. The summer temperatures of St. Petersburg (67° F.) and of Moscow (62° F.) admit yet of the cultivation of this plant.

Capparis spinosa, L.

South Europe and North Africa. A somewhat shrubby and trailing plant, deserving even for the sake of its handsome flowers a place in any garden. It sustains its life in the most arid deserts. The frosts of our lowlands do not destroy this plant. The flower-buds and young berries preserved in vinegar with some salt form the Capers of commerce. Samples of Capers, prepared from plants of the Botanic Garden, are placed in our Industrial Museum, together with many other industrial products emanating from the writer's laboratory. A closely allied and probably equally useful plant, Capparis nummularia, is indigenous to Northern Australia. The Caper-plant is propagated either from seeds or suckers; it is well able to withstand either heat or drought. The buds after their first immersion into slightly salted vinegar are strained and afterwards preserved in bottles with fresh vinegar. Chemical principle: Glycosid.

Capsicum annuum, L.

Central America. An annual herb, which yields the Chillies and thus also the material for Cayenne Pepper. Chemical principle: Capsicin, an acrid soft-resinous substance.

Capsicum baccatum, L.

The Cherry-Capsicum. A perennial plant. From Brazil brought to tropical Africa and Asia, where now other Pepper-Capsicums are likewise naturalized.

Capsicum frutescens, L.

Tropical America. The berries of this shrubby species are likewise converted into Cayenne Pepper.

Capsicum longum, Candolle.

Some of the hottest parts of America. An annual herb, also yielding Cayenne Pepper. Our summers admit of the successful growth of at least the annual species of Capsicum in all the lowlands.

Carthamus tinctorius, L.

From Egypt to India. The Safflower. A tall annual rather handsome herb. The florets produce yellow, rosy, ponceau and other red shades of dye, according to various admixtures. Pigment principles: Carthamin and Carthamus-yellow. For domestic purposes it yields a dye ready at hand from any garden. In India the Carthamus is also cultivated for the sake of the oil, which can be pressed from the seeds.

Carum Ajowan, Bentham. (*Ptychotis Ajowan*, Candolle.)

India. The fruits of this annual herb form an excellent culinary condiment with the flavor of thyme. Its peculiar oil is accompanied by Cymol and Thymol.

Carum Carui, L.

The Caraway-plant. Perennial. Europe, North and Middle Asia. It might be naturalized in our Alps and also along our sea shores. The Caraway-oil is accompanied by two chemical principles : Carven and Carvol.

Carum ferulifolium, Koch. (*Bunium ferulifolium*, Desfont.)

A perennial herb of the Mediterranean regions. The small tubers are edible.

Carum Petroselinum, Bentham. (*Apium Petroselinum*, L.)

The Parsley. The biennial well-known herb, indigenous to South Europe and the Orient. Essential oil peculiar with Stearopten.

Caryota urens, L.

India. One of the hardier Palms, ascending according to Dr. Thomas Anderson the Himalayas to an altitude of 5000 feet, yet even there attaining a considerable height, though the temperature sinks in the cooler season to 40° Fahrenheit. The trunk furnishes a sago-like starch. This Palm flowers only at an advanced age, and after having produced a succession of flowers dies away. From the sap of the flowers Toddy and palm-sugar are prepared, like from the Cocos and Borassus Palm, occasionally as much as 12 gallons of Toddy being obtained from one tree in a day. The fibre of the leaf-stalks can be manfactured into very strong ropes, also into baskets, brushes and brooms. The outer wood of the stem serves for turnery.

Cassia acutifolia, Delile.

Indigenous or now spontaneous in Northern and tropical Africa and South-west Asia. Perennial. The merely dried leaflets constitute part of the Alexandrian and also Tinnevelly Senna. In Victoria it will be only in the warmest northern and eastern regions, where Senna can perhaps be cultivated to advantage.

Cassia angustifolia, Vahl.

Northern Africa and South-western Asia, indigenous or cultivated. Perennial. Yields Mecca-Senna.

Cassia Marylandica, L.

An indigenous Senna plant of the United States of North America. Perennial.

Cassia obovata, Colladon.

South-west Asia ; widely dispersed through Africa as a native or disseminated plant. Perennial. Part of the Alexandrian and also Aleppo Senna is derived from this species. Several of the Australian desert Cassias of the group of C. artemisioides may also possess purgative properties. The odor of their foliage is almost that of Senna.

Catha edulis, Forskoel.

Arabia and Eastern Africa. The leaves of this shrub under the designation Kafta or Cat are used for a tea of a very stimulating effect, to some extent to be compared to that of Erythroxylon Coca. To us here the plant would be mainly valuable for medicinal purposes.

Cedronella cordata, Bentham.

United States of North America. A perennial herb, fragrant like the foregoing.

Cedronella triphylla, Moench.

Madeira and Canary Islands. A shrubby plant with highly scented foliage. The volatile oil obtainable from it resembles that of Melissa, but is somewhat camphoric.

Cephaelis Ipecacuanha, Richard.

Brazil in woods of mountains, consociated with Palms and Fern-trees. It is not unlikely, that this herb, which is perennial and yields the important medicinal Ipecacuanha root, would live in our warmer forest regions, such as those of East Gipps Land. Active principles : Emetin and Ipecacuanha-acid.

Ceroxylon andicola, Humboldt.

The Wax-palm of New Granada, ascending the Andes to 11,000 feet. One of the most majestic and at the same time one of the most hardy of all palms, attaining occasionally a height of 180 feet. The trunk exudes a kind of resinous wax, about 25 lbs. being obtainable at a time from each stem; this by admixture to tallow is used for candles. There are several other andine palms, which could be reared in our forests or in sheltered positions at our dwellings, but some of them are not even yet phytographically circumscribed.

Cervantesia tomentosa, Ruiz and Pavon.

Forest-mountains of Peru. This tree yields edible seeds. It is likely to prove hardy in our lower forest regions.

Chaerophyllum bulbosum, Linné.

Middle Europe and Western Asia. The Parsnip-Chervil. A biennial herb. The root a good culinary esculent.

Chaerophyllum sativum, Lamarck.

(Anthriscus Cerefolium, Hoffm.)

The Chervil. Middle and South Europe, Western Asia. An annual herb, available for salads and condiments, but the root deleterious.

Chamaerops excelsa, Thunberg.

South China. This fan-palm is highly desirable, although not tall as the name would indicate.

Chamaerops Fortunei, Hooker.

North China. The Chusan-palm. It attains a height of about 12 feet and endures like the following species considerable frost. The leaves can be employed for plaiting palm-hats. Other hardy palms might be naturalized and used for various purposes, irrespective of their ornamental features.

Chamaerops humilis, Linné.
The dwarf Fan-Palm of South Europe and North Africa. It is very decorative for garden plantations, particularly also eligible for scenic effect.

Chamaerops Hystrix, Fraser.
The Blue Palmetto of Florida and Carolina. Another dwarf Fan-Palm.

Chamaerops Martiana, Wallich.
Ascends the mountains of Nepaul to 5000 feet. Attains a height of 50 feet and is altogether a noble object.

Chamaerops Richieana, Griffith.
Arid mountains of Affghanistan. Has also proved hardy even in England.

Chelidonium majus, L.
Europe and Western Asia. The Celandine. A perennial herb of medicinal value. Chemical principles: Chelerythrin and Chelidonin ; also a yellow pigment: Chelidoxanthin.

Chenopodium ambrosioides, L.
Tropical America. An annual medicinal herb. Chenopodium anthelminticum is a perennial variety of this species.

Chenopodium auricomum, Lindley.
From the Darling River to Carpentaria and Arnhem's Land. A tall perennial herb, furnishing a nutritious and palatable spinage. It will live in arid desert regions.

Chenopodium Quinoa, Willdenow.
From New Granada to Chili. A large-leaved quick-growing annual species, cultivated for the sake of its amylaceous seeds, but perhaps of more value as a culinary vegetable.

Cicer arietinum, L.
South Europe and Orient. The Gram. An annual herb, valuable as a pulse for pasture animals. The seeds can also be converted into peameal or be used otherwise for culinary purposes.

Cichorium Endivia, L.

South Europe, Orient, Middle Asia. A biennial plant, used since ancient times as a culinary vegetable.

Cichorium Intybus, L.

Chicory. A well-known perennial plant, indigenous to Europe, North Africa and North and West Asia. The roots can be used as a substitute for Coffee. This plant requires a rich deep loamy soil, but fresh manure is detrimental to the value of the root. It is also a good fodder-plant especially for sheep. The root can also be dressed and boiled for culinary purposes. The leaves useful for salad.

Cimicifuga racemosa, Elliot.

The Black Snake-root of North America. A perennial herb of medicinal value, the root possessing emetic properties.

Cinchona Calisaya, Ruiz.*

Yellow Perubark-tree. Andes of Peru and Bolivia, 5-6000 feet above the ocean. This tree attains a height of 40 feet. It yields the yellow bark, and also part of the crownbark. It is one of the richest yielder of quinin, and produces besides Cinchonidin.

Cinchona micrantha, Ruiz and Pavon.

Cordillieres of Bolivia and Peru. This tree attains a height of 60 feet, and from it part of the Grey and Huanuco Bark as well as Lima Bark are obtained. It is comparatively rich in Cinchonin and Quinidin, contains however also Quinin.

Cinchona nitida, Ruiz and Pavon.

Andes of Peru and and Ecuador. This tree rises to 80 feet under favorable circumstances. It also yields Grey Bark and Huanuco Bark, besides Loxa Bark. It will probably prove one of the hardiest species. It contains predominantly Cinchonin and Quinidin.

Cinchona officinalis, L. (partly.)*

(*Cinchona Condaminea*, Humboldt)

Andes of New Grenada and Peru, at a height of 6000 to 10,000 feet. Yields Crown or Brown Peru Bark, besides part of Loxa Bark. Comparatively rich in Quinin and

Cinchonidin. The temperature of the middle regions of
the Andes, where this tree grows, is almost the same as that
of the Canary Islands. Superabundance of moisture is particularly to this species pernicious. The Crispilla variety
endures a temperature occasionally as low as 27° F.

Cinchona clancifolia Mutis is considered by Weddell a
variety of C. officinalis. This grows on places, where the
mean annual temperature is that of Rome, with however
less extremes of heat and cold. It yields part of the Pitaya-
Bark.

Cinchona Pitayensis must also be referred to C. officinalis
as a variety. This attains a height of 60 feet and furnishes also a portion of the Pitaya Bark. It is this particular Cinchona, which in Upper India yielded in some
instances the unprecedented quantity of 11 per cent. alkaloids,
nearly 6 per cent. Quinin, the rest Quinidin and Cinchonin.

In Java some of the best results were obtained with Cinchona Hasskarliana Miq., a species seemingly as yet not
critically identified.

Cinchona succirubra, Pavon.*

Middle andine regions of ·Peru and Ecuador. A tree,
attaining a height of 40 feet, yielding the red Peru-Bark,
rich in Quinin and Cinchonidin. It is this species, which is
predominantly cultivated on the mountains of Bengal. All
these Chinchonas promise to become of importance for culture in the warmest regions of our forest-land, on places not
readily accessible or eligible for cereal culture. The Peruvian proverb that Cinchona trees like to be "within sight of
snow" gives some clue of the conditions, under which they
thrive best. They delight in the shelter of forests, where
there is an equable temperature, no frost, some humidity at
all times both in air and soil, where the ground is deep and
largely consists of the remnants of decayed vegetable substances and where the subsoil is open. Drippage from
shelter-trees too near will be hurtful to the plants. Closed
valleys and deep gorges, into which cold air will sink, are
also not well adapted for cinchona-culture. In our Colony
we ought to consociate the Perubark-plants with naturally

growing fern-trees but only in our warmest valleys of richest soil. The best temperature for Cinchonas is from 53° to 66° F.; but they mostly will endure in open places a minimum of 32° F.; in the brush shades of the Botanic Garden of Melbourne, where years ago already Cinchonas were raised by the thousands, they have even resisted uninjured a temperature of a few degrees less, wherever the wind had no access, while under such very slight cover the Cinchonas withstood also a heat of a few degrees over 100° F. The plants are most easily raised from seeds, best under some cover such as mats and they are seeding copiously already several years after planting. The contents of alkaloids in the bark can be much increased by artificial treatment, if the bark is only removed on one side of the stem and the denuded part covered with moss, under which in one year as much bark is formed as otherwise requires three years' growth, such forced bark moreover containing the astounding quantity of as much as 25 alkaloids, because no loss of these precious substances takes place by gradual disintegration through age. The Cinchona-plants are set out at distances of about 6 feet. The harvest of bark begins in the fourth or fifth year. · The price varies in Europe from 2s. to 9s. per lb. according to quality. The limits assigned to this small literary compilation do not admit of entering further into details on this occasion, but I may yet add, that in the Darjeeling district over three millions of Cinchona plants were in cultivation in 1869, raised in Government plantations.

Citrus Aurantium, L.*

The Orange (in the widest sense of the word). A native of South Asia. A tree of longevity, known to have attained an age of 600 years and more. Any specific differences, to distinguish C. Aurantium from C. medica, if they once existed, are obliterated now through hybridisation at least in the cultivated forms. As prominent varieties of C. Aurantium may be distinguished:—

Citrus Bigaradia, Duhamel. The Bitter Orange. This furnishes from its flowers the Neroli Oil so delicious and costly as a scent. It is stated, that Orange-flowers to the value of £50 might be gathered from the plants of an acre within a year. The rind of the fruit is used for candied orange-peel. Bitter principle : Hesperidin in the rind, Limonin in the seed.

Citrus dulcis, Volkamer. The Sweet Orange, of which many kinds occur. The St. Michael Orange has been known to bear in the Azores on sheltered places 20,000 fruits on one tree in a year. Neroli Oil is obtained from the flowers of this and allied varieties.

Citrus Bergamium, Risso. From the fruit-rind of this variety Bergamotte Oil is obtained, but also oil from the flowers. The Mellarosa variety furnishes a superior oil and exquisite confitures.

Citrus decumana, Linné. The Shaddock or Pompelmos. The fruit will exceptionally attain a weight of 20 lbs. The pulp and thick rind can both be used for preserves.

Citrus nobilis, Lourciro. The Mandarin-Orange. The thin peel separates most readily from the deliciously flavored sweet pulp. There are large and small fruited Mandarin Oranges ; the Tangerine variety is one of them.

Citrus medica, Linné.*

The Citron (in the widest sense of the word). Indigenous to Southern Asia. For convenience's sake it is placed here as distinct from the preceding species. As prominent varieties of the Citrus medica may be distinguished :—

Citrus Cedra, Gallesio. The real Citron. From the acid tubercular fruit essential oil and citric acid can be obtained, irrespective of the ordinary culinary use of the fruit. A large variety with thick rind furnishes candied the Citrionate or Succade. The Cedra oil comes from a particular variety.

Citrus Limonium, Risso. The real Lemon. From the fruit of this is largely pressed the Lemon juice, while the thin smooth aromatic peel serves for the production of volatile oil or for condiments. The juice of this fruit is particularly rich in citric acid. A large variety is the Rosaline Lemon.

Citrus Lumia, Risso. The sweet Lemon, including the Pear-Lemon with large pear-shaped fruit. Rind thick and pale ; pulp not acid. This variety serves for particular condiments.

Citrus Limetta, Risso. The real Lime. The best lime-juice is obtained from this variety, of which the Perette constitute a form.

Citrus Australasica, F. von Mueller.

Coast forests of extra-tropic East Australia. A shrubby species with oblong or almost cylindrical fruits of lemon-like taste, measuring 2 to 4 inches in length. They are thus very much larger than those of Atalantia glauca of the coast and the desert-interior of tropic Australia, which are also of similar taste. These plants are entered together with the following on this list, merely to draw attention to them, as likely capable of improvement of their fruit through culture.

Citrus Planchoni, F. von Mueller.

(*C. Australis*, Planchon, partly.)

Forests near the coast of sub-tropic East Australia. A noble tree, fully 40 feet high with globular fruits about the size of a walnut, called Native Oranges. The species has first appeared under the above name in the "Report on the Vegetable Products of the Intercolonial Exhibition of 1867."

Citrus Japonica, Thunberg.

The Kumquat of Japan. A shrubby Citrus with fruits of the size of a Gooseberry, from which on account of their sweet peel and acid pulp an excellent preserve can be prepared.

Cochlearia Armoracia, L.

The Horseradish. Middle Europe and Western Asia. Perennial. The volatile oil of the root allied to that of Mustard.

Cochlearia officinalis, L.

Shores of Middle and North Europe, North Asia and North America. A biennial herb, like the allied C. Anglica and

C. Danica valuable as an antiscorbutic; hence deserving naturalization. It contains a peculiar volatile oil.

Coffea Arabica, L.

Mountains of South-west Abyssinia. The Coffee-plant. This shrub or small tree has been admitted into this list not without great hesitation, merely not to be passed. The cultivation within Victorian boundary can only with any prospect of success be tried in the warmest and simultaneously moistest regions, such as East Gipps Land, frost being detrimental to the Coffee-plant. In Ceylon the Coffee regions are between 1000 and 5000 feet above the ocean, but Dr. Thwaites observes that the plant succeeds best at an elevation from 3000 to 4500 feet, in places where there is a rainfall of about 100 inches a year. The temperature there rises hardly ever above 80° F., and almost never sinks below 45° F. Coffee requires moist weather whilst it ripens its fruit, and a season of drier weather to form its wood. For further particulars see the papers of the Planters' Association of Kandy. Chemical principles : Coffein, a peculiar tannic acid and Quina acid.

Colchicum auctumnale, L.

Middle and South Europe, West Asia. The Meadow Safron. The seeds and roots of this pretty bulbous-tuberous herb are important for medicinal use. The plant has been introduced by the writer with a view of being cultivated on moist meadows in our ranges. Active principle : Colchicin.

Colocasia antiquorum, Schott.

From Egypt through South Asia to the South Sea Islands, apparently also indigenous in the warmer parts of East Australia. The Taro. The stem-like tuberous starchy roots lose their acridity by the process of boiling, roasting or baking. The plant proved hardy in the Botanic Garden of Melbourne. The tops of the tubers are replanted for a new crop. Taro requires a rich moist soil and would grow well on banks of rivers. For scenic culture it is a very decorative plant. Colocasia esculenta is a variety of this species.

Colocasia Indica, Kunth. (*Alocasia Indica*, Schott.)

South Asia, South Sea Islands and East Australia. Cultivated for its stem and tubers on swamps or rivulets. This
stately plant will rise in favorable localities to a height of
12 feet, the edible trunk attaining a considerable thickness,
the leaves sometimes measuring 3 feet in length. In using
the stem and root for food great care is needed to expel by
the heating process all acridity. Colocasia odora and C.
macrorrhiza seem varieties of this species. Several other
Aroid plants deserve attention for test-culture on account
of their edible roots, among them Cyrtosperma edulis,
Seemann, from the Feegee Islands.

Conium maculatum, L.

The Hemlock. Europe, North Africa, North and West
Asia. A biennial herb, important for medicinal purposes.
It should however not be allowed to stray from its plantations, as it is apt to be confounded with culinary species of
Anthriscus, Chaerophyllum and Myrrhis, and may thus
cause as a most dangerous plant disastrous mistakes. Active
principles : Coniin, in the fruit also Conhydrin.

Conopodium denudatum, Koch.

Western Europe. The small tuberous roots of this herb,
when boiled or roasted, are available for food and known as
Earth Chesnuts. The plant is allied to Carum Bulbocasta-
num.

Convolvulus floridus, L. fil.

Canary Island. A shrubby not climbing or winding species.
With the following it yields the Atlantic Rosewood from
stem and root.

Convolvulus scoparius, L. fil.

Teneriffe. One of the Rosewood plants.

Convolvulus Scammonia, L.

Mediterranean regions and Asia Minor. A perennial
herb. From the root is obtained the purgative resin Scam-
monia.

Corchorus capsularis, L.*

From India to Japan. One of the principal Jute plants. An annual, attaining a height of about a dozen feet, when closely grown, with almost branchless stem. A nearly allied but lower plant, *Corchorus Cunninghami*, F. v. Mueller, occurs in tropical and subtropical East Australia. Jute can be grown where cotton and rice ripen, be it even in localities comparatively cold in the winter, if the summer's warmth is long and continuous. The fibre is separated by steeping the full grown plant in water from five to eight days, and it is largely used for rice and cotton bags, carpets and other similar textile fabrics, and also for ropes. About 60,000 tons are annually exported from India to England, and a large quantity also to the United States. Jute is sown on good land, well ploughed and drained, but requires no irrigation, although it likes humidity. The crop is obtained in the course of four or five months, and is ripe when the flowers turn into fruit capsules. Good paper is made from the refuse of the fibre.

Corchorus olitorius, L.*

South Asia and North Australia. Furnishes, with the foregoing species, the principal supply of Jute fibre. As it also is an annual, it can be brought to perfection in our summers. The foliage can be used for spinage. The fibre is not so strong as hemp, but very easily prepared. It will not endure exposure to water. The allied *Corchorus trilocularis*, L., of Indian origin, is likewise a native of eastern tropical and subtropical Australia.

Cordyline Banksii, J. Hooker.

New Zealand. This lax and long leaved palm-lily attains a height of 10 feet; its stem is usually undivided. This and the following species have been admitted into this list for a double reason, because not only are they by far the hardiest, quickest growing and largest of the genus, and thus most sought in horticultural trade for scenic planting; but also because they furnish from the leaves a superior fibre for ropes and other purposes. The small seeds are produced in great abundance, and germinate with extreme readiness. These Palm-lilies ought to be naturalized in our ranges by mere dissemination.

Cordyline Forsteri, F. v. Mueller.
(*C. Australis*, J. Hooker, not Endlicher.)
New Zealand. The stem of this noble thin-leaved plant attains a height of 40 feet, and is branched.

Cordyline indivisa, Kunth.
New Zealand. The stem. of this thick and rigid-leaved palm-like species rises to a height of 20 feet, and remains undivided. Leaves finally 5 inches broad; yield the Toi-fibre.

Cordyline Baueri, J. Hooker.
(*C. Australis*, Endlicher, not J. Hooker.)
Norfolk Island. The stem of this stately species attains a height of 40 feet, and becomes in age ramified. It is very intimately allied to the New Zealand Cordyline Forsteri.

Coriandrum sativum, L.
Orient and Middle Asia. An annual or biennial herb, much in use for condiments. The essential oil peculiar.

Corynosicyos edulis. (*Cladosicyos edulis*, J. Hooker.)
Guinea. A new cucumber-like plant, with edible fruits about 1 foot long, and 3 inches in diameter.

Crambe maritima, L.
Sea Kale. Sand coasts of Europe and North Africa. A perennial herb; the young shoots used as a wholesome and agreeable vegetable.

Crambe Tataria, Wulfen.
From Southern Europe to the Orient. Perennial. Likewise used for culinary purposes.

Crataegus aestivalis, Torrey and Gray.
The Apple Haw. Southern States of North America. The small juicy fruit of an agreeable acid taste.

Crataegus apiifolia, Michaux.
North America. Highly serviceable for hedges.

Crataegus coccinea, L.

North American Whitethorn. A valuable hedge plant; also very handsome. Spines strong.

Crataegus cordata, Aiton.

Southern States of North America. Also much employed for hedges.

Crataegus Crus-Galli, L.

North America. The Cockspur Thorn. Regarded as one of the best species for hedges. Spines long and stout.

Crataegus Oxyacantha, L.

Europe, North Africa, North and West Asia. The ordinary Hawthorn or Whitethorn. Recorded here as one of the most eligible among deciduous hedge plants.

Crataegus parvifolia, Aiton.

North America. For dwarf hedges. Spines long, slender, sharp and numerous.

Crataegus pyracantha, Persoon.

The Firethorn. South Europe. This species is evergreen. It is likewise adapted for hedges, but slower in growth than Hawthorn, but not difficult to rear.

Crataegus tomentosa, L.

North America. Fruit edible. By the species mentioned the list of American Hedgethorns is, probably, not yet exhausted.

Crithmum maritimum, L.

The real Samphir. Sea shores of Middle and South Europe, North Africa and the Orient. A perennial herb. Settlers on the coast might readily disseminate and naturalize it. It is held to be one of the best plants for pickles, the young leaves being selected for that purpose.

Crocus sativus, L.

The Dye-Safron. South Europe and Orient. The Stigmata of this particular autumnal flowering Crocus constitute the costly dye substance. The best is collected from the flowers, just as they daily open in succession. At our stage of colonisation it would not be remunerative to grow Safron commercially; but as the plant is well adapted for our clime, it might be planted out into various unoccupied mountain localities, with a final view to naturalize it, and to render it thus available at a later period from native sources.

Crotalaria juncea, L.

The Sunn Hemp. Indigenous to South Asia, and also widely dispersed through tropical Australia. An annual herb, rising under favourable circumstances to a height of 10 feet. In our colony Sunn can only be cultivated in the warmest and moistest localities. It comes in four or five months to maturity. The plant can also be grown as a fodder-herb for cattle. It requires rich friable soil. If a superior soft fibre is desired, then the plant is pulled while in flower; if strength is the object, then the plant is left standing until it has almost ripened its seeds. The steeping process occupies about three days. For the purpose of obtaining branchless stems it is sown closely.

Crotalaria retusa, L.

Asia, America and Australia within the tropics. A perennial herb. Its fibre resembles that of C. juncea, and is chiefly used for ropes and canvas. Others of the multitudinous species of Crotalaria deserve to be tested for their fibres.

Crozophora tinctoria, Necker.

South Europe, North Africa and Orient. An annual herb. The turnsole-dye is prepared by exposure of the juice to the air, or by treating it with Ammonia.

Cucumis cicatrisatus, Stocks.

Scinde, where it is called " Wungee." The edible ovate fruit is about 6 inches long.

Cucumis Citrullus, Seringe.

(*Citrullus vulgaris*, Schrader.)

Mediterranean regions. The Water-Melon. It is simply mentioned here, to indicate the desirability of naturalizing it in the interior-deserts, where no Cucurbita and only a single kind of edible Cucumis (*C. acidus*, Jacquin), with fruits not larger than a pigeon's egg, is indigenous. In South African deserts it has become spontaneously established, and retained the characters of the cultivated fruit.

Cucumis Colocynthis, L.
(*Citrullus Colocynthis*, Schrader.)

From the Mediterranean regions to India. An annual herb. The medicinal extract of Colocynth is prepared from the small gourd of this species. Active principle : Colocynthin.

Cucumis Conomon, Thunberg.
Japan. An annual. The large fruit is used for preserves.

Cucumis Melo, L.
The Melon. Originally from the country about the Caspian Sea. The best varieties might also be naturalized in our sand-deserts, particularly on places where some moisture collects. Some of the Bokhara varieties are remarkably luscious and large. Apparently remunerative results have been gained in Belgium from experiments to cultivate Melons for sugar and treacle. The seeds, thus obtained in quantity, become available for oil-pressing. The root contains Melonemctin.

Cucumis Momordica, Roxburgh.
Cultivated in India. It produces Cucumbers 2 feet long, bursting slowly when ripe into several divisions. Young the fruit is used like Cucumbers, aged like Melons.

Cucumis sativus, L.
The Cucumber. Egypt. Indicated here merely for completeness' sake, also because Gherkin pickling ought to become a more extended local industry.

Cucumis utilissimus, Roxburgh.
Mountains of Bengal. An annual like the other species. Fruit of the size and shape of an ostrich's egg with the flavor of Melons. These fruits will keep for several months.

Cucurbita maxima, Duchesne.

Large Gourd. Turkey. Instances are on record of fruits having weighed over 2 cwt. Also this species is eligible for naturalization in the interior. Amongst other purposes it serves for calabashes.

Cucurbita Melopepo, L.

The Squash. May be regarded as a variety of C. Pepo. It will endure storage for months.

Cucurbita moschata, Duchesne.

The Musky Gourd. Doubtless also from the Orient.

Cucurbita Pepo, L.

The Pumpkin and Vegetable Marrow. Countries on the Caspian Sea. Its naturalization in the desert would be a boon. The seeds on pressure yield a fixed oil; they are also anthelmintic. *C. melanosperma,* A. Braun, is not edible.

Cuminum Cyminum, L.

North Africa. The fruits of this annual herb are known as Cumin and used for certain condiments, as also in medicine. *Cuminum Hispanicum,* Merat, is similar. Essential oil peculiar.

Cycas revoluta, Thunberg.

The Japan Fern-palm. The trunk attains in age a height of about 6 feet, and is rich in sago-like starch. The slow growth of this plant renders it to us valuable for no other purpose than scenic decorative culture. *Cycas angulata,* R. Br., may also prove hardy, and would prove a noble horticultural acquisition, as it is the most gigantic of all Cycadeæ, attaining a height of 70 feet in tropical East Australia. Possibly like the Zamia stems also the trunks of Cycas admit of translocation even at an advanced age.

Cynara Cardunculus, L.

The Cardoon. Mediterranean regions. A perennial herb. The bleached leaf-stalks serve as esculents.

Cynara Scolymus, L.

The Artichoke. South Europe and North Africa. The receptacles and the base of the flower scales well known as a vegetable. The plant is perennial and here merely mentioned as entitled to extended culture in grouping this with other stately plants. Several other species are worthy of cultivation.

Cynosurus cristatus, L.

The Crested Dogstail-Grass. Europe, North Africa, West Asia. A perennial grass, particularly valuable as withstanding drought, the roots penetrating to considerable depth. The stems can also be used for bonnet plaiting. Though inferior in value for hay this grass is well adapted for permanent pasture, as it forms a dense turf without suffocating other grasses or fodder-herbs.

Cyperus corymbosus, Rottboell.

India. This stately perennial species may be chosen to fringe our lakes and ponds. It is extensively used for mats in India.

Cyperus Papyrus, L.

The Nile Papyrus. Though no longer strictly an utilitarian plant, as in ancient times, it could scarcely be passed on this occasion, as it ought to become valuable in horticultural trade. Its grand aspect recommends it as very decorative for aquatic plantations.

Cyperus Syriacus, Parlatore.

The Syrian or Sicilian Papyrus. This is the Papyrus-plant usual in garden cultivation. The plants in our Botanic Garden attain a height of 8 feet, but suffer somewhat from frost. Other tall Cyperi deserve introduction, for instance *C. giganteus*, Rottboell, from West India and Guiana, these kinds of plants being hardier than others from the tropics. I have not ventured to recommend the introduction of *Cyperus esculentus*, L., a Mediterranean species, remarkable for its sweet tubers, known as Earth Almonds. It is stoloniferous like the allied *Cyperus rotundus*, L., which has invaded the culture ground of many countries as an obnoxious irrepressible weed. The tubers of Cyperus esculentus contain about 16 per cent. oil.

Cyperus vaginatus, R. Brown.

Widely dispersed over the Australian continent, but not yet noticed in Tasmania and New Zealand. It is restricted to swampy localities, and thus is not likely to stray into ordinary fields. It is our best indigenous fibre-plant, and it is likewise valuable as being with ease converted into pulp for good writing paper, as shown by me some years ago. Its perennial growth allows of regular annual cutting. Within Victorian territory this Galingale-rush is particularly common on the Murray-flats.

Cytisus scoparius, Link. (*Spartium scoparium*, L.)

The Broom-bush. Europe, North Asia. Of less significance as a broom-plant than as one of medicinal value. It can also be used for tanning purposes. An alkaloid (Spartein) and a yellow dye (Scoparin) are obtainable from this Broombush.

Dactylis caespitosa, Forster. (*Poa Forsteri*, Steudel.)

Fuegia, Falklands Island, South Patagonia. The Tussockgrass. Thrives in cold countries near the sea in pure sand, at the edge of peat-bogs. It would likely prosper in our alpine moors. It is perennial, and reaches to a height of 7 feet. It is very nutritious, and much sought by herds. The base of the stem is nutty and edible.

Dactylis glomerata, L.*

Europe, North Africa, North and Middle Asia. The Cocksfoot-grass. Perennial. One of the best of tall pasture grasses, adapted as well for dry as moist soil, thus even available for wet clays. It will live also under the shade of trees in forests. Its yield of fodder is rich and continuous, but its stems are hard. It is already largely cultivated, and has become naturalized.

Daucus Carota L.

Europe, North Africa, extra-tropic Asia east to Japan. The Carrot. Admits of naturalization along our shores. Beyond the ordinary culinary utilization it serves for the distillation of a peculiar oil. The chemical substances Carotin and Hydrocarotin are derived from it.

Digitalis purpurea, L.

Greater part of Europe. The Fox-glove. A biennial and exceedingly beautiful herb of great medicinal value, easily raised. Chemical principles: Digitalin, Digitaletin and three peculiar acids.

Dioscorea aculeata, L.*

The Kaawi-Yam. India, Cochin-China, South Sea Islands. Stem prickly, as the name implies, not angular. Leaves alternate, undivided. It ripens later than the following species, and requires no reeds for staking. It is propagated from small tubers. This Yam is of a sweetish taste, and the late Dr. Seemann regarded it as one of the finest esculent roots of the globe. A variety of a blueish hue, cultivated in Central America (for instance at Caracas), is of very delicious taste. In the warmest parts of our colony this and the following species are likely to come to perfection.

Dioscorea alata, L.*

The Uvi-Yam. India and South Sea Islands. The stems are four-angled and not prickly. The tubers, of which there are many varieties, will attain under favorable circumstances a length of 8 feet, and the prodigious weight of one hundred pounds! This species, and the preceding one, are the two principal kinds cultivated in tropical countries. D. alata is in culture supported by reeds. It is propagated from pieces of the old root, and comes in warm climes to perfection in about seven months. The tubers may be baked or boiled. It is this species, which has been successfully cultivated in New Zealand, and also in the Southern States of North America.

Dioscorea globosa, Roxburgh.

India. Roxburgh states this to be the most esteemed Yam in Bengal.

Dioscorea hastifolia, Nees.

Extra-tropic Western Australia, at least as far south as 32°. It is evidently one of the hardiest of the Yams, and on that account deserves particularly to be drawn into culture. The tubers are largely consumed by the aborigines for food; it is the only plant on which they bestow any kind of cultivation, crude as it is.

Dioscorea Japonica, Thunberg.* (*D. Batatas*, Decaisne.)

The hardy Chinese and Japan Yam. This species, which is not prickly, has been cultivated some years in our Botanic Garden. The material here for comparison is not complete, but seems to indicate, that *D. transversa*, R. Br. and *D. punctata*, R. Br., are both referable to D. Japonica. If this assumption should prove correct, then we have this Yam along the coast tracts of North and East Australia as far south as latitude 33°. In Australia we find the wild root of good taste.

Dioscorea nummularia, Lamarck.

The Tivoli Yam. Continental and Insular India, also South Sea Islands. A high climbing prickly species, with opposite leaves. Roots cylindrical as thick as an arm ; their taste exceedingly good.

Dioscorea oppositifolia, L.

India and China. Not prickly. One of the edible Yams.

Dioscorea pentaphylla, L.

Continental and Insular India, also South Sea Islands. Likewise a good Yam. A prickly species, with alternate divided leaves.

Dioscorea purpurea, Roxb.

India. In Bengal considered next best to D. alata.

Dioscorea sativa, L.

South Asia, east as far as Japan, also in the South Sea Islands, and North and tropical East Australia, likewise recorded from tropical Africa. Stem cylindrical, not prickly. The acrid root requires soaking before boiling. It has proved hardy in the Southern States of North America.

Dioscorea spicata, Roth.

India. Root used like those of other species.

Dioscorea tomentosa, Koenig.

Ooyala Yam. India. The nomenclature of some of the Asiatic species requires further revision.

Dioscorea trifida, L. fil.

Central America. One of the Yams there cultivated. Various other tuberous Dioscoreæ occur in tropical countries; but their respective degree of hardiness, taste and yield are not recorded or ascertained. The length of the Victorian warm season is probably sufficient for ripening all these Yams.

Diospyros Kaki, L. fil.

The Date-plum of China and Japan. A slow growing not very productive tree, here recorded for completeness. The fruit is yellow or pink or dark purple, variable in size, but never larger than an ordinary apple. It has ripened at Sydney. *D. Virginiana*, L., has been recorded among the timber-trees.

Dipsacus fullonum, L.

Fuller's Teazel. Middle and South Europe and Middle Asia. A tall biennial herb. The thorny fruit-heads in use for fulling in cloth factories. The import during one of the last years into England was valued at £5000. The plant is most easily raised. The use of these Teazels has not yet been superseded by any adequate machinery.

Dolichos Lablab, L.

Warmer parts of Africa; probably thence spread widely through the tropics. An annual herb, sometimes lasting through several years. The young pods as well as the ripe seeds available for culinary use, but not of all varieties. It delights in rich soil, and ripens in hot countries within three months; its yield is about fortyfold according to Roxburgh. The whole plant forms excellent stable-feed for cattle.

Dracocephalum Moldavica, L.

North and Middle Asia. An annual showy scent-herb.

Ecballion Elaterium, Richard.

Mediterranean regions and Orient. The Squirting Cucumber. An annual. The powerful purgative Elaterium is prepared from the pulp of the fruit. Chemical principles: Elaterid, Elaterin, Hydroelaterin.

Ehrharta Diplax, F. v. Mueller.

(*Microlaena avenacea,* J. Hooker.)

New Zealand. This tall perennial grass is fond of wood‐lands and deserves introduction. It is likely to prove a rich pasture-grass. A few other Australian species, particularly of the section Tetrarrhena, are readily accessible to us, and so indeed also the South African Ehrhartas, all adapted for our clime, the majority perennial and several of superior value. *Ehrharta caudata,* Munro, is indigenous in Japan.

Ehrharta stipoides, Labillardière.

Extra-tropic Australia, also New Zealand. A perennial grass, which keeps beautifully green all through the year. For this reason its growth for pasturage should be encouraged, particularly as it will live on poor soil. Mr. W. H. Bacchus, of Bacchus-Marsh, considers it nearly as valuable as Kangaroo-Grass, and in the cool season more so. He finds it to bear over-stocking better than any other native grass, and to maintain a close turf. It is however not always copiously seeding.

Eleusine Coracana, Gaertner.

Southern Asia, east to Japan. Though annual, this grass is worthy of cultivation on account of its height and nutri-tiveness. The large grains can be used like Millet.

Eleusine stricta, Roxburgh.

India. The increase of grain of this annual grass in rich soil is at times five hundredfold. *E. Tocusso,* Fresenius, is a valuable kind from Abyssinia, seemingly allied to E. stricta. The Arabian and Himalaian *E. flagellifera,* Nees, is perennial. Other species of Eleusine are deserving of trial.

Elymus arenarius, L.*

The Sea Lyme-Grass. Europe and North Asia, on sand-coasts. One of the most important and vigorous of grasses for binding drift-sand on the sea shores. The North American *E. mollis*, Trinius, is allied to this species.

Elymus condensatus, Presl.

The Bunch-Grass of British Columbia and California. This is favorably known as adapted for sandland.

Ervum Lens, L. (*Lens esculenta*, Moench.)

Mediterranean regions, Orient. The Lentil. Annual, affording in its seeds a palatable and nutritious food.

Euclea myrtina, Burchell.

South Africa. Berry small, black, but edible. To us this plant would hardly be more than an ornamental bush.

Euclea undulata, Thunberg.

South Africa. Berry small, red, edible. Other shrubby species from the same portion of the globe yield also esculent fruits, which under superior culture may vastly improve.

Erythroxylon Coca, Lamarck.*

Peru. This shrub is famed for the extaraordinarily stimulating property of its leaves, which pass under the names of Spadic and Coca. They contain two alkaloids, Cocain and Hygrin, also a peculiar tannic acid. Whether any of the many other species of Erythroxylon possess similar properties seems never yet to have been ascertained.

Eupatorium triplinerve, Vahl. (*E. Ayapana*, Ventenat.)

Central America. A perennial somewhat shrubby herb, possibly hardy in the warmer parts of our Colony. It is used as a medicinal plant, also as an alexipharmic. It contains Eupatorin and much essential oil, peculiar to the plant.

Fagopyrum cymosum, Meissner.

The perennial Buck-Wheat or rather Beech-Wheat of the Indian and Chinese Highlands.

Fagopyrum emarginatum, Babington.

Chinese and Himalaian Mountains, where it is cultivated for its seeds. Annual.

Fagopyrum esculentum, Moench.

Central Asia. The ordinary Buck-Wheat. This annual herb succeeds on the poorest soil. The crushed amylaceous seeds can be converted by boiling or baking into a palatable and wholesome food. As an agrarian plant it can with advantage be raised as a first crop on sandy heath-land, newly broken up, for green manure. The period, required for the cyclus of its vegetation, is extremely short. Thus it can be reared on our higher Alps.

Fagopyrum Tataricum, Moench.

Middle and North Asia. Yields for the higher mountain regions a still safer crop than the foregoing, otherwise the remarks offered in reference to F. esculentum apply also to T. Tataricum.

Fagopyrum triangulare, Meissner.

In the Himalaian Mountains, ascending naturally to regions 11,500 feet high. An annual. *F. rotundatum*, Babington, seems a variety of this species. It is cultivated for food like the rest.

Festuca elatior, L.*

The Meadow Fescue. Europe, North Africa, North and Middle Asia. A perennial grass, attaining a height of several feet. There are several varieties of this species. The tallest follows rivers readily as far down as the tides reach. The ordinary form is well adapted for permanent pastures, has tender leaves, produces excellent hay and is early out in the season. It can be mixed advantageously with F. ovina. It is superior to ryegrass in produce and improves with age. *F. arundinacea*, Schreb., *F. pratensis*, Huds. and *F. loliacea*, Huds. are varieties of this species.

Festuca Hookeriana, F. v. Mueller.

Alps of Australia and Tasmania. A tall perennial grass, evidently nutritious, required to be tried for pastoral culture, and perhaps destined to become a meadow grass of colder countries.

Festuca ovina, L.

Sheep-Fescue. Europe, North and Middle Asia, North America, found also in South America and the Alps of Australia and New Zealand. This species like F. elatior is obtainable with facility. *F. duriuscula*, L. and *F. rubra*, L. are varieties. A perennial grass, thriving on widely different soil, even moory and sandy ground. It yields a good produce, maintains its virtue, resists drought, and is also well adapted for lawns and the swards of parks.

The space does not admit of entering here into further details of the respective value of many species of Festuca, which might advantageously be introduced from various parts of the globe for rural purposes.

Ficus Carica, L.*

Orient. The ordinary Figtree. It attains an age of several hundred years. In our latitudes and clime a prolific tree. The most useful and at the same time the most hardy of about a thousand recorded species of Ficus. The extreme facility with which it can be propagated from cuttings, the resistance to heat, the comparatively early yield and easy culture recommend the Figtree to be chosen, where it is an object to raise masses of tree-vegetation in widely treeless landscapes of the warmer zones. Hence the extensive plantations of this tree made in formerly woodless parts of Egypt; hence the likelihood of choosing the Fig as one of the trees for extensive planting through favorable portions of our desert-wastes, where moreover the fruit could be dried with particular ease. Caprification is unnecessary, even in some instances injurious and objectionable. Two main-varieties may be distinquished, that which produces two crops a year and that which yields but one. The former includes the grey or purple Fig, which is the best, the white Fig and the golden Fig, the latter being the finest in appearance but not in quality. The main-variety, which bears only one crop a year, supplies the greatest quantity of Figs for drying, among which the Marseillaise and Bellonne are considered the best. The **Barnisote** and the **Aubique** produce delicious large fruits, but they must be dried with fire-heat, and are usually consumed fresh. The ordinary drying is effected in the sun. For remarks on this and other points, concerning the Fig, the valuable tract, recently published by the Rev. Dr. Bleasdale, should be consulted. The first crop of figs grows on wood of the preceding year, the last crop however on wood of the current year. Varieties of particular excellence are known from Genua, Savoy, Malaga, Andalusia.

Flemingia tuberosa, Dalzell.

Western India. The tubers of this herb are said to be edible. Another species, F. vestita, it on record as cultivated in North-western India for its small esculent tubers.

Foeniculum officinale, Allioni.

The Fennel. Mediterranean regions, particularly on limestone soil. A perennial or biennial herb, of which two primary varieties occur—the so-called sweet variety having fruits almost twice as large as the other. The herb and fruits are in use as condiments and the latter also for medicine. The fruits are rich in essential oil, containing much Anethol.

Fourcroya Cubensis, Haworth.

West India and continental tropical America. A smaller species than the following, but equally utilized for fibre and impenetrable hedges. *F. flavo-viridis*, Hooker, from Mexico, is still smaller.

Fourcroya gigantea, Ventenat.

Central America. With species of Yucca, Agave, Dracaena, Cordyline, Phormium, Doryanthes and this and a few other Furcroyas, we have gigantic liliaceous plants available industrially for fibre. Frost injures the leaves of this species. Scape up to 30 feet high.

Fourcroya longaeva, Karw. and Zuec.

High mountains of Guatemala and Mexico, at an elevation of about 10,000 feet. One of the most gigantic and magnificent of all liliaceous or amaryllideous plants, in volumen only surpassed by Dracaena Draco, the Dragon-tree of the Canary Islands. This is the only known high-stemmed species, the trunk attaining a height of 50 feet and the huge panicle of flowers 40 feet more. It dies, like many allied plants, after flowering. The species is recorded here as a fibre plant, but with us would mainly or solely be kept for its ornamental grandeur.

Fragaria Chiloensis, Aiton.

In various of the colder parts both of North and South America. Chili-Strawberry.

Fragaria collina, Ehrhart.

In various parts of Europe. Hill-Strawberry.

Fragaria grandiflora, Ehrhart. (*F. Ananas*, Miller.)

Various colder parts of America. Closely allied to F. Chiloensis. Ananas Strawberry.

Fragaria Illinoensis, Prince.

North America. Hovey's Seedling and the Boston kind from this plant.

Fragaria pratensis, Duchesne. (*Fragaria elatior*, Ehrhart.)

In mountain-forests of Europe. Cinnamon-Strawberry. Hautbois.

Fragaria vesca, L.

Naturally very widely dispersed over the temperate and colder parts of the Northern Hemisphere. Wild Wood Strawberry. From this typical form probably some of the other Strawberries arose. Middle forms and numerous varieties now in culture were produced by hybridisation. These plants, though abounding already in our gardens, are mentioned here, because even the tenderest varieties could be naturalized in our ranges. Any settler living near some brook or rivulet might readily set out some plants, which with others, similarly adapted, would gradually spread with the current.

Fragaria Virginiana, Miller.

North America. Scarlet Strawberry.

Gaultieria Shallon, Pursh.

North-western America. This handsome spreading bush would yield its pleasant edible berries in abundance, if planted on our snowy mountains, where it would likely become naturalized.

Gaylussacia frondosa, Torrey and Gray.

The Blue Tangleberry of North America. A bush with deciduous foliage. Berry sweet.

Gaylussacia resinosa, Torrey and Gray.

The Black Huckleberry of North America. A dwarf shrub with deciduous leaves. It likes swampy woodlands, and thus would find ample space in our forest-ranges. Berry of pleasant taste. Perhaps some of the South American species produce also edible fruits.

Geitonoplesium cymosum, All. Cunningham.

Through the whole East Australian forests. It is mentioned here to draw attention to the fact, that special culture may convert this into an Asparagus plant, as Mr. P. O'Shanesy has found, that the young shoots offer a fair substitute for Asparagus

Genista monosperma, Lamarck.

Mediterranean regions. One of the best of broom-bushes for arresting sand-drift. *G. sphaerocarpa.* Lam., is of like use, and comes also from the Mediterranean Sea.

Gentiana lutea, L.

Sub-Alpine tracts of Middle and South Europe. A perennial most beautiful herb, yielding the medicinal Gentian-root. It could be easily raised in our higher mountains. Chemical principles : Gentian-bitter and Gentianin.

Gladiolus edulis, Burchell.

Interior of South Africa. The bulb-like roots are edible, and taste like chesnuts, when roasted.

Glycine hispida, Bentham. (*Soja hispida,* Moench.)

An annual herb of India, China and Japan. The beans are one of the main ingredients of the condiment known as Soja. *Glycine Soja,* Siebold and Zuccarini, is said to be a distinct plant, but probably serving the same purpose.

Glycyrrhiza echinata, L.

South Europe and Orient. From the root of this herb at least a portion of the Italian Liquorice is prepared. The root is thicker than that of the following. The Russian Liquorice root is derived from this species. It is less sweet.

Glycyrrhiza glabra, L.

South Europe. The extract of the root of this herb constitutes the ordinary Liquorice. The plant grows here most vigorously. The liquorice is of some utility in medicine, but also used in Porter Breweries. Chemical principle : Glycyrrhizin.

Gossypium arboreum, L.*

The Tree-Cotton. India, Arabia. A tall perennial species, but not forming a real tree, yielding cotton in the first season already. Leaves long-lobed. Bracts with few teeth. Petals yellow or in age pink or purple. Seeds brown, disconnected, after the removal of the cotton-fibre greenish-velvety. The cotton of long staple, but a variety occurs with short staple. The New Orleans Cotton (*G. sanguineum,* Hassk.,) belong to this species. Dr. Seemann connects also the ordinary *G. herbaceum,* L., as a variety with *G. arboreum.* The cotton-fibre is crisp, white, opaque, and not easily separable.

Gossypium Barbadense, L.*

West India. Sea Island Cotton. Leaves long-lobed. Petals yellow. Seeds disconnected, black, after the removal of the cotton-fibre naked. The cotton of this species is very long, easily separable and of a silky lustre. This species requires low-lying coast tracts for attaining to perfection. Perennial, and yielding like the rest a crop in the first season. Cultivated largely in the Southern States of North America, also in South Europe, North Africa, Queensland and various other countries.

Gossypium herbaceum, L.*

Scinde, Cabul and other parts of tropical and sub-tropical Asia, much cultivated in the Mediterranean countries.

Perennial. Leaves short-lobed. Petals yellow. Seeds disconnected, after removal of the cotton-fibre grey-velvety. Distinguished and illustrated by Parlatore as a species, regarded by Seemann as a variety of *G. arboreum*. Staple longer than in the latter kind, white, opaque, not easily seeding. Even this species, though supposed to be herbaceous, will attain a height of 12 feet. A variety with tawny fibre furnishes the Nankin Cotton.

Gossypium hirsutum, L.*

Upland or Short-staple Cotton. Tropical America, cultivated most extensively in the United States, Southern European and many other countries. Perennial. Seeds brownish-green, disconnected, after the removal of the cotton-fibre greenish-velvety. Staple long, white, almost of a silky lustre, not easily separable. A portion of the Queensland Cotton is obtained from this species. It neither requires the coast tracts nor the highly attentive culture of G. Barbadense.

Gossypium religiosum, L.*   (*G. Peruvianum*, Cavan.)

Tropical South America. Kidney Cotton, Peruvian or Brazilian Cotton. Leaves long-lobed. Petals yellow. Seeds black. connected. The cotton is of a very long staple, white, somewhat silky and easily seeding from the seeds. A tawny variety occurs. This is the tallest of all cotton-bushes, and it is probably this species, which occurs in the valleys of the Andes as a small tree, bearing its cotton while frosts whiten the ground around.

Gossypium Taitense, Parlatore.

(*G. religiosum*, Banks and Solander.)

In several islands of the Pacific Ocean. A shrub. Petals white. Seeds disconnected, glabrous after the removal of the fulvous cotton-fibre, which seedes not with readiness.

Gossypium tomentosum, Nuttall.*

(*G. Sandvicense*, Parlat. *G. religiosum*, A. Gray.)

Hawaia. Perennial. Petals yellow. Seeds disconnected, after the removal of the tawny cotton-fibre fulvous-velvety, not easily parting with their cotton.

For limitation of species and varieties Parlatore's specie *dei cotoni* (Florence, 1866,) and Todaro's asservazioni su cotone may be consulted; information on culture may be sought in Porter's " Tropical Agriculturist " and in Mallet's work on " Cotton " (London, 1862).

There are many parts of our Colony, in which all these species of Gossypium could be cultivated, and where a fair or even prolific cotton crop may be obtained. Good cotton for instance has been produced on the Goulbourn River, the Loddon, the Avoca and the Murray Rivers, particularly in places where water could be applied. All cultivated kinds of Cotton-plants are either naturally perennials or become such in favorable climes, although they may be treated strictly as annuals. Some of them will indeed in particular instances grow to the height of 20 feet. The geographic parallels, between which cotton-culture is usually placed, are stretching in various girdles between the 36° N.L. and 36° S.L. The primary advantages of this important culture are : A return in a few months, comparatively easy field operations, simple and not laborious process of collecting the crop, and requirement of but little care in the use of the gin-machine in finally preparing the raw material for the market, the woolly covering of the seeds constituting the cotton of commerce. The oil obtained by pressure from the seeds is useful for various technic purposes, and the oil-cake can be used like most substances of similar kind for very fattening stable-feed. Sea Island Cotton was raised in splendid perfection in the northern parts of Victoria fully 15 years ago from seeds, extensively distributed by the writer ; but the want of cheap labor has hitherto militated against the extensive cultivation of the Cotton, and so also against the culture of Tea and many other industrial plants. Cotton having been raised far away from the influence of the sea-air, it would be worthy of attempts, to naturalize various kinds of Cotton in the oases of our deserts, irrespective of regular culture. Our native Gossypium of the interior produces no fibre, worth collecting. Cotton-plants have a predilection for gently undulating or sloping ground, with light soil and a moderate supply of moisture. In the most favorable climes, such as that of Feegee, Cotton produces flowers and fruits throughout the year, but the principal ripening falls in the dry season. From 200 to 300 plants or more can be placed on an acre. As many as 700 pods have been gathered from a single plant at one time, 12 to 20 capsules yielding an ounce of mercantile cotton. Weeding is rendered less onerous by the vigorous growth of the plants. Cotton comes well in for rotation of crops. Major Clarke has ascertained that crossing cannot be effected between the Oriental and Occidental kinds of cotton. A high summer temperature is needed for a prolific cotton harvest. Intense heat, under which even maize will suffer, does not injuriously affect cotton, provided the atmosphere is not dry in the extreme. The soil should not be wet, but of a kind that naturally absorbs and retains humidity, without over saturation. In arid regions it is necessary to irrigate the cotton-plant. Heavy rains at the ripening period are injurious if not destructive to the Cotton crop. Dry years produce the best returns, yet aqueous vapour in the air is necessary for the best yield. In colder localities the balls or capsules continue to ripen after the frosts prevent the formation of new ones. Porous soils resting on limestones and metamorphic rocks are eminently adapted for cotton culture. The canebrake soil of the North American cotton regions absorbs ammonia to a prodigous extent.

Guadua angustifolia, Kunth.

(Bambusa Guadua, Humboldt and Bonpland.)

New Granada, Ecuador and probably others of the Central American States. This Bamboo attains a height of 40 feet, and might prove hardy in sheltered places of our lowlands.

Guadua latifolia, Kunth.

(Bambusa latifolia, Humb. and Bonpl.)

One of the tall Bamboos of Central America, from whence several other lofty Bamboos may be obtained, among them the almost climbing Chusqueas. This Gadua is stouter than any Indian Bamboo. In tropical America native Bamboos are planted for hedges.

Guizotia oleifera, Candolle.

India and probably also Abyssinia. The Ramtil oil is pressed from the seeds of this annual herb, which yields its crop in three months. The oil is much used like Sesamum oil, as well for culinary as technic purposes.

Hedeoma pulegioides, Persoon.

The Pennyroyal of North America. An annual herb of aromatic taste, employed in medicine.

Hedysarum coronarium, L.*

The Soola Clover. South Europe. One of the best of perennial fodder-herbs. It carries with it also the recommendation of being extremely handsome.

Helianthus annuus, L.*

The Sunflower. Peru. This tall showy and large-flowered annual is not without industrial importance. As much as 50 bushels of seeds or rather seed-like nutlets have been obtained from an acre under very favorable circumstances, and as much as 50 gallons of oil can be pressed from such a crop. The latter can be used not only for machinery, but even as one of the best for the table. Otherwise the seeds afford an excellent fodder for fowl. The stalks furnish a good textile fibre and the blossoms yield a brilliant lasting yellow dye. About 6 lbs. of seeds are required for an acre. The plant likes calcareous soil. Several allied North American species deserve perhaps rural culture. The return from a Sunflower field is attained within a few months.

Helianthus tuberosus, L.

Brazil. Sunflower Artichoke. Inappropriately passing under the name Jerusalem Artichoke. The tubers are saccharine and serve culinary purposes. The stem is rich in textile fibre. The percentage of crystalline sugar is largest during the cold season, namely 5–6/100. During the summer the starch-like Inulin prevails. This plant can only be brought to full perfection in a soil rich in potash.

Heliotropium Peruvianum, L.

Andes of South America. A perennial somewhat shrubby plant. Among various species of Heliotrop this one can best be utilized for the distillation of the scented oil.

Helleborus niger, L.

Forest mountains of Middle and South Europe. The Christmas Rose of British gardens. A perennial handsome herb. The roots are used in medicine.

Hibiscus cannabinus, L. (*H. radiatus*, Cavanill.)

Tropical Asia, Africa and Australia. An annual showy herb. The stem yields a hemp-like fibre; the leaves serve as sorrel-spinage. Several other Hibisci can be utilized in the same manner.

Hibiscus esculentus, L.

West India and Central America. A tall herb. The mucilaginous seed-capsules are known as Ochro, Bandakai or Gobbo, and used as culinary vegetables. Our summers bring them to maturity. The leaves of this and allied species can be used as pot-herbs.

Hierochloa redolens, R. Br.

South-eastern Australia, almost confined to the Alps; in Tasmania and New Zealand also found in the lowlands, occurring likewise in the Antarctic islands and the southern extremity of America. A tall perennial nutritious grass, with the odor of Anthoxanthum. It is worthy of dissemination on moist pasture land. H. borealis of the colder regions of the Northern Hemisphere accompanies here in the south H. redolens, but is a smaller grass.

Hordeum deficiens, Steudel.

The Red Sea Barley. One of the two-rowed Barleys, cultivated in Arabia and Abyssinia. Allied to this is *H. macrolepis*, A. Br., a native of Abyssinia.

Hordeum distichon, L.

Central Asia. The ordinary two-rowed Barley. To this species belong: the ordinary English Barley, the Chevalier, the Annat, the Dunlop, the long-eared, the black, the

Italian and the Golden Barley along with other kinds. A variety with grains free from the sepals constitutes the Siberian and the Haliday Barley, which however is less adapted for malt. Dry Barley-flour, heated at the temperature of boiling water during several hours, constitutes Hufeland's meal for invalids. Barley-culture might be carried on in many parts of our Alps.

Hordeum hexastichan, L.

Orient. The regularly six-rowed Barley. This includes among other varieties the Scotch, the Square and the Bear Barley. Seeds less uniform in size than those of H. distichon. The so-called skinless variety is that, in which the grain separates from the calyx.

Hordeum secalinum, Schreber.

(*H. pratense*, Hudson.)

Europe, North and Middle Asia, North America. Perennial. Famed as the best fattening grass of many of the somewhat brackish marsh pastures on the North Sea. It never fruits when kept down by cattle, and surpresses finally nearly all other grasses and weeds.

Hordeum vulgare, L.

Orient. The four-rowed Barley, though rather six-rowed with two prominent rows. Several varieties occur, among them: the Spring, Winter and Black Barley, the Russian, the French, the Naked and the Wheat Barley. Chemical principles of malt: Asparagin; a protein substance: Diastase; an acid and Cholesterin-fat.

Hordeum zeocriton, L.

Central Asia. Also a two-rowed Barley. To this species belong the Sprat, the Battledore, the Fulham and the Putney Barley.

Hovenia dulcis, Thunberg.

Himalaia, China, Japan. The pulpy fruit-stalks of this tree are edible. *H. inaequalis*, D. C., and *H. acerba*, Lindl., are mere varieties of this species.

Humulus Lupulus, L.*

The Hop-plant. Temperate zone of Europe, Asia and North America. This twining perennial unisexual plant has proved to yield enormously on river banks in rich soil or on fertile slopes, where irrigation could be effected, particularly so within our territory along the river valleys of Gipps Land and in other similar localities. A pervious especially alluvial soil, fertile through manure or otherwise, appliances for irrigation natural or artificial, and also shelter against storms are some of the conditions for success in hop-growth, and under such conditions the rearing of hops will prove thus far profitable in countries and localities of very different mean temperature. A dry summer-season is favorable to the ripening and gathering of hops. On the Mitchell River, in Gipps Land, 1500 lbs. have been obtained from an acre. In Tasmania large crops have been realized for very many years. The plant might be readily naturalized on river banks and in forest valleys. The scaly fruit cones form the commercial hops, whose value largely depends on the minute glandular granules of Lupuline. Hops impart their flavor to beer, and principally by their tannic acid prevent acetous fermentation and precipitate albuminous substances from the malt. Hop-pillows are recommended to overcome want of sleep. Many of the substitutes of hops are objectionable or deleterious. The refuse hops of breweries possess double the value of stable manure. Active principles of hop leaves and fruits: A peculiar volatile and a bitter acid substance. The fibre of the stem can be made into cords and paper.

Hydrastis Canadensis, L.

North America. The Yellow Poccoon. A perennial herb, utilized in medicine. The root contains two alkaloids: Berberin and Hydrastin.

Hyascyamus niger, L.

The Henbane. Europe, North Africa, extra-tropic Asia. An important medicinal herb of one or two years' duration. It contains a peculiar alkaloid: Hyoscyamin.

Hyphæne Argun, Martius.

Nubia. Probably hardy in the warmer parts of our Colony.

Hyphaene coriacea, Gaertner.

Equatorial Eastern Africa. The dichotomous Palm of the seacoast-regions. It attains a height of 80 feet.

Hyphaene crinita, Gaertner. (*H. Thebaica*, Martius.)

Abyssinia, Nubia, Arabia and Egypt as far as 31° N., and southward to the Zambesi, Nyassa and Sofala. The Ginger-bread-palm or Doum-palm. It is much branched and attains a height of about 30 feet. The mealy husk of the fruit is edible. Grows away from the sea.

Hyphaene ventricosa, Kirk.

Zambesi. Loftier than the other species. Stem turgid towards the middle. Fruit large.

Hypochœris apargioides, Hook and Arn.

Chili. A perennial herb. The root is used for culinary purposes like that of the Scorzonera Hispanica.

Hyphochœris Scorzoneræ, F. v. M.

(*Achyrophorus Scorzonerae*, Cand.)

·Chili. Of the same use as H. apargioides. Allied species of probably similar utility exist in Western South America.

Ilex Paraguensis, St. Hilaire.

Uruguay, Paraguay and Southern Brazil. The Maté. This Holly-bush is inserted into this list rather as a stimulating medicinal plant, than as a substitute for the ordinary Tea-plant. Chemical principles :. Coffein, Quina-acid and a peculiar tannic acid, which latter can be converted into Viridin-acid.

Illicium anisatum, L.

China and Japan. The Star-Anis. An evergreen shrub or small tree. The starry fruits used in medicine and as a condiment. Their flavour rests on a peculiar volatile oil with Anethol. This species and a few others deserve culture also as ornamental bushes.

Indigofera Anil, L.

Recorded as indigenous to West India, and as extending naturally through Continental America from Carolina to Brazil. A shrub several feet high. Pods sickle-shaped, short, compressed. One of the principal Indigo plants under cultivation both in the eastern and western hemispheres. Only in the warmest parts of our Colony can we hope to produce Indigo with remunerative success. But many of the hardier species seem never yet tested for pigment. Already 114 are recorded alone from extra-tropical Southern Africa. An Indigofera of Georgia, said to be wild, perhaps I. Anil, yields an excellent product. The pigment in all instances is obtained by maceration of the foliage, aeration of the liquid and inspissation of the sediment.

Indigofera argentea, L. (*I. coerulea*, Roxb.)

Tropical and extra-tropical Northern Africa, Arabia, India. A shrub several feet high, closely allied to I. Anil, and likewise a good Indigo-plant.

Indigofera tinctoria, L.

Warmest part of Asia, as far east as Japan, recorded also from tropical Africa and even Natal. A shrubby plant, attaining a height of 6 feet. Pods straight, cylindrical, many-seeded. Extensively cultivated in warm zones for Indigo, and probably hardy in our northern and eastern lowland regions.

Inula Helenium, L.

The Elecampane. Middle and South Europe, Middle Asia eastward to Japan. A perennial herb. The bitter and somewhat aromatic root, for the sake of its stimulating and tonic properties, is used in medicine. It contains also the amylaceous Inulin and the crystalline Helenin.

Ipomœa Batatas, Poiret.* (*Batatas edulis*, Choisy).

The Sweet Potato. Tropical South America. First brought to Europe from Brazil. It proved well adapted also for our part of Australia and for New Zealand. The tubers afford a patatable food, more nutritious than ordinary potatoes. Varieties with red, white and yellow roots occur.

Each tuber weighs generally from 3 lbs. to 5 lbs., but may occasionally attain to 56 lbs. The yield is from 200 to 300 bushels from an acre.

Ipomœa paniculata, R. Brown.

Almost a cosmopolitan plant on tropical coasts ; thus indigenous to North Australia and the warmer parts of East Australia. The tubers also of this species are edible. If hardy, the plant would deserve cultivation.

Ipomœa purga, Wenderoth.

Mountains of Mexico. The true Jalap. This species yields the medicinal Jalap root. It has recently been cultivated with apparent success even at New York. Thus it is entitled to a trial in our warm woodlands. Active principle : the resinous Convolvulin.

Ipomœa simulaus, Hanbury.

Mexico. From this species the Tampico Jalap, or rather the Sierra Gorda Jalap, is derived. *I. operculata*, Mart., yields the Brazilian Jalap.

Isatis indigotica, Fortune.

North China. Perennial, almost shrubby. The use is similar to that of the following plant.

Isatis tinctoria, L.

Dyer's Woad. From the Mediterranean regions through part of the Orient, apparently extending as far as Japan. A tall herb of two years' duration. The blue dye is obtained from the fermented leaves. Many other species of Isatis, mostly Asiatic, may produce perhaps dye with equal advantage. Boissier enumerates merely as Oriental 28 kinds.

Jasminum grandiflorum, L.

From India to Japan. Flowers white. Extensively cultivated in South Europe. The delicate scent is withdrawn either by fixed oils or alcoholic distillation. The pecuniary yield obtainable from Jasmin cultivation seems vastly over-rated, even if inexpensive labour should be obtainable.

Jasminum odoratissimum, L.

Madeira. Shrubby like the rest. Flowers yellow. Used like the foregoing and following for scent. This may be prepared by spreading upon wool or cotton, slightly saturated with olive oil or other fixed oil, the flowers, and covering them with other layers so prepared. The flowers are renewed from time to time until the oil is thoroughly pervaded by the scent, when the latter is withdrawn by Alcohol. Other modes of extracting the oil exist.

Jasminum officinale, L.

From the Caucasus to China. Flowers white. This is the principal species cultivated in South Europe for its scent.

Jasminum Sambac, Aiton.

From India to Japan. It would probably endure our cool season in the northern and eastern regions. It has the richest perfume of all. The bush attains a height of 20 feet, and is almost climbing. The flowers are white, and must be collected in the evening before expansion. The relative value of many other species of Jasmin, nearly all from the warmest parts of Asia, seems in no instance to have been ascertained, as far as their oils or scents are concerned. Our Australian species are also deliciously fragrant, amongst which *J. lineare*, Br., occurs in our Victorian deserts, while also *J. didymum*, Forst.; *J. racemosum*, F. v. M.; *J. simplicifolium*, Forst.; *J. calcareum*, F. v. M., and *J. suavissimum*, Lindl., reach extra-tropic latitudes.

Jubæa spectabilis, Humboldt.

The tall and stout Coquito-Palm of Chili. Well adapted for our extra-tropic latitudes. A kind of treacle is obtained from the sap of this Palm. The small kernels are edible.

Justicia Adhatoda, L.

India; enduring the climate of the lowlands of Victoria. This bush possesses anti-spasmodic and febrifugal properties. It can be utilized also as a hedge-plant.

Kentia Baueri, Seemann.

The Norfolk Island Palm. Height 40 feet.

Kentia Belmoriana, M. and M.

The Curly Palm of Lord Howe's Island. About 40 feet high. With its congeners, evidently destined to grace our gardens, and to become also important for horticultural traffic abroad.

Kentia Canterburyana, M. and M.

Umbrella Palm of Lord Howe's Island. Likewise a tall and hardy palm.

Kentia Mooreana, F. v. M.

Dwarf Palm of Lord Howe's Island, where it occurs only on the summits of the mountains.

Kentia sapida, Blume.

The Nika Palm of New Zealand and the Chatham Islands. It also attains a height of 40 feet and is one of the hardiest of all palms. The unexpanded flower-spikes can be converted as palm-cabbage into food.

Lactuca virosa, L.

Middle and South Europe, North Africa, Middle Asia. A biennial. The inspissated juice of this Lettuce forms the sedative Lactucarium.

Lathyrus pratensis, L.

Europe, North and Middle Asia. The Meadow Pea. A good perennial pasture-herb.

Lathyrus sativus, L.

Middle and South Europe. The Jarosse. An annual forage-herb; the pods also available for culinary purposes. Probably other species of Lathyrus could advantageously be introduced.

Lavandula angustifolia, Ehrhart. (*L. vera*, Candolle.)

Countries around and near the Mediterranean Sea. The Lavender-plant of somewhat shrubby growth, from which by distillation the best oil of Lavender is prepared. It lives on dry soil, but is less hardy than the following.

Lavandula latifolia, Villars. (*L. spica*, Candolle.)

South Europe, North Africa. Also from this species much Lavender oil is obtained.

Lavandula Stœchas, L.

South Europe, North Africa. This shrub can also be utilized for oil distillation and other purposes, for which the two other Lavenders are used. The quality of the oil of these species seems to differ according to their locality of growth.

Lawsonia alba, Lamarck.

North and Middle Africa, Persia, Arabia, India and North-western Australia. The Henne or Henna-Bush. It may become of use as a dye-plant in parts of our Colony free of frost. The orange pigment is obtained from the grinded foliage.

Lavatera arborea, L.

Tree-Mallow of Middle Europe and the countries at the Mediterranean Sea. A tall biennial plant of rapid growth. The ribbon-like bast is produced in greater abundance than in most other malvaceous plants. The Tree-Mallow might easily be naturalized on our shores. Perhaps it might serve with allied plants for green manure.

Leersia oryzoides, Swartz.

Middle and South Europe, various parts of Asia, Africa and America. A perennial nutritious swamp-grass. Other Leersias from both hemispheres are deserving of introduction.

Lepidium sativum, L.

The Cress. Orient. Annual. Irrespective of its culinary value Cress is of use as one of the remedies in cases of scurvy. Active principle: A volatile oil and the bitter Lepidin.

Lepidosperma gladiatum, La Billard.

The Sword-Sedge of the sea coasts of extra-tropic Australia. One of the most important plants for binding sea-sand, also yielding a paper material as good as Sparta.

Leptospermum lævigatum, F. v. M.

(Fabricia laevigata, Gaertner.)

The "Sandstay." Sea-shores and sand-deserts of extra-tropic Australia, but not extending to Western Australia.

This shrub or small tree is the most effectual of all for arresting the progress of drift-sand in a clime like ours. It is most easily raised by simply scattering in autumn the seeds on the sand and covering them loosely with boughs.

Ligustrum Japonicum, Thunberg.

The Japan Privet. A shrub, evergreen or nearly so, promising to become a valuable hedge-plant. It grows like the ordinary European Privet readily from cuttings.

Linum usitatissimum, L.*

The Flax-plant. Orient. A well-known annual, which yields the fibre for linen and the linseed oil. Flax-culture is doubtless destined to become an important industry among us. Few plants find a wider congeniality of soil and climate, and few give a quicker return. Good and deep soil well drained is requisite for successful flax-culture· Change of seed-grain is desirable. Thick sowing extends the length of the fibre. To obtain the best fibre, the plant must be pulled when the seeds commence to ripen. If the seeds are allowed in part to mature, then both fibre and seed may be turned to account. If the seed is left to ripen completely, then the fibre is generally discarded. The seed yields by pressure about 22 per cent. of oil. The residue can either be prepared as Linseed Meal or be utilized as admixture to stable-fodder. The demand for both fibre and oil is enormous. The value of our import of raw fibre in 1871 was already £15,634, while the import of oil was £22,469. Two principal varieties are under culture : a tall sort, with smaller flowers, closed capsules and dark seeds ; a dwarf sort, more branched (even if closely sown) with larger flowers and capsules, the seed-vessels opening spontaneously and with elasticity, while the seeds are of a a pale color. None of the perennial species of Linum are so manageable in culture as the ordinary annual flax.

Lippia citriodora, Kunth.

Peru, Chili, La Plata States, Brazil. An evergreen shrub, yielding scented oil.

Lithospermum hirtum, Lehmann.

North American Alkanna. A showy perennial herb ; the root yields a red dye.

Lithospermum canescens, Lehmann.

North American Alkannet. This, as the vernacular name indicates, offers also a dye root.

Lithospermum longiflorum, Sprengel.

North America. A red pigment can also be extracted from the root of this species.

Livistona Australis, Martius.

East Australia. Our own and only Palm-tree in Victoria, occurring in East Gipps Land (in the latitude of Melbourne), and there attaining a height of 80 feet. The young leaves can be plaited as a material for cabbage-tree hats.

Livistona Chinensis, R. Brown.

South China and Japan. A very decorative fan-palm, hardy in our lowlands.

Lolium perenne, L.*

Europe, North Africa, Western Asia. The perennial Rye-Grass, mentioned here for completeness' sake. *L. Italicum*, Al. Br., the Italian Rye-Grass, seems to be only a variety. One of the most important of all pasture-grasses, also almost universally chosen for lawn-culture. It produces an abundance of seeds, which are readily collected and easily vegetate. It arrives early to perfection. Nevertheless the produce and nutritive powers are considerably less than those of Dactylis glomerata, Alopecurus pratensis and Festuca elatior ; but it pushes forward earlier than the last mentioned grass, while the ripening of seeds is less defective than in Alopecurus. Rye-grass though naturally living but a few years, maintains its ground well by the ease, with which it disseminates itself spontaneously. Several sorts, which scarcely can be called varieties, are under cultivation. Rye-grass stands the dry heat of our summers well. It is likely to spread gradually over the whole of the Australian continent, and may play an important part in our pastoral affairs and also in ameliorating the clime of the desert districts.

Lupinus albus, L.

The White Lupine. Countries at the Mediterranean Sea, also in the Orient. An annual quick-growing herb, valuable for fodder and for green manure. The lentil-like seeds, after the bitter principle (Lupinin) has become removed through boiling, become edible. It would lead too far, to enumerate here many others of the numerous species of Lupines, of which unquestionably very many are eligible for agrarian purposes, while all are acceptable as hardy, elegant and easily grown garden plants. One (*L. perennis*, L.) extends in America to the Northern States of the Union and Canada ; fourteen are recorded from South Europe, seventeen from Brazil, and numerous species from other parts of America, where the limits of the genus are about Monte Video southward and about Nootka Sound northward. The majority of the species is perennial. The Egyptian *L. Termis*, Forsk., is closely allied to L. albus, and of equal use.

Lupinus luteus, L.

The Scented Yellow Lupine. Countries in the vicinity of the Mediterranean Sea. This likewise annual species is predominently in use through Middle Europe, to improve sandy soil. It can also be employed like some other Lupines as a fodder herb. About 90 lbs. of seeds are required for an acre.

Lupinus varius, L.

The Blue Lupine. Also a Mediterranean annual, used like the above congeners ; but a few others are under cultivation as Blue Lupines. Some of the American, particularly Californian species, are regarded for agrian purposes superior to the Mediterranean kinds.

Maclura aurantiaca, Nuttall.

The Osage Orange, or North American Bow-wood, or Yellow-wood. Texas, Arkansas, Louisiana. This thorny deciduous shrub or tree can be well trained into hedges.

It is unisexual, and will in favourable localities on rich
river banks attain a height of 60 feet, with a stem 2 to 3
feet thick, thus becoming available as a timber-tree. Here
it is recorded as a hedge plant ; as such our own thorny
Maclura Calcar Galli (*Morus Calcar Galli*, A. Cunningh.)
of extra-tropical East Australia, which moreover possesses
small edible fruits, deserves attention for live fences. Neither
of the two is readily subject to blight or attacks of insects.
The latter produces suckers and from the root a yellow dye.

Maharanga Emodi, A. de Candolle.

Nepaul. The root produces like that of Alkanna tinctoria a
red dye.

Mallotus Philippinensis, J. M.

(*Rottlera tinctoria*, Roxburgh.)

South Asia and East Australia, in jungle-country, extending
into New South Wales. Though not of great importance
this bush should not be passed on this occasion, inasmuch
as the powdery substance, investing the seed-capsules, constitutes the Kamala, which can be employed not only as
an orange dye, but also as an anthelminthic remedy. The
Hindoo silk-dyers use it for an orange colour, obtained by
boiling the Kamala with carbonate of soda.

Manihot Aipi, Pohl.

The Sweet Cassava. Tropical South America, but traced as
far south as the Parana River. The root is reddish and
harmless; it can therefore be used, unlike those of the following species, without any further preparations than boiling,
as a culinary esculent, irrespective of its starch being also
available for tapioca. Both are somewhat woody plants,
several feet high, and they are too important to be left
altogether unnoticed on this occasion, although we have no
evidence, that they will prove productive even in those parts
of Victoria, which are free of frost. The Aipi has ligneous
tough fibres, stretching along the axis of the tubers, while
generally the roots of the following species are free of this
central woody substance.

Manihot utilissima, Pohl.
The Bitter Cassava or Tapioca-plant. Tropical South
America. Closely allied to the former, producing varieties
with roots of poisonous acridity, and with tubers perfectly
harmless. The tubers attain a length of 3 feet; they can
be converted into bread or cakes, the volatile poison of
the milky sap being destroyed through pressing of the
grated root in first instance, and the remaining acridity is expelled by the heating process. The starch, heated in a moist
state, furnishes the Tapioca. Manihot is abundantly cultivated at Caracas, where the singularly uniform temperature
throughout the year is only 60° to 70° F. It is a very
exhausting crop, and stands thus in need of rich soil and
manuring. The propagation is effected by cuttings from
the ligneous part of the stem. The soil, destined for Cassava,
must not be wet. In warm countries the tubers are available in about 8 months, though they still continue to grow
afterwards. The growth of the plant upwards is checked
by breaking off the buds. The Bitter Cassava is the more
productive of the two. The yellowish tubers attain sometimes a weight of 30 lbs. They do not become soft by boiling like Aipi.

Maoutia Puya, Weddell.
India, on mountains up to 4000 feet. It is taller than
Boehmeria nivea, and furnishes a similar fibre. This shrub
belongs to a tribe of the nettle order, not possessing
burning acridity. None of the true nettles, such as the
Girardinias, nor allied stinging plants have been recommended in this index, although from some an exquisite
fibre is derived, as the writer wishes to guard against the
introduction of any burning species, which possibly might
disseminate itself in a mischievous manner in our ranges,
and then probably could not again be suppressed.

Maranta arundinacea, L.
The true Arrow-root plant. West India. The plant is introduced into this list not without hesitation, as it seems to require
a warmer clime than ours to attain perfection. It furnishes
most of the genuine West Indian Arrowroot, although other

species, such as M. nobilis, M. Allouya, M. ramosissima, are also cultivated for a similar starch of their tubers.

Matricaria Chamomilla, L.

The annual Chamomile. Europe, North and Middle Asia. A highly useful herb in medicine. In many parts of the European continent it is much more extensively used than the ordinary perennial Chamomile. The infusion of the flowers has rather a pleasant taste without strong bitterness. The flowers serve as a tonic and especially as a sudorific, and possess a peculiar volatile oil. *Marrubium vulgare*, L., is not prominently mentioned, as it is already rather copiously naturalized.

Medicago sativa, L.*

Orient; now spread through Middle and South Europe and Middle Asia. The purple Medick, Alfalfa or Lucerne. A perennial fodder-herb of great importance, and already largely utilized in our colony, perhaps descended from the English Medicago falcata, which also deserves naturalization. Lucerne keeps here green and fresh in the hottest season of the year, even in dry and comparatively barren ground, but developes itself for field-culture with the greatest vigour on river banks, particularly in soil rich in lime. Its deeply penetrating roots render the plant particularly fit for fixing fenced embankments or hindering the washing away of soil subject to occasional inundations.

Melilotus alba, Desrouss.

The Cabul or Bockhara Clover. Middle and Southern Europe, North Africa, Middle Asia. A biennial herb. On account of its fragrance it is of value for admixture to hay. It is also a good bee-plant. Flowers white. Odorous principle: Cumarin.

Melilotus officinalis, Desrouss.

Europe and Middle Asia. Also biennial, or lasting through several years if prevented from flowering. Contains also Cumarin. An allied species is *M. macrorrhiza*, Pers. Both serve purposes similar to those for which M. alba is employed.

Melissa officinalis, L.

The Balm-herb. South Europe and Middle Asia. A perennial herb, valuable for its scent, which depends on a peculiar volatile oil. It is also valuable as a bee-plant.

Melocanna bambusoides, Trinius. (*Beesha Rheedei*, Kunth.)

The berry-bearing Bamboo, from Chittagong and other mountainous parts of India. It is a thornless Bamboo, growing on dry slopes of hills. Height up to 70 feet; circumference towards base 1 foot; growth beautifully erect.

Melocanna humilis, Roeper.

India. More slender than the preceding species, and attaining only a height of 20 feet.

Melocanna Travancorica. (*Beesha Travaneoriea*, Beddome.)

A new Bamboo from Travancore, worthy of introduction.

Mentha piperita, L.*

The Peppermint. Middle Europe. This well-known perennial herb is important for its peculiar essential oil, which here by culture is produced in good quality. This distilled oil is in considerable demand, and would be best obtained from plants cultivated in the mountain regions or naturalized along the forest rivulets. Eminent authorities refer the Peppermint as a variety to Mentha aquatica, L., the Water-mint of Europe, North Africa, West and North Asia, from which the true Crisp Mint (*M. crispa*, L.) is again derived, as well as the Bergamot-mint (*M. citrata*, Ehrh.)

Mentha Pulegium, L.

The true Penny-royal. Europe, Western Asia, North Africa. A perennial scent herb, yielding a peculiar ethereal oil. It likes moist soil.

Mentha rotundifolia, L.

Middle and South Europe, North Africa, Western Asia. Fond of wet places, which by the culture of this and other mints may be profitably utilized. In odor this mint approaches to Melissa. The French and Italian Crisp Mint is partly derived from this species. Closely allied to the following, and often regarded as a variety of *M. viridis*, L.

Mentha silvestris, L.

The Horse Mint. Europe, North Africa, temperate Asia. Perennial. One of the Crisp Mints is derived from this species.

Mentha viridis, L.

The Spear Mint. Middle and South Europe. Perennial. A particular sort of Crisp Mint (*M. crispata*, Schrad.) belongs to this species.

Our native Mints, M. Australis, M. gracilis and M. saturejoides, R. Br., yield also oil of good flavor. M. Australis is far the largest and most abundant of these plants.

Menyanthes trifoliata, L.

Inappropriately called the Bog-bean. Europe, North and Middle Asia, North America. In springy and spongy bogs. A perennial herb of great beauty, which could be naturalized with facility in our Alps. The root is starchy. The whole plant is pervaded with a bitter principle, largely derived from Menyanthin. The plant is used medicinally as a tonic and febrifuge.

Microseris Forsteri, J. Hooker.

The Native Scorzonera of extra-tropical Australia and New Zealand. A perennial herb deserving attention, as likely its roots would enlarge and improve through culture. On the summits of our snowy mountains the plant developes itself most luxuriantly. The aborigines use the root for food. The plant would prove hardy in Middle Europe.

Morus alba, L.*

The White Mulberry-tree. China. This tree in several varieties provides the food for the ordinary Chinese Silk-insect (*Bombyx Mori*). Silk was produced in Italy already 600 years ago, and there this branch of industry has florished ever since. In China, Silk was reeled since 4500 years. This may demonstrate the permanency of an industry, which we wish to establish here extensively under a similar sky. "One pound of silk is worth its weight in silver, and this pound may be produced (so far as the food of the Bombyx is concerned) from 30 lbs. of Mulberry leaves or from a single tree, which thus may be brought to yield annually the material for 16 yards of Gros de Naples." The White Mulberry-tree is of extremely easy growth from cuttings, also readily raised from well-matured seeds. It is usually unisexual, and attains finally a very large size. It can be grown in climes, where no longer Olives will thrive. Spots for Mulberry-culture must not be over-moist, when the leaves are to be utilized for the Bombyx. In 1870, according to the *British Trade Journal*, the produce of cocoons amounted in Europe to £16,588,000; in Asia to £28,112,000; in Africa to £44,000; in the South Sea Islands to £24,000; in America to £20,000;—thus giving a general total of £44,788,000. Superior varieties of Mulberry can be grafted with ease on ordinary stock. *M. Indica* L., *M. macrophylla* Morett., *M. multicaulis* Perott., *M. Morettiana* Jacq., *M. Chinensis* Bertol., *M. latifolia* Poir., *M. Italica* Poir., *M. Japonica* Nois., *M. Byzantina* Sieb., *M. nervosa* Del., *M. pumila* Nois., *M. tortuosa* Audib., as well as the Constantinople Mulberry, are merely forms of M. alba, to which probably also *M. Tatarica*, L. and *M. pabularia*, Jacquem., belong. The variety known as M. Indica produces black fruits. The planting of Mulberry-trees has recently assumed enormous dimensions in California, where in 1870 between seven and eight millions were planted. The process of rearing the silk-insect is simple and involves no laborious exertions. The cocoons, after they have been properly steamed, dried and pressed, find readily purchasers in Europe, the price ranging according to quality from 3s. to 6s. per lb. The eggs of the Silkworm sell at a price from 16s. to £2 per ounce, and in 1870 Japan had to provide two millions of ounces of Silk-ova for Europe, where the worms had extensively fallen victims to disease. Instances have been recorded in California, where 8 tons of leaves were gathered in the first year from the Mulberry-trees of 1 acre, and 30 tons in the next year. As an example of the profit thus to be realized, a Californian fact may be cited, according to which £700 were the clear gain from 3½ acres, the working expenses having been £93. The Commissioner of Agriculture of the United States has estimated, that under ordinary circumstances an acre should support from 700 to 1000 Mulberry-trees, producing 5000 lbs. of leaves fit for food, when four years old. On this quantity of leaves can be reared 140,000 worms, from which ova at a nett profit ranging from £80 to £240 per acre will be obtained by the work of one person. Mr. C. Brady, of Sydney, thinks the likely proceeds of silk-culture to be from £60 to £150 for the acre. The discrepancies in calculations of this kind are explained by differences in clime, soil, attention and treatment.

The White Mulberry-tree has been very copiously distributed from the Melbourne Botanic Garden since many years. A very palatable fruit is obtained from a variety cultivated in Beloochistan and Affghanistan. *Morus Tatarica*, L., resembles M. alba. Its juicy fruit is insipid and small. The leaves are not generally used for Silkworms.

The results of Mr. Brady's experience on the varieties of the Morus alba are as follows :—In the normal form the fruits are white with a purplish tinge more or less deep, the bark is pale, the leaf is also of a pale hue, not very early nor very tender, nor very abundant. It may be grown on moist ground as long as such is drained, or it will live even on poor loose gravelly soil bordering on running water. The Cevennes variety is a free grower, affords a large quantity of leaves though of rather thick consistence ; all varieties of the Morus Bombyx like these leaves at all stages of their age. It is also called the rose-leaved variety. The silk which it yields is substantial in quantity and also good in quality. It does best on rich dry slopes. The bushy Indian variety has a fine leaf of beautiful green, which though light in weight is abundantly produced. It can be cut back to the stem three or four times a year ; the leaves are flat, long and pointed, possess a fine aroma, and are relished by every variety of the ordinary Silk-insect, though not all thrive equally well on it. The silk derived from this variety is excellent, but not always so heavy in quantity as that produced from the rosy variety. It prefers rich low-lying bottoms, is a greedy feeder, but may thus be made to cover an extraordinary breadth of alluvial or manured land in a marvellous short space of time. At Sydney, Mr. Brady can provide leaves from this Indian variety all through the year by the removal of cuttings, which will strike their root almost at any season. It ripens also seeds readily, and should be kept at bush size. It requires naturally less space than the other kinds. A fourth variety comes from North China; it has heart-shaped flat thickish leaves, which form very good food for the Silkworm. Mr. Brady, as well as Mr. Martelli, recommend very particularly the variety, passing under the name Morus multicaulis for the worms in their earliest stages. The former recommends the Cape variety also; the latter wishes also the variety, called Morus Morettiana, to be used on account of its succulent nutritious foliage, so well adapted for the insect while yet very young, and also on account of producing the largest amount of food within the shortest time. The Manilla variety, known as Morus multicaulis, comes several weeks earlier into bearing than most other sorts, and should therefore be at hand for early hatched worms.

Morus nigra, L.*
The Black Mulberry-tree. South Russia and Persia. Highly valuable for its pleasant refreshing fruits. It is a tree of longevity, instances being on record of its having lived through several centuries. It is also very hardy. The leaves also of this species afford food for the ordinary silk-moth. The tree occurs usually unisexual. *M. atropurpurea*, Roxb., from Cochin-China, is an allied tree. The cylindrical fruit-spike attains a length of two inches.

Morus rubra has been recorded already in the Appendix to our Acclimatisation Society's Report for 1870-1871, among the timber-trees.

Musa Cavendishii, Lambert.
(*M. regia*, Rumph.; *M. Chinensis*, Sweet.)
The Chinese Banana. A comparatively dwarf species, the stem attaining only a height of about 5 or 6 feet. Its robust and dwarf habit render it particularly fit for exposed

localities, and this is one of the reasons, why it is so extensively cultivated in the South Sea Islands. The yield of
fruit is profuse (as much as 200 to 300 fruits in a spike),
and the flavor excellent. This as well as M. sapientum and
M. paradisiaca ripen still their fruits in Madeira and
Florida.

Musa Ensete, Gmelin.

Bruce's Banana. From Sofala to Abyssinia, in mountain
regions. This magnificent plant attains a height of 30 feet,
the leaves occasionally reaching to the length of 20 feet,
with a width of 3 feet, being perhaps the largest in the whole
empire of plants, exceeding those of Strelitzia and Ravenala,
and surpassing even in quadrat-measurement those of the
grand water-plant Victoria Regia, while excelling in com-
parative circumference also the largest compound frond of
Angiopteris erecta, or divided leaf of Godwinia Gigas,
though the compound leaves of some palms are still larger.
The inner part of the stem, and the young spike of the
Ensete can be boiled to serve as a table esculent, but the
fruit is pulpless. This plant produces no suckers, and
requires several years to come into flower and seed, when
it dies off like the Sago plant, the Caryota palm and others,
which flower but once without reproduction from the root.

Musa Livingstoniana, Kirk.

Mountains of Sofala, Mozambique and the Niger regions.
Similar to M. Ensete; seeds much smaller. Possibly requiring no protection here in favorable places.

Musa paradisiaca, L.

The ordinary Plantain or Pisang. India. Among the most
prolific of plants, requiring the least care in climes adapted
for its growth. Stem not spotted. Bracts purple inside.
In this as well as the foregoing and the following new shoots
are produced from the root, to replace annually the fruit-
bearing stem. The fruit of this is chiefly prepared by some
cooking process. Only a few varieties are distinguished,
and they seem to have sprung from the wild state of M.
sapientum. The writer did not wish to pass this and the

allied plants unnoticed, as they will endure our clime in the warmest localities of the colony, where under more careful attention they are likely to mature with regularity their fruit. They require rich and humid soil. Plantain meal is prepared by simply reducing the dried pulp to powder. It is palatable, digestible and nourishing.

Musa sapientum, L.

The ordinary Banana or Sweet Plantain. India. One of the most important plants yielding nutritious delicious fruits. The stem is spotted. Bracts green inside. The leaves and particularly the stalks and the stems of this and other species of Musa can be utilized for producing a fibre similar to Manilla Hemp. The fruit of this is used chiefly unprepared; it is generally of a yellow color. Numerous varieties are distinguished. As much as a hundredweight of fruit is obtained from a plant annually in tropical climes. At Caracas, where the temperature is seldom much above or below 60° F., the Plantain and Banana plants are very productive, being loaded with fruits 12 to 15 inches long, on mountains about 5000 feet high. In our dry Murray regions the winter temperature seems too low for the successful development of these plants, except on sheltered spots.

Musa troglodytarum, L. (*M. uranoscopos*, Rumph.)

India, and apparently indigenous also in the Feegee and other islands of the Pacific Ocean. The fruit-stalk of this species stands upright; the edible fruits are small, reddish or orange-colored. The Chinese *M. coccinea*, Ait., a dwarf ornamental species, has also the fruit-spike straight.

Myrica Faya, Aiton.

Madeira, Azores and Canary Islands. A small tree. The drupaceous fruits are used for preserves. *M. sapida*, Wallich., an Indian mountainous species, has also edible fruits.

Myrtus Ugni, A. Gray.

The Chilian Guava. A hardy shrub, freely bearing its small but pleasantly aromatic berries.

Nardostachys Jatamansi, Cand.

Mountains of Bengal and Nepaul. A perennial herb, famous already at ancient times as a medicinal plant. The root contains an ethereal oil and bitter principle. This drug is often also obtained from *N. grandiflora*, Cand.

Nelumbo lutea, Caspary.* (*Nelumbium luteum*, Willd.)

In North America, north to 44° ; also in Jamaica. This magnificent perennial water-plant carries with it the type of Nelumbo nucifera, but seems more hardy and thus better adapted for our latitudes, the Pythagorean Bean not descending in Australia naturally beyond the 23°, although also this species may perhaps live in the warmer parts of our Colony. The tuberous roots of both species resemble the Sweet Potato and are starchy : the seeds are of particularly pleasant taste. To us the plants would be of great value as ornamental aquatics. The leaves of N. lutea are from 1 foot to 2 feet in diameter. The flowers measure one-half to one foot across. The capsular fruit contains from 20 to 40 nut-like seeds. The plant in congenial spots displaces nearly all other water vegetation by the vigor of its growth.

Nelumbo nucifera, Gaertner.* (*Nelumbium speciosum*, Willd.)

The Pythagorean Bean. Egypt; at the Caspian and Aral Seas (46° N.) ; Persia ; through India, where in Cashmere it occurs at an elevation of 5000 feet; China ; Japan; Amur (16° N.); tropical Australia as far south as 23°. The occurrence of this grand plant at the Ima, at Pekin and at Astrachan proves sufficiently, that we can naturalize it in Victoria. The Nelumbo requires deep water with a muddy bottom. The large white or rosy flowers are very fragrant. The seeds retain their vitality for several years. According to the ancient Egyptian method they are placed in balls of muddy clay and chaff and then sunk into the water.

Nephelium Litchi, Cambess.

South China, Cochin-China and Philippine Islands. An evergreen tree, producing the Litchi-fruit. The pulpy arillus is of extremely pleasant taste, though not large.

Nephelium Longanum, Cambess.

India and Southern China. The Longan-fruit is obtained from this tree; it is smaller than that of the Litchi-tree.

Nicotiana multivalvis, Lindley.

The Native Tobacco of the Columbia River. An annual. This with the following species can be utilized for certain kinds of Tobacco.

Nicotiana Persica, Lindley.

The Shiraz Tobacco. Persia. Annual. This can be brought to perfection only in cool mountain regions. The mode of culture is somewhat different to that of the ordinary Tobacco. Moderate irrigation is favorable. The plants when ripe are cut off and stuck into the ground again until they become yellow. They are then heaped together for a few days in the drying-house. They are then packed into thin strata and placed into bags, for pressure and daily turning.

Nicotiana quadrivalvis, Pursh.

The Native Tobacco of the Missouri. An annual.

Nicotiana repanda, Willd.

Cuba, Mexico, Texas. Annual. It is utilized for some of the Havannah Tobaccoes.

Nicotiana rustica, L.

Tropical America. Annual. Some sorts of Eastern India Tobacco, of Manilla Tobacco and of Turkey (for instance Latakia) Tobacco are derived from this particular species.

Nicotiana Tabacum, L.*

The ordinary Tobacco-plant of Central America. Annual. Various districts with various soils produce very different sorts of Tobacco, particularly as far as flavor is concerned, and again various climatic conditions will affect vastly the Tobacco-plant in this respect. We can thus not hope to produce for instance Manilla or Havannah Tobacco in our latitudes, but we can anticipate to produce good sorts of our own, more or less peculiar, or we may aspire to producing in our rich and frostless forest valleys a Tobacco similar to that of Kentucky, Maryland, Connecticut and Virginia, parts of Victoria resembling in climate very much these countries. Frost is detrimental to the Tobacco-plant ; not only particularly when young must it be guarded against it, but frost will also injure the ripe crop. Mr. Politz considers the scarcity of dew in some of our districts to militate against the production of the best kinds, otherwise the yield as a rule is large, and the soil in many places well adapted for this culture. Leaves of large size are frequently obtained. The moister and warmer northern and eastern regions of our Colony are likely to produce the best Tobacco, if the final preparation of the leaf for the manufacturer is effected by experienced skill. The cruder kinds are obtained with ease, and so leaves for covering cigars. Virgin soil with rich loam is the best for Tobacco-culture, and such soil should also contain a fair proportion of lime and potash, or should be enriched with a calcareous manure and ashes, or with well decomposed stable manure. The seedlings, two months or less old, are transplanted. When the plants are coming into flower the leading top-shoots are nipped off, and the young shoots must also be broken off. A few weeks afterwards the leaves will turn to a greenish yellow, which is a sign that the plants are fit to be cut, or that the ripe leaves can gradually be pulled. In the former case the stems are split ; the drying is then effected in barns by suspension from sticks across beams. The drying process occupies four or five weeks and may need to be assisted by artificial heat. Stripped of the stalks the leaf-blades are then tied into bundles to undergo sweating or a kind of slight fermentation. It does not answer to continue tobacco-culture beyond two years on the same soil uninterruptedly. A prominent variety is *Nicotiana latissima*, Miller, or *N. macrophylla*, Lehm., yielding largely the Chinese, the Orinoco and the Maryland Tobacco. The dangerously powerful Nicotin, a volatile acrid alkaline oily liquid, and Nicotianin, a bitter aromatic lamellar substance, are both derived from Tobacco in all its parts and are therapeutic agents.

Niemeyera prunifolia, F. v. Mueller.

The Australian Cainito. An evergreen tree, sparingly dispersed from the North of New South Wales through the coast forests of Queensland. The fruit is of plum-like appearance and edible. Culture is likely to improve its quality.

Ocimum Basilicum, L.

The Basil. Warmer parts of Asia and Africa. An annual herb, valuable for condiments and perfumery. Several varieties exist, differing considerably in their scent. A crystalline substance is also obtained from this and similar species. *O. canum*, Sims, is closely allied.

Ocimum gratissimum, L.

Recorded from India, the South Sea Islands and Brazil, as indigenous. Somewhat shrubby. This is also a scent-plant like the following, and is one of the best of the genus. *O. viride*, Willd., from tropical Africa seems a variety.

Ocimum suave, Willd.

East Africa. A shrubby species.

Ocimum sanctum, L.

Arabia, India, tropical Australia. A perennial herb. The odor of the variety occurring in North Australia reminds of Anis; the smell of the variety growing in East Australia resembles cloves. *O. tenuiflorum*, L., seems to be another variety. Probably other species, as well cis- as trans-Atlantic, can be used like Basil.

Olea Europæa, L.*

The Olive-tree. From South-western Asia; naturalized in the countries around the Mediterranean Sea. A tree not of great height, but of many centuries' duration and of unabating fecundity. The well-known Olive Oil is obtained from the fruit. Certain varieties of the fruit, preserved in vinegar or salt liquid before perfectly ripe, are also much used for the table. For this purpose the fruit is generally macerated previously in water containing potash and lime. The gum-resin of the Olive-tree contains the crystalline Olivil. The oil of the drupaceous fruit is a most important

product of countries with climates similar to that of
Victoria. Its chemical constituents are :—30 per cent.
crystalline Palmitin; 70 per cent. Olein, through which
Olive-oil belongs to those kinds, which are not drying. The
wild variety of the Olive-tree has usually short blunt leaves
and thorny branches. Long continued droughts, so detrimental to most plants, will affect the Olive but slightly. It
thrives best on a free loamy calcareous soil, even should it
be strong and sandy, but it dislikes stiff clay. Proximity to
the sea is favorable to it, and hill-sides are more eligible for
its culture than plains. The ground must be deeply
trenched. Manuring with well decayed substances is requisite annually, or every second or third year according
to circumstances. Irrigation will add to the productiveness
of the plant. Mons. Riondet distinguishes three main
varieties, of which he recommends two : 1, the Cayon, a
small-sized tree, which comes into bearing already after
three or four years, but it bears fully only every second
year ; its oil is fine with some aroma. 2, the Pendulier, a
larger tree, with long drooping branches, yielding an oil of
first-rate quality. Mons. Reynaud " Culture de l'Olivier,"
separates 12 varieties, as cultivated in France, and recommends among them :—1, the Courniau or Courniale, also
called Plante de Salon, bearing most prolifacly a small fruit
and producing an excellent oil. 2, the Picholine, which by
pruning its top branches is led to spread over eight square
yards or more. It is of weeping habit, yields a good oil in
fair quantity and resists well the attack of insects. 3, the
Mouraou or Mourette, a large tree furnishing also oil of a
very fine quality. Olive-trees require judicious pruning
immediately after the fruit is gathered, when the sap is
comparatively at rest. They may be multiplied from seeds,
cuttings, layers, suckers, truncheons or estacas and old
stumps, the latter to be split. The germination of the seeds
is promoted by soaking the nutlets in a solution of lime and
woodash. The seedlings can be budded or grafted after a
few years. Truncheons or estacas may be from one to many
feet long and from one inch to many inches thick ; they are
placed horizontally into the ground. Olive plantations at

Grasse are worth from £200 to £250 per acre. For many details the tract on the " Culture of Olive and its Utilization," here recently issued by the Rev. Dr. Bleasdale should be consulted, as it rests largely on its author's observations during a long stay in Portugal. The olive oil imported last year into Victoria was valued at £15,538.

The following notes are derived from the important " Tratado del Cultivo del Olivo en Espana," by the Chev. Capt. José de Hidalgo-Tablada (second edit., Madrid 1870). The Olive-tree will resist for a short time considerable frost (— 15° C.) provided the thawing takes place under fogs or mild rain (or perhaps under a dense smoke). It requires for ripening its fruit about one-third more annual warmth than the Vine. The Olive zones of South Europe and North Africa are between the 18° and 44° N.L. An elevation of about 550 feet corresponds in Spain, as far as this culture is concerned, to one degree further north. Olives do not grow well on granitic soil. The fruit produced on limestone formations is of the best quality. Gypsum promotes the growth of the tree (which thus may perhaps prosper in parts of the Murray-desert, underlaid with Gypsum). An equable temperature serves best ; thus exposure to prevailing strong winds is to be avoided. The winter temperature should not fall below — 7° C. The content of oil in the fruit varies from 10 to 20 per cent.; sometimes it even exceeds the latter proportion. In the Provence at an average 24 lbs. of Olive Oil are consumed by each individual of the population ; in Southern Germany nearly 60 lbs., in Andalusia about 30 lbs. For obtaining the largest quantity of oil the fruit must be completely ripe. Hand-picked Olives give the purest oil. Knocking the fruits from the branches with sticks injures the tree and lessens its productiveness in the next year. About 30 Olive-trees can be planted conveniently on an acre for permanence ; each tree under ordinary circumstances will produce fruits for 4 lbs. to 5 lbs. of oil annually. Spain alone produces about 250,000,000 lbs. of Olive Oil a year.

SPANISH VARIETIES.

A.—Varieties of early maturation, for colder localities :—

1. Var. *pomiformis*, Clem.
   Manzanillo. (French: Ampoulleau.) Fruit above an inch in diameter, spherical, shining black. Putamen broad and truncate.

2. Var. *regalis*, Clem.
   Sevillano. (French : Pruneau de Catignac.) Fruit about an inch in diameter, ovate-spherical, blunt, bluish-black.

3. Var. *Bellotudo* or Villotuda.
   Fruit about an inch long, egg-shaped ; pericarp outside dark-red, inside violet.

4. Var. *Redondillo*.
   Fruit ovate-spherical, nearly an inch long. Pericarp outside bluish-black, inside whitish. A rich yielder.

5. Var. *ovalis*, Clem.
   Lechin, Picholin, Acquillo. (French : Saurine.) Fruit broad-oval, two-thirds of an inch long. A copious yielder.

6. Var. *argentata*, Clem.
   Nevadillo blanco ; Doncel ; Zorzalena ; Moradillo ; Oji-blanco ; Olivo lucio. Fruit broad-ovate, an inch long, very blunt, not oblique. Quality and quantity of oil excellent.

7. Var. *Varal blanco*.
   (French : Blanquette.) Fruit ovate, globular, three-fourths of an inch long, neither pointed nor oblique, outside blackish-red.

8. Var. *Empeltre*.
   Fruit ovate, an inch long, equable. Rich in oil of excellent quality, also one of the best for pickles. Pericarp outside violet, inside white.

9. Var. *Racimal*.
   (French: Bouteillan, Boutinicne, Ribien, Rapugette.) Fruit violet-colored, globose-ovate, about an inch long ; neither pointed nor oblique. Bears regularly also on less fertile soil, and is one of the earliest to ripen.

10. Var. *Varal negro*.

Alameno. (French: Cayon, Nasies.) Fruit violet-black, spotted, globose-ovate, nearly an inch long, somewhat pointed. Bears richly.

11. Var. *Colchonudo*.

Fruit spheric, outside red, inside white, one inch in diameter, slightly pointed. Produces a large quantity of good oil.

12. Var. *Ojillo de Liebre*.

Ojo de Liebre. Fruit nearly spheric, outside violet-black; about one inch long, somewhat oblique. One of the less early varieties.

13. Var. *Carrasquena*.

(French: Redouan de Cotignat.) Fruit black-red, almost spherical, slightly oblique, about an inch long. Valuable both for oil and preserves, but liable to be attacked by various insects.

14. Var. *Hispalensis*, Clem.

Gordal; Ocal; Olivo real. Fruit black-grey, oblique, spherical, measuring fully an inch. Rather a large and quick-growing tree. Fruit used in the green state for preserves, not used for table-oil.

15. Var. *Verdejo*.

Verdial. (French: Verdal, Verdan.) Fruit black-violet, oblique-spheric, pointed, about one inch long. Furnishes good oil and resists best of all the cold.

B.—Varieties of late maturation, for warmer localities:—

16. Var. *maxima*, Clem.

Madrileno; Oivo moreal. Fruit over an inch long, cordate-globose, strongly pointed. Less valuable for oil than for preserves.

17. Var. *rostrata*, Clem.

Cornicabra. (French: Cournaud, Corniaud, Courgnale, Pl. de Solon, Pl. de la Fanc; Cayon, Rapunier, Grasse.) Strong and tall, less tender. Fruit black-reddish, over an inch long, oval, much pointed. Good for oil.

18. Var. *ceratocarpa*, Clem.

Cornezuelo. (French: Odorant, Luquoise, Luques.) Fruit fully an inch long, oval, pointed.

19. Var. *Javaluno*.
Fruit black-grey, over an inch long, egg-shaped, somewhat oblique, gradually pointed. Rich in good oil; can also be chosen for preserves; much subject to attacks of insects.

20. Var. *Picudo*.
Fetudilla. Fruit fully an inch long, egg-shaped, blunt at the base, pointed at the apex, with black-grey pulp. Pericarp easily separable. Employed both for oil and preserves.

21. Var. *Nevadillo negro*.
Fruit egg-shaped, fully an inch long, with turned pointed apex. One of the richest of all varieties in yield. Endures considerable cold and ripens not quite late.

All these Spanish varieties show rather long lanceolate leaves of more or less width.

FRENCH VARIETIES.

(Some verging into the Spanish kinds.)

22. Var. *angulosa*, Gouan.
Galliningue, Laurine. For preserves.

23. Var. *Rouget*.
Marvailletto. Produces a fine oil.

24. Var. *atrorubens*, Gouan.
Salierne, Sayerne. Fruit dusted white. Furnishes one of the best of oils.

25. Var. *variegata*, Gouan.
Marbée, Pigale, Pigau. Purple fruit with white spots.

26. Var. *Le Palma*.
Oil very sweet, but not largely produced.

27. Var. *atrovirens*, Ros.
Pointue, Punchuda. Fruit large with good oil.

28. Var. *rubicans*, Ros.
Rougette. Putamen small. Yield annual and large.

29. Var. *alba*, Ros.
Olive blanche, Blancane, Vierge. This with many others omitted on this occasion is an inferior variety.

30. Var. *Caillet Rouge.*
Figanier. Small tree. Fruit large, red. Oil good and produced in quantity.

31. Var. *Caillet Blanche.*
Fruit almost white, produced annually and copiously, yielding a rather superior oil.

32. Var. *Raymet.*
Fruit large, reddish. Oil copious and fine. This variety prefers flat country.

33. Var. *Cotignac.*
Pardignière. Fruit middle-sized, blunt. Oil obtained in quantity and of excellent quality. This wants much pruning.

34. Var. *Bermillaon.*
Vermillon. Yields also table-oil and resists cold well.

Many other apparently desirable varieties occur, among which the Italian Oliva d'ogni mese may be mentioned, which ripens fruits several times in the year, and furnishes a pleasant oil and also berries for preserves.

Onobrychis sativa, La Marck.*
The Sanfoin or Cocks-head Plant. South and Middle Europe, Middle Asia. A deep-rooting perennial fodder-herb, fond of marly soil, and living in dry localities. It is thus well adapted also for the limestone formation of the lower Murray River.

Ophelia Chirata, Grisebach. (*Agathotes Chirata*, D. Don.)
Widely dispersed over the higher mountain regions of India. A perennial herb, considered as one of the best of tonics; it possesses also febrifugal and antarthritic properties. Its administration in the form of an infusion, prepared with cold water, is the best. Besides *O. elegans*, Wight., some of the other Upper Indian, Chinese and Japanese species deserve probaly equal attention.

Opuntia coccinellifera, Miller.
Mexico and West India. The Cochineal Cactus. On this and O. Tuna, O. Hernandezii and perhaps a few others subsists the Coccus, which offers the costly Cochineal dye. Three gatherings can be effected in the year. About 1200

tons used to be imported annually into Britain alone, and a good deal also to other countries, valued at about £100 for the ton. The precious Carmin-pigment is prepared from Cochineal.

Opuntia elatior, Miller.
Central America. A hedge plant with formidable thorns.

Opuntia Ficus Indica, Miller.
Central America, north as far as Florida. Serves for hedges. Pulp of fruit edible.

Opuntia Hernandezii, Candolle.
Mexico. Affords also food for the Coccus Cacti.

Opuntia spinosissima, Miller.
Mexico and West India. Stem columnar with pendant branches. Also a good hedge-plant.

Opuntia Tuna, Miller.
West India, Ecuador, New Granada, Mexico. Irrespective of its value as the principal Cochineal plant, this Cactus is also of use for hedges. It will attain a height of 20 feet. The pulp of the fruit is edible. With the other species hardy at least in our lowlands.

Opuntia vulgaris, Miller.
Central America, northward to Georgia, southward to Peru. Adapted for hedges and like the rest inflammable, thus particularly valuable along Railway-lines. The fruit almost smooth, also eatable. A dye can also be prepared from its pulp and that of allied species. Numerous other species are here industrially eligible for hedging purposes.

Origanum Dictamnus, L.
Candia. Like the following a scent-plant of somewhat shrubby growth.

Origanum Majorana, L.
North Africa, Middle Asia, Arabia. A perennial herb, used for condiment, also for the distillation of its essential oil.

Origanum Maru, L.
Palestine. Perennial and very odorous.

Origanum Onites, L.

Countries at the Mediterranean Sea. Somewhat shrubby and strongly scented.

Origanum vulgare, L.

The ordinary Marjoram. All Europe, North Africa, North and Middle Asia. A scented herb of perennial growth, containing a peculiar volatile oil. It prefers limestone soil. *O. hirtum*, Link., *O. virens* Hoffmannsegg and *O. normale* D. Don, are closely allied plants of similar use. Several other Majorams, chiefly Mediterranean, are of value.

Ornithopus sativus, Brotero.

South Europe and North Africa. An annual herb, larger than the ordinary Birdsfoot-clover. It is valuable as a fodder-plant on sterile soil.

Oryza sativa, L.*

The Rice-plant. South Asia and North Australia. Annual like most cereals. The many rivulets in our ranges afford ample opportunities for irrigating rice-fields: but these can be formed with full advantage only in the warmer parts of the colony, where rice will ripen as well as in Italy, China, or the Southern States of the American Union. Among the numerous varieties of Indian Rice may be noted as prominent sorts: The Early Rice, which ripens in four months and is not injured by saline inundations. The hardier Mountain Rice, which can be raised on comparatively dry ground, and which actually perishes under lengthened inundation, but which is less productive. The Glutinous Rice, which succeeds as well in wet as almost dry places, and produces black or reddish grains. In the rich plains of Lombardy, irrigated from the Alps, the average crop is estimated at 48 bushels for the acre annually. The spirit distilled from Rice and molasses is known as Arrack.

Oryza latifolia, Humb. and Bonpl.

Central America. This species is said to be perennial and to attain a height of 18 feet. It deserves here trial-culture, and may prove a good fodder-grass on wet land in warm localities. *O. perennis*, Moench., seems closely allied.

Oxalis crassicaulis, Zuccar.

Peru. This seems one of the best of those Woodsorrels, which yield a tuberous edible root. Amongst others *O. tuberosa*, Mol. and *O. succulenta*, Barn. from Chili, as well as *O. carnosa* Mol. and *O. conorrhiza* Jacq. from Paraguay, might be tried for their tubers.

Pachyrrhizus angulatus, Rich.

From Central America rendered spontaneous in many tropical countries. A climber, the horizontal starchy roots of which attain a length of 8 feet and a thickness of many inches. It requires rich soil. The root is edible, though inferior to Yam. From the stems a tough fibre is obtained. The plant proved hardy at Sydney.

Paliurus ramosissimus, Poir. (*P. Aubletia*, Schult.)

China and Japan. A thorny tree, which could be utilized for hedging.

Paliurus Spina Christi, Mill. (*P. aculeatus*, Lam.)

The Christ Thorn. From the Mediterranean Sea to Nepaul. A deciduous bush or finally tree, which can be trimmed into hedges.

Panicum amarum, Elliot.

North America. A perennial species, fit to be grown on drifting coast-sand.

Panicum barbinode, Trinius.

Brazil. Valuable as a fodder-grass.

Panicum ciliare, Retzius.

From South Europe and Southern Asia spread through all countries with a warm climate, but apparently also indigenous in East Australia. It readily disseminates itself on barren ground, and is likely to add to the value of our desert-pastures, although it is annual. Stock relish this grass. *P. sanguinale*, L. and *P. glabrum*, Gaudin, are allied species.

Panicum Crus-Galli, L.

The Barn-yard Grass. Occurring now in all warm countries, but probably of Oriental origin, as it seems not recorded in ancient classic literature. A rich but annual grass of ready spontaneous dispersion. *P. colonum*, L. and *P. Crus-Corvi* L. are varieties of it. Regarded by R. Brown as indigenous to Eastern and Northern Australia, where many other excellent fodder-species occur, some perennial. It will succeed also on somewhat saline soil, particularly on brackish water-courses.

Panicum decompositum, R. Brown.   (*P. laevinode*, Lindl.)

The Australian Millet. One of the most spacious of native nutritious grasses. The aborigines convert the small millet-like grains into cakes. This grass will thrive on poor soil.

Panicum frumentaceum, Roxb.

The Shamalo or Deccan Grass. Probably introduced from tropical Africa into South Asia. It serves as a fodder-grass and produces also a kind of millet.

To this species is allied *P. sarmentosum*, Roxb. from Sumatra, which is now likewise much cultivated in tropical countries. It is perennial.

Panicum Italicum, L.

This grass notwithstanding its specific name is of Indian origin, but appears to be likewise a native of North Australia. It is annual and worthy to be cultivated as a tender green-fodder, attaining a height of 5 feet. The grain is not only one of the best for poultry, but that of some varieties can also be utilized as millet. *P. Germanicum*, Roth. is a form of this species.

Panicum Koenigii, Spreng.   (*P. Helopus*, Trin.)

India. A good fodder-grass.

Panicum maximum, Jacq.*   (*P. jumentorum*, Pers.)

The Guinea-Grass. Tropical Africa ; elsewhere not indigenous. This perennial grass attains a height of 8 feet in tropical countries. It is highly nutritious and quite adapted for the warmer parts of our colonial territory.

Panicum miliaceum, L.*   (*P. miliare*, Lam.)

The true Millet. South Asia and North Australia, but cultivated in Southern Europe already at Hippocrates's

aud Theophrastos' time. Annual, attaiuiug a height of
4 feet. Several varieties occur, one with black grains.
They all need a rich but friable soil. It is one of the best
of all grains for poultry, but furuishes also a palatable and
nutritious table-food. It ripens still in Middle Europe.

Panicum pilosum, Swartz.
Tropical America. A perennial fodder-grass.

Panicum repens, L.
At the Mediterranean Sea, also in South Asia and North
Australia. Regarded by the Cinghalese as a good fodder-
grass. It is perennial and well suited for naturalization on
moist soil or river-banks or swamps.

Panicum prostratum, Lam. (*P. setigerum*, Retz.)
Egypt, South Asia, North Australia, perhaps also indigenous
to tropical America. Perennial. Recommendable for pastures.

Panicum spectabile, Nees.*
The Coapim of Angola. From West Africa transferred to
many other tropical countries. A rather succulent very
fatteuing grass, attaining a height of about 4 feet. It
may be assumed, that hitherto about 300 well-defined
species of Panicum are kuown, chiefly tropical and sub-
tropical, thus very few extending naturally to Europe, or
the United States of North America, or Japan, or the
southern part of Australia. Though mostly from the hot
zones these grasses endure in many instances our clime,
and some of them would prove great acquisitions, particularly the perennial species. Numerous good kiuds occur in
Queensland and North Australia spontaueously. Panicum
is the genus richest in species among grasses.

Papaver somniferum, L.*
The Opium-Poppy. Orieut. The capsules of this tall annual,
so showy for its flowers, are used for medicinal purposes ;
from the miuute but exceedingly uumerous seeds, oil of a
harmless and most palatable kind can be pressed remuneratively ; but a still more important use of the plant is that
for the preparation of Opium, of which a quantity valued in

the Custom's returns at £91,455 was imported during 1871 into Victoria, and this does not provide for a large portion of Morphia used in medicine. Both the black and pale seeded varieties can be used for the production of Opium. The return of Poppy-culture, whether for opium or for oil, is within a few months. Our milder and somewhat humid open forest tracts proved most productive for obtaining opium from this plant; but it can be reared also in colder localities, good Opium, rich in Morphia, having even been obtained in Middle Europe and the northern United States, the summers there being sufficiently long to ripen the Poppy with a well elaborated sap. The Morphia contents in Opium from Gipps Land was at an average somewhat over 10 per cent. Opium was prepared in our Botanic Garden for the Exhibition of 1866; but palticularly Mr. J. Bosisto and Mr. J. Hood have given to this branch of rural industry here commercial dimensions. The Smyrna variety is particularly desirable for Opium; it enables the cultivator to get from 40 lbs. to 75 lbs. of Opium from an acre, generally worth 30s. to 35s. per pound. The ground for poppy-culture must be naturally rich, or otherwise be well manured; dressing with ashes increases the fecundity of the plant. The seed, about 9 lbs. to an acre, is generally sown broadcast, mixed with sand. In the most favorable places as many as three crops are obtained during a season. The collecting of the Opium, which consists merely of the indurating sap of the seed-vessels, is commenced a few days after the lapse of the petals. Superficial, horizontal or diagonal incisions are made into the capsules as they successively advance to maturity. This operation is best performed in the afternoons and evenings, and requires no laborious toil. The milky opium-sap thus directed outward, is scraped off next morning into a shallow cup, and allowed to dry on a place away from sunlight; it may also be placed on Poppy-leaves. From one to six successive incisions are made to exhaust the sap, according to season, weather, locality or the knife-like instrument employed. In the Department of Somme (France) alone Opium to the value of £70,000 annually is produced, and poppy-seed to the value of £170,000. Our seasons here, as a rule, are favorable for collecting Opium, and thus this culture is here rendered less precarious than in many other countries. Our Opium has proved as good as the best Smyrna kinds. The petals are dried for packing the Opium, The main value of Opium depends on its contents of Morphia, for which the genus Papaver, as far as hitherto known, remains the sole source. But not less than eleven Alkaloids have been revealed in Opium by the progressive strides of organic chemistry: Codein, Metamorphin, Morphia or Morphin, Narcein, Narcotin, Opianin, Papaverin, Porphyroxin, Pseudo-morphin and Thebain. It contains besides an indifferent bitter principle: Meconin and Meconic Acid (*Vide* " Wittstein's Chemische Analyse von Pflanzentheilen.") Various species of Papaver produce more or less Opium and Morphia.

Parinarium Nonda, F. v. Mueller.

The Nonda-tree of North-east Australia. It may prove hardy in East Gipps Land, and may live perhaps in the dry and hot air of our deserts, where it deserves trial-culture for the sake of its edible mealy plum-like fruit. A few other species with esculent drupes occur in different tropical countries.

Parkinsonia aculeata, L.

From California to Monte Video. A thorny shrub, clearly adapted for the warmer parts of Victoria, where it might be utilized with the following plant for evergreen hedges. The flowers are handsome.

Parkinsonia Africana, Sonder.

South Africa. A tall bush. A third species, *P. microphylla*, Torr., occurs on the Colorado.

Paspalum distichum, Burm.

From India to South-eastern Australia. A creeping swamp-grass, forming extensive cushions. It keeps beautifully green throughout the year, affords a sufficiently tender blade for feed, and is exquisitely adapted to cover silt or bare slopes on banks of ponds or rivers.

Paspalum scrobiculatum, L.

Through the tropics of the Eastern Hemisphere widely dispersed, extending to South-east Australia. A valuable pasture-grass. A superior variety is cultivated in India for a grain crop. This grass furnishes a good ingredient to hay. The stem sometimes attains a height of 8 feet.

Passiflora alata, Aiton.

Peru and Brazil. This Passion-flower and all the following (and probably other species) furnish Granadilla fruits.

Passiflora coccinea, Aublet.

From Guiana to Brazil.

Passiflora coerulea, L.

South Brazil and Uruguay. One of the hardiest of all Passion-flowers, and with many others well adapted for covering bowers, rookeries and similar structures. Many of the Equatorial species come from mountainous regions and may thus endure our lowland clime.

Passiflora edulis, Sims.

Southern Brazil.

Passiflora filamentosa, Willd.

Southern Brazil.

Passiflora incarnata, L.

North America from Virginia and Kentucky southward. The fruits are called Maypops.

Passiflora laurifolia, L. (P. tinifolia, Jussieu.)

The Water-Lemon. From West India to Brazil.

Passiflora ligularis, Juss.

From Mexico to Bolivia.

Passiflora lutea, L.

North America from Pennsylvania and Illinois southward. Berries small.

Passiflora maliformis, L.

From West India to Brazil.

Passiflora quadrangularis, L.

Brazil. One of the most commonly cultivated Grana-dillas.

Passiflora serrata, L.

From West India to Brazil.

Passiflora suberosa, L. (*P. pallida, L.*)

From Florida to Brazil. A careful investigator, Dr. Maxw. Masters, has recently defined about 200 species of Passion-flowers.

Peireskia aculeata, Miller.

West India. The Barbadoes Gooseberry. A tall shrub, adapted for hedges in localities free of frost. The Cochineal Insect can be reared also on this plant. The berries are edible. Several other species exist in tropical America, among which *P. Bleo*, Humb., is particularly handsome, but they may not all be sufficiently hardy for utilitarian purposes in our clime. Otherwise the Bleo is used for salad.

Peireskia portulacifolia, Haw.

West India. This attains the size of a fair tree.

Pennisetum thyphoideum, Rich.*

(*Penicillaria spicata*, Willd. *Panicum coeruleum*, Miller.)

Tropical Asia, Nubia and Egypt. The Bajree. An annual, ripening its millet crop in about three months in warm countries. The stems are thick and reach a height of 6 feet. This grass requires a rich and loose soil, and on such it will yield upwards of a hundred fold. It furnishes also a good hay, and is also valuable as green-fodder. Some of the many other species of Pennisetum are doubtless of pastoral value. A plant allied to P. thyphoideum occurs in China: namely *P. cereale*, Trin. This affords also millets or corn for cakes.

Pentzia virgata, Lessing,

South Africa. A small bush, recommended to be established in our deserts for sheep-fodder. Several other species occur in South Africa.

Perilla arguta, Benth.

Japan. An annual herb. An infusion of this plant is used to impart to table vegetables and other substances a deep red color. *P. ocimoides*, L., of Upper India, serves probably similar purposes.

Persea gratissima, Gaertner.

From Mexico to Peru and Brazil in forest-tracts near the coast. The Avocado Pear. Suggestively mentioned here as likely available for East Gipps Land, French Island and other mild localities of our country, inasmuch as it has become naturalized in Madeira, the Azores and Canary Islands. A noble evergreen spreading tree. The pulp of the large pear-shaped fruit is of delicious taste and flavor. Persea Teneriffæ (*P. Indica*, Spreng.), indigenous to Madeira, the Canary Islands and Azores, is a tree with hard and remarkably beautiful wood.

Peucedanum graveolens, Benth. (*Anethum graveolens*, L.)

The Dill. South Europe, North Africa, Orient. Annual. The well-known aromatic fruitlets used as a condiment. *P. Sowa*, Benth. (*Anethum Sowa*, Roxb.) is a closely allied Indian annual herb.

Peucedanum officinale, L.

The Sulphur Root. Middle and South Europe, North Africa, Middle Asia. Perennial. The root used in veterinary medicine. It contains like that of the following species the crystalline Peucedanin.

Peucedanum Ostruthium, Koch. (*Imperatoria Ostruthium*, L.)

Mountains of Middle Europe. A perennial herb, which could be grown in our Alps. The acrid aromatic root is used in medicine, particularly in veterinary practice. It is required for the preparation of some kinds of Swiss Cheese. *P. Cervaria*, Cuss. and *P. Orcoselinum*, Moench., are also occasionally drawn into medicinal use.

Peucedanum sativum, Benth. (*Pastinaca sativa*, L.)

The Parsnip. Europe, North and Middle Asia. Biennial. The root palatable and nutritious.

Phalaris Canariensis, L.

The Canary Grass. An annual grass from the Canary Islands, now widely dispersed as a spontaneous plant over the warmer zones of the globe. Thus it has also become naturalized in Australia. It is grown for its seeds, which form one of the best kinds of fodder for many sorts of small cage-birds. The flour is utilized in certain processes of cotton manufacture, and liked for some kinds of cakes. The soil for the culture of the Canary-grass must be friable and not too poor. It is an exhaustive crop. As allied annual species of similar use, but mostly of less yield, may be enumerated : *P. brachystachys* Link., from Italy; *P. minor* Retz, and *P. truncata* Guss., from various countries at the Mediterranean Sea. Other species, including some from Asia, are deserving of trial; but the perennial British *P. arundinacea*, L., is too harsh to serve for wholesome fodder, nor does it furnish Canary seed.

Phaseolus adenanthus, G. Meyer.

(*P. Truxillensis*, Humb. *P. rostratus*, Wallich).

Almost cosmopolitan within the tropics, where irrespective of navigation and other traffic it becomes dispersed by migrating birds; truly spontaneous also in tropical Australia. A perennial herb with large flowers, resembling those of *Vigna vexillata*, Benth. Cultivated for its seeds, which are rather small ,but copiously produced.

Phaseolus coccineus, Kniphof.* (*P. multiflorus*, Willd).

The Turkish Bean or Scarlet-Runner. A native of the Orient, if Sprengel's identification is correct, according to which this plant was known in Arabia and Persia at Avicenna's time; but according to other opinions it is a native of Mexico. A twining showy perennial, as useful as the ordinary French Bean. Its seeds usually larger than those of the latter plant, purple with black dots, but sometimes also pure blue and again quite white. The flowers occur sometimes white. The root contains a narcotic poison.

Phaseolus lunatus, L.

Considered as a native of tropical America, but also recorded as wild from many parts of tropical Africa and Asia. Biennial according to Roxburgh. Much cultivated in the warm zone for its edible beans, which are purple or white. A yellow-flowered variety or closely allied species is known as the Madagascar Bean and proved hardy and productive here. *P. perennis*, Walt., from the United States of North America, is another allied plant.

Phaseolus Mungo, L. (*P. Max*, L.)

The Green Gram. South Asia and tropical Australia. An annual very hairy plant, not much climbing. Frequently reared in India, when rice fails or where that crop cannot be produced. The seeds are but small, and the herb is not available for fodder. This plant requires no irrigation, and ripens in two and a-half to three months. The grain tastes well and is esteemed wholesome. The harvest is about thirtyfold.

Phaseolus vulgaris, L.*

The ordinary Kidney Bean or French Bean or Haricot. India, from whence it came to Europe through the conquest of Alexander the Great; but apparently it is also wild in North-western Australia. Though this common and important culinary annual is so well known, it has been deemed desirable, to refer to it here with a view of reminding, that the Kidney-bean is nearly twice as nutritive than wheat. The meal from Beans might also find far augmented use. As constituents of the Beans should be mentioned a large proportion of starch (nearly half), then much Legumin, also some Phaseolin (which like Amygdalin can be converted into an essential oil) and Inosit-Sugar. Lentils contain more Legumin but less starch, while Peas and Beans are in respect to the proportion of these two nourishing substances almost alike. *Phaseolus nanus*, L., the Dwarf-bean, and *P. tumidus*, Savi, the Sugar-bean or Sword-bean or Egg-bean, are varieties of P. vulgaris. Several other species of Phaseolus seem worthy of culinary culture.

Phleum pratense, L.*

The Catstail or Timothy Grass. Europe, North Africa, North and Middle Asia. One of the most valuable of all perennial fodder-grasses. Its production of early spring-herbage is superior to that of the Cocksfoot-grass. It should enter largely into any mixture of grasses for permanent pasturage. It will live also on moist and cold clay-ground. This grass and perhaps more yet the allied *Phleum alpinum*, L., are deserving of an extensive transfer to our moory Alps. For hay it requires mowing in a young stage. The seed is copiously yielded and well retained.

Phœnix dactylifera, L.*

The Date-Palm. North Africa, also inland ; Arabia, Persia. This noble palm attains finally a height of 80 feet. It is unisexual and of longevity :—"Trees of from 100 to 200 years old continue to produce their annual crop of dates." Though from the sap sugar or palm wine can be obtained, and from the leaves hats, mats and similar articles can be manufactured, we here would utilize this palm beyond scenic garden ornamentation only for its fruits. It is in the oases of our desert-tracts, swept by burning winds, where the Date-palm would afford in time to come a real boon, although it might be grown also in the valleys of our mountains and in any part of our lowlands. Several bunches of flowers are formed in a season, each producing often as many as 200 dates. Many varieties of dates exist, differing in shape, size and color of the fruit; those of Gomera are large and contain no seed. The unexpanded flower-bunches can be used for palm-cabbage ; the fibre of the leaf-stalks for cordage. The town Elcho in Spain is surrounded by planted forest of about 80,000 Date-palms, and the sale of leaves for decorative purposes produces irrespective of the value of the date-fruits a considerable income to the town, and so it is at Alicante. As far north as the Gulf of Genoa exists also a date-forest. The ease, with which this palm grows from seeds, affords facility in adapted climes to imitate these examples, and we certainly ought to follow them in all parts of Australia.

Phœnix paludosa, Roxb.

India. A stout species, not very tall. Of value at least for decorative culture.

Phœnix pusilla, Gaertner.

India and South China. A dwarf species, likely also to be hardy here. *P. farinifera*, Roxb., appears to be identical. It is adapted for sandy and otherwise dry and barren land, but prefers the vicinity of the sea. Berry shining black, with a sweet mealy pulp.

Phœnix reclinata, Jacquin.

South Africa in the eastern districts. A hardy species, but not tall, often reclining. It is adapted for ornamentation. The seeds are frequently drawn into local use as a substitute for coffee.

Phœnix silvestris, Roxb.

India, almost on any soil or in any situation. It has proved at Melbourne a very hardy species. Its greatest height is 40 feet. Berries yellowish or reddish, larger than in P. pusilla. Where this palm abounds much sugar is obtained from it by evaporation of the sap, which flows from incisions into the upper part of the trunk, a process not sacrificing the plant, as for 20 years the sap can thus be withdrawn. A kind of Arack is obtained by fermentation and distillation of this sap. Each plant furnishes the juice for about 8 lbs. of Date-sugar annually, but in some instances much more. About 50,000 tons of sugar are produced a year in Bengal alone from this and some other palms.

Phœnix spinosa, Thonning.

Tropical Africa, ascending mountain regions, thus perhaps hardy here with us. Dr. Kirk found the green bunches, if immersed in water for half a day, suddenly to assume a scarlet hue, and then the astringent pulp to become edible and sweet.

Phormium tenax, J. R. and G. Forster.*

The Flax-lily of New Zealand, where it occurs as far south as 46° 30', occurring also in the Chatham Islands and Norfolk Island, though not on Lord Howe's Island. It seems important, that this valuable plant should here be brought universally under culture, particularly on any inferior spare ground or on the sea-beaches or any rocky declivity, where it may be left unprotected to itself, as no pastoral animal will touch it. It is evident, that the natural upgrowth will soon be inadequate to the demand for the plant. Merely torn into shreds the leaves serve at once in gardens and vineyards as cordage, and for this purpose, irrespective of its showy aspect, the Phormium has been distributed from our Botanic Garden since the last 14 years. From the divided roots any plantation can gradually be increased, or this can be done more extensively still by sowing the seeds. In all likelihood the plant would thrive and become naturalized in the Auckland's and Campbell's Group, in Kerguelen's Land, the Falkland Islands, the Shetland Islands and many continental places of both hemispheres. Among the varieties three are better characterized than the rest : The Tehore, the Swamp and the Hill variety. The first and the last mentioned produce a fibre fine and soft, yet strong, and the plants attain a height of only about 5 feet, whereas the Swamp-variety grows to double that height, producing a larger yield of a coarser fibre, which is chiefly used for rope or paper making. As might be expected, the richer the soil the more vigorous the growth of the plant ; it likes moreover now and then to be overflown by fresh or brackish water, but it will not live if permanently sunk into wet. In swampy ground trenches should be dug to divert the surplus of humidity. Fibre free from gum-rosin properly dressed withstands moisture as well as the best Manilla rope. Carefully prepared the fibre can also be spun into various textile durable fabrics, either by itself or mixed with cotton, wool or flax. In October last, the sale of Phormium fibre in London was 11,500 bales, ranging in price from £19 to £31. The tow can also be converted into paper, distinguished for its strength and whiteness. The London price of Phormium fibre for this purpose is from £10 to £20 per ton.

For further details on the utilization of this plant the elaborate reports of the New Zealand Commission for Phormium should be consulted. One of the dwarf varieties is *Phormium Colensoi*, J. Hook.

Physalis Alkekengi, L.

The Strawberry-Tomato or Winter-Cherry. Middle and South Europe, North Africa, Middle Asia, extending to Japan, said to have come originally from Persia. A perennial herb. The berry, which is red and of a not unpleasant taste, has some medicinal value. The leaves contain a bitter principle : Physalin.

Physalis angulata, L.

In many tropical countries, extending as a native plant to the northern parts of the United States and to Japan. An annual herb. Yellowish ; the berries edible. *P. minima* L. (*P. parviflora*, R. Br.) appears to be a variety and extends also into tropical Australia.

Physalis Peruviana, L.

Temperate and tropical America, widely naturalized in many countries of the warmer zones. With double inaptness called the Cape Gooseberry. A perennial herb ; but for producing its fruit well, it requires early renovation. The acidulous berries can be used as well as a table-fruit as for preserves. Doubtless several other kinds of Physalis can be utilized in the same manner. In colder countries the P. Peruviana becomes annual.

Pimpinella Anisum, L.

The Anise Plant. Greece, Egypt, Persia. An annual. The seed-like fruits enter into various medicines and condiments, and are also required for the distillation of oil, rich in Anethol.

Pimpinella Saxifraga, L.

Europe, North and Middle Asia. A perennial herb ; its root used in medicine ; a peculiar volatile oil can be distilled from the root. *P. magna*, L., is a closely allied species, and *P. nigra*, W., is a variety. The root of the last is particularly powerful.

Pimpinella Sisarum, Benth. (*Sium Sisarum, L.*)
East Asia. A perennial herb. The bunches of small tubers afford an excellent culinary vegetable.

Pipturus propinquus, Weddell.
Insular India, South Sea Islands and warmer parts of East Australia. This bush is higher and rather more hardy than Boehmeria nivea; but in fibre it is similar to that plant. *P. velutinus,* Wedd., is closely allied. The few other species serve probably as well for fibre.

Pistacia Lentiscus, L.
The Mastix Tree. Mediterranean regions. A tall ever-green bush, exuding the Mastix Resin mostly through incisions into its bark. In Morocco it is extensively used for hedges.

Pistacia Terebinthus, L.
Countries around the Mediterranean Sea. A tall bush or small tree with deciduous foliage. The fragrant Cyprian or Chio Turpentine exudes from the stem of this species. *P. vera,* L., is inserted already among the timber trees.

Pisum sativum, L.*
The Common Pea. Mediterranean countries and Western Asia. This annual of daily use could hardly be left disregarded on this occasion. Suffice it to say, that the herbage as a nutritious fodder deserves more attention than it receives. The green fruit contains Inosit-sugar and Cholesterin-fat. A second species, *P. Aucheri,* Jaub. and Spach., which is perennial, occurs in alpine elevations on the Taurus.

Plectocomia Himalaiana, Griffith.
Sikkim, up to 7000 feet. This Rattan-Palm requires moist forest-land. Its canes are not durable, but this palm is an object worthy of horticulture and would prove the hardiest among its congeners.

Poa angustifolia, L. (*P. serotina,* Ehrh. *P. fertilis,* Host.)
Europe, North Asia, North America. A perennial pasture-grass, allied to P. nemoralis. An excellent grass for moist meadows and river-banks.

Poa aquatica, L. (*Glyceria aquatica,* Sm.)

Europe, North and Middle Asia, North America. This conspicuous water-grass attains a height of 6 feet. It is perennial, and deserves naturalization in our swamps.

Poa Brownii, Kunth. (*Eragrostis Brownii,* Nees.)

Tropical and Eastern extra-tropical Australia, extending rather widely through our Colony. It is here mentioned as a valuable perennial species, keeping beautifully green in our driest summers, even on poor soil. The section Eragrostis of the genus Poa contains numerous species in the hotter parts of the globe. Of these many would doubtless be hardy here and prove of pastoral value.

Poa cynosuroides, Retz.

North-eastern Africa, South Asia. A harsh perennial grass, not serviceable for fodder, but mentioned by Royle as a fibre-plant of North-western India, where it is valued as a material for ropes. In this respect it may not surpass the rough tufty variety of our own *Poa Australis,* R. Br., so common on our river-bankss, from the leaves of which excellent nets are made by the natives.

Poa distans, L.

Europe, North Africa, Middle and Northern Asia, North America. Perennial. It is one of the limited number of tender grasses, suited for moist saline soil, and thus affords pasturage on coast marshes.

Poa fluitans, Scopoli. (*Glyceria fluitans,* R. Brown.)

Europe, North Africa, Middle and North Asia, North America. The Manna-Grass. Perennial. Excellent for stagnant water and slow-flowing streams. The foliage is tender. The seeds are sweet and palatable, and are in many countries used for porridge.

Poa maritima, Hudson.

Europe, North Africa, North Asia, North America. Its long creeping roots help to bind the coast-sand. This grass can also be depastured.

Poa nemoralis, L.

Europe, North and Middle Asia, North America. This perennial grass can be grown on shady forest-land, as the name implies, but it accommodates itself also to open places, and will grow even among rocks. It endures alpine winters.

Poa pratensis, L.

The ordinary English Meadow-Grass. A perennial species, fit for any meadows, thriving early, and able to live also in alpine localities. Better adapted for pasture than hay, but by no means one of the very best grasses, though it resists drought. It forms excellent sward, and with advantage can be used for intermixing it with other pasture-grasses.

Poa trivialis, L.*

Europe, North Africa, Middle and Northern Asia. Also a good perennial grass for mixture on pasture-land. One of the best grasses for sowing on ground recently laid dry. Sinclair regarded the produce of this Poa as superior over many other kinds, and noticed the marked partiality, which horses, oxen and sheep evince towards it. To thrive well it wants rather moist and rich soil and sheltered places.

These few species of Poa have been singled out as recommendable, because they are well tested. Future experiments beyond Europe will add others to lists of recommendations like this.

Podophyllum peltatum, L.

North America. A perennial forest-herb, not without importance for medicinal purposes. The root contains the bitter alkaloid Berberin. *Podophyllum Emodi,* Wall., occurring in the Indian mountains at a height from 6000 to 14,000 feet, can probably be used like the American species. The berries of both are edible, though the root and leaves are poisonous.

Pogostemon Patchouli, Pellet.

Mountains of India. A perennial herb, famed for its powerful scent arising from a volatile oil. *P. parviflorus,* Benth. and *P. Heyneanus,* Benth. belong to this species.

Polygala Senega, L.

North America. A perennial herb. The root is of medicinal value; its acrid principle is Saponin.

Prangos pabularia, Lindley.

Plateaus of Mongolia and Tibet. A perennial fodder-herb, much relished by sheep, eligible for cold and arid localities, and deserving naturalization on our alpine pasture-ground. Other perennial species exist near the Mediterranean Sea, on the Atlas, the Caucasus and the Indian Highlands. P. pabularia is regarded by some as the Silphium of Arrianus.

Pringlea antiscorbutica, W. Anderson and R. Br.*

The Cabbage or Horse-Radish of Kerguelen's Island. The perennial long roots taste somewhat like Horse-Radish. The leaves in never-ceasing growth are crowded cabbage-like into heads, beneath which the annual flower-stalks arise. The plant ascends mountains in its native island to the height of 1400 feet, but luxuriates most on the sea-border. To Arctic and other Antarctic countries it would be a boon. Probably it would live not only on our shores, but also on our Alps. Whalers might bring us the roots and seeds of this remarkable plant, which seems to have never entered into culture yet. Not even its flowers in a perfect state are known. The plant was used by the celebrated Captain Cook and all subsequent navigators, touching at yonder remote spot, as Cabbage, and it proved to possess powerful properties against scurvey. Dr. Hooker observes, that Pringlea can sectionally be referred to Cochlearia. The whole plant is rich in a pungent volatile oil. Through culture important new culinary varieties may likely be raised from this plant. The taste of this vegetable in its natural growth is like Mustard and Cress, and the Kerguelen's Land Cabbage, when boiled, proved a wholesome and agreeable substitute for the ordinary Cabbage.

Prosopis dulcis, Kunth.

From Mexico to the southern parts of the La Plata States. A thorny shrub, growing finally to a tree, adapted for live-fences. This is one of the species, yielding the sweetish

Algaroba-pods for cattle-fodder, and utilized even in some instances for human food. As allied plants, besides the following, may be mentioned: *P. horrida*, Humb., occurring from the base of the Andes to the sand-shores of Peru; *P. juliflora*, Cand., growing from Mexico and West India to Ecuador; *P. Siliquastrum*, Cand., extending from the Chilian Andes apparently into the Argentine Province Catamarka. A short communication on the American Algaroba-trees was presented to our Parliament by the writer in 1871.

Prosopis glandulosa, Torrey.

Colorado, Arkansas, Texas. The pods of this thorny ever green shrub or tree are also succulent. It exudes a gum, not unlike Gum Arabic, and this is obtained so copiously, that children could earn from 2 dollars to 3 dollars a day in Texas while gathering it, latterly about 40,000 lbs. being bought by druggists there. The tree attains a height of 30 feet, and its wood is excessively hard. The pods of several species are rich in tannin.

Prosopis pubescens, Bentham.

Texas, California, New Mexico. Likely available for hedges, with other species of other countries.

Prosopis spicifera, L.

India. A thorny tree, also with edible pods, possibly hardy here.

Prosopis Stephaniana, Kunth.

Syria and Persia. A shrubby species for hedge-growth.

Prunus Americana, Marshall. (*P. nigra*, Aiton.)

Canada, Eastern United States of America. A thorny tree, furnishing the Yellow and Red Plum of North America. The fruit is roundish and rather small, but of pleasant taste.

Prunus Chisasa, Michaux.

North America, west of the Missisippi. On the prairies it is only 3 to 4 feet high. Fruit spherical, red, rather small, with a tender usually agreeable pulp. Other species with edible fruit occur in North America, such as *P. pumila*, L.,

P. Pennsylvanica, L., *P. Virginiana,* L., *P. serotina,* Ehrh., but their fruits are too small to render these plants of importance for orchard culture, though they may also become enlarged by artificial treatment.

Prunus maritima, Wangenheim.

The Beach Plum of North America. A shrubby species, of service not only for covering coast-sands, but also for its fruit, which is crimson or purple, globular and measuring from a-half to one inch. It is not necessary to enter here any notes on the generally known species of Prunus, which have engaged already for years the keen attention of many orchard-cultivators also in this Colony. Thus we possess in this country numerous though not all the best varieties of the Cherry (*P. avium,* L. and *P. Cerasus,* L.), of the Plum (*P. domestica,* L.), of the Apricot (*P. Armeniaca,* L.) and of the Cherry-Plum (*P. myrobalana,* L.), the latter Canadian, the others European and Oriental. Information on these and other varieties, to which we have added independently also here, may be sought in "Hogg's Fruit Manual." The Almond (*Amygdalus communis,* L.) and the Peach (*Amygdalus Persica,* L.) belong also generically to Prunus, as indicated in 1813 by F. G. Hayne (" Arznei Gewaechse," iv., 38) and finally settled by J. D. Hooker (Benth. and Hook., gen. pl. i., 610), for which therefore now the names P. Amygdalus and P. Persica should be adopted.

Prunus spinosa, L.

The Sloe or Blackthorn. Wild in many parts of Europe. With its flowers it is one of the earliest plants to announce the spring. Its tendency to throw out suckers renders the bush less adapted for hedges of gardens than of fields, but these suckers furnish material for walking-sticks. The small fruits can be made into preserves. *P. insititia,* L., the Bullace, with larger and sometimes yellow fruits, extends to North Africa and Middle Asia. Dr. Hooker and other phytographers consider P. domestica not specifically distinct from P. spinosa. Of medicinal value are *P. Lauro-Cerasus,* L., the evergreen Cherry-Laurel from the Orient, and *P. Padus,* L., the deciduous Birds Cherry, which extends from Europe to North Africa and West Asia. These and most other species contain in their foliage and in some other parts Amygdalin. Perhaps some of the species from Eastern Asia, California and tropical America are eligible for improving their fruit through horticultural skill. The Sloe and others might with advantage be naturalized on our forest streams.

Psamma arenaria, Roem. and Schult.

(P. littoralis, Beauv. Calamagrostis arenaria, Roth.)

The Moram or Marrem or Bent Grass. Sand-coasts of Europe, North Africa and Middle North America. One of the most important of reedy grasses, with long creeping roots, for binding the moving drift sands on the sea shore, for the consolidation of which in Europe chiefly this tall grass and Elymus arenarius are employed *Psamma Baltica*, R. and S., from the Baltic and North Sea, serves the same purpose. Both can also be used in the manner of Sparta for paper material.

Psidium Araca, Raddi.

From West India and Guyana to Peru and Southern Brazil, where it is found in dry high-lying places. This is one of the edible Guavas, recorded already by Piso and Marcgrav. The greenish-yellow berry is of exquisite taste.

Psidium arboreum, Vellozo.

Brazil; province Rio de Janeiro. This Guava-fruit measures about one inch, and is of excellent flavor.

Psidium Cattleyanum, Sabine.*

The Purple Guava. Brazil and Uruguay. One of the hardiest of the Guava-bushes, attaining finally a height of 20 feet. The purple berries are seldom above an inch long, but of delicious flavor and taste, resembling thus far strawberries. *P. buxifolium*, Nutt., of Florida, seems nearly related to this species.

Psidium cinereum, Martius.

Brazil : provinces Minas Geraes and Sao Paulo. Also yielding an edible fruit.

Psidium cordatum, Sims.

The Spice Guava. West India. This one attains the height of a tree. Its fruit edible.

Psidium cuneatum, Cambess.

Brazil; province Minas Geraes. Fruit greenish, of the size of a Mirabelle Plum.

Psidium grandifolium, Martius.

Brazil; provinces Rio Grande do Sul, Parana, Sao Paulo, Minas Geraes, where the climate is similar to Southern Queensland. A shrub of rather dwarf growth. The berries edible, size of a walnut.

Psidium Guayava, Raddi.*

(*P. pomiferum*, L. *P. pyriferum*, L.)

The large Yellow Guava. From West India and Mexico to South Brazil. For this handsome evergreen and useful bush universal attention should be secured anywhere in our warm lowlands, for the sake of its aromatic wholesome berries, which will attain the size of a hen's egg and can be converted into a delicious jelly. The pulp is generally cream-colored or reddish, but varies in the many varieties, which have arisen in culture, some of them bearing all the year round. Propagation is easy from suckers, cuttings or seeds. Many other berry-bearing Myrtaceae (of the genera Psidium, Myrtus, Myrcia, Marliera, Calyptranthes, Eugenia) furnish edible fruits in Brazil and other tropical countries, but we are not aware of their degrees of hardinesss. Berg enumerates as esculent more than half a hundred for Brazil alone, of which the species of Campomanesia may safely be transferred to Psidium.

Psidium incanescens, Martius.

Brazil; from Minas Geraes to Rio Grande do Sul. This Guava-bush attains a height of 8 foot. Berry edible.

Psidium polycarpon, Al. Anderson.*

From Guiana to Brazil, also in Trinidad. A comparatively small shrub, bearing prolifically and almost continuously its yellow berries, which are of the size of a large cherry and of exquisite taste.

Psidium rufum, Martius.

Brazil, in the province Minas Geraes, on sub-alpine heights. This Guava-bush gains finally a height of 10 foot, and is likely the hardiest of all the species, producing palatable fruit.

Ptychosperma Alexandrae, F. v. Mueller.

The Alexandra Palm. Queensland, as well in tropical as extra-tropical latitudes. The tallest of Australian Palms, and one of the noblest form in the whole empire of vegetation. It exceeds 100 feet in height, and is likely destined to grace any shady moist grove free from frost in this and other countries, as it seems less tender than most palms. The demand for seeds has already been enormous.

Ptychosperma Cunninghami, Wendland.

East Australia, as far south as Illawarra; thus one of the most southern of all palms. This also is a very high species, destined to take here a prominent position in decorative plantations. Several species occur in Feegee and other islands of the Pacific Ocean, and again others might be obtained from India, but they are probably not so hardy as ours. Though strictly speaking of no industrial value these palms are important for horticultural trade, and are objects eminently fitted for experiments in acclimation.

Ptychosperma elegans, Blume.

(*P. Seaforthia,* Miq. *Seaforthia elegans,* R. Br.)

Litoral forests of tropical Australia. Also a lofty magnificent Feather-Palm. Its leaflets are erose. It may prove hardy.

Pycnanthemum incanum, Michaux.

North America. A perennial herb, in odor resembling both Pennyroyal and Spearmint. It likes to grow on rocky woodland, and on such it might be easily naturalized.

Pycnanthemum montanum, Michaux.

The Mountain-Mint of North America. A perennial herb of pleasant aromatic mint-like taste. These two particular species have been chosen from several North American kinds to demonstrate, that we may add by their introduction to the variety of our odorous garden herbs. They may also be subjected with advantage to distillation.

Pyrularia edulis, Meissner.

Nepaul, Khasia, Sikkim. A large umbrageous tree. The drupaceous fruit is used by the inhabitants for food. A few other species occur in Upper India, one on the high mountains of Ceylon and one in North America. The latter, *P. pubera*, Mich., can be utilized for the oil of its nuts.

Pyrus coronaria, L.

The Crab-Apple of North America. This showy species is mentioned here as worthy of trial-culture, since it is likely, that it would serve well as stock for grafting. It seems unnecessary to refer here to any of the forms of *Pyrus communis*, L., *P. Malus*, L., *P. Cydonia*, L., and *P. Germanica*, J. Hook. (*Mespilus Germanica*, L.), but it may passingly be observed, that curious fruits have been produced latterly in North America by the hybridisation of the Apple with the Pear. A bitter Glycosid, namely Phlorrhizin, is obtainable from the bark of Apple and Pear Trees, particularly from that of the root, while a volatile Alkaloid, namely Trimethylamin, can be prepared from the flowers.

Quercus Mongolica, Fischer.*

Mandschuria. One of the two species, on which mainly (if not solely) the silk insect peculiar to Oak trees is reared, as shown by Dr. Hance. *Q. serrata*, Thunb. (*Q. obovata*, Bunge), the second of the principal Oaks for the production of silk, has been mentioned previously in the Acclimatisation Society's list of trees yielding timber, and has through the exertions of the writer found its way already to Australia.

Rafnia amplexicaulis, Thunberg.

South Africa. The root of this bush is sweet like Liquorice, and is administered in medicine. *Rafnia perfoliata*, E. Meyer, also from South Africa, furnishes likewise a medicinal root.

Reseda Luteola, L.

The Weld. Middle and South Europe, Middle Asia, North Africa. A herb of one or two years' duration. A yellow dye (Luteolin) pervades the whole plant.

Reseda odorata, L.

The true Mignonette. North Africa and Syria. A herb of one or very few years' duration. The delicate scent can best be concentrated and removed by enfleurage.

Rhamnus catharticus, L.

The Buckthorn. Middle and South Europe, North Africa, Middle Asia. It can be utilized as a hedge-plant. The berries are of medicinal value, as indicated by the specific name. The foliage and bark can be employed for the preparation of a green dye.

Rhamnus chlorophorus, Lindl.

China. From the bark a superior green pigment is prepared. *R. utilis*, from the same country, serves for the like purpose. This kind of dye is particularly used for silk, and known as Lokao.

Rhamnus infectorius, L.

On the Mediterranean Sea, and in the countries near to it. The berry-like fruits of this shrub are known in commerce as Graines d'Avignon and Graines de Perse, and produce a valuable green dye. Other species seem to supply a similar dye material, for instance *R. saxatilis*, L., *R. amygdalinus*, Desf., *R. oleoides*, L.

Rhapis flabelliformis, L. fil.

China and Japan. This exceedingly slender palm attains only a height of a few feet. The stems can be used for various small implements. It is one of the best plants for table decoration.

Rhaponticum acaule, Cand.

On the Mediterranean Sea. A perennial herb. The root is edible.

Rheum australe, Don.*

(*R. Emodi*, Wall. *R. Webbianum*, Royle.)

Himalaian regions up to 16,000 feet. From this species at least a portion of the medicinal Rhubarb is obtained, most likely several species furnish Rhubarb-root, and its quality depends probaby much on the climatic region and the geologic formation, in which the plant grows. Should we wish to cultivate any species here for superior medicinal roots, then clearly localities in our higher and drier alpine tracts should be chosen for the purpose. Hayne regards the presence of much yellowish pigment in the seed-shell as indicating a good medicinal Rhubarb-plant. As much as 5 lbs. of the dried drug are obtained from a single plant, several years old. An important orange-red crystalline substance, Emodin, allied to Crysophanic acid, occurs in genuine Rhubarb.

Rheum Rhaponticum, L.

From the Volga to Central Asia. This species together with *R. Tataricum*, L. fil., *R. undulatum*, L., and a few others, all Asiatic (one extending to Japan) provide their acidulous leaf-stalks and unexpanded flower-mass for culinary purposes. Rhubarb leaves can also be used in the manner of Spinage. *R. palmatum*, L., often considered to yield the best Rhubarb root, is an insular plant of North-eastern Asia, but may in the alpine deserts far inland become a source of the genuine root, so long ascribed to it. That is the only one with deeply jagged leaves.

Rhus copallina, L.

North America, extending to Canada. A comparatively dwarf species. This can also be used for tanning. A resin for varnishes is also obtained from this shrub.

Rhus Coriaria, L.*

The Tanner's Sumach. Countries around the Mediterranean Sea. The foliage of this shrub or small tree, reduced to powder, forms the Sumach of commerce. Many localities in our colony are particulary well adapted for the growth of this bush. It is remarkably rich in Tannic acid, yielding as much as 30 per cent., and extensively used for the production of a superior Corduan- or Maraquin-leather. The cultivation presents no difficulty. Sumach can also be used for ink and various particularly black dyes. Under favorable circumstances as much as a ton of Sumach is obtained from an acre.

Rhus Cotinus, L

The Scotino. Countries at the Mediterranean Sea. The wood of this bush furnishes a yellow pigment. The Sotino, so valuable as a material for yellow and black dye, and as a superior tanning substance, consists of the grinded foliage of this plant.

Rhus glabra, L.

North America, extending to 54° N.L. This Sumach shrub will grow on rocky and sterile soil. It produces a kind of gall, and can also be used as a good substitute for the ordinary Sumach. This species can easily be multiplied from suckers. It will live on poor soil. American sumachs contain generally from 15 to 20 per cent. Tannin.

Rhus lucida, L.

South Africa. This shrub proved here of particular adaptability for forming hedges. About half a hundred South African species are known, of which probably some could be utilized like ordinary Sumach, but hitherto we have remained unacquainted with the nature and degree of any of their tanning and coloring principles.

Rhus semialata, Murray.

China and Japan. This shrub produces a kind of nut-galls.

Rhus typhina, L.

The Staghorn Sumach. North America, extending to Canada. This species will grow to a tree of 30 feet high. Its wood is of an orange tinge. Through incisions into the bark a kind of Copal is obtained. The leaves can be used like ordinary Sumach. This bush can be reared on inferior land.

Ribes aureum, Pursh.

Arkansas, Missouri, Oregon. This favorite bush of our shrubberies would likely on our forest-streams produce its pleasant berries, which turn from yellow to brown or black. Allied to this is *R. tenuiflorum*, Lindl., of California and the nearest States, with fruits of the size of red currants, of agreeable flavor, and either dark purple or yellow color.

Ribes divaricatum, Douglas.

California and Oregon. One of the Gooseberries of those countries. Berries smooth, black, about one-third of an inch in diameter, pleasant to the taste. Culture might improve this and many of the other species. R. Nuttalli (*R. villosum*, Nutt., not of Gay, nor of Wallich) is an allied plant also from California.

Ribes Floridum, l'Herit.

The Black Currant of North America. The berries resemble in odor and taste those of R. nigrum. Allied to this is *R. Hudsonianum*, Rich., from the colder parts of North America.

Ribes Griffithi, J. Hook. and T. Thoms.

Himalaia, at a height of 10,000 to 13,000 feet. Allied to R. rubrum, bearing similar but larger berries of somewhat austere taste. The naturalization of this Currant-bush on our highest alps may prove of advantage. *R. laciniatum*, H. and T., is likewise a Himalaian species with red berries, and so *R. glaciale*, Wall. Furthermore *R. villosum*, Wall. (*R. leptostachyum*, Decaisne) comes from the Indian highlands and seems worthy of introduction.

Ribes Grossularia, L.

The ordinary Gooseberry. Europe, North Africa, Western Asia, on the Himalaian Mountains up to a height of 12,000 feet. This bush, familiar to every one, is mentioned here merely to indicate the desirability of naturalizing it in our alpine regions, where no fruits equal to it in value exist.

Ribes hirtellum, Michaux.

The commonest smooth Gooseberry of North America. It likes moist ground.

Ribes nigrum, L.

The Black Currant. Middle and Northern Asia, Europe, North America, ascending the Himalaian and Tibet mountains to a height of 12,000 feet. Commonly cultivated already in the cooler parts of Victoria, but also particularly fit to be dispersed through our forests and over our alps.

Ribes niveum, Lindl.

One of the Oregon Gooseberry-bushes. Berries small, black, of a somewhat acid taste and rich vinous flavor.

Ribes rotundifolium, Michaux.

North America. Yields part of the smooth Gooseberries of the United States. The fruit is small, but of delicious taste.

Ribes rubrum, L.

The ordinary Red Currant. Europe, North America, North and Middle Asia, in the Himalaian Mountains ceasing where R. Griffithi commences to appear. One of the best fruit-plants for jellies and preserves that could be chosen for the colder mountain altitudes of our Colony. The root-bark contains Phlorrhizin. Perhaps other species, than those recorded here, among them some from the Andes, may yet deserve introduction, irrespective of their showiness, for their fruits.

Ricinus communis, L.*

The Castoroil-plant. Indigenous to the tropical and subtropical zones of Asia and Africa. A shrubby very decorative plant, attaining the size of a small tree. It was well known to the Egyptians 4000 years ago, and is also mentioned already in the writings of Herodotos, Hippocrates, Dioscorides, Theophrastos, Plinius and other ancient physicians, philosophers and naturalists. The easy and rapid growth, the copious seeding and the early return of produce, render this important plant of high value in a clime like ours, more particularly as it will thrive on almost any soil, and can thus be raised even on arid places, without being scorched by hot winds. It may thus become an important plant also for culture in our desert-tracts, and is evidently destined to be one of our most eligible oil-plants for technical uses, irrespective of the value of its oil for medicinal purposes. The seeds contain about 50 per cent. oil. To obtain the best medicinal oil, hydraulic pressure should be employed, and the seeds not be subjected to heat; the seed-coat should also be removed prior to the extracting process being proceeded with. A screw-press suffices however for ordinary supply to obtain the oil. By decantation and some process of filtration it is purified. For obtaining oil to be used for lubrication of machinery or other technologic purposes, the seeds may be pressed and prepared by various methods under application of heat and access of water. Castoroil is usually bleached simply by exposure to solar light, but this procedure lessens to some extent the laxative properties of the oil. It dissolves completely in waterless alcohol and in ether, and will become dissolved also in spirit of high strength, to the extent of three-fifths of the weight of the latter. Solutions of this kind may become valuable for various technic purposes, and afford some tests for the pureness of the oil. If pressed under heat it will depose margaritin. Heated in a retort about one-third of the oil will distil over, and a substance resembling india-rubber remains, which saponizes with alkalies. Other educts are at the same time obtained, which will likely become of industrial value. These facts are briefly mentioned here merely to explain, that the value of this easily produced oil is far more varied than is generally supposed, and this remark applies with equal force to many other chemical compounds from vegetable sources, briefly alluded to in this present enumerative treatise. The seeds contain also a peculiar alkaloid : Ricinin. The solid chemic compound of Castor-oil is the crystalline Isocetin-Acid (a Glycerid). The oil contains also a non-crystalline acid peculiar to it (Ricin-acid). For the production of a particular kind of silk the Ricinus-plant is also important, inasmuch as the hardy Bombyx Cynthia requires for food the leaves of this bush. The value of Castoroil imported last year into Victoria was according to the Custom-returns not less than £23,755. Even a few of the seeds if swallowed, will produce poisonous effect.

Rosa contifolia, L.

The Cabbage Rose. Indigenous on the Caucasus and seemingly also in other parts of the Orient. Much grown in South Europe and South Asia for the distillation of Rosewater and Oil or Attar of Roses. From 12,000 to 16,000 roses, or from 250 lbs. to 300 lbs. of rose-petals are required according to some calculations, for producing a single ounce of Attar through ordinary distillation. The flowers require to be cut just before expansion ; the calyx is separated and rejected ; the remaining portions of the flowers are then subjected to aqueous distillation, and the saturated rosewater, so obtained, is repeatedly used for renewed distillation, when from the overcharged water the oil separates on a cold place and floats on the surface. But some other methods exist for producing the oil, for instance it may be got by distilling the rosebuds without water at the heat of a saltwater bath. The odor may also he withdrawn by alcoholic distillation from the Roses, or be extracted by the " enfluerage " process. The latter is effected by placing the flowers, collected while the weather is warm, into shallow frames covered with a glass-plate, on the inner side of which a pure fatty substance has been thinly spread. The odor of the flowers is absorbed by the adipose or oleous substance, though the blossoms do not come with it in direct contact ; fresh flowers are supplied daily for weeks. The scent is finally withdrawn from its matrix by maceration with pure alcohol. Mr. Jos. Bosisto's method for obtaining the most delicate and precious volatile oils will likely be applicable also to the Rose, and prove more advantageous both in labor and gain than any other process. Purified Eucalyptus-oil can be used for diluting Rose-oil, when it is required for the preparation of scented Soap.

Rosa Damascena, Miller.

Orient. Allied to the preceding species, and also largely used for the production of essential Oil of Roses.

Rosa Gallica, L.

The French or Dutch Rose. Middle and South Europe, Orient. The intensely colored buds of this species are par ticularly chosen for drying. These however may be got also from other kinds of Roses.

Rosa Indica, L.

Noisette Rose. From Upper India to China and Japan. Some Roses of the sweetest scent are derived from this species.

Rosa laevigata, Michaux (*R. Sinica*, Aiton.)

The Cherokee Rose. China and Japan. Considered one of the best Hedge-roses, and for that purpose much employed in North America. It serves also well for bowers. Allied to the foregoing species.

Rosa moschata, Miller.

North Africa and South Asia as far east as Japan. From the flowers of this extremely tall climbing species also essential oil is obtained. The Attar thus derived from Roses of not only different varieties but even distinct species must necessarily be of various quality.

Rosa sempervirens, L.

From South Europe through Southern Asia to Japan. One of the best Rose-bushes for covering walls, fences and similar structures. Also the flowers of this species can be utilized for Rose-oil.

Rosa setigera, Michaux.

North America, where it is the only climbing Rose-bush. It deserves introduction on account of its extremely rapid growth, 10 feet to 20 feet in a season. Its flowers however are nearly inodorous.

Other original species of Roses deserve our attention, Dr. J. Hooker admitting about 30, all from the Northern Hemisphere. But on the snow-clad unascended mountains of Borneo, Sumatra, New Guinea and Africa south of the Equator yet perhaps new Roses may be discovered, as they have been traced south to Abyssinia already.

Rosmarinus officinalis, L.

The Rosmary. Countries around the Mediterranean Sea. This well-known bush is mentioned here as a medicinal plant, from which a distilled oil is rather copiously obtainable. One of our best plants for large garden edgings. The oil enters into certain compositions of perfumery.

Rubia cordifolia, L. (*R. Mungista*, Roxb.)

From the Indian Highlands through China and Siberia to Japan; also occurring in various parts of Africa, as far south as Caffraria and Natal. This perennial plant produces also a kind of Madder. Probably other species yield likewise Dye-roots. The genus is represented widely over the globe, but as far as known not in Australia.

Rubia tinctorum, L.

The Madder. Countries around the Mediterranean Sea. A perennial herb of extremely easy culture. The roots merely dried and pounded form the dye. The chemical contents are numerous; in the herb: Rubichloric and Rubitannic acid; in the root: Alizarin, Purpurin, Rubiacin, Rubian, Ruberythrin acid, and three distinct resins; also Chlorogenin, Xanthin and Rubichloric acid. On the five first depend the pigments produced from the root. Madder is one of the requisites for Alizarin Ink.

Rubus Canadensis, L.*

The Dewberry of North America. A shrub of trailing habit. Fruit black, of excellent taste, ripening earlier than that of *R. villosus*, Ait., which constitutes the High Blackberry of the United States, with large fruits.

Rubus Chamæmorus, L.

The Cloud-Berry. North Europe, North Asia, North America, particularly in the frigid zone. A perennial but herbaceous plant; a pigmy amongst its congeners. Nevertheless it is recommended for introduction to our spongy mossy alpine moors, on account of its grateful amber-colored or red fruit. All the species can readily be raised from seeds. *R. Arcticus*, L., also with edible fruit, is in the high north usually its companion. Near to us we have a similar little herb, living for a great part of the year in snow, namely *Rubus Gunnianus*, Hook. It occurs on the alpine heights of Tasmania, from whence it might be easily transferred to our snowy mountains and those of New Zealand. The fruit of R. Gunnianus is red and juicy, but not always well developed.

Rubus cuneifolius, Pursh.

The Sand Blackberry. North America. A dwarf shrub. The fruit is of agreeable taste.

Rubus deliciosus, Torrey.

On the sources of the Missouri. An erect shrub. Fruit Raspberry-like, large and grateful.

Rubus fruticosus, L.*

The ordinary Blackberry or Bramble. All Europe, North Africa, Middle and Northern Asia. This shrub bears well in our clime. In some countries it is a favorite plant for hedges. It likes above all calcareous soil, though it is content with almost any, and deserves to be naturalized on the rivulets of our ranges. *R. corylifolius*, Sm., *R. subcretus*, Andr. and *R. leucostachys*, Sm., are varieties like many other named kinds of European Blackberries, or perhaps belong to the closely allied *R. caesius*, L., the English Dewberry; or in some instances hybrid forms may have arisen from the two, although the generality of these various Blackberry-bushes bear their fruits freely enough.

Rubus Idaeus, L.*

The ordinary Raspberry. Europe, Northern and West Asia. It is mentioned here, to point out the desirability of naturalizing the plant in our mountains and on river-banks. It would live also on our highest alps, where the native Raspberry (*R. parvifolius*, L.) produces much finer fruits than in our lowlands. The fruits contain Stereopten.

Rubus macropetalus, Douglas.*

California and Oregon. An unisexual shrub. Fruit black, oval-cylindric, particularly sweet.

Rubus occidentalis, L.*

The Black Raspberry or Thimbleberry. North America. A species with woody stems and nice fruits, with a glaucous bloom, well flavored and large. It ripens early.

Rubus odoratus, L.*

North America. A kind of Raspberry. A handsome species on account of its large purple flowers. Berry edible. Culture would doubtless enhance the value of the fruits of many of these Rubi. Hybridising might be tried.

Rubus strigosus, Michaux.

North America. Closely allied to the European Raspberry. Its fruits large, also of excellent taste. It would lead too far to enumerate other kinds of Rubus, although about a hundred genuine species occur, which render the genus one of very wide dispersion over the globe.

Rubus trivialis, Michaux.*

Southern States of North America. Another shrubby species with good edible fruits, which are large and black. The plant will thrive in dry sandy soil.

Rumex Acetosa, L.

The Kitchen Sorrel. Europe, Middle and North Asia to Japan, also in the frigid zone of North America. A perennial herb. The tender varieties, particularly the Spanish one, serve as pleasant aciduous vegetables, but must be used in moderation, as their acidity like that of the species of Oxalis (Wood-sorrel) depends on Binoxylate of potash.

Rumex scutatus, L.

The French Sorrel. Middle and South Europe, North Africa, Orient. Also perennial, and superior to the foregoing as a culinary plant. Both and the following are of use against scurvy and most easily reared.

Rumex vesicarius, L.

South Europe, Middle Asia, North Africa. An annual herb of similar utility as the two former ones.

Ruta graveolens, L.

The Rue. Mediterranean countries and the Orient. The foliage of this acrid and odorous shrub, simply dried, constitutes the Rue-herb of medicine. The allied *R. silvestris*, Mill., is still more powerful in its effect. These plants and others of the genus contain a peculiar volatile oil and a Glycosid (Rutin).

Sabal Adansoni, Guernscut.

Dwarf Palmetto. South Caroliua, Georgia and Florida. A stomless Fan-Palm, with the two following and Chamaerops Hystrix attaining the most northerly positions of any American palms.

Sabal Palmetto, Roem. and Schult.*

Extends from Florida to North Carolina. The stem attains a height of 40 feet. This noble Palm ought to grow on our sandy coast-tracts, as in such it delights to live.

Sabal serrulata, R. and S.

South Carolina, Georgia and Florida. The stem grows to 8 feet high. The leaves can be used for cabbage-tree hats and other purposes, for which palm-leaves are sought.

Saccharum officinarum, L.

The Sugar-Cane. India, China, South Sea Islands, not indigenous in any part of America or Australia. Sugar-cane having been cultivated in Spain and other countries on the Mediterranean Sea, it will be worthy of further trial, whether in the warmest parts of our Colony under similar climatic conditions sugar from cane can be produced to advantage. Though the plant will live unprotected in the vicinity of Melbourne, it thrives there not sufficiently for remunerative culture. But it may be otherwise in East Gipps Land or along the Murray River and its lower tributaries. In the United States the profitable culture of cane ceases at 32° N.L., in China it extends only to the 30° N.L. In the last-mentioned country the culture of Sugar-cane dates from the remotest antiquity ; moreover we have from thence a particular kind (*S. Sinense*, Roxb.), which is hardier and bears drought better than the ordinary cane ; this kind needs renewal only every second or third year, and ripens in seven months if planted early in spring, but if planted in autumn and left standing for fully a year the return of sugar is larger. Moderate vicinity to the sea is favorable for the growth of canes.

The multiplication of all sorts of Sugar-cane is usually effected from top cuttings, but this cannot be carried ou from the same original stock for au indefinite period without deterioration; and as seeds hardly ever ripeu on the caues, new plants must from time to time be brought from the distance. Thus New Caledonia has latterly supplied its wild-growing splendid varieties for replanting many sugar-fields in Mauritius. The Bourbon variety is praised as one of the richest for sugar: the Batavian variety (*S. violaceum*, Tussac) is content with less fertile soil. Many other varieties are known. Excessive raius produce a rank luxuriance of the canes on expense of the saccharine principle. Rich manuring is necessary to attain good crops, unless in the best of virgin soil. The lower leaves of the stem must successively be removed, also superabundant suckers, to promote the growth upwards, and to provide ventilation and light. Out of the remnants of Sugar-cane Molasses, Rum and Taffia can be prepared. The average yield of Sugar varies from 1 ton 6 cwt. to 3 tons for the acre. For fuller information the valuable local work of Mr. A. McKay, "The Sugar-cane in Australia," should be consulted. The stately *S. spontaneum*, L., which extends from India to Egypt, is available for scenic culture. It attains a height of 15 feet. Other tall kinds of Saccharum occur in South Asia.

Sagittaria lancifolia, L.

From Virginia to the Antilles. This very handsome aquatic plant can doubless be utilized like the following species. It attains a height of 5 feet.

Sagittaria obtusa, Muehlenberg. (*S. latifolia*, Willd.)

North America, where it replaces the closely allied S. sagittifolia. A few other conspicuous species are worthy of introduction.

Sagittaria sagittifolia, L.

Europe, North and Middle Asia, east to Japan. One of the most showy of all hardy water-plants; still not alone on that accouut deserving naturalization, but also because its root is edible. If once established this plant maintains its ground well, and might occupy spots neither arable nor otherwise utilized.

Salix nigra, Marshall. (*S. Purshiana,* Sprengel.)
The Black Willow of North America. It attains a height
of 25 feet. This species was not included in the list of trees,
published by the Acclimatisation Society in its last year's
report. The Black Willow is one used for basket-work,
although it is surpassed in excellence by some other species,
and is more important as a timber-willow. Mr. W. Scaling,
of Basford, includes it among the sorts, which he recommends in his valuable publication "The Willow" (London,
1871). From his treatise, resting on unrivalled experience,
it will be observed, that he anew urges the adoption of the
Bitter Willow (also called the Rose-Willow or the Whipcord-
Willow), *S. purpurea,* L., for game-proof hedges, this species
scarcely ever being touched by cattle, rabbits and other
herbivorous animals. Not only for this reason, but also for
its very rapid growth and remunerative yield of the very
best of Basket material he recommends it for field hedges.
Cuttings are planted only half-a-foot apart, and must be
entirely pushed into the ground. The annual produce from
such a hedge is worth 4s. to 5s. for the chain. For additional strength the shoots can be interwoven. In rich
bottoms they will grow from 7 feet to 13 feet in a year.
The supply of basket material from this species has fallen
very far short of the demand in England. The plant grows
vigorously on light soil or warp land, but not on clay.
S. rubra, Huds., is also admirably adapted for hedges. The
real Osier, *S. viminalis,* L., is distinguished by basketmakers
as the soft-wooded Willow, and is the best for rods requiring
two years' age, and also the most eligible for hoops, but
inferior to several other species for basket manufacture.
S. triandra, L., is a prominent representative of the hard-
wooded Basket Willows, and comprises some of the finest
varieties in use of the manufacturers. A crop in the third
year after planting from an acre weighs about 12 tons,
worth £3 for the ton. *S. fragilis,* L., and *S. alba,* L., are
more important as timber-willows, and for growing hoop-
shoots. Their rapidity of growth recommends them also for
shelter plantations, to which advantage may be added their
inflammability and their easy propagation ; the latter

quality they share with most Willows. Mr. Scaling's renewed advocacy for the formation of Willow-plantations comes with so much force, that his advice is here given though condensed in a few words. Osier-plantations come into full bearing already in the third year; they bear for ten years and then slowly decline. The raw-produce from an acre in a year averages 6 tons to 7½ tons, ranging in price from £2 10s. to £3 10s. for the ton (unpeeled). Although 7000 acres are devoted in Britain to the culture of Basket Willows (exclusive of spinneys and plantations for the farmers' own use), yet in 1866 there had to be imported from the Continent 4400 tons of Willow-branches, at a value of £44,000, while besides the value of the made baskets imported in that year was equal to the above sum. Land comparatively valueless for root or grain crop can be used very remuneratively for Osier-plantations. The soft-wooded Willows like to grow in damper ground, than the hard-wooded species. The best peeled Willow-branches fetch as much as £25 for the ton. Peeling is best effected by steam, by which means the material is also increased in durability. No Basket Willow will thrive in stagnant water. Osier-plantations in humid places should therefore be drained. The cuttings are best taken from branches one or two years old, and are to be planted as close as 1 foot by 1½ foot. No part of the cutting must remain uncovered, in order that only straight shoots may be obtained; manuring and ploughing between the rows is thus also facilitated, after the crop has been gathered, and this, according to the approved Belgian method, must be done by cutting the shoots close to the ground after the fall of the leaves.

Salvia officinalis, L.

The Garden Sage. Countries at the Mediterranean Sea. A somewhat shrubby plant of medicinal value, pervaded by essential oil. Among nearly half a thousand species of this genus some are gorgeously ornamental.

Sambucus nigra, L.

The ordinary Elder. Europe, North Africa, Middle Asia. The flowers are of medicinal value, and an essential oil can be obtained from them. The wood can be utilized for shoe-pegs and other purposes of artisans. The berries are used for coloring of port wine and for other purposes of dye.

Santalum cygnorum, Miquel.

South-western Australia, where this tree yields scented Sandal-wood.

Santalum Preissianum, Miq. (*S. acuminatum*, A. de Cand.)

The Quandang. Desert-country of extra-tropical Australia. The fruits of this small tree are called Native Peaches. As both the succulent outer part and kernel are edible, it is advisable to raise the plant in desert-tracts, where the species does not occur, since moreover it becomes gradually sacrificed on many native places by pasture operations.

Santalum Yasi, Seemann.

The Sandal-tree of the Feegee Islands, where it grows on dry and rocky hills. It is likely to prove hardy here, and deserves with a few other species from the South Sea Islands, yielding scented wood, test-culture in the warmest parts of our Colony.

Saponaria officinalis, L.

The Soapwort or Fuller's Herb. Europe, North and Middle Asia. A perennial herb of some technologic interest, as the root can be employed with advantage in some final processes of washing silk and wool, to which it imparts a peculiar gloss and dazzling whiteness, without injuring in the least the most sensitive colors. Experiments, instituted in the laboratory of the Botanic Garden of Melbourne, render it highly probable, that Saponin, which produces the froth from the soapwort, is also present in the bark of *Acacia* (*Albizzia*) *lophantha*, W. At all events a substance, closely resembling Saponin, was unexpectedly detected (in the course of other investigations entrusted to Mr. Rummel) in the bark of this Acacia, and this substance occurred in so large a proportion as to constitute 10 per cent. of the dry bark.

Satureja hortensis, L.

The Summer Savory. Countries around the Mediterranean Sea. An annual scent herb, from which an essential aromatic oil can be distilled. The culture of this and allied plants is easy in the extreme.

· Satureja montana, L.

The Winter Savory. On arid hilly places at and near the Mediterranean Sea. A perennial somewhat shrubby herb, frequently used as a culinary condiment along with or in place of the foregoing species, although it is scarcely equal to it in fragrance.

Satureja Thymbra, L.

Countries at or near the Mediterranean Sea. A small evergreen bush, with the flavor almost of Thyme. The likewise odorous *S. Graeca*, L., and *S. Juliana*, L., have been transferred by Bentham to the closely cognate genus Micromeria; they are in use since Dioscorides' time, though not representing, as long supposed, the Hyssop of that ancient physician.

Saussurea Lappa, Bentham. (*Haplotaxis Lappa*, De Caisne.)

Cashmere. The aromatic root of this perennial species is of medicinal value, and by some considered to be the Costus of the ancients.

Schizostachyum Blumei, Nees.

Java. A lofty Bamboo. A few other species, less elevated, occur in China, the South Sea and Philippine Islands and Madagascar. The genus might well be united with Melocanna. The Bamboos being brought once more thus before us, it may be deemed advisable, to place together into one brief list all those kinds, which are recorded either as very tall or as particularly hardy. Accordingly, from Major-General Munro's admirable monography ("Linnean Transact.," 1858,) the succeeding enumeration is compiled, and from that masterly essay, resting on very many years' close study of the richest collections, a few prefatory remarks are likewise offered, to vindicate the wish of the writer of seeing these noble and graceful forms of vegetation largely transferred to every part of Australia, where they would impress a grand tropical feature on the landscapes. Even in our far southern latitudes Bamboos from the Indian

lowlands have proved to resist our occasional night frosts
of the low country. But in colder places the many sub-alpine
species could be reared. Be it remembered that Chusque
aristata advances to an elevation of 15,000 feet on the
Andes of Quito, indeed to near the zone of perpetual ice.
Arundinaria falcata, A. racemosa and A. spathiflora live on
the Indian highlands, at a zone between 10,000 feet and
11,000 feet, where they are annually beaten down by snow.
We may further recognize the great importance of these
plants, when we reflect on their manifest industrial uses, or
when we consider their grandeur for picturesque scenery,
or when we observe their resistance to storms of heat, or
when we watch the marvellous rapidity, in which many
develope themselves. Their seeds, though generally only in
long intervals produced, are valued in many instances higher
than rice. The ordinary great Bamboo of India is known
to grow 40 feet in 40 days, when bathed in the moist heat of
the jungles. The Bourbon Bamboo forms an impenetrable
sub-alpine belt of extraordinary magnificence in yonder
island. One of the Tesserim Bambusas rises to 150 feet,
with a diameter of the mast-like cane sometimes measuring
fully 1 foot. The great West Indian Arthrostylidium is
sometimes nearly as high and quite as columnar in its form,
while the Dendrocalamus at Pulo Geum is equally colossal.
The Platonia Bamboo of the highest wooded mountains of
Parama sends forth leaves 15 feet in length and 1 foot in
width. Arundinaria macrosperma as far north as Philadelphia rises still in favorable spots to a height of nearly
40 feet. Through perforating with artistic care the huge
canes of various Bamboos musical sounds can be melodiously
produced, when the air wafts through the groves, and this
singular fact may possibly be turned to practice for checking
the devastations from birds on many a cultured spot.
Altogether 20 genera with 170 well-marked species are
circumscribed by General Munro's consummate care; but
how may these treasures yet be enriched, when once the
snowy mountains of New Guinea through Bamboo jungles
become ascended, or when the alps on the sources of the
Nile, which Ptolemæus and Julius Cæsar already longed to

ascend, have become the territory also of phytologic researches, not to speak of many other tropical regions as yet left unexplored. Europe possesses no Bamboo; Australia as far as hitherto ascertained only one (in the interior of Arnhem's Land). Almost all Bamboos are local, and there seems really no exception to the fact, that none are indigenous to both hemispheres, all true Bambusas being Oriental.

The introduction of these exquisite plants is one of the easiest imaginable, either from seeds or the living roots. The Consuls at distant ports, the missionaries, the mercantile and navigating gentlemen abroad and so particularly also any travellers could all easily aid in transferring the various Bamboos from one country to the other—from hemisphere to hemisphere. Most plants of this kind here with us, once well established in strength under glass, can be trusted out to permanent locations with perfect and lasting safety, at the commencement of the warm season. Indeed Bamboos are hardier than most intra-tropical plants, and the majority of them are not the denizens of the hottest tropical lowlands, but delight in the cooler air of mountain regions. In selecting the following array from General Munro's monography it must be noted, that it comprises only a limited number, and that among those, which are already to some extent known, but as yet cannot be defined with precision in their generic and specific relation, evidently some occur, which in elegance, grace and utility surpass even many of of those now specially mentioned:—

Arundinaria Japonica, S. and Z. Japan. Height to 12 feet.
Arundinaria macrosperma, Mich. North America. Height to 35 feet.
Arundinaria verticillata, Nees. Brazil. Height to 15 feet.
Arundinaria debilis, Thwaites. Ceylon; ascends to 8000 feet. A tall species.
Arundinaria acuminata, Munro. Mexico. Height to 20 feet.
Arundinaria falcata, Nees. Himalaia; ascends to 10000 feet. Height to 20 feet.

Arundinaria tesselata, Munro. South Africa ; ascends to 6500 feet. Height to 20 feet.

Arundinaria callosa, Munro. Himalaia ; ascends to 6000 feet. Height to 12 feet.

Arundinaria Khasiana, Munro. Himalaia ; ascends to 6000 feet. Height to 12 feet.

Arundinaria Hookeriana, Munro. Sikkim ; ascends to 7000 feet. Height to 15 feet.

Arundinaria suberecta, Munro. Himalaia ; ascends to 4500 feet. Height to 15 feet.

Thamnocalamus Falconeri, J. Hook. Himalaia ; ascends to 8000 feet. Tall.

Thamnocalamus spathiflorus, Munro. Himalaia ; ascends to 10000 feet. Tall.

Phyllostachys bambusoides, S. and Z. Himalaia, China, Japan. Height to 12 feet.

Phyllostachys nigra, Munro. China, Japan. Height to 25 feet.

Arthrostylidium longiflorum, Munro. Venezuela ; ascends to 6000 feet.

Arthrostylidium Schomburgkii, Munro. Guiana ; ascends to 6000 feet. Height to 60 feet.

Arthrostylidium excelsum, Griseb. West India. Height to 80 feet ; diameter 1 foot.

Arthrostylidium racemiflorum, Steudel. Mexico ; ascends to 7500 feet. Height to 30 feet.

Aulonemia Quexo, Goudot. New Granada, Venezuela, in cool regions. Tall, climbing.

Merostachys ternata, Nees. South Brazil. Height to 20 feet.

Merostachys Clausseni, Munro. South Brazil. Height to 80 feet.

Merostachys Kunthii, Ruprecht. South Brazil. Height to 30 feet.

Chusquea simpliciflora, Munro. Panama. Height to 80 feet. Scandent.

Chusquea abietifolia, Grisebach. West India. Tall, scandent.

Chusquea Culcou, E. Desv. Chili. Height to 20 feet. Straight.

Chusquea uniflora, Steudel. Central America. Height to 20 feet.

Chusquea Galleottiana, Ruprecht. Mexico ; ascends to 8000 feet.

Chusquea montana, Philippi. Chili Andes. Height to 10 feet.

Chusquea Dombeyana, Kunth. Peru ; ascends to 6000 feet. Height to 10 feet.

Chusquea Fendleri, Munro. Central America ; ascends to 12000 feet.

Chusquea scandens, Kunth. Colder Central America. Climbing, tall.

Chusquea Quila, Kunth. Chili. Tall.

Chusquea tenuiflora, Philippi. Chili. Height to 12 feet.

Chusquea Gaudichaudiana, Kunth. South Brazil. Very tall.

Chusquea capituliflora, Trinius. South Brazil. Very tall.

Platonia nobilis, Munro. New Granada, colder region.

Nastus Borbonicus, Gmel. Bourbon, Sumatra ; ascends to 4000 feet. Height to 50 feet.

Guadua Tagoara, Kunth. South Brazil ; ascends to 2000 feet. Height to 30 feet.

Guadua latifolia, Kunth. Central America. Height to 24 feet.

Guadua macrostachya, Rupr. Guiana to Brazil. Height to 30 feet.

Guadua capitata, Munro. South Brazil. Height to 20 feet.

Guadua angustifolia, Kunth. Andes of South America. Height to 40 feet.

Guadua virgata, Rupr. South Brazil. Height to 25 feet.

Guadua refracta, Munro. Brazil. Height to 30 feet.

Guadua paniculata, Munro. Brazil. Height to 30 feet.

Bambusa Tulda, Roxb. Bengal to Burmah. Height to 70 feet.

Bambusa nutans, Wall. Himalaia ; ascends to 7000 feet.

Bambusa tuldoides, Munro. China, Hong Kong, Formosa.

Bambusa pallida, Munro. Bengal to Khasia; ascends to 3500 feet. Height to 50 feet.

Bambusa polymorpha, Munro. Burmah, in the Teak region. Height to 80 feet.

Bambusa Balcooa, Roxb. Bengal to Assam. Height to 70 feet.

Bambusa flexuosa, Munro. China. Height to 12 feet.

Bambusa Blumeana, Schultes. Java. Tall.

Bambusa arundinacea, Roxb. Southern India. Height to 50 feet.

Bambusa spinosa, Roxb. Bengal to Burmah. Height to 100 feet.

Bambusa vulgaris, Wendl. (*B. Thouarsi,* K.) Ceylon and other parts of India. Height to 50 feet.

Bambusa Beecheyana, Munro. China. Height to 20 feet.

Bambusa marginata, Munro. Tenasserim ; ascends to 5000 feet. Tall, scandent.

Bambusa regia, Th. Thomson. Tenasserim. Height to 40 feet.

Bambusa Brandisii, Munro. Tenasserim ; ascends to 4000 feet. Height to 120 feet, circumference 2 feet.

Gigantochloa maxima, Kurz. (*Bambusa verticillata,* Willd.) Java. Height to 100 feet

Gigantochloa atter, Kurz. Java. Height to 40 feet.

Gigantochloa heterostachya, Munro. Malacca. Height to 30 feet.

Oxytenanthera Abyssinica, Munro. Abyssinia to Angola ; ascends to 4000 feet. Height to 50 feet.

Oxytenanthera nigro-ciliata, Munro. Continental and insular India. Height to 40 feet.

Oxytenanthera albo-ciliata, Munro. Pegu, Moulmein. Tall, scandent.

Oxytenanthera Thwaitesii, Munro. (*Dendrocalamus mona-delphus,* Thwait.) Ceylon ; ascends to 5000 feet. Height to 12 feet.

Melocanna bambusoides, Trin. Chittagong, Sylhet. Height to 70 feet.

Schizostachyum Blumei, Nees. Java. Very tall.

Cephalostachyum capitatum, Munro. Himalaia ; ascends to 6000 feet. Height to 30 feet.

Cephalostachyum pallidum, Munro. Himalaia ; ascends to 5000 feet. Tall.

Cephalostachyum pergracile, Munro. Burmah. Height to 40 feet.

Pseudostachyum polymorphum, Munro. Himalaia ; ascends to 6000 feet. Very tall.

Teinostachyum attenuatum, Munro. (*Bambusa attenuata,* Thw.) Ceylon ; ascends to 6000 feet. Height to 25 feet.

Teinostachyum Griffithi, Munro. Burmah. Tall and slender.
Beesha Travancorica, Beddome. Madras. Tall.
Beesha Rheedei, Kunth. Southern India, Cochin-China.
Height to 20 feet.
Beesha stridula, Munro. Ceylon.
Beesha capitata, Munro. Madagascar. Height to 50 feet.
Dendrocalamus strictus, Nees. India to Japan. Height to
100 feet.
Dendrocalamus sericeus, Munro. Behar ; ascends to 4000
feet. Tall.
Dendrocalamus flagellifer, Munro. Malacca. Very tall.
Dendrocalamus giganteus, Munro. Burmah, Penang. Ex-
ceedingly tall. Circumference 2 feet.
Dendrocalamus Hookeri, Munro. Himalaia ; ascends to 6000
feet. Height to 50 feet.
Dendrocalamus Hamiltoni, Nees. Himalaia ; ascends to
6000 feet. Height to 60 feet.
Dinochloa Tjankorreh, Buchse. Java, Philippines; ascends
to 4000 feet. Climbing.

Scilla esculenta, Ker. (*Camassia esculenta,* Lindl.)
The Quamash. In the Western extra-tropic parts of North
America, on moist prairies. The onion-like bulbs in a
roasted state form a considerable portion of the vegetable
food, on which the aboriginal tribes of that part of the globe
are living. It is a pretty plant, and might be naturalized
here on our moist meadows.

Schoenocaulon officinale, A. Gray.
(*Asa-Graya officinalis,* Lindl.)
(*Sabadilla officinalis,* Brandt and Dierbach.)
Mountains of Mexico. A bulbous-rooted herb with leafless
stem, thus far specially distinct from any Veratrum. It
furnishes the Sabadilla-seeds and yields two alkaloids : Veratrin and Sabadillin ; a resinous substance : Helonin; also
Sabadillic and Veratric acid. The generic names adopted
for this plant by Lindley and by Dierbach are coetaneous.

Scorzonera deliciosa, Gusson.*
Sicily. One of the purple-flowered species, equal if not
superior in its culinary use to the allied Salsify.

Scorzonera Hispanica, L.*

Middle and South Europe, Orient. The perennial root of this yellow-flowered herb furnishes not only a wholesome and palatable food, but also serves as a therapeutic remedy much like Dandelion. Long boiling destroys its medicinal value. Some other kinds of Scorzonera may perhaps be drawn into similar use, there being many Asiatic species.

Scorzonera tuberosa, Pallas.

At the Wolga and in Syria. Also this species yields an edible root, and so perhaps the Chinese *S. albicaulis*, Bunge, the Persian *Sc. Scowitzii*, Cand., the North African *Sc. undulata*, Vahl., the Greek *Sc. ramosa*, Sibth., the Russian *Sc. Astrachanica*, Cand., the Turkish *Sc. semicana*, Cand., the Iberian *Sc. lanata*, Bieberst. At all events careful culture may render them valuable esculents.

Sebæa ovata, R. Brown.

Extra-tropic Australia and New Zealand. This neat little annual herb can be utilized for its bitter tonic principle (Gentian-bitter). *S. albidiflora*, F. v. M., is an allied species from somewhat saline ground. These plants disseminate themselves most readily.

Secale cereale, L.*

The Rye. Orient, but perhaps wild only in the country between the Caspian and Black Seas. Mentioned here as the hardiest of all grain-plants for our highest alpine regions. There are annual and biennial varieties, while a few allied species, hitherto not generally used for fodder or cereal culture, are perennial. The Rye, though not so nutritious as wheat, furnishes a most wholesome well-flavored bread, which keeps for many days, and is most extensively used in Middle and North Europe and Asia. This grain moreover can be reared in poor soil and cold climates, where Wheat will no longer thrive. In produce of grain Rye is not inferior to Wheat in colder countries, while the yield of straw is larger, and the culture less exhaustive. It is a hardy cereal, not readily subject to disease, and can be grown on some kinds of peaty or sandy or moory ground. The sowing must not be effected at a period of much wetness. Wide sand tracts would be uninhabitable, if it was not for the facility to provide human sustenance from this grateful corn. It dislikes moist ground. Sandy soil gives the best grain. It is a very remarkable fact, that since ages in some tracts of Europe Rye has been prolifically cultivated from year to year without interruption. In this respect Rye stands favorably alone among alimentary plants. It furnishes in cold countries also the earliest green-fodder, and the return is large. When the Rye-grain becomes attacked by *Cordyceps purpurea*, Fr., or very similar species of fungi, then it becomes dangerously unwholesome, but then also a very important medicinal substance, namely Ergot, is obtained. The biennial Wallachian variety of Rye can be mown or depastured prior to the season of its forming grain. In alpine regions Wallachian Rye is sown with Pine-seeds, for shelter of the Pine seedlings in the first year.

Sechium edule, Swartz.

West India. The Chocho or Chayota. The large root of this climber can be consumed as a culinary vegetable, while the good-sized fruits are also edible. The plant comes in climates like ours to perfection.

Selinum anesorrhizum, F. v. M.

(*Anesorrhiza Capensis*, Ch. and Schl.)

South Africa. The root of this biennial herb is edible. *A. montana*, Eckl. and Zeyh., a closely allied plant, yields likewise an edible root, and so it is with a few other species of the section Anesorrhiza.

Sesamum Indicum, L.

The Gingili. Southern Asia, extending eastwards to Japan. This annual herb is cultivated as far as 42° N.L. The oil, fresh expressed from the seeds, is available for table use. One of the advantages of the culture of this plant consists in its quick return of produce. The soot of the oil is used for China-ink.

Sesbania aculeata, Persoon.

The Danchi. Intra-tropical and sub-tropical Asia, Africa and Australia. This tall annual plant has proved adapted for our desert-regions. It yields a tough fibre for ropes, nets and cordage, valued at from £30 to £40 for the ton Several congeneric plants can be equally well utilized.

Shepherdia argentea, Nuttall.

The Buffalo Berry. From the Missouri to Hudson's Bay. This bush bears red acidulous edible berries.

Sison Amomum, L.

Middle and South Europe. A herb of one or two years' duration. It grows best on soil rich in lime. The seeds can be used for condiment.

Smilax officinalis, Humboldt.

New Granada and other parts of Central America. This climbing shrub produces at least a portion of the Columbian Sarsaparilla.

Smilax medica, Cham. and Schl.

Mexico. This plant produces mainly the Sarsaparilla root of that country.

Smilax papyracea, Duhamel.

Guyana to Brazil. The origin of the principal supply of Brazilian Sarsaparilla is ascribed to this species, although several others of this genus, largely represented in Brazil, may yield the medicinal root also. In our fern-tree gullies these plants would likely succeed in establishing themselves. *Smilax australis*, R. Br., extends from the tropical coast-parts of Australia to East Gipps Land. Neither this, nor the East Australian *S. glycyphylla*, Smith, nor the New Zealand *Ripogonum scandens*, Forst., have ever been sub-jected to accurate therapeutic tests, and the same may be said of numerous other Smilaces, scattered through the warmer countries of the globe. The Italian Sarsaparilla, which is derived from the Mediterranean *S. aspera*, L., has been introduced into medicine.

Smyrnium Olusatrum, L.

The Alisander. Middle and South Europe, North Africa, Western Asia. A biennial herb, which raw or boiled can be utilized in the manner of Celery. The roots and the fruitlets serve medicinal purposes.

Solanum Aethiopicum, L.

Tropical Africa. Cultivated there and elsewhere on account of its edible berries, which are large, red, globular and uneven. The plant is annual.

Solanum Dulcamara, L.

Middle and South Europe, North Africa, Middle Asia. A trailing half-shrub, with deciduous leaves. The stems are used in medicine, and contain two alkaloids: Dulcamarin and Solanin.

Solanum edule, Schum. and Thonn.

Guinea. The berry is of the size of an apple, yellow and edible.

Solanum indigoferum, St. Hilaire.

Southern Brazil. A dye-shrub, deserving here trial-culture.

Solanum Gilo, Raddi.

Tropical America; much cultivated there for the sake of its large spherical orange-colored berries, which are eatable.

Solanum Lycopersicum, L (*Lycopersicum esculentum*, Mill.)

The Tomato. South America. Annual. Several varieties exist, differing in shape and color of the berries. It is one of the most eligible plants with esculent fruits for naturalization in our desert-country. As well known the Tomato is adapted for various culinary purposes.

Solanum Melongena, L.

(*S. ovigerum*, Dunal. *S. esculentum*, Dunal.)

The Egg-plant. India and some other parts of tropical Asia. A perennial plant, usually renewed in cultivation like an annual. The egg-shaped large berries are known under the name of Aubergines or Bringals or Begoons as culinary esculents. Allied plants are: *S. insanum*, L., *S.*

S. longum, Roxb., *S. serpentinum,* Desf., *S. undatum,* Lam.,
S. ferox, L., *S. pseudo-saponaceum,* Blume, *S. album,* Lour.,
which bear all large berries, considered harmless, but may
not all represent well-marked species. Absolute ripeness
of all such kinds of fruits is an unavoidable requisite, as
otherwise even wholesome sorts may prove acrid or even
poisonous. Probably many other of the exceedingly
numerous species of the genus Solanum may be available
for good-sized edible berries.

Solanum macrocarpum, L.

Mauritius and Madagascar. A perennial herb. The berries
are of the size of an apple, globular and yellow. *S. Thon-
ningi,* F. Jacq., from Guinea, is a nearly related plant. *S.
calycinum,* Moc. et Sess., from Mexico, is also allied.

Solanum muricatum, l'Herit.

The Pepino of Peru. A shrubby species with egg-shaped
edible berries, which are white with purple spots, and attain
a length of 6 inches.

Solanum Quitoense, La Marck.

Ecuador, Peru. A shrubby plant. The berries resemble
in size, color and taste small oranges, and are of a peculiar
fragrance. To this the *S. Plumierii,* Dun., from the West
Indian Islands is also cognate and the *S. Topiro,* Kunth, from
the Orinoco.

Solanum tuberosum, L.*

The Potato. Andes of South America, particularly of
Chili, but not absolutely trans-equatorial, as it extends into
Columbia. It is also wild in the Argentine territory. As
a starch plant, the Potato interests us on this occasion particularly. Considering its prolific yield in our richer soil, we
possess as yet too few factories for Potato-starch. The
latter by being heated with mineral acids or malt can be
converted into Dextrin and Dextro-Glucose for many purposes of the arts. Dextrin, as a substitute for gum, is also
obtainable by subjecting Potato-starch in a dry state to a
heat of 400° F. Alcohol may be largely produced from the
tubers. The berries and shoots contain Solanin.

Solanum torvum, Swartz.

From West India to Peru. A shrubby species with yellow spherical berries of good size, which seem also wholesome. Other species from tropical America have shown themselves sufficiently hardy for inducing us to recommend the test-culture of such kinds of plants. Many of them are highly curious and ornamental.

Solanum Uporo, Dunal.

In many of the islands of the Pacific Ocean. The large red spherical berries of this shrub can be used like Tomato.

Solanum vescum, F. v. Mueller.

The Gunyang. South-east Australia. A shrub yielding edible berries, which need however to be fully ripe for securing absence of deleterious properties.

Solanum xanthocarpum, Schrad. and Wendl.

North Africa and South Asia. A perennial herb. The berries are of the size of a cherry, and either yellow or scarlet.

Sophora Japonica, L.

China and Japan. A deciduous tree. The flowers produce ⸱ a yellow or with admixtures a green dye, used for silk.

Spartina juncea, Willd.

Salt marshes of North America. A grass with creeping roots ; it can be utilized to bind moist sand on the coast. A tough fibre can readily be obtained from the leaves. *S. polystachya,* W. and *S. cynosuroides,* W. are stately grasses, the former also adapted for saline soil, the latter for fresh-water swamps.

Spartium junceum, L.

Countries around the Mediterranean Sea. The flowers of this bush provide a yellow dye. A textile fibre can be separated from the branches.

Spigelia Marylandica, L.

North America, north to Pennsylvania and Wisconsin. A perennial handsome herb, requiring as a vermifuge cautious administration   S. *anthelmia*, L. is an annual plant of tropical America and possesses similar medicinal properties, in which probably other species likewise share.

Spilanthes oleracea, N. Jacq.

The Para Cress.   South America.   An annual herb of considerable pungency, used as a medicinal salad.

Spinacia oleracea, L.

Sibiria.   The ordinary Spinage.   An agreeable culinary annual of rapid growth.   It is of a mild aperient property.

Spinacia tetrandra, Stev.

Caucasus.   Also annual and unisexual like the preceding plant, with which it has equal value, though it is less known.

Stenotaphrum glabrum, Trin.*

South Asia, Africa, warmer countries of America, not known from any part of Europe or Australia.   Here called the Buffalo-Grass.   It is perennial, creeping and admirably adapted for binding sea-sand and river-banks, also for forming garden edges, and for establishing a grass-sward on lawns much subjected to traffic; it is besides of some pastoral value.

Stilbocarpa polaris, De Caisne and Planchon.

Auckland's and Campbell's Islands, and seemingly also in the southern extremity of New Zealand.   A herbaceous plant with long roots, which are saccharine and served some wrecked people for a lengthened period as sustenance.   The plant is recommended here for further attention, as it may prove through culture a valuable addition to the stock of culinary vegetables of cold countries.

Stipa tenacissima, L.*   (*Macrochloa tenacisima*, Kunth.)

The Esparto or Atocha.   Spain, Portugal, Greece, North Africa, ascending the Sierra Nevada to 4000 feet.   This grass has become celebrated since some years, having afforded already a vast quantity of material for British paper-mills.   It is tall and perennial, and may prove here a valuable acquisition, inasmuch as it lives on any kind of poor soil, occurring naturally on sand and gravel as well as on

clayey or calcareous or gypseous soil, and even on the very
brink of the coast. But possibly the value of grasses of
our own, allied to the Atocha, may in a like manner become
commercially established, and mainly with this view paper
samples of several grass-kinds were prepared by the writer
(vide "Report, Industrial Exhibition, Melbourne, 1867").
Even in the scorching heat and the arid sands of the Sahara
the Atocha maintains itself, and it may thus yet be destined
to play an important part in the introduced vegetation of
any arid places of our desert-tracts, particularly where lime
and gypsum exist. The very tenacious fibre resists decay,
and is much employed for the manufacture of ropes.
During 1870 the import of Esparto ropes into England was
18,500 tons, while the raw material to the extent of about
130,000 tons was imported. Extensive culture of this grass
has commenced in the south of France. It is pulled once
a year, in the earlier part of the summer. The propagation
can be effected from seeds, but is done usually by division
of the root. Ten tons of dry Esparto, worth from £4 to £5
each, can under favorable circumstances be obtained from
an acre. The supply has fallen short of the demand. Good
writing paper is made from Esparto without admixture; the
process is similar to that for rags, but cleaner. The price of
Esparto-paper ranges from £40 to £50 for the ton. *Stipa
arenaria*, Brot., is a closely allied and still taller species,
confined to Spain and Portugal. Consul W. P. Mark
deserves great praise for having brought the Atocha into
commercial and manufactural recognition.

Styrax officinale, L.

Countries on the Mediterranean Sea. A tall bush or small
tree. The fragrant solid Storax-resin exudes from this
plant, or is particularly obtained by pressure of the bark.

Symphytum officinale, L.

The Comfrey. Europe, Western Asia. A perennial herb.
The root is utilized in veterinary practice. *S. asperrimum*,
Sims, from the Caucasus, is recommended by some as a pro-
lific plant for green-fodder.

Tacca pinnatifida, G. Forster.

Sand-shores of the South Sea Islands. From the tubers of this herb the main supply of the Feegee Arrowroot is prepared. It is not unlikely, that this plant will endure our coast clime. The Tacca-starch is much valued in medicine, and particularly used in cases of dysentery and diarrhœa. Its characteristics are readily recognized under the microscope. Several other kinds of Tacca are distinguished, but their specific limits are not yet well ascertained. Dr. Seemann admits two (*T. maculata* and *T. Brownii*) for tropical Australia, one of these extending as a hill-plant to Feegee. From the leaves and flower-stalks light kinds of bonnets are plaited. A Tacca, occurring in the Sandwich Islands, yields a large quautity of the so-called Arrowroot exported from thence. Other species (including those of Ataccia) occur in India, Madagascar, Guinea and Guiana, all deserving tests in reference to their value as starch-plants.

Tamarindus Indica, L.

Tropical Asia and Africa. This magnificent large expansive tree extends northwards to Egypt, and was found by the writer of this list in North-western Australia. It is indicated here not without hesitation, to suggest new trials of its acclimation on the lower Murray River and in East Gipps Land. The acid pulp of the pods forms the medicinal Tamarind, rich in formic and butyric acid, irrespective of its other contents.

Tanacetum vulgare, L.

The Tansy. North and Middle Europe, North Asia, North-western America. A perennial herb of well-known medicinal value, which mainly depends on its volatile oil.

Telfairia pedata, Hooker.

Mozambique. A cucurbitaceous climber with perennial stems, attaining a length of 100 feet, with fringed lilac flowers of extraordinary beauty and with fruits attaining a weight of 60 lbs., and containing at times as many as 500 large seeds. The latter in a boiled state are eatable, or a large quantity of oil can be pressed from them. The root is fleshy. Our summers in the Murray-country are likely to bring this plant regularly into bearing. A second huge species of similar use, *T. occidentalis*, J. Hook., occurs in Guinea.

Terfezia Leonis, Tulasne.

South Europe, North America. This edible truffle, together with other species of this and other genera, is deserving of naturalization in Australia.

Tetragonia implexicoma, J. Hook.

Extra-tropic Australia, New Zealand, Chatham's Island. A frutescent widely expanding plant, forming often large natural festoons, or trailing and climbing over rocks and sand, never away from the coast. As a Spinage-plant it is as valuable as the succeeding species. It is well adapted for the formation of bowers in arid places. *T. trigyna*, Banks and Soland., seems identical.

Tetragonia expansa, Murray.

The New Zealand Spinage, occurring also on many places or the coast and in the desert-interior of Australia. Known also from New Caledonia, China, Japan and Valdivia. An annual herb, useful as a culinary vegetable, also for binding drift-sand.

Teucrium Marum, L.

Countries at the Mediterranean Sea. A small somewhat shrubby plant, in use for the sake of its scent, containing a peculiar Stearopten. *T. Scordium*, L. from Europe and Middle Asia, *T. Chamaedrys*, L., *T. Polium*, L. and *T. Creticum*, L. from South Europe, are occasionally drawn into medical use. All these together with many other species from various countries are pleasantly odorous.

Thea Chinensis, Sims.*

The Tea-shrub of South-eastern Asia. This evergreen and ornamental bush has proved quite hardy in our lowland clime, where in exposed positions it endures without any attention as well our night frosts as also the free access of scorching summer winds. But it is in our humid valleys with rich alluvial soil and access to springs for irrigation, where only the most productive tea-fields can be formed.

The plant comes into plentiful bearing of its product as early as the Vine and earlier than the Olive. Its culture is surrounded with no difficulties, and it is singularly exempt from diseases if planted in proper localities. Pruning is effected in the cool season, in order to obtain a large quantity of small tender leaves from young branches. Both the Chinese and Assam tea are produced by varieties of one single species, the Tea-shrub being indigenous in the forest-country of Assam. Declivities are best adapted and usually chosen for tea-culture, particularly for Congo, Pekoe and Souchong, while Bohea is often grown in flat countries. For many full details Fortune's work, " The Tea-Districts of China," might be consulted.

The tea of commerce consists of the young leaves, heated, curled and sweated. The process of preparing the leaves can be effected by steam machinery ; one of particular construction has been suggested recently by Mr. Joachimi according to requirements explained by the writer. In 1866 three machines for dressing tea have been patented in England, one by Messrs. Campbell and Burgess, one by Mr. Thomson and one by Mr. Tayser. To give an idea of the quantity of Tea, which is consumed at the present time, it may be stated, that from June to September, 1871, 11,000,000 lbs. of tea were shipped from China alone to Australia, and that the produce of tea in India from January to June of this year has been 18,500,000 lbs. Seeds of the Tea-bush are now in many parts of this colony locally to be gathered from plants distributed by the writer, and for years to come the cultivation of the Tea-bush, merely to secure local supplies of fresh seeds, ready to germinate, will in all likelihood prove highly lucrative. Tea contains an alkaloid : Coffein, a peculiar essential oil and Bohea-acid along with other substances.

Thrinax parviflora, Swartz.

West India, and also on the continent of Central America. The stem of this Fan-palm attains a height of 25 feet. It belongs to the sand-tracts of the coast and may endure our clime. The fibre of this Palm forms material for ropes.

T. argentea, Lodd., is a closely allied palm. The few other species of the genus deserve also trial-culture here.

Thymelæa tinctoria, Endl. (*Passerina tinctoria,* Pourr.)
Portugal, Spain, South France. A small shrub. It yields a yellow dye. Cursorily it may be noted here, that some of our Pimeleæ contain a blue pigment, which has not yet been fully tested. Their bark produces more or less of Daphnin and of the volatile acrid principle, for which the Bark of *Daphne Mezereum,* L. is used. These are remarkably developed in the Victorian *Pimelea stricta,* Meissn. The bark of many is also pervaded by a tough fibre, that of the tall *Pimelea clavata,* Labill., a West Australian bush, being particularly tenacious.

Thymus capitatus, Hoffm. and Link. (*Satureja capitata,* L.)
Around the whole Mediterranean Sea. Since the times of Hippocrates, Theophrastos and Galenus this small scented shrub has been employed in medicine.

Thymus Mastichina, L.
Spain, Portugal, Morocco. A half-shrub of agreeable scent, used also occasionally in medicine.

Thymus Serpillum, L.
Europe, Western Asia. A perennial herb of some medicinal value. It would live on our highest alps. An essential oil can be obtained from it. One particular variety is lemon-scented.

Thymus vulgaris, L.
The Garden-Thyme. South Europe. This small shrubby plant is available for scent and for condiments. It is also well adapted for forming garden-edges. The essential oil of this plant can be separated into the crystalline Thymol and the liquid Thymen and Cymol. *T. aestivus,* Reut., and *T. hiemalis,* Lange, are closely cognate plants. Several other species with aromatic scent occur at the Mediterranean Sea.

Tragopogon porrifolius, L.
The Salsify. Middle and Southern Europe, Middle Asia. The root of this herb is well known as a useful culinary vegetable.

Trapa bicornis, L. fil.*

The Leng or Ling or Links of China. The nuts of this water-plant are extensively brought to market in that country. The horns of the fruit are blunt. The kernel, like that of the two following species, is of excellent taste. The plant is regularly cultivated in lakes and ponds of China.

Trapa bispinosa, Roxb.*

Middle and South Asia, extending to Ceylon and Japan; found also in Africa as far south as the Zambesi. Here in our culture it lasts through several years. In some countries, for instance in Cashmere, the nuts form an important staple of food to the population. To this species probably belong *T. Cochin-chinensis*, Lour. and *T. incisa*, Sieb. and Zucc.

Trapa natans, L.*

The ordinary Waternut. Middle and South Europe, Middle Asia, North and Central Africa. Recorded as an annual. *T. quadrispinosa*, Roxb., from Sylhet, is an allied plant.

Trifolium agrarium, L.

The perennial Yellow Clover or Hop-Clover. All Europe, Western Asia. Of considerable value in sandy soil as a fodder-herb. It is easily naturalized.

Trifolium Alexandrinum, L.*

The Bersin-Clover. North-eastern Africa, South-western Asia, South Europe. Much grown for forage in Egypt. Recorded as annual.

Trifolium fragiferum, L.

The Strawberry-Clover. Europe, North Africa, Middle and North Asia. A perennial species, well adapted for clay soils.

Trifolium hybridum, L.*

The Alsike-Clover. Europe, North Africa, Western Asia. A valuable perennial pasture-herb, particularly for swampy localities.

Trifolium incarnatum, L.

Tho Carnation-Clover. Middle and South Europe. Though annual only, it is valued in some of the systems of rotation of crops. It forms particularly a good fodder for sheep. A white flowering variety exists.

Trifolium medium, L.*

The Red Zigzag Clover. Europe, North and Middle Asia. A deep-rooting perennial herb, much better adapted for dry sandy places than *T. pratense*. It would also endure the inclemency of the climo of our higher alpine regions if disseminated there. *T. Quartinianum*, A. Rich., is an allied plant from Abyssinia, where several endemic species exist.

Trifolium pratense, L.*

The ordinary Red Clover. All Europe, North Africa, North and Middle Asia, extending to Japan. A biennial or under special circumstances also perennial herb, of great importance for stable-fodder. It prefers rich soil and particularly such, which is not devoid of lime. Also this species would live in our alps, where it would much enrich the pastures.

Trifolium repens, L.*

The ordinary White Clover. Europe, North Africa, North and Midele Asia, sub-Arctic America. Perennial. Most valuable as a fodder-plant on pastoral land. It has a predilection for moist soil, but springs again from dry spots after rain. It has naturally spread over many of our humid valleys, and its growth should be encouraged in such localities.

Trifolium subrotundum, Hochstett.

The Mayad-Clover. North and Middle Africa, ascending to 9000 feet. A perennial species, in its native countries with advantage utilized for Clover-culture. This by no means closes the list of the Clovers, desirable for introduction, inasmuch as about 150 well-marked species are recognized, many doubtless of pastoral value. But the notes of rural observers on any of these kinds are so sparingly extant, that much uncertainty about the yield and nutritive value of the various kinds continues to prevail. Most Clovers come from the temperate zone of Europe and Asia ; only two are indigenous to the eastern of the United States of North America, none occurs in Australia, few are found in South Africa, several in California and the adjoining countries, several also in Chili ; no species is peculiar to Japan.

Trigonella Foenum Graecum, L.
Countries on the Mediterranean Sea. The seeds of this annual herb find their use in veterinary medicine.

Trigonella suavissima, Lindley.
Interior of Australia, from the Murray River and its tributaries to the vicinity of Shark's Bay. This perennial, fragrant, clover-like plant proved a good pasture-herb. A lithogram, illustrating this plant, occurs in the work on the " Plants Indigenous to Victoria." Some of the many European, Asian and African plants of this genus deserve our local tests.

Tripsacum dactyloides, L.
Central and North America. A reedy perennial grass, more ornamental than utilitarian. It is the original Buffalo-Grass, and attains a height of 7 feet, assuming the aspect of Maize. It is of inferior value for fodder.

Triticum vulgare, Villars.*
The Wheat. Apparently arisen through culture from *Aegilops ovata*, L., and then a South European, North African and Oriental plant. This is not the place, to enter into details about a plant universally known. It may therefore suffice merely to mention, that three primary varieties must be distinguished between the very numerous sorts of cultivated Wheat : 1. Var. muticum (*T. hybernum*, L.), the Winter Wheat or Unbearded Wheat ; 2. Var. aristatum (*T. aestivum*, L.), the Summer Wheat or Bearded Wheat ; 3. Var. adhaerens (*T. Spelta*, L.), Wheat with fragile axis and adherent grain. Metzger enumerates as distinct kinds of cultivated Wheat :—

T. vulgare, Vill., which includes among other varieties the ordinary Spring Wheat, the Fox Wheat and the Kentish

Wheat. It comprises also the best Italian sorts for plaiting straw-bonnets and straw-hats, for which only the upper part of the stem is used, collected before the ripening of the grain and bleached through exposure to the sun while kept moistened.

T. turgidum, L., comprising some varieties of White and Red Wheat, also the Clock Wheat and the Revet Wheat.

T. durum, Desfont., which contains some sorts of the Bearded Wheat.

T. Polonicum, L., the Polish Wheat, some kind of which is well adapted for Peeled Wheat.

T. Spelta, L., the Spelt Corn or Dinkel Wheat, a kind not readily subject to disease, succeeding on soil of very limited fertility, not easily attacked by birds, furnishing a flour of excellence for cakes, also yielding a superior grain for Peeled Wheat. For preparing the latter it is necessary to collect the spikes while yet somewhat green and to dry them in baking-houses.

T. diccocum, Schrank. (*T. amyleum*, Ser.) The Emmer Wheat. Its varieties are content and prolific on poor soil, produce excellent starch, are mostly hardy in frost and not subject to diseases. To this belongs the Arras Wheat of Abyssinia, where a few other peculiar sorts of Wheat are to be found.

T. monococcum, L. St. Peter's Corn, which is hardier than most other Wheats; exists in the poorest soils, but produces grains less adapted for flour than Peeled Wheat.

Tropaeolum majus, L.

Peru. This showy perennial climber passes with impropriety under the name of Nasturtium. The herbage and flowers serve as Cress and also are considered antiscorbutic. A smaller species, *T. minus*, L., also from Peru, can likewise be chosen for a Cress-salad; both besides furnish in their flower-buds and young fruits a substitute for Capers. A volatile oil of burning taste can be distilled from the foliage of both; and this is more acrid even than the distilled oil of Mustard-seeds. In colder countries these plants are only of one year's duration. Numerous other species, all highly ornamental, occur in South America and a few also in Mexico.

Trophis Americana, L.

West Indian Archipelagus. The foliage of this milky tree has been recommended as food for the silk-insect. In Cuba and Jamaica it is used as provender for cattle and sheep.

Tuber aestivum, Vittad.

The Truffle mostly in the markets of England. The white British Truffle, *Chairomyces meandriformis*, Vitt., though large is valued less. In the Department Vaucluse (France) alone about 60,000 lbs. of Truffles are collected annually at a value of about £4000. Many other kinds of Truffles are in use. Our own native Truffle, *Mylitta australis*, Berk., attains sometimes the size of a Cocos nut, and is also a fair esculent. It seems also quite feasible to naturalize the best of edible fungi of other genera, although such may not be amenable to regular culture.

Tuber cibarium, Sibthorp.

Middle and South Europe. The Black Truffle. Like all others growing under ground, and generally found in forest-soil of limestone formations. It attains a weight over 1 lb. Experiments for naturalization may be effected with every prospect of success by conveying the Truffle in its native soil to us, and locating it in calcareous places of our forest-regions. As condiment or merely in a roasted state it affords an aromatic food. *T. melanosporum*, Vitt., from France, Germany and Italy, is of a still more exquisite taste than *T. cibarium*, indeed of Strawberry flavor. Again *T. magnatum*, Pico, from Italy, is of delicious fragrance.

Ullucus tuberosus, Lozano. (*Melloca tuberosa*, Lindl.)

Andes of New Granada and Peru, up to an elevation of 9000 feet. A perennial herb, the tubers of which are edible.

Urginia Scilla, Steinheil. (*Scilla maritima*, L.)

South Europe, North Africa. The medicinal Squill. The plant needs not regular cultivation, but settlers living near

the coast might encourage its dissemination, and thus obtain
the bulbs as drug from natural localities. Its peculiar bitter
principle is called Scillitin.

Uvularia sessilifolia, L.

North America, in forests. This pretty herb is mentioned
as yielding a good substitute for Asparagus.

Vaccinium alatum, Dombey. (*Thibaudia alata*, Dunal.)

Frigid regions of the Andes of Peru. A tall evergreen
shrub, with pink berries of the size of a cherry. This
highly ornamental plant could be grown in our sub-alpine
regions.

Vaccinium bicolor, F. v. M. (*Thibaudia bicolor*, R. and P.)

Cold zone of the Peruvian Andes. A high evergreen bush,
with red berries of the size of a Hazel nut. All Thibaudias
seem best to form a section in the genus Vaccinium, some
species of the latter, for instance *Vaccinium Imrayi*, Hook.,
from Dominica, mediating the transit. The species of the
section Thibaudia are, as a rule, producing red berries of
acidulous grateful taste. Many others may deserve therefore culture in our forest ravines or on our alpine heights.
They occur from Peru to Mexico, also in West India. One
species, Vaccinium melliflorum (*Thibaudia melliflora*, R. and
P.), has its flowers rich in honey-nectar.

Vaccinium caespitosum, Mich.

Canada and Northern States of North America. A
deciduous-'eaved small bush, with blueish edible berries.
V. ovalifolium, Sm., is an allied species.

Vaccinium corymbosum, L.*

The Swamp-Blueberry or blue Huckle-berry. Canada and
United States of North America. A good-sized shrub with
deciduous foliage. Berries blueish-black of sweetish taste,
ripening late in the season.

Vaccinium erythrocarpum, Michaux.

(*Oxycoccus erectus* Pursh.)

Carolina and Virginia, on high mountains. An upright
bush of a few feet in height, with deciduous leaves. The

transparent scarlet berries, according to Pursh, are of excellent taste.

Vaccinium grandiflorum, Dombey.

(*Ceratostemma grandiflorum*, R. and P.)

Andes of Peru. A tall evergreen shrub. The berries of a pleasant acidulous taste.

Vaccinium humifusum, Graham.

North-western America, on the Rocky Mountains. Berries of this bush well flavored.

Vaccinium Leschenaultii, Wight. (*Agapetes arborea*, Dunal.)

India, Neilgherries and Ceylon. This evergreen species attains the size of a tree, flowering and fruiting throughout the year. The fruits resemble cranberries.

Vaccinium leucanthum, Cham.

Mountains of Mexico. An arborescent species. The blackish berries are edible.

Vaccinium macrocarpon, Aiton.*

(*Oxycoccus macrocarpus*, Pers.)

The large Cranberry. From Canada to Virginia and Carolina, particularly in sandy and peaty bogs, and in cold mossy swamps. A trailing evergreen bush, with stems attaining a length of 3 feet. It is this species, which has become so extensively cultivated in the eastern parts of the United States, where on moory land, often not otherwise to be utilized, enormous quantities of this fruit have been produced by regular culture at a highly profitable scale. The berries are of the acid taste, pleasant aroma and scarlet brightness of the British Cranberry, but considerably larger.

Vaccinium meridionale, Swartz.

Jamaica, from the summits of the highest ranges down to the Coffee-regions. It attains a height of 30 feet and is evergreen. The small berries are of the taste and color of those of V. Vitis Idæa.

Vaccinium Mortinia, Bentham.

Mountains of Columbia. A shrub several feet high. The fruits resemble those of V. Myrtillus, but are more acid. They come under the name Mortina to the Quito market.

Vaccinium Myrtillus, L.*

The British Whortleberry or Bilberry. Throughout Europe, North and Middle Asia, remotest North America, in heathy and turfy forest-land. A shrub, few feet high or less, deciduous, erect, of great value for its copious supply of berries. They are, as well known, black with a blueish-grey hue and of exceedingly grateful taste. The naturalization of this plant on our alpine ranges and in our cooler woodlands, particularly in our forests of Fagus Cunninghami, would prove a boon. The berries can be utilized for their dye. The whole bush contains Quina acid.

Vaccinium myrtilloides, Michaux.

Michigan, Canada, Newfoundland, Labrador. The large edible berries are called Bluets. This little bush is adapted for our higher alpine country.

Vaccinium Oxycoccus, L.* *(Oxycoccus palustris,* Pers.)

The British Cranberry. Through Europe, North and Middle Asia, North America, on turf-moss in moory heaths. A creeping evergreen shrub of particular neatness. The berries give a most agreeable preserve and are of anti-scorbutic value. This species is particularly eligible for the spongy mossy bogs of our snowy mountains.

Vaccinium parvifolium, Smith.

North-western America. A tall shrub. The berries are excellent for preserves.

Vaccinium Pennsylvanicum, Lamarck.*

(V. angustifolium, Aiton.)

The early Blue-berry or Blue Huckleberry. North America, on dry woody hills. A dwarf-bush with deciduous foliage, producing fruit in abundance. The berries are large, blueish-black and of sweet taste. *V. Canadense,* Kalm, according to Dr. Asa Gray, is closely allied.

Vaccinium uliginosum, L.

British Bog Bilberry. Europe, North and Middle Asia, North America. A deciduous bush, with blackish berries, similar to those of V. Myrtillus, but hardly of equal excellence.

Vaccinium vacillans, Solander.

North America, in sandy forest-lands. A deciduous small bush, coming with its blue berries later into season than V. Pennsylvanicum.

Vaccinium Vitis Idaæ, L.

Europe, North and Middle Asia, North America. A dwarf-shrub with evergreen leaves. The purplish-red berries are sought for jellies and other preserves.

It is as yet impossible to say, how many other species of Vaccinium are producing good-sized and well-flavored fruits. But the genus ranges in many species from Continental Asia to the Indian Archipelagus, and has a wide extension also in South America, occupying in hot countries higher mountain regions. But few reliable notes on the tropical species are extant, as far as the fruits are concerned.

Valeriana Celtica, L.

Alps of Europe. The root of this perennial herb is particularly aromatic.

Valeriana edulis, Nuttall.

North-western America, from Oregon to the Rocky Mountains. The thick spindle-shaped root of this herb affords food to the natives of that part of the globe. When baked the root proves agreeable and wholesome. When we consider the wild states of the plants, from which many of our important root-crops arose, then this Valeriana and several other plants, suggestively mentioned in these pages, may well be admitted for trial-culture.

Valeriana officinalis, L.

Europe, North and Middle Asia, in swampy grass-land, with a predilection for forests and river-banks. This perennial herb would do particularly well on our alps. It is the only one among numerous congeners of Europe, Asia and America, which is drawn to a considerable extent into medicinal use. The root and herb contain Valerianic acid and a peculiar tannic acid ; the root furnishes an esential oil, which again resolves itself into Valerol (70 per cent.), Valerecn, Barneol and Valerianic acid. The order of Valerianeæ is not represented by any native plant in Australia.

Valerianella olitoria, Moench.
Lamb's Lettuce. Europe, North Africa, North and Middle Asia. A fair and early Salad-plant. It is an annual plant, and has several congeners in Europe and Asia.

Veratrum album, L.
Europe, North and Middle Asia, extending eastwards to Japan. It delights particularly in sub-alpine localities. The root furnishes Veratrin, Jervin and Sabadillic acid.

Veratrum viride, Aiton.
Canada and United States of North America. A near relative of the former plant. Its root has come recently into medicinal use.

Vicia Ervilia, Willdenow. (*Ervum Ervilia*, L.)
South Europe, North Africa, South-western Asia. An annual herb, praised as a valuable fodder-plant on dry calcareous soil.

Vicia Faba, L.*
The Straight Bean. Orient, particularly on the Caspian Sea. This productive annual herb affords not only its seeds for table use, but provides also a particularly fattening stable food. The seeds contain about 33 per cent. starch.

Vicia sativa, L.* (*V. angustifolia*, Roth.)
The ordinary Vetch or Tare. Europe, North Africa, North and Middle Asia. One of the best of fodder-plants, but only of one or two years' duration. Many of the other European and Asiatic species of Vicia are deserving our attention.

Vigna Sinensis, Endl.* (*Dolichos Sinensis*, L.)

Tropical Asia and Africa. The cultivation of this twining annual pulse-herb extends to Southern Europe and many other countries with a clime like ours. The pods are remarkable for their great length, and used like French Beans. *Vigna Catjang,* A. Rich. and *Vigna sesquipedalis* are varieties of this species. In fair soil the produce is fortyfold.

Viola odorata, L.

The Violet. Middle and South Europe, North Africa, Middle Asia. Passingly alluded to here, as this modest though lovely plant should be extensively naturalized in our forest-glens, to furnish its delicate scent for various compositions of perfumery.

Vitis acetosa, F. v. Mueller.

Carpentaria and Arnhem's Land. Stems rather herbaceous than shrubby, erect. The whole plant is pervaded with acidity, and proved valuable in cases of scurvy. The berries are edible. This species, if planted here, would likely spring annually afresh from the root.

Vitis aestivalis, Michaux.*

The Summer Grape of the United States of North America. Flowers fragrant. The berries are deep blue, of pleasant taste, and ripen late in the season.

Vitis Baudiniana, F. v. Mueller. (*Cissus Antarctica*, Vent.)

East Australia. With V. hypoglauca the most southern of all Grapes, none extending to New Zealand. It is evergreen, and here a vigorous plant for bowers, but suffers even from slight frosts. The berries are freely produced and edible, though not large.

Vitis cordifolia, Michaux.* (*Vitis riparia*, Mich.)

The Winter Grape or Frost Grape. From Canada to Florida. A deciduous vine. The scent of the flowers reminds of Reseda. The berries are small, either blackish or amber-colored, and very acid. They can be used for preserves, and are only fully matured when touched by frosts. A succession of seedlings may give us a superior and simultaneously a very hardy vine.

Vitis hypoglauca, F. v. Mueller.

East Australia, as far south as Gipps Land. An evergreen climber of enormous length, forming a very stout stem in age. The black berries attain the size of small cherries. Also this species may perhaps be vastly changed in its fruit by continued culture.

Vitis Indica, L.

On the mountains of various parts of India, ascending an altitude of 3000 feet in Ceylon. The small berries are edible. The plant should be subjected to horticultural experiments. This is an apt opportunity to draw attention to the various Indian species of Vitis with large edible berries; for instance: *V. laegivata*, Bl., *V. thyrssiflora*, Miq., *V. mutabilis*, Bl., *V. Blumeana*, Steud., all from the mountains of Java, and all producing berries as large as cherries, those of V. Blumeana being particularly sweet. Further may here be inserted *V. imperialis*, Miquel, from Borneo, *V. auriculata*, Wall. and *V. elongata*, Wallich, both the last from the mountainous mainland of Coromandel, and all producing very large juicy berries even in the jungle wilderness. *V. quadrangularis*, L., stretches from Arabia to India and Central Africa, and has also edible fruits. Many such plants may be far more eligible for Grape-culture in hot wet climes than the ordinary vine. About 250 species of Vitis are already known, mostly from intra-tropical latitudes, and mostly evergreen ; but in regard to their elevation above the ocean, and to the nature of their fruits, we are almost utterly without data.

Vitis Labrusca, L.*

The Isabella Grape. North America, from Canada to Texas and Florida, also in Japan. The Schuylkill Grape is derived from this species. A pale-fruited variety furnishes the Bland's Grape. Another yields the American Alexander-Grape. The berries are large among American kinds and are of pleasant taste. Flowers fragrant. This and the other hardy North American vines seem never to be attacked by the Oidium disease.

Vitis Schimperiana, Hochstetter.

From Abyssinia to Guinea. This vine may become valuable with many other Central African kinds for tropical culture, and may show itself hardy here. Barter compares the edible berries to clusters of Frontignac Grape.

Vitis vinifera, L.*

The Grape Vine. Turkey, Persia, Tartary. This is not the place to discuss at length the great industrial questions, concerning this highly important plant, even had these not engaged already since many years the attention of a large number of our colonists. The whole territory of Victoria stretches essentially through the vine-zone, and thus most kinds of vine can be produced here, either on the lowlands or the less elevated mountains in various climatic regions and in different geologic formations.

The Corinthian variety, producing the " Currants " of commerce, thrives also well in some districts, where with Raisons it promises to become a staple article of our exports beyond home consumption. Dr. W. Hamm, of Vienna, has recently issued a Vine-map of Europe, indicating the distribution of the different varieties and the principal sources of the various sorts of Wine. The writer would now merely add, that the preservation of the Grapes in a fresh state, according to M. Charmeux's method, and the sundry modes of effecting the transit of ripe Grapes to long distances, ought to be turned to industrial advantage. The pigment of the dark wine-berries is known as Oenolic acid. The juice contains along with Tartaric acid also Grape acid. All these chemically defined substances have uses of their own in art and science.

Vitis vulpina, L.* (*Vitis rotundifolia*, Mich.)

The Muscadine or Fox-Grape. South-eastern States of North America. This species includes as varieties also the Bullace, the Mustang, the Bullet-Grape, both kinds of the Scuppernangs and the Cotowba Grape. The berries are of a pleasant taste, but in some instances of a strong flavor; they are the largest among American Grapes.

Voandzeia subterranea, Thouars.

Madagascar and various parts of Africa, as far south as Natal. This Earth-Pea is annual, and pushes its pods under ground in the manner of Arachis hypogæa for maturation. The pods are edible, and much consumed in tropical countries.

Wallichia oblongifolia, Griffith.

Himalaia, as far as 27° North. There one of the hardiest of all Palms. It is not a tall one, yet a graceful and useful object for cultural industries. Several species exist.

Wettinia augusta, Poeppig.

Peru, on mountains several thousand feet high. This Palm is therefore likely to endure our clime.

Wettinia Maynensis, Spruce.

Cordilleras of Peru. Like the foregoing it attains a height of 40 feet, and advances to elevations of 3000 feet or 4000 feet. Before finally parting from the American Palms, it may be appropriate to allude briefly to some of the hardier kinds, which were left unnoticed in the course of this compilation. From Dr. Spruce's important essay on the Palms of the Amazon River may be learnt, that besides other species, as yet imperfectly known from the sources of this great river, the following kinds are comparatively hardy; thus they might find places for cultivation or even naturalization within the limits of our Colony:—*Geonema undata*, Klotzsch; *Iriartea deltoïdea*, R. and P.; *Iriartea ventricosa*, Mart., which latter rises in its magnificence to fully 100 feet; *Iriartea exorrhiza*, Mart.; this with the two other Iriarteas ascends the Andes to 5000 feet.—*Oenocarpus multicaulis*, Spruce; ascends to 4000 feet; from 6 to 10 stems are developed from the same root, each from 15 feet to 30 feet high.—*Euterpe ;* of this two species occur in a zone between 3000 feet and 6000 feet.—*Phytelephas microcarpa,* R. and P. ; eastern slope of the Peru Andes, ascending to 3000 feet.—*Phytelephas macrocarpa,* R. and P. ; also on the eastern side of the Andes, up to 4000 feet ; it is this superb species which yields by its seeds part of the vegetable ivory.— *Phytelephas aequatorialis,* Spruce ; on the west slope of the Peruvian Andes, up to 5000 feet ; this Palm is one of the grandest objects in the whole vegetable creation, its leaves attaining a length of 30 feet ! The stem rises to 20 feet. Palm-ivory is also largely secured from this plant. Though aequinoctial it lives only in the milder regions of the mountains ; therefore in the equable temperature of East Gipps Land it would likely prosper without protective cover.— *Carludovica palmata,* R. and P., on the east side of the Andes of Peru and Ecuador, up to 4000 feet ; the fan-shaped leaves from cultivated specimens furnish the main material for the best Panama-hats. The illustrious Count de Castelnau saw many Palms on the borders of Paraguay during his great Brazilian Expedition. Most of these together with the Palms of Uruguay and the wide Argentine territory would likely prove adapted for acclimation in our latitudes ; but hitherto the limited access to those countries has left us largely unacquainted with its vegetable treasures also in this direction. Von Martius demonstrated, already in 1850, the occurrence of the following Palms in extra-tropic South America :—*Ceroxylon australe,* Mart., on high mountains in Juan Fernandez at 30° S.L. ; *Jubœa spectabilis,* Humb., in Chili at 40° S.L. ; *Trithrinax Brasiliana,* Mart., at 31° S.L. ; *Copernicia cerifera,* Mart., at 29° S.L. ; *Acrocomia Totai,* Mart., at 28° S.L. ; *Cocos australis,* Mart., at 34° S.L. ; *Cocos Yatai,* Mart., at 32° S.L. ; *Cocos Romanzoffiana,* Cham., at 28° S.L. ; *Diplothemium littorale,* Mart., at 30° S.L. All the last mentioned Palms occur in Brazil, the Acrocomia and Trithrinax extending to Paraguay, and Cocos australis to Uruguay and the La Plata State.

While some Palms, as indicated, descend to cooler latitudes, others ascend to temperate and even cold mountain regions. Among the American species are prominent in this respect: *Euterpe andicola*, Brogn., *E. Haenkeana*, Brogn., *E. longivaginata*, Mart., *Diplothemium Porallyi*, Mart. and *Ceroxylon pithyrophyllum*, Mart., all occurring on the Bolivian Andes at an elevation of about 8000 feet.—*Ceroxylon andicola*, Humb., *Kunthia montana*, Humb., *Oreodoxa frigida*, Humb., and *Geonoma densa*, Linden, reach also on the Andes of New Granada a height of at least 8000 feet.—*Ceroxylon Klopstockia*, Mart., advances on the Andes of Venezeula to a zone 7500 feet altitude, where Karsten saw stems 200 feet high with leaves 24 feet long! There also occur *Syagrus Sancona*, Karst. and *Platenia Chiragua*, Karst. at elevations of 5000 feet, both very lofty Palms. From the temperate mountain regions of sub-tropical Mexico are known among others: *Chamaedora concolor*, Mart., *Copernicia Pumos*, Humb., *C. nana*, Kunth, and *Brahea dulcis*, Mart., at elevations from 7000 feet to 8000 feet.

Xanthorrhiza apiifolia, l'Herit.

North America. A perennial almost shrubby plant of medicinal value. The root produces a yellow pigment, similar to that of *Hydrastis Canadensis*, L. Both contain also Berberin.

Ximenia Americana, L.

Tropical Asia, Africa and America, passing however the tropics in Queensland, and gaining also an indigenous position in Florida. This bush may therefore accommodate itself to our clime in localities free of frost. The fruits are edible, resembling yellow plums in appearance ; their taste is agreeable. The wood is scented.

Yucca filamentosa, L.

The Adam's Needle. From Carolina and Florida to Texas and Mexico. An almost stemless species. It would hardly be right, to omit here the plants of this genus altogether, as they furnish a fibre of great strength, similar to that of the Agaves. Moreover all these plants are decorative, and live in the poorest soil, even in drifting coast-sand. They are also not hurt, as is the case with the Fourcroyas, by the frosts of our lowlands. Among the species with stems of several feet in height may be recorded *Y. gloriosa*, L. and *Y. aloifolia*, L., both from the sandy south coast of North America.

Zalacca secunda, Griffith.

Assam, as far north as 28°. A stemless Palm with large feathery leaves, exquisitely adapted for decorative purposes. Before we finally quit the Asiatic Palms we may yet learn from Von Martius's great work, how many extra-tropic members of this princely order were known in 1850 already, when that masterly work was concluded. Martius enumerates as belonging to the boreal extra-tropic zone in Asia: From Silhet at 24° N.L.: *Calamus erectus*, Roxb.; *C. extensus*, Roxb.; *C. quinquencrvius*, Roxb.;—from Garo at 26° N.L.: *Wallichia caryotoides*, Roxb.; *Ptychosperma gracilis*, Miq.; *Caryota urens*, L.; *Calamus leptospadix*, Griff.;—from Khasya in 26° N.L.: *Calamus acanthospathus*, Griff.; *C. macrospathus*, Griff.; *Plectocomia Khasyana*, Griff.;—from Assam about 27° N.L.: *Areca Nagensis*, Griff.; *A. triandra*, Roxb.; *Livistona Jenkinsii*, Griff.; *Daemonorops nutantiflorus*, Griff.; *D. Jenkinsii*, Griff.; *D. Guruba*, Mart.; *Plectocomia Assamica*, Griff.; *Calamus tenuis*, Roxb.; *C. Flagellum*, Griff.; *C. Heliotropium*, Hamilt.; *C. floribundus*, Griff.; *Phœnix Ouseloyana*, Griff.;—from Upper Assam between 28° and 29° N.L.: *Caryota obtusa*, Griff.; *Zalacca secunda*, Griff.; *Calamus Mishmelensis*, Griff.;—from Darjiling at 27° N.L.: *Wallichia obtusifolia*, Griff.; *Licuala peltata*, Roxb.; *Plectocomia Himalaiana*, Griff.; *Calamus schizospathus*, Griff.;—from Nepaul between 28° and 29° N.L.: *Chamaerops Martiana*, Wall.;—from Guhrval in 30° N.L.: *Calamus Royleanus*, Griff.;—from Saharampoor in 30° N.L.: *Borassus flabelliformis*, L.;—from Duab in 31° N.L.: *Phœnix silvestris*, Roxb.;—from

Kheree in 30° N.L. : *Phœnix humilis*, Royle; — from Dekan: *Bentinckia Coddapanna*, Berry, at an elevation of 4000 feet.

Miquel mentions as Palms of Japan (entirely extra-tropical) : *Rhapis flabelliformis*, Aiton; *R. humilis*, Blume ; *Chamaerops excelsa*, Thunb. ; *Livistona Chinensis*, Br. and *Arenga saccharifera*, La Bill. or a species closely allied to that Palm.

Zea Mays, L.*

The Maize or Indian-Corn. Indigenous to the warmer parts of South America. St. Hilaire mentions as its native country Paraguay. Found in Central America already by Columbus. This conspicuous though annual cereal grass interests us on this occasion as being applicable here to far more uses than those, for which it has hitherto been employed. In North America, for instance, Maize is converted into a variety of dishes for the daily table, being thus boiled in an immature state as "green corn." Mixed with other flour it furnishes good bread. For some kind of cakes it is solely used, also for Maizena, Maccaroni and Polenta. Several varieties exist; the Inca-maize of Peru being remarkable for its gigantic size and large grains. Maize is not readily subject to the ordinary corn diseases; but to prosper it requires fair access to potash and lime. Good writing and printing papers can be prepared from Maize-straw. Meyen calculated, that the return from Maize under most favorable circumstances in tropical countries would be 800-fold, and under almost any circumstance it is the largest yielder among cereals in warm countries. As a fattening saccharine green-fodder Maize is justly appreciated. Any Ergot from it is used, like that of Rye, for medicinal purposes. Maize-Corn contains about 75 per cent. of starch. Dierbach recommends Mellago or Treacle from Maize, instead of that prepared from the roots os *Triticum repens*, L., and the molasses, so obtained, serve also culinary uses.

Zingiber officinale, Roscoe.

The Giuger. India and China. Possiby this plant may be productive in the hottest parts of our colony, and give satisfactory results. The multiplication is effected by division of the root. For candied ginger only the young succulent roots are used, which are peeled and scalded prior to the immersion into the saccharine liquid.

Zizania aquatica, L.* (*Hydropyrum esculentum*, Liuk.)

The Canada Rice. In shallow streams and around ponds and lakes from Canada to Florida. This tall grass might be readily naturalized. Although its grain can be utilized for bread-corn, we would wish to possess the plant chiefly to obtain additional food of a superior kind for water-birds.

Zizania latifolia, Hance.*

(*Hydropyrum latifolium*, Grisebach.)

The Kau-sun of China. In lakes of Amur, Manschuria, China and Japan. Nearly related to the preceding species. From Dr. Hance we know, that the solid base of the stem forms a very choice vegetable, largely used in China, where this tall water-grass undergoes regular cultivation like the Trapa.

Zizania miliacea, Michaux.

Southern part of North America, West India. Likewise tall and perennial, but more restricted to the tide-water meadows and ditches, according to Pursh ; but according to Chapmau's note generally distributed like Z. aquatina, with which it has similar use. In South Brazil occurs a similar grass, namely *Z. microstachya*, Nees.

Zizyphus Jujuba, La Marck.

From India to China. This shrub or tree can only be expected to bear its pleasant fruits in the warmest parts of our colony. The fruit is red or yellow, and of the size of a large cherry.

Zizyphus rugosa, La Marck.

Nepaul and other mountainous parts of India. A small tree, hardier than the last. The drupe of this is also edible, and the same may be said of a few other Indian species.

Zizyphus vulgaris, La Marck.

Orient, particularly Syria. A small tree, well-adapted for our clime. Fruits scarlet, about an inch long, with edible pulp; they are known as South European Jujubs.

CONCLUDING REMARKS.

THE writer in concluding this small contribution towards the literature of industrial plants could not but feel, that he over-stepped already the limits originally assigned to this communication. Yet thus far extended as it is, it excludes many important genera and species altogether, not merely such as Atalantia, Cynodon, Debregeasia, Villeburnia, Zamia and others, which were inadvertently passed, but also numerous others of perhaps secondary note, yet sufficiently significant to be reserved for a supplemental treatise. Nevertheless to about seven hundred prominent utilitarian plants now primary local attention has been directed in a connected form, which with the three hundred timber-trees, enumerated in last year's Report of the Acclimatisation Society, gives us a list of about one thousand plants for our cultural choice. But besides indirectly or passingly the writer has alluded to very many more; and these indications ought to aid many of our colonists to trace out still further novel resources for their requirements in husbandry or technology or any other purpose. It is the intention at an early opportunity to add to these lists, and to group also the products of the various timber-trees together in an augmented index, as many of these furnish also medicinal substances, dyes, oils, gums, resins, esculent fruits and other articles of our wants. Thus notes for instance on Camphor, vegetable tallow, real manna, maple-sugar, hickory-nuts, sandarac, turpentine, kauri, &c., must be sought among the timber-trees. Simultaneously then a geographic grouping of all these indicated plants will be effected, in order that at a glance may be indicated, what from each particular country in various parts of the globe may be secured. The range of each recorded species is now already given with a view of affording a clearer insight into the adaptability of different climatic tracts and altitudes of this colony or countries within the same isothermal lines for special plants. Furthermore to give to benefactors abroad, who may wish to let us participate in their treasures of plants a more exact indication of our varied climatic zones, it was found expedient to append to this Record a very succinct Meteorologic Schedule. Space did not admit of an enumeration of the many works of different nations, which may be consulted with advantage for following up the indications now given, but a list of the principal publications will be prepared for the supplement promised. It should however be stated, and this with regret, that the new work on vegetable industrial productions, published very recently by Mr. J. Smith of Kew, and resting largely on the notes of the late Alexander Smith, derived from the collections of Hooker's Museum, did not yet reach this country. Notes may hereafter also be added, distinguishing those plants, which give an immediate return in one season, and those, which produce their yield only in variously extended periods. Likewise might be discriminated between those plants, from which commercial raw products are obtained, and those which require costly machinery or toilsome application, to perfect the mercantile article. The brief chemical notes are largely derived from Professor Wittstein's "Chemische Analyse von Pflanzentheilen," of which important work with the author's friendly concession a translation by the writer is early to appear. By these means industrial enquiry may here also be advanced, modern therapeutic for instance depending often with far more exactness on alkaloids or other chemically defined substances, than on the administration of a plant as a whole. In conclusion the writer trusts, that by the issue of these pages our transoceanic interchanges may become extended, and the vegetable treasures of distant countries may be rendered more extensively our own, while some slight advantage may also arise from these unpretensive data to countries endowed with climatic regions not dissimilar to those of Victoria.

TEMPERATURE OF AIR IN SHADE FOR THE LAST FOURTEEN YEARS.

From the Observatory Records of Melbourne.

	HIGHEST.	LOWEST.	MEAN.
At Melbourne	111·2	27·0	57·6
At Sandhurst	117·4	27·5	59·0
At Ballarat	109·0	22·0	53·2
At Portland	103·0	30·0	61·5
At Port Albert	...	...	56·5

RAINFALL AT MELBOURNE.

	INCH.		INCH.		INCH.
In 1857	28·90	In 1862	22·08	In 1867	25·79
1858	26·02	1863	36·43	1868	18·27
1859	21·80	1864	27·40	1869	24·59
1860	25·40	1865	15·94	1870	33.75
1861	29·15	1866	22·41	1871	30·17

TEMP. OF AIR IN SHADE AT TWOFOLD BAY, 1871.

(Corresponding to the lowlands of East Gipps Land.)
From the Observatory Records of Sydney.

	MEAN.	M.MAX.	M.MIN.	E.MAX.	E.MIN.	R'FALL
January	68·1	75·0	61·2	...	...	4.570
February	67.6	72·9	62·3	...	...	12·350
March	64·0	70·4	57·7	...	...	1·500
April	61·5	68·4	54·5	...	...	2·540
May	59·4	64·6	54·2	...	..	12·000
June	53·5	59·9	47·1	...	...	5·640
July	52·7	60·3	45·0	72·0	39·1	0·790
August	52·8	60·8	44·7	68·0	41·1	0·690
September	56·7	63·8	49·5	73·0	44·1	1·530
October	58·1	65·9	50·2	76·0	42·1	8·270
November	63·4	71·6	55·2	81·0	47·1	2·390
December	70·4	79·7	61·1	106·0	54·1	1·470

60·7° mean annual temperature.   53·740 inches rainfall for the year.

TEMP. OF AIR IN SHADE AT TWOFOLD BAY, 1872.
From the Magistrate's Office at Eden.

	MAX. Deg.	MINIM. Deg.	R'FALL Inches.
January	88.0	61·0	3·15
February	83·0	63·0	1·15
March	81·0	58·0	1·92
April	62·0	55·0	1·03
May	62·0	47·0	1·08

INDICATED GENERA,

CONTAINING

Alimentary Plants :

1. YIELDING HERBAGE :

Atriplex, Beta, Brassica, Chenopodium, Corchorus, Crambe, Hibiscus, Musa, Pringlea, Rheum, Rumex, Spinacia, Tetragonia.

2. YIELDING ROOTS :

Apios, Arracacha, Asparagus, Beta, Butomus, Carum, Chaerophyllum, Cichorium, Colocasia, Conopodium, Cyperus, Daucus, Dioscorea, Flemingia, Geitonoplesium, Gladiolus, Helianthus, Hypochoeris, Ipomæa, Manihot, Microseris, Oxalis, Pachyrrhizus, Peucedanum, Rha. ponticum, Scilla, Scorzonera, Sechium, Selinum, Stilbocarpa, Tragopogon, Ullucus, Uvularia, Valeriana.

3. YIELDING GRAIN :

Andropogon, Avena, Eleusine, Hordeum, Oryza, Panicum, Pennisetum, Secale, Zea, Zizania.

4.—YIELDING TABLE PULSE :

Cajanus, Cicer, Dolichos, Ervum, Lupinus, Phaseolus, Pisum, Vigna.

5.—YIELDING VARIOUS ESCULENT FRUITS :

Arachis, Corynosicyos, Cucumis, Cucurbita, Cynara, Fagopyrum, Sechium, Telfairia, Trapa, Voandzoa.

S. TRUFFLES :

Terfezia, Tuber.

Bamboo Plants:

Arundinaria, (*Arundo*), Bambusa, Guadua, Melocanna, Schizostachyum; (many other genera mentioned under Schizostachyum).

Coffee Plants :
Coffea (doubtful).

Condiment Plants :
Acorus, Allium, Apium, Archangelica, Artemisia, Borrago, Brassica, Capparis, Capsicum, Carum, Chærophyllum, Citrus, Cochlearia, Coriandrum, Crithmum, Cuminum, Foeniculum, Glycine, Illicium, Lepidium, Mentha, Ocimum, Olea, Origanum, Peucedanum, Pimpinella, Prunus (*Amygdalus*), Satureja, Sison, Smyrnium, Spilanthes, Tropæolum, Thymus, Valerianella, Zingiber.

Dye Plants :
Alkanna, Anthemis, Carthamus, Crocus, Crozophora, Helianthus, Indigofera, Isatis, Lawsonia, Lithospermum, Maharanga, Mallotus, Opuntia, Peireskia, Perilla, Reseda, Rhamnus, Rhus, Rubia, Sambucus, Saponaria, Solanum, Sophora, Spartium, Thymelæa, Xanthorrhiza.

Fibre Plants :
Agave, Apocynum, Bœhmeria, Broussonetia, Camelina, Cannabis, Corchorus, Cordyline, Crotalaria, Cyperus, Fourcroya, Gossypium, Helianthus, Hibiscus, Humulus, Lavatera, Linum, Maoutia, Musa, Pachyrrhizus, Phormium, Pipturus, Poa, Sesbania, Spartium, Yucca.

Fuller's Plant :
Dipsacus.

Fodder Plants :
1. GRASSES :
Agrostis, Alopecurus, Andropogon, Anthistiria, Anthoxanthum, Avena, Bromus, Cynosurus, Dactylis, Ehrharta, Eleusine, Festuca, Hierochloa, Hordeum, Leersia, Lolium, Panicum, Paspalum, Pennisetum, Phalaris, Phleum, Poa, Secale, Stenotaphrum, Tripsacum, Triticum.

2. OTHER HERBAGE :
Cichorium, Pentzia, Prangos, Symphytum.

3. STABLE PULSE (PODS AND HERB) :
Cicer, Dolichos, Hedysarum, Lathyrus, Lupinus, Medi-

cago, Melilotus, Onobrychis, Ornithopus, Pisum, Trifolium, Trigonella, Vicia.

4. OTHER FRUITS :
Argania, Helianthus, Prosopis.

Gum Plants: ·
Acacia, Astragalus, Olea, Prosopis.

Hedge Plants :
Acacia, Agave, Crataegus, Justicia, Ligustrum, Maclura, Opuntia, Paliurus, Parkinsonia, Peireskia, Prosopis, Prunus, Rhus, Rosa, Rubus, Salix.

Hop Plant :
Humulus.

Medicinal Plants :
1. YIELDING HERBAGE OR FLOWERS :
Achillea, Aconitum, Aletris, Aloe, Althaea, Anemone, Anthemis, Arctostaphylos, Arnica, Artemisia, Atropa, Barosma, Canuabis, Cassia, Catha, Chelidonium, Chenopodium, Cochlearia, Conium, Cytisus, Digitalis, Erythroxylon, Eupatorium, Hyoscyamus, Ilex, Justicia, Lactuca, Marrubium, Matricaria, Mentha, Menyanthes, Ophelia, Polygala, Prunus, Rafnia, Ricinus, Rosmarinus, Ruta, Salvia, Sambucus, Sebæa, Solanum, Spigelia, Tanacetum.

2. YIELDING BARK :
Alstonia, Cinchona.

4. YIELDING ROOTS :
Acorus, Actaea, Anacyclus, Archangelica, Aristolochia, Cephaelis, Cimicifuga, Colchicum, Convolvulus, Gentiana, Glycyrrhiza, Helleborus, Hydrastis, Inula, Ipomaea, Nardostachys, Peucedanum, Pimpinella, Podophyllum, Saponaria, Saussurea, Schoenocaulon, Smilax, Symphytum, Urginia, Xanthorrhiza, Valeriana, Veratrum.

4. YIELDING FRUITS (OR ONLY SEEDS) :
Cucumis, Ecballion, Foeniculum, Illicium, Mallotus, Rhamnus, Rheum, Ricinus, Smyrnium, Trigonella.

Oil Plants :

Prunus (*Amygdalus*), Arachis, Argania, Brassica, Came-
lina, Cannabis, Cucurbita, Cyperus, Gossypium, Guizotia,
Helianthus, Linum, Olea, Papaver, Ricinus, Sesamum,
Telfairia.

Orchard Plants :

Amelanchier, Anona, Brabejum, Cervantesia, Citrus,
Diospyros, Euclea, Ficus, Fragaria, Gaultheria, Gaylus-
sacia, Hovenia, Morus, Musa, Myrica, Myrtus, Nephelium,
Niemeyera, Opuntia, Parinarium, Passiflora, Peireskia,
Persea, Physalis, Prunus, Psidium, Pyrularia, Pyrus,
Ribes, Rubus, Santalum, Sechium, Shepherdia, Solanum,
Tamarindus, Vaccinium, Vitis, Ximenia, Zizyphus.

Palm Plants :

Bactris, Calamus, Caryota, Ceroxylon, Chamaerops, Hyphaene, Jubæa, Kentia, Livistona, Phœnix, Plectocomia,
Ptychosperma, Rhapis, Sabal, Thrinax, Wallichia, Wettinia, Zalacca. (Many other American genera under
Wettinia ; many other Asian genera under Zalacca.)

Paper Plants :

Arundo, Broussonetia, Cyperus, Lepidosperma, Stipa,
Zea. (See also Fibre Plants.)

Resin Plants :

Pistacia, Rhus, Styrax.

Sand-coast Plants :

Agrostis, Asparagus, Crambe, Crithmum, Dactylis, Elymus,
Ehrharta, Genista, Lepidosperma, Leptospermum, Pani-
cum, Paspalum, Phormium, Poa, Prunus, Psamma, Sabal,
Spartina, Stenotaphrum, Stipa, Tacca, Tetragonia, Thrinax,
Urginia, Yucca.

Scent Plants :

Acacia, Adesmia, Andropogon, Anthoxyanthum, Boronia,
Cedronella, Citrus, Convolvulus, Dracocephalum, Hedeoma,
Heliotropium, Jasminum, Lavandula, Lippia, Melissa,
Mentha, Ocimum, Origanum, Pogostemum, Prunus
(*Amygdalus*), Pycnanthemum, Reseda, Rosa, Rosmarinus,
Satureja, Styrax, Teucrium, Thymus, Viola.

Silk Plants:
Morus, Quercus, Ricinus, Trophis.

Starch Plants:
Alstroemeria, Canna, Cycas, Fagopyrum, Hordeum, Maranta, Oryza, Secale, Solanum, Tacca, Triticum, Zea.

Sugar Plants:
Andropogon, Beta, Cucumis, Saccharum, Zea.

Tannic Plants:
Cytisus, Prosopis, Rhus.

Tea Plants:
Andropogon, Thea.

Tobacco Plants:
Nicotiana.

Water Plants:
Acorus, Aeschynomene, Butomus, Cyperus, Menyanthes, Nelumbo, Oryza, Poa, Sagittaria, Trapa, Zizania.

Wicker Plants:
Salix. (Also genera mentioned under Bamboo Plants).

ELWOOD COOPER.

THE subject of this sketch is a man who is is inseperably connected with the history of the marvelous horticultural developments which have, in recent years, brought fame and wealth to our chosen land. For the following article and the portrait which accompanies it, we are indebted to that ably edited and always readable journal, the *Press and Horticulturist*, of Riverside:

A pleasant drive of thirteen miles out from Santa Barbara, over splendid roads, brings one to Ellwood, the famous ranch and home of Ellwood Cooper, the president of the State Board of Horticulture, consisting of 2,000 acres extending from low water mark of the Pacific ocean back to the highest elevation on the sloping hills. Four hundred acres of this ranch are devoted to fruits, prominent among which is the olive, there being seven thousand olive trees on the place from one to four years old. Mr. Cooper commenced planting the olive in 1872, and is the pioneer in that industry in the State. Others have followed his lead extensively in the planting and cultivation of the olive, for which that section was peculiarly adapted. It has been demonstrated by Mr. Cooper to be one of the most profitable trees to be grown, not only for the oil, but also for the preserved fruit.

In addition to his olive industry the ranch contains twelve thousand five hundred almond trees, four thousand English walnuts, and over one thousand fruit trees, comprising almost every variety of fruit grown from the temperate zone to the tropics. The ranch is sheltered by eucalyptus trees placed on the boundary line, which are a great protection to the fruit trees and considerably modify the climate. They number over 150,000 trees comprising twenty-five varieties of the eucalyptus genus.

In addition to his fruit industry, Mr. Cooper has many hundred acres devoted to grain and grazing, and has a herd of 150 Jersey cattle from which he supplies butter to Santa Barbara and San Francisco.

Everything on this ranch is a monument to the capabilities of the climate, aided by a perfect state of cultivation. The Marquis of Lorne, in an article in the *Youth's Companion* on the subject of "Opportunities for young men in America," thus refers to Mr. Cooper:

"The second is a gentleman who has a magnificent farm on the Pacific, and has shown that California can produce better olive oil than France, Spain, or Italy; grapes as good as any man can desire; English walnuts and European almonds, in crops whereof the old countries hardly ever dream; oranges, lemons, and Japanese persimmons, with other fruits and crops too numerous to mention; and all hedged from the gentle sea-winds by belts and bands of Australian eucalypti, which grows in ten years to 100 feet. But such a Paradise is not for the beginner, who must make his money before he indulges in so many broad acres."

We have been thus particular in describing "Ellwood," as it is not only a model ranch, showing what intelligent cultivation

can do in this sunny clime, but because the proprietor is one of the most prominent horticulturists in the State, and what he has done in a few years others may do.

Ellwood Cooper was born in Lancaster county, Pennsylvania, in 1829; went to Philadelphia when quite a youth and engaged in a store to learn the ways of mercantile and city business life, where, after one years' experience, he joined an importing and shipping house, which was his original aim. In 1855 he engaged with an East India firm as head clerk, and moved to Port au Prince, St. Domingo, where he lived for ten years, being made a partner in the house after the first year. His arduous duties and the debilitating heat undermined his health and compelled him to leave and go north to New York, where he connected himself with a house doing an extensive business, having vessels trading with many different countries, and building ships as well as running a line of steamboats.

This sort of slavery was not congenial, especially after ten years in the beautiful warm climate of the West Indies, unfitting him to endure the inclement weather of the Atlantic seaboard cities, and in 1870 he cut loose from mercantile life, and buying his present home, before starting, came to California and commenced a new life at the age of 41, in this Eldorado of the coast, laying the foundation for the beautiful "Ellwood" ranch, joining with enthusiasm in the work of tree planting, fruit raising, sheep husbandry, and cattle growing.

Having a son and two daughters who needed better educational facilities than were offered at that time, he founded the Santa Barbara College, for fitting pupils for the State University.

Mr. Cooper has been a constant contributor to the papers, and is the author of three books: "Report of trade with statistics, between United States and Santa Domingo," "Fruit Culture and Eucalyptus Trees," and "Treatise on Olive Culture."

His first effort in trying to arouse the attention of fruit growers to the emission of insect pests was in 1875, and he has been an active worker in that field ever since. He has been a

ELLWOOD COOPER, President of the State Board of Horticulture.

member of the State Board of Horticulture since its first inception, and in 1883 was elected President of the Board, an office he still holds.

Bone Manure for Fruit Trees.

Bones seem peculiarly grateful food to fruit trees. Barry remarks that "In taking up trees from soil where bones have been used as manure, we find every particle within reach of the roots completely enveloped in masses of fibre." Hoare, in his treatise on the grape vine, states that "a large bone, which was dug out of a vine border, was covered with a network of fibres, inside and out, and the roots, instead of passing into the soil beyond, when they reached the end of the bone, had turned over the edge and passed inside." Lindley says that superphosphate of lime "greatly facilitates the emission of roots by newly transplanted trees." Clear bone dust is an excellent manure, and nothing is needed with it to make a perfect fertilizer but a mixture of potash. either German potash salts or wood ashes. Let no bones be allowed to go to waste on the farm, but all of them carefully preserved and made into manure.—[Planters' Journal.

PACIFIC FRUIT GROWER

Published monthly by

REYMERT & BROOK

Office: 141½ East First St., Los Angeles, Calif.

HARRY BROOK, Editor.   F. D. REYMERT, Business Manager.

Entered at Postoffice at Los Angeles, Calif., as second class matter.

SUBSCRIPTIONS.

$1.50 per year, in advance. Club of five, $6; Club of ten, $10. Single copies 15 cents. Remit by postoffice or express money order or postal note.

ADVERTISEMENTS

Rates furnished on application. No advertisements of swindles or humbugs inserted. Copy must be received by the 20th.

CONTRIBUTIONS.

Contributions are solicited from practical fruit growers and others interested in the fruit industry. Experiences of growers with new varieties or with insect pests, etc., are specially welcome. Unless you wish you need not attempt to put the matter in shape. Send the facts and we will attend to the rest. Lengthy contributions should be sent early in the month to insure a place in the following number.

JULY, 1887.

WE have received from J. E. Cutter, of Riverside, a package of "King" oranges. The trees from which these were gathered were imported from Cochin China some years ago, under seal of the government of that country and have been first fruited in California by Mr. Cutter. This orange is flattish in shape, has a rough moderately thick skin, salmon pink flesh, which parts very readily. The flavor is exquisite, equalling that of any orange we have ever tasted. Mr. Cutter says this orange does not appear to ripen until June, which will insure for it a good market after other oranges have been gathered.

IMPORTED Sultana raisins bring twenty-five per cent. more than the California product, owing to the fact that imported Sultanas are bleached before drying. Many unsuccessful efforts have been made to imitate the European method of bleaching. In a forthcoming circular, Executive Officer Wheeler, of the Viticultural Commission, will recommend the following process of bleaching: A solution of concentrated lye is used instead of sulphur fumes. The solution tried with success consists of about eight pounds of lye to forty gallons of water. The solution is kept in large, shallow vats, and the fruit on trays is dipped into it, remaining from one to two minutes and then being put into the drier after a short period for draining. The cost of this process of bleaching is said to be less than $1.00 for a ton of grapes.

GEO. W. MEADE is undoubtedly the most enterprising fruit packer on the coast. He is a man who takes a genuine interest in his business, of which he has made a close study. Mr. Meade's reputation is by no means confined to this coast. On a recent visit East he was interviewed by a reporter of the Chicago Independent Grocer, to whom he gave some interesting information regarding the Pacific Coast fruit business. In the course of an editorial founded upon this information, the journal above mentioned makes the following pertinent remarks, which are worthy the attention of our fruit men:

There is, however, one grievous mistake which Californians should rectify at once, and that is the practice of imitating the foreign goods in labeling. Why should California prunes be called French prunes, or why should California raisins be called London layers? With the tremendous strides which these products of the Pacific Coast are making, it will be harder a year hence to rectify this matter. It would have been much easier a year ago than it is to-day, and we cannot impress too strongly upon our friends in California the necessity of taking immediate action upon this matter. Let us have our California goods distinctively American, for we know that the State can and has produced goods second to none at home or abroad, and even at this late date any errors that have heretofore been made should promptly be rectified, in order that the task which will force itself upon us may not come up at a time when it will certainly lead to great complication and untold annoyance. The con-

sumer is rapidly being educated regarding the superiority of California products and now is the time to take prompt action and start in the right direction.

A DISPATCH from Sacramento announces that L. W. Buck, manager of the California Fruit Union, refuses to give the prices obtained at the recent auction sales of California fruits in the East, on the ground that to do so might prejudice dealers in California. What the fruit growers of Northern California are now asking is whether the Fruit Union is managed in the interest of dealers or of the fruit growers. If the hocus pocus of a previous year is going to be repeated Mr. Buck will find that the fruit growers will not remain patient so long as they did then. It looks as if Mr. Buck was endeavoring to run a plain business proposition after the style of a secret society, of which he is High Muck-a-Muck, and that in doing so he was in danger of making a very numerous ass of himself.

WE are pleased to note that the Sacramento Bee has commenced to agitate the taxing of large tracts at their full value, with the object of forcing their owners to divide them up. Nearly ten years ago the writer spent several days on the Morris Grant, belonging to J. B. Haggin, adjoining Sacramento city, for the purpose of writing a description of the same, its colonization being at that time contemplated. This immense tract of over 40,000 acres adjoins the city limits of the capital of the State. The Central Pacific runs for seven miles through the center of the tract, and for the whole distance not a house was visible, the land being used as a sheep pasture. We believe it exists in the same condition to-day, and yet our northern brethren wonder that the boom seems to give them a wide berth. It would scarcely be supposed that anyone—except the owners—would object to the proposition that persons who keep large tracts of land unimproved should pay taxes at the same rate as small farmers who work and produce something, and yet, strange to say, even our northern exchanges take exception to the Bee's proposition and refer to it as if it concealed some dangerous communistic theory.

THE LONDON FRUIT MARKET.

WHEN the United States fruit market is overdone with California products, as some of our friends are always prognosticating it will be, we may commence to turn our attention to supplying the English market with our choice fruits. Our excellent London exchange, the Horticultural Times, in its issue of April 23d, gives the following quotations as the ruling wholesale prices of the fruits named. We have changed the prices to their equivalent in dollars and cents: Strawberries, $1.25 to $3.00 per pound; hot-house grapes 50c to $2.00 per pound; Alicante grapes, 42c to $1.25 per pound. English hot-house grapes are of very fine quality, large, thin-skinned and delicious, resembling our black Hamburgs. The Alicante grapes come packed in sawdust, from Spain, and may be found for sale in the London grocery stores all the year round. They are of the White Malaga variety, large and sweet, and may at some seasons be purchased at retail as low as 12½c a pound. Immense quantities of grapes are grown for the London market in the Channel Islands (Jersey and Guernsey) under glass, acres being covered in that way. The London market would alone consume all California can offer in the way of fine fresh fruit, and cry for more. Price is no object when anything choice can be offered. The editor of the PACIFIC FRUIT GROWER has frequently seen large Louise Bonne de Jersey pears, weighing perhaps 2½ pounds each, displayed in the window of a leading London fruiterer, at the modest price of £12 (86c) per dozen. The usual retail price for English hot-house pineapples, of which large quantities are grown for the market, is $5 apiece, and of English hot-house peaches 60 cents apiece.

www.ingramcontent.com/pod-product-compliance
Lightning Source LLC
Chambersburg PA
CBHW032306280326
41932CB00009B/711

* 9 7 8 3 7 4 1 1 3 6 3 1 3 *